THE CONFESSIONS

OF A PSYCHEDELIC CHRISTIAN

THE CONFESSIONS

OF A PSYCHEDELIC CHRISTIAN

Sebastián Gaete

Copyright © 2020 by Sebastián Gaete

All rights reserved.

ISBN: 9798623455925

Imprint: Independently published

For Raphael, Claudio and Flora

Contents

BOOK ONE

Introduction	1
1. Holy River Isis!	7
2. Heaven and Hell	16
3. The Gateless Gate	25
4. Pantheism is not Sexed-up Atheism	32
5. Something that our Mind cannot Grasp	40
6. A Walk in the Forest	50
7. Spiritual Autism	57
8. The Portal of God is Non-Existence	70
9. Seven Gods	80
10. Light in the Tunnel	93
11. The Clearing	100
12. The Tent	106
13. The Chakras	110
14. The Presence of God	115
15. Words and Things	131
16. Word Magic	140
17. In Dreams	146
18. Isis and Osiris	153
19. Attention, Attention, Attention	164
20. Earth Medicine	171
21. Three Trees	177

BOOK TWO

1. Mystery	209
2. The Divided Brain	213
3. The Bitter Truth	214
4. Faith Never Dies	216
5. The Hermeneutics of Faith	219
6. All Shall be Well	222
7. Filter Bubbles	223
8. The Tibetan Wheel of Life	227
9. The Madman's Argument	230
10. Personality Disorders	233
11. The Iceman Cometh	236
12. Talk to the Soul	237
13. Soul Building	240
14. No Yoga, No Joy	242
15. After Virtue	245
16. Vive la Resistance!	248
17. Mind your Q's	250
18. Thus Spoke Ayahuasca	253
19. The Temple and the Pub	254
20. Remembering and Forgetting	259
21. Three, Two, One: Heaven, Earth, Hell	263
22. How to Make Hell on Earth	268
23. Training and Enlightenment	271
24. Pachananda	275
25. Jacob's Ladder	277
26. The God of the Living	279
27. Infinite Matter or Infinite Consciousness?	280
28. Bad Science, Bad Religion, Bad Philosophy, Bad Politics	284
29. Bad Art and No Burgers	287
30. Book Medicine	289
31. Atheist Delusions	292
32. Mystical Atheism	294
33. Cognitive Filters	296
34. Sola Ratio, Sola Scriptura	300
35. Tradition, Meditation, Revelation	303

36. Borders	305
37. Why Left and Right Disgust Each Other	308
38. Where do Bored Muggles go?	312
39. What's at the Top of the Tree?	315
40. Redemption	320
41. Three Orientations to Life	324
42. Latter-Day Prophets in the Age of Equality	325
43. Rousseau's Chains	328
44. Reason and Civility	332
45. The Darkness and the Light	334
46. Why Marx was Half Right	336
47. Do Not Waste Time	339
48. Tetris and Zen	341
49. What's Behind the Wall?	343
50. Waking Up	346
51. The Eye of God	348
52. The Ray of Creation	350
53. Meditation	352
54. Flat Batteries	355
55. Balance and Volume	356
56. Express Yourself	359
57. Ghosts, Spirits and Angels	361
58. The World, the Flesh and the Devil	362
59. Orthodoxy	365
60. The Magic of Christianity	369
61. The Philosopher Monk	375
62. The Warrior King	379
63. The One True Refuge	382
64. Integral Yoga	385
65. A Simple Cure for Spiritual Narcissism	390
66. I Believe	391
67. The True Vine	394
68. The Armour of Christ	398
69. Holy, Virtuous and Wise	400
70. Two Trees	403
References	407
Quotations	421

Introduction

At the heart of this book is an experience. It is the experience of *waking up*. What does this over-used, hackneyed expression actually mean? It means different things to different people of course, but here's what it means to me.

When I went for a walk by the river Isis in Oxford high on LSD with a couple of friends, I woke up. When I drank ayahuasca in a shamanic ceremony in the Sussex countryside, I woke up. When I smoked DMT in a converted industrial estate in Clapton, I woke up. On an intensive meditation retreat at a Zen monastery in Northumberland, I woke up. Walking alone on the Walthamstow marshes, I woke up. Praying at church in Highgate, I woke up.

In all these separate occasions, my ego simply vanished. It felt like waking up from a dream, the dream of an unreal, fictional self. However, because this is such an unusual, out of the ordinary, even once-in-a-lifetime event, it's very difficult if not impossible to describe to people who haven't experienced it for themselves. If they consider themselves to be spiritual, they may assume they've had it when they haven't, whereas if they're not particularly interested in spiritual things, all they will hear is a string of mystical clichés.

Those who have had this "waking up" experience will instantly recognise it as soon as they hear about it. It doesn't matter if the words are clumsy or clichéd, as long as they are genuine. Those who have had the experience know. Buddha recognises Buddha.

*

My DMT experience was only about fifteen minutes long. That was long enough. It took me "all the way", so to speak (I became one with all humanity, literally). When I came back from being One Giant Eternal Person and the other people in the room slowly separated themselves from me, and I from them, I slowly sat up.

I listened to the others relate their own experiences. They had had some visuals, some visions and some insights, but that was it. They nattered away just as they had before smoking. I was amazed and not a little disappointed. From the way they spoke and moved I could see that nothing had fundamentally changed. They were still fast asleep. They were still lost in the dream of ego.

When I was invited to speak, I was speechless. What could I say? After half a minute or so, I finally found some half-way adequate words. I spoke them slowly and deliberately and, to their ears I imagine, enigmatically, possibly pretentiously.

There was really nothing I could say, just as there was nothing I could say to my friends when I woke up by the river Isis. There's nothing you *can* say. All you can do is to try to stay awake for as long as possible, before sleep descends again. It's actually quite awkward, because your behaviour can seem odd, or aloof, or admonitory. And egos don't like that. So they look for ways to bring you down to size, or "down to Earth". The safest policy is to keep quiet.

This is the paradox of religion. People generally like the idea of it in theory, but when someone starts acting out, as if it were something real, something more than just metaphor, they don't like it at all. Religion is all very well if it stays in its box. If you're dressed as a priest or a monk you can act all holy. But not if you're a real person in the real world.

Which is why it's so important that Jesus didn't have priestly authority. He wasn't part of the establishment. He was just an ordinary guy. Except, of course, that he was a holy man who insisted on preaching religion whenever he went for a walk. "Isn't this the carpenter's son? Isn't his mother called Mary, and his brothers James, Joseph, Simon, and Judas?" (Matthew 13:55). Apparently he said he was the son of God! In the end, of course, as everyone knows, he was crucified for it.

For a short time after my DMT experience, I was a holy man. I was sitting on holy ground. My body was a temple of holiness. My mind was a bejeweled palace. But the others could obviously only see the outer aspect, which was that "I looked like a shaman". It seemed to make them uncomfortable.

They appeared to resent the fact not only that I clearly thought my experience was deeper than theirs, but that I was visibly changed, that I had "woken up". Was I just showing off?

It seems that we are socially hardwired against holiness. The very idea actually makes some people's skin crawl. Perhaps we like the dreams of our egos and don't really want to wake up. We want the people around us to be dreaming too, and automatically assume that everyone else is an ego just like us, and so read ego back into any and every word and gesture.

As a result, people who want to wake up and stay awake have to self-isolate in monasteries, ashrams and hermitages. Or else, if they are to survive in the social world, they must master the art of dissimulation and act like an ego accommodating other egos, and play the game, just like everyone else.

As a self-confessed psychedelic Christian, I must find a way to reconcile these two worlds and to love God with all my heart, soul, mind and strength and to love my neighbour as myself. I won't pretend it's easy, but the alternative is either to stop loving my neighbour or to stop loving God, and that is no longer an option.

*

This is not a book about crazy psychedelic experiences. The psychedelics are not really that important, except as gateway drugs to waking up. If tripping is your thing and you're fascinated by far out, mind bending "insane in the membrane" psychedelia, this is not the book for you. Equally, if you're an armchair intellectual interested in the phenomena of religious experience and mind expansion from a purely detached, academic point of view, this is not for you.

Beyond all the stories, reflections and meditations, this book is, to coin a phrase, "a serious call to a devout and holy life"[1]. If you feel called, read on.

BOOK ONE

1. Holy River Isis!

It was a glorious summer's day. I had done my finals and had finally escaped the academic prison that Cambridge had become. Sitting on the edge of a soggy sofa in a fashionably squalid student house in Oxford with my old pal Justin and his Wadham buddy James, listening to something weird on the record player, with no job prospects (I read English Literature) and no idea what to do with my life, a bag of weed on the table and a tab of acid in the palm of my hand, Wordsworth's immortal line suddenly came to me: "Bliss was it in that dawn to be alive, but to be young was very heaven!"[2]

We dropped the acid and went for a walk down to the river Isis. The sun beat down and Oxford sparkled with the optimism of youth. Justin and James were jabbering away about something vaguely interesting but inconsequential, and I leant them only half an ear. I was too much enjoying the sunshine to want to waste it in conversation. I also somehow knew that this was going to be a Big One, and my real focus was on my level of awareness and my surroundings, which I constantly scanned for clues that I was "coming up".

We stopped at a small ornamental bridge over the river. The water was shallow where it gently lapped a small ramp, which emerged onto the bank, for no visible purpose. Justin and James were still deep in conversation. I gazed down at the water gently flowing beneath the bridge. The sun danced off the water in a thousand brilliant points of light. A posse of ducks slowly glided past, creating trails of impossibly intricate patterns as they broke up the reflected sunlight. I was mesmerised.

I tried to follow the dancing patterns of light, but it was too fast. All I could manage was a general impression, which, I realised, was all I ever saw. But today, I wanted to see more than a general impression. I wanted to see Reality. And the LSD would help me. But however much I tried to follow the flashing pattern, as the tiny points of light momentarily shone and disappeared, with others almost instantaneously taking their place, I just couldn't keep up.

I was always one step behind. The time lapse between perception and brain processing was just long enough that I could see little more than a shimmering blur.

*

Then a voice in my head said, "Make your mind water". So I did. I flowed with the water. Suddenly, I was in. I could see the individual points of light skipping over the water with tremendous speed, but I was with them. I could see them with perfect clarity. There was no gap between the water and my mind.

I stared with intense concentration and growing amazement. How long could I keep this up for? Was it bad for my eyes maybe? All sorts of shapes and images started to emerge from the dancing lights. I saw Cleopatra's golden barge, followed by a bewildering palimpsest of Egyptian figures and symbols and mythical beasts. It was like a procession of the weird and the wonderful in glittering lights. Most of it, although perfectly clear and well-defined, I didn't recognise at all.

After a while I got tired of this lightning fast game of cat and mouse, and let the shimmering light show go on unseen. I started to think about the nature of reality. It occurred to me that this was exactly what the pre-Socratic philosophers had done all those years ago. I thought about Thales, who famously said that, "the world is water". I imagined him sitting gazing at the sun dancing on the water somewhere on the Aegean coast, just as I was doing now. I felt that our minds were somehow connected and that the two and a half millennia between us was no more than a temporary misunderstanding. I was seeing through his eyes, as he was seeing through mine.

We both understood in that timeless instant that we were gazing at the same water, and that the water *never stopped*. It had flowed and sparkled and shimmered and rippled and danced, creating an infinity of complex forms without end, since the time of Thales and long before, since the early dawn of the Earth itself. We looked away, exhausted, but the water just kept on moving, forever and ever. We could only witness an infinitesimal portion of its infinite being and becoming.

"The world is water": all things come into being and disappear endlessly and ceaselessly, like the irrepressible dance of water in stream and river and sea. There is no end and no beginning to the infinite dance of forms. Everything is in motion, shifting and changing, combining and transforming. That's why it's impossible to step into the same river twice, as Heraclitus said. Everything is constantly in flux. There is no fixity, no stability, no permanence, no being. There is no being, only endless and eternal becoming.

I gazed at the shifting waters below me, sometimes catching the glint of the sun, sometimes not, shape-shifting, swirling, ebbing and flowing. I knew that I had been hallucinating. All of those beautiful forms and shapes I saw were nothing but a spectacular illusion created by my over-active imagination. It was all just an illusion. There was no Cleopatra's barge. I just made it all up. I was high on acid, after all. But then again, didn't I always do that anyway? Take the passing show as real? Mistake the appearance of things for the reality? Project my mind onto the world?

If this is all just an illusion, I thought, what is reality? Well, the water itself is real, even if the shapes projected onto it aren't. Not the ever-changing surface, but the actual substance and depth of water below the surface is real. Underneath the glitter and spectacle of endless becoming on the surface was the constant and eternal being of the water, hidden from view but always there and always the same.

Then the simple but, at the time, extraordinary truth struck me like a bolt of lightning. The surface show *is* the water! The depths and the surface are aspects of one thing. It's "not-two". The surface show is not just an illusion: it's the cosmic play, the dance of *lila*, of Reality itself. Being and Becoming are one and the same!

I have no idea how long I had been ruminating like this, staring at the abstract shapes of light and shade below me, but when I emerged from my philosophical reverie and looked up and around at the trees and sky laid out before me, I saw the world transformed. I had entered the "Pure Land".

*

Everything was alive. Everything was on fire with overflowing life. It was just as Thomas Traherne described it: "The green trees when I saw them first ... transported and ravished me, their sweetness and unusual beauty made my heart to leap, and almost mad with ecstasy, they were such strange and wonderful things"[3].

At the time I didn't know Traherne, but I did know William Blake. I thought of that line from *The Marriage of Heaven and Hell*, "If the doors of perception were cleansed, everything would be seen as it is, infinite."[4] Now, finally, after years of trying, I had broken through to the other side and everything was, indeed, infinite. This was the real thing, the Big One, a genuine, full-blown *satori*. So this was Enlightenment!

Time seemed to stop. I turned my head and saw a flower. The flower was so real, the looking was so real. Everything was so absolutely, unbelievably *real*. I remember thinking that that moment of looking at a flower was worth more than my whole life up to that point. My life had been nothing more than a long, hazy dream. But now I had woken up.

It was as if time had stopped, although things continued exactly as they had before. It was as if my mind had stopped, although I could still think. There was a special quality of stillness in my awareness that I had never experienced before. And I was not the person I had thought I was. The person I thought I was had vanished like a wisp of white cloud in a bright blue sky.

As I looked around me, with this strange, unfamiliar mixture of stillness and wonder, it was as though I was seeing the world for the first time. Traherne describes it perfectly: "Eternity was manifest in the light of day, and something infinite behind everything appeared"[5].

I realised that this world that I was standing in was the same world that had always existed. All of the past history of the Earth seemed somehow contained in this present moment. I saw the miracle of existence, the miracle of life. And I *myself* was part of it. I wasn't just a passive observer standing to one side of Reality. I was right in the middle of it.

But I wasn't just part of it, I was the most amazingly complex and *conscious* part of it. I myself was the growing tip of the consciousness of this beautiful planet. I myself was the culmination of billions of years of evolution. I wasn't twenty-two at all. I was billions of years old!

I understood, in the core of my being, that I was the same as everything else. "At the water level", I thought, "it's all one". The water, the trees, the bushes, plants, flowers, insects, animals, people, *everything*, everything was just a different form and manifestation of the same thing. At the water level, it was all the same. Everything had grown up out of the same "Earth stuff", like different forms of the same body of water, different waves on the same sea. *That's* what Thales meant.

Not only that, but one small part of all this Earth stuff saw and understood that it was all one: *me*. But I wasn't "me" any more. I was just part of the one Earth. When I looked at the trees, it was as if the trees were looking at themselves. It was as if they could see themselves for the first time, as if they had *woken up*. It felt like the Earth itself was looking at itself through my eyes. Through "me", the Earth had evolved to the point where it had become aware of itself. Not only had "I" woken up - so had *everything*.

*

There were a few houses beyond the trees on the other side of the river. There were fences and gardens. In a flash I saw the illusion of property. Everything was part of the Earth, and everything was mine, because they were all *me*. At first the fences and hedges offended me by their artificial parceling of the world, but then I realized that even the parceling and dividing, the houses and fences and gates, *all of it* was mine. The owner of the house and garden might believe that it belonged to him, but in fact it belonged to me and to everyone and everything, because it belonged to the Earth.

I was the Earth, but at the same time I was a human being. I was both the host and the guest. This was my *home*. At last, I felt like I truly belonged. I was filled with "oikophilia", the love of home. Growing up, I had always felt like a bit of an outsider, at school, at uni, even at home with my family.

I never felt fully at home in England, my adoptive country, nor in Chile, my homeland. Now I felt that wherever I was, wherever I went, I would be completely at home, because I belonged here, on Earth. Nobody could tell me I was trespassing on their property, or that I had no right to be where I was, because this was my rightful home.

We walked on in silence. I knew that it was impossible to communicate what I was experiencing. I was transformed and the world was transformed, but actually everything was exactly the same, and just as it should be. I understood that this was "nothing special", because it was just reality, and that as soon as I made it into something special, in my mind it would become other than reality, and therefore *un*real, and then I would fall back into the mind's dream of reality. So I kept my mouth shut. What could I possibly say anyway? I was afraid that if I started talking about it, I would lose it. Best to communicate through my actions and my simple presence.

Justin and James didn't seem to notice anything at all. So much for my Enlightened presence! Would they have recognised Christ or Buddha? Probably not. Even without looking at their faces, I could tell that they were lost in their own dream world, believing that it was the real world. Everyone we passed as we walked along the river was dreaming too. I could see how everyone was basically sleepwalking through their own private dreams. Everyone was just pretending to be awake, by waking up for a split second every now and then, before falling back to sleep again. I felt a great surge of sadness and compassion, but there was absolutely nothing I could do about it.

We approached a young woman sunbathing on the grass. From a distance she looked young and healthy and beautiful, but when she turned her face towards us, I saw that she was in fact full of corruption. Her outward appearance was just a disguise. I held her gaze and looked into her corrupted soul. She suddenly panicked, hastily gathered her things and ran off, scrambling desperately over a fence and disappearing across a field. "What the fuck was that all about?" said Justin. I said nothing.

Further on, we passed another bridge, this time an unsightly rusty old railway bridge, covered in graffiti. Justin and James were bemoaning Man's desecration of the natural landscape.

They saw the bridge as an imposing iron structure rudely slammed over a delicate and fragile Earth. It must have represented for them the tragic environmental degradation of the planet by our insatiably greedy and destructive species. I shared the sentiment, but I didn't see the bridge as they saw it. They presumably saw the bridge as solid and enduring and the trees as fragile and weak. Through the eyes of the Earth, however, the bridge barely existed. Nature was eternal. The Earth was eternal. But the bridge was nothing more than a passing twig on the river. It didn't bother me in the slightest.

We paused by the brick wall, which was covered in graffiti. It was a mixture of ugly tags and obscenities. It seemed to me that the wall was the inside of someone's skull. Every scratch and marking, every word and phrase, was a desperate attempt to make sense of the crazy world this human mind found themselves in. Desperation, anger and frustration were laid bare before me. I felt the raw pain of humanity, of human consciousness straining to *understand*. Amongst the chaos and confusion, one word jumped out at me. Someone had written just one word: "LOVE". I couldn't help but smile. They'd got there in the end!

We soon came to another bridge. It was intimidatingly high, but there were young teenage boys jumping off it into the water. I was amazed and impressed by their bravado. Suddenly, the water seemed welcomingly cool in the blazing heat of the sun. "Let's have a swim!" I said. "What? Don't be stupid."

I waded in, fully clothed. Justin and James looked on from the bank with a mixture of worry and baffled amusement. So I splashed them. There was a young boy in the water who had just jumped off the bridge. Treading water, we exchanged a few words. He was friendly enough, but looked kind of naughty. There was an edge to him, an edge of "corruption", just like I had seen in the young woman earlier. He couldn't have been more than twelve or thirteen years old, and I could see a sweet childhood innocence mixed in with the corruption. Perhaps "experience" is a better word.

I became aware of his awareness. It seemed to come and go. One minute he was with me, the next he was somewhere else. He had disappeared into his mind. I remember thinking to myself, "but I'm still here".

I could see how people came in and out of reality, in and out of the present. I also noticed the difference between children and adults. Children could meet me, so to speak, in the present, although they soon disappeared back into their minds. Adults, on the other hand, rarely, if ever, emerged from their minds at all. "But I'm still here", I thought, as he swam off to join his mates.

I didn't notice that the current had taken me downstream, far from the bridge and away from the bank. I tried to swim ashore, but the current was too strong. I wasn't getting anywhere.

I stopped struggling for a moment and felt the weight of my clothes and my heavy sandals pulling me down. Like a bolt from the blue, I suddenly remembered that I was high on acid. Justin and James were nowhere to be seen. "I might drown", I thought. It occurred to me that my beautiful dream of Enlightenment could well end up as the nightmare reality of a stupid drug-induced death. Had I seen too much? Was this the pay off? I thought I was invincible, like the apocryphal LSD casualties who jump out of windows believing they can fly, and reality was about to teach me the ultimate lesson in humility.

"What a shame" I thought. But I didn't feel afraid. If I died now, I would die happy, because I had *made* it. I least I would die Enlightened! It just seemed a bit of a shame to die now, just when I had seen the light, but maybe that's how it had to be.

Then I thought, "Well, I might as well make a bit of an effort". So I kicked off and swam vigorously towards the shore. It turned out not to be so difficult after all, and I was soon climbing out, dripping wet, with one sandal somewhere at the bottom of the river. I stumbled up the bank to the path. I was quite attached to my sandals, which were new and quite stylish, with a metal ring in the middle, and I regretted the brief moment of panic when I kicked one off. But I was glad to be alive. I had sacrificed one sandal to the water, and now I sacrificed the other to the dusty earth. It felt very symbolic, a sacrifice to the elements in exchange for my life.

*

So it was that, barefoot, I walked aimlessly but purposively along the banks of the river Isis, like a wild prophet, half hoping to find my way back to the house, and half expecting to wander the world forever. I had various adventures along the way. I met the same naughty boys again, who were trying to haul an old boat into the river. It was like something out of *Huckleberry Finn*. I helped them carry it over and lower it down into the water, and it instantly sank.

As I walked along, I had a strange sensation, as though I were straddling two worlds, as though I was a time traveller from the distant past, or perhaps the distant future. At one point, I joined two young girls in their twenties, students maybe, who were having a picnic on the grass in the shade of tree, and got talking to them. I remember, absurdly, talking about Spike Milligan. I was a little surprised that they didn't offer me any food or drink. After a while, although I had been faultlessly polite and charming (in my eyes anyway!), I sensed that they were beginning to feel a little uncomfortable randomly talking to a strange barefoot madman, so I said goodbye and went on my way.

I have no idea how I found my way back to the house, since I had no idea where it was or even what the address was, and this was a time before mobile phones, but I got there somehow. One of the housemates, a pretty black girl, whose name I forget, was there, but there was no sign of Justin or James. The kitchen was a horrible mess, with piles of dirty plates and pans everywhere. I poured myself a much needed glass of water and set to washing and cleaning until it was spotless. Then I went into the garden to commune with the plants. I was still in raptures. When the boys eventually returned, it was getting dark. They were visibly relieved to see me. They'd been looking for me for hours, apparently.

That night we all watched *A Room with a View*. Every time a spliff came my way I politely refused. I didn't need it. The film made complete sense, and I shed quiet, hot tears, which I managed to conceal in the semi-darkness. I went to bed in the early hours, exhausted but calmly elated. The next morning, I woke up with the mother of all hangovers, and my beatific vision was no more.

2. Heaven and Hell

That amazing experience by the river Isis didn't come completely out of the blue. I got my first taste of Zen at the tender age of twelve, when my father took me to a Japanese ex-monk's Tuesday meditation evenings in a semi in North Finchley. Since then, I had read my way through my dad's bookshelf (a heady mixture of Buddhism and postmodernism), and raved my way through my teens. My church was *Whirl-y-gig* and my spirituality was getting high.

Aldous Huxley's *The Doors of Perception* and *Heaven and Hell* were gospel to my young, impressionable mind, eloquent witnesses to the truth of Suchness and Higher Consciousness. It was all very exciting. But now, lying in the half light of a stale student room in Oxford one summer morning with a cracking headache, I had incontrovertible proof, through direct first-hand experience, that all this Enlightenment business was actually, literally true. It wasn't just fanciful, wishful thinking. It wasn't metaphorical or symbolic mumbo-jumbo, or exaggerated poetic license. It was plain *fact*.

Heaven was, indeed, a place on Earth. I already knew that hell was. I had already been to hell, at an all-night rave in a country mansion in Hay on Wye, in North Wales, just a couple of years before.

This was my personal glimpse into the abyss, a voyage into the depths of madness, psychosis and paranoid schizophrenia. Once recovered (it actually took me about a year to fully recover from the periodic flash-backs and panic attacks), I seriously considered pursuing a career as a psychiatric nurse, knowing now what the horrors of madness really were.

Some time after this harrowing experience, I happened to watch a film version of Franz Kafka's paranoid classic, *The Trial*. The screenplay was by Harold Pinter, and it starred Kyle MacLachlan (of Twin Peaks fame) as "K". It was an almost blow-by-blow account of my own bad trip. I was transfixed. I lived the whole experience over again, vicariously, in my parents' front room. Clearly, Kafka had been there, and so too possibly, had Pinter.

*

With hindsight, I probably shouldn't have got stoned on the coach trip there and shouldn't have taken a micro-dot and half an E on arrival. Set and setting were not good. I didn't know anyone there, apart from the couple of friends I arrived with, who I quickly got separated from. On one of the dance floors, I had an altercation with a clown (I was mildly hallucinating) and it was as if my mind shattered into pieces, like a plate at a Greek wedding. It was all downhill from there.

I was on trial. Like K, I spent the whole night searching for "the Law". I needed to be acquitted of a serious, existential crime, but I had no idea what it was. All I knew was that I was guilty and somehow had to prove my innocence. But "the Law" was also "the Truth". I didn't know what was real any more, and I was hell-bent on finding out. This was my mission: to find out what the hell was going on and to find absolution and forgiveness for whatever it was I had done wrong. As the night progressed, I drew closer and closer to the Law, which lay at the centre of all the craziness like a spider at the centre of its web.

There were four or five dramatic turning points. Something extremely weird would happen, and with a dreadful mental crash, I felt another turn of the screw in my brain. I was on a spiral inexorably pulling me into the middle of an irresistible vortex. I was wrapping myself ever tighter in the invisible threads of the spider's web and inching ever closer to its patient jaws. There was nothing I could do. The more I fought it, the more powerful it became, this centripetal force pulling me into the dark centre of my mind.

Eventually, I found myself sitting on a wall in front of the house as the sun came up, smoking my last cigarette before my execution. "Do you want a cigarette?" Never had those simple words been so pregnant with meaning and foreboding. How could I refuse? I knew that the person offering it to me was none other than the Devil himself. He was calmly sitting next to me, biding his time with infinite demonic patience.

I was strangely relieved. It was almost over. After all my frantic struggling, I had reached the innermost circle of hell. This was my final judgment. I thought I could outwit the forces of darkness, but they were far cleverer and far stronger than I. With an inner sigh of resignation, I understood what should have been obvious all along: the Truth I had been looking for was the fact of my own death.

The Devil turned out to be a tall, wiry black man. Between drags, he whispered ponderously and enigmatically into my ear. After a few ambiguous statements, which I took to be further confirmation, in cryptic, coded language, of my impending doom, I began to wonder why he was stringing me along so much. Why didn't he just get on with it? Then he said something about being black. In that very instant, I knew, with huge relief, that this *couldn't* be the Devil. Why would the Devil be going on about being black? What did that have to do with my execution? Maybe he was just a black guy with a chip on his shoulder off his face on drugs!

I think I actually laughed out loud, which can't have helped his own nascent paranoia. I thanked him for the cigarette and went back inside. It would have been good to take a walk in the surrounding countryside, but there was still the slim possibility that I would be stabbed to death and thrown into a lake.

As luck would have it, I bumped into my friends, hours after having been separated from them, and they managed to talk me round. I explained, with heart-rending pathos, that however hard I tried, I just couldn't work out what was real. My Chinese friend, Colin, with the profound sagacity of a Taoist Master, uttered five simple words that probably saved my sanity, if not my life: "Just accept it - you're fucked!"

The Truth dawned on me with the warmth of the rising sun. The vice on my head loosened its grip. Yes! I'm fucked! I have no idea what's going on! Just like that, the quest was over. I gave up on my crazy, desperate mission. Everything relaxed. It was ok. I didn't have to work it out. I didn't have to fight. I didn't have to find justification for my existence in this crazy place. And I didn't have to continue down this one-way road to destruction. Once I accepted it, the nightmare simply evaporated, like a faerie mist.

My psychotic episode was soaked in paranoid delusions and driven by hyper-vigilance and hyper-rationalisation. My brain was working overtime, spinning one theory after another in a desperate attempt to make sense of what obviously didn't. It wasn't so much a case of irrationality, as a case of misplaced hyper-rationality. However brilliant my judgment and insight into the probability of the reality of my predicament, it was all just more strands in the tangled web of the convoluted logic of my madness.

*

My experience of heaven two years later was the exact opposite. On my trip by the river Isis, the world seemed to expand outwards to embrace all existence, whereas by the Wye, everything was pulled into a tight fist at the centre of my shattered mind. In that hellish night in Wales, everything pointed towards me. It was all about me. This is the essence of paranoia: a kind of twisted narcissism. On that heavenly sunny day in Oxford, on the other hand, nothing was about me. It was all everything else: the trees, the Earth, the universe. I wasn't a prisoner of my self. I was *free*.

In *Heaven and Hell*, Aldous Huxley reflects on the contrasting effects of good and bad trips on psychoactive drugs like LSD. I had to agree with his conclusion that what we call "hell" is an extreme contraction of the ego, while what we call "heaven" is an extreme expansion.

The black hole at the centre of the mental vortex of hell is really nothing but "I". The Devil sitting at the centre of the innermost ring of hell is a projected, psychotic image of "I". In hell the world contracts and revolves around this central core, but in heaven, there is no core. In between these two extremes lies the ordinary, sober state, where "I" and "the world" somehow find a poised equilibrium, which is what we generally call "sanity".

I should probably have learnt my lesson and learnt to make do with sanity after the horror of my "Wye trip" (or my "Why trip"), but something drove me to keep pushing on the envelope of reality. I knew what hell was and I knew *where* it was. So I knew how to avoid it.

All I had to do was to push in the opposite direction, in the direction of expansion rather than contraction, and surely, I would find happier and greener pastures. As William James said, there are many realities out there, just waiting to be tapped into:

"Our normal waking consciousness, rational consciousness as we call it, is but one special type of consciousness, whilst all about it, parted from it by the flimsiest of screens, there lie potential forms of consciousness entirely different. We may go through life without suspecting their existence; but apply the requisite stimulus, and at a touch they are there."[6]

*

For James, the requisite stimulus was nitrous oxide, laughing gas. For me, as it was for Huxley, it was LSD. LSD was my gateway drug into both heaven and hell. It is psycho-mimetic, because it recreates psychotic conditions, but it is also, potentially, mystico-mimetic. Like other psychedelic compounds, it is an *entheogen*: it can "generate God within". But could I generate God without the drugs?

This was one of the big questions that naturally arose as a result of my brief sojourn in heaven. I was already more committed to a broadly Buddhist conception of self-reliance and self-mastery than to the drug-fuelled psychedelic pre-millenial revolution of the '90s. The Buddha advocated meditation in pursuit of Enlightenment and explicitly ruled out the use of intoxicants for his followers. As part of their vows, Buddhists must refrain from partaking in "the wine of delusion". In this, he departed from the older schools of Indian mysticism, where *soma*, the mysterious "food of the gods", and the widespread use of charis, marijuana and hashish, were central to the mystical visions of Saddhus and Brahmins.

I decided that if it could be done without drugs, it should be. Drugs had their obvious disadvantages, not least of which was the very real danger of going permanently mad. I knew that "set and setting" (a positive mind-set and safe environment) were of fundamental importance in negotiating psychedelic experiences, but even then, drugs were probably too hazardous over the long term.

Also, it was *cheating*. If I couldn't sustain the enlightened awareness once the effects of the drug had worn off, it was because I was so far from the real enlightened state when I was sober, that I just pinged back to my habitual deluded state like a rubber band. I was haunted by the refrain "Was that trip really necessary?" It could only make me more dissatisfied with myself and so more dependent on drugs. There was the potential for psychological and maybe even physical addiction. And I could easily get distracted from genuine *satori* by who knows what phantasmagoria of *makyo*. Who knows if I would ever find my way out of the countless rabbit holes I might get lost in?

I'm sure that lots of people must have "heavenly" experiences similar to mine. Perhaps they are content to treat them as just a "good trip", another notch on the psychedelic bedpost. Most people, I imagine, remember these "spots of time", these partings of the veil of reality, with fondness, like a beautiful remembered dream. I couldn't do that, though. I couldn't just file it away as nothing but a happy *memory*! It wasn't just a memory, because it wasn't just an experience. It was conclusive evidence and incontrovertible proof that reality was not this collective dream we think of as real.

This was precisely the Buddha's claim. Our ordinary waking consciousness is unreal, a delusion. We must wake up to how things *really* are. Waking up from the dream of false consciousness is *satori*, Enlightenment. And my "Isis trip" was confirmation of the objective truth of the Buddha's claim.

From the Buddhist point of view, there is a spectrum of reality, with hell at one end and heaven at the other. The midpoint between them, the realm of Earth, is not really "reality", flanked on both sides by two unrealities, one pleasant, one unpleasant. This would be the conventional, rational view. For hard-headed rationalists, heaven is just as much a deluded state as hell is. No, Earth is just one point along a spectrum of consciousness that finds its apotheosis in Enlightenment. In other words, our normal waking consciousness is not absolutely real, it is just *half-way* real.

*

I decided not to go down the psychedelic route to Enlightenment. I also decided not to go down the monastic route, although I did think about it a lot. At one point I came seriously close to becoming a postulant at a Zen monastery, because I despaired of ever getting enlightened in the "real world". I soon realised that my state of consciousness was so intimately related to that of everyone else, that it was almost impossible to maintain any other state in the midst of ordinary life.

I remember one occasion very clearly. I was meditating upstairs in my room one evening in a shared house in Greenwich. I managed to break through to a beautiful, heightened state of awareness, where my mind stopped, and I became intensely aware of even the subtlest movement of my body, and of everything around me. The way I *intentionally* closed the curtains will remain with me for the rest of my life.

When I was called down for supper, I immediately saw that my friends were on a completely different wavelength. I knew they would be, of course, but I wanted to test my altered state to see if it could survive the social onslaught. I could see layer upon layer of delusion as they merrily chatted away, and I merrily, but knowingly, joined them. After maybe half an hour at the most, my lucid awareness was gone. My delusion and theirs was one seamless delusion. And it wasn't just because of the wine.

I realised that because everyone I knew, and everyone I met, family, friends, even casual acquaintances and strangers, were in the same ordinary rational state of consciousness, I was automatically pulled into it whenever I had any dealings with *anyone*. It seemed that the only way to live in this deluded world was to be deluded myself. Now I understood the powerful draw of the anchorite's cell and the monastery cloisters. It was the only way to escape the "world trance".

*

Was it possible to be "in the world but not of the world"? This was the challenge. Could I minimise social influences and social contact at the same time as leading an ordinary life, while also making time for meditation and spiritual practice? I tried Buddhism; I tried Qi Gong; I tried the Fourth Way. I joined the School of Economic Science, which offered "Good Company" and "the Householder's Way". This seemed to offer the answer to my dilemma. But in the end, after only three years, I decided to leave, when I discovered the miraculous Amazonian brew, *ayahuasca*.

Ayahuasca turned me on to the power of the imagination and the power of the body. It's all about visions and energy. This was a world away from the reified mansions of philosophy and meditation. I saw (or rather, was *shown*) how philosophical detachment and transcendental meditation can be as much of an obstacle to the spirit as the ordinary distractions of the world. Ayahuasca is a great teacher. It teaches with compassion but with great force. It is "the vine of the dead", but it teaches *life*. It doesn't teach an escape from the world, but full immersion in it. It's all about life. Life is spirit and spirit is life, and the energy and consciousness which runs the whole show is what we call *love*.

It also reveals the dark side, the "sickness unto death", and, of course, the snakes. In my first purge (the violent vomiting which often accompanies the experience), I saw dozens of thick, black, writhing snakes come out of my mouth and disappear into the ground. It felt like an exorcism. I emerged from the experience refreshed, energised, lightened, relaxed and *happy*. What a medicine!

The ayahuasca experience is the subject for another book. Research into its effects is still in its infancy, and, as with LSD and Ecstasy, once the utopian hysteria has died down, we discover that it is not, in fact, the cure for all our ills. This is because, unlike the prescription drugs of the pharmacological industry, which purport to chemically straighten out our twisted minds without any effort on our part, it all depends on *us*.

Ayahuasca, and psychedelics in general, require active participation. They offer insight and healing, but only through conscious dialogue, through conscious relationship.

Taking ayahuasca is a sacred act, which must be taken in a sacred setting, since it opens the channels between human consciousness and … and what exactly? Plant Consciousness? Gaia Consciousness? Higher Consciousness? God? At the end of the day, these are just words. The essential nature of spiritual experience will always remain a mystery.

Psychedelics, of which DMT (the active ingredient in the ayahuasca brew) is just one, are no substitute for spiritual practice. They are powerful aids to meditation, visualisation, somatic energetics, emotional catharsis, deep psychotherapy, etc. etc., but they must be approached with the utmost care and respect. As soon as use turns into abuse, all the good work is lost. And they are not for everyone.

3. The Gateless Gate

An Enlightenment experience is called *satori* in Japanese. It is impossible to convey the content of this experience to someone who hasn't had a taste of it themselves. It is *ineffable*. This is why Zen Masters don't waste time discussing or debating the content or meaning of Enlightenment. If you asked a Zen Master, "what is Enlightenment?" he (or she) would probably just show you the best posture for zazen (sitting meditation). Words are pointless. Only direct, personal experience can answer the question.

Why? Because satori is not just one experience among others. It is an "ASC", an altered (or alternative) state of consciousness. Any description of it, if addressed to an "OSC", an ordinary state of consciousness, will automatically be translated into terms that make sense within the ordinary frame of reference. Alternatively, if the ordinary mind can't make sense of it, it just won't make sense!

Zen Masters are renowned for their bizarre and paradoxical utterances and behaviour. They make no concession to the state of consciousness of their students, in order that they might be jolted into *kensho* (a brief glimpse of Reality) or full-blown satori. The only way to make sense of the Master's strange words and actions is to meet them in the same state of consciousness. Thus the famous *koans* of the Rinzai School encourage trainees to break through habitual thinking by frustrating all the possible solutions offered by the OSC.

Satori is ineffable. It is also "nondual" and "egoless". These terms point to two further aspects of satori, which are themselves essentially ineffable. Let's take the first one first: "nonduality". On the face of it, this seems a rather straightforward and unproblematic concept. If there is no duality, there must be unity: "All is One". But what exactly does this mean? It is easy to say, and perhaps even easy to understand on an intellectual level. But what would the actual experience be like? How would it differ from our ordinary way of seeing things?

Clearly, if there is no duality, then there must also be no distinction between "self" and "other", which accounts for the condition of *anatta*, "no ego". This also makes perfectly rational sense.

But again, understanding this conceptually brings us no closer to the actual experience, which the OSC can only *imagine*, not experience.

*

The day after my own Enlightenment experience, everything was back to normal. It was overcast. And I was back in duality. Depressed at my inability to recreate the awareness of the day before, I went back to the riverside clutching a copy of Meister Eckhart's writings for good measure. I sat and gazed at the water. I meditated cross-legged on a rock. I read a few choice passages from the book. I meditated some more. Nothing. No magic. No parting of the veil of reality. The ducks seemed to be laughing at me. Meister Eckhart seemed abstract, pretentious, boring.

I found myself on the horns of a classic dilemma. Yesterday I was "Enlightened", but today I was "Deluded". I knew that I could create all sorts of stories, theories and ideas about yesterday. I could immortalize it in poetry, philosophize about it, mythologize it, even write a book about it. But the more special I made it, the less special my present reality seemed. The more attached I was to my enlightenment yesterday, the further it receded from the light of today. Only a few hours ago, and it was already lost in the mists of legend.

The day before, I remembered thinking, "this is nothing special". I knew that if I made it into something special, it wouldn't be real for me any more, because my OSC would be "nothing special" and therefore real. I would slip straight back into deluded thinking. But in the ASC, which I knew was really "nothing special", I also knew that I was experiencing reality for the first time in my life, and that what I had previously taken to be reality was just a dream in comparison. So it was kinda special!

Yesterday, my so-called ASC (by rights, it *should* be the OSC) seemed completely natural, totally real and perfectly ordinary. Now, however, looking back on it with my ordinary mind, it seemed a million miles away, another world, another reality, like Lewis Carroll's Wonderland or C.S. Lewis' Narnia. And there was absolutely nothing I could do about it. I felt as though I had been banished from Eden.

I knew that if I went to a Zen Master to tell him (or her) all about it and seek confirmation of my Enlightenment experience, he (or she) would just point at my empty hands and say, "Where is your Enlightenment now? Show me your Enlightenment *now!*" I would have to muster all my resolve to resist the temptation to tell him (or her) to eff off. But in my heart I would know that it was true: the more I obsessed over the past, even if it *was* a completely genuine Enlightenment experience, the less I was able to be in the present moment, and so the further I was from Enlightenment now. I was just dreaming about a time when I was awake, which, precisely because it was such a lovely dream, made it all the harder to wake up *now*!

I understood then the intractable problem of dualistic religion. The duality creates a great chasm between the "sacred" and the "profane", keeping us firmly and eternally on the profane side, with God and his angels eternally and sacredly cavorting on the other. We can establish some kind of communication across the chasm, through supplication and prayer, and catch occasional glimpses of divinity, but essentially we belong here, in the "real world", the "fallen world".

If we didn't make any distinction between the two worlds, the world of "enlightenment" and the world of "delusion", we could have no way of knowing that there was another, deeper reality. There's no way round it. Shakyamuni Buddha taught his disciples about "Enlightenment" and Jesus taught his disciples about the "Kingdom of God" as a way of pointing to a radically different way of experiencing the world. Were they talking about the same thing? Were they talking about what I'm talking about? It sounds like it to me, but who knows?

Whatever they did mean, or might have meant, the same problem rears its paradoxical head. The more "other" the other reality they point to, the more separate and inaccessible it seems, but the less "other", the less visible and clearly distinct it is, and the more likely it is to get subsumed into our ordinary awareness, co-opted, appropriated and colonized by the OSC.

If the nondual view is the true, enlightened, view, and the dualistic view is simply wrong and deluded, then not only is dualistic religion wrong and deluded, but the very duality between delusion and enlightenment must be wrong and deluded.

The term "nonduality" is itself dualistic, because it defines itself in opposition to "duality" (although nondualists attempt to avoid this inherent contradiction by doing away with the hyphen).

There clearly *is* a difference between delusion and enlightenment, so duality must be true. Yet if from the enlightened perspective there is no difference, then nonduality must be true. If we assume that enlightenment represents the true version of reality, nonduality trumps duality. But almost everyone, almost all of the time, lives in a non-enlightened state, so put to a vote, duality trumps nonduality. Even if it *seems* as if there is no difference between delusion and enlightenment when you're enlightened, we know that actually, of course there is *really*. How can we resolve this conundrum? Or are we just putting hair on the tortoise and a tail on the hare?

*

There is a third option: scientific materialism, which dismisses the whole crazy debate by pointing out that there clearly is no such thing as "Enlightenment" or "Kingdom of God", and therefore neither duality *nor* nonduality. They are just figments of a febrile imagination. Any ASC is just an altered state, a chemical imbalance, an aberration and a deviation from the objective empirical evidence of the OSC, which is as real as we'll ever get. Common sense and majority opinion carry the day. There is no "other world" and there certainly are no "other worlds". There is only *this* world, which you would do well to cleave to as closely as possible, if you want to avoid losing your grip on reality and on your marbles. Oh yes, and massacring millions of innocent people because they don't happen to agree with your particular brand of imaginary god and heaven.

Scientific materialists like to think that they are the enlightened ones. They are, after all, heirs of the European Enlightenment, which conclusively and comprehensively blew away the mists and cobwebs of medieval mysticism, scholasticism and superstition. Now we are all atheists, apart from a few irrational "Flat Earthers", because we believe in Reason, not God.

Does the arrow of progress necessarily point unambiguously "Faith" to "Reason"? Is materialism really an advance in the cultural, moral and spiritual evolution of humanity? The people that Jesus and Buddha addressed must have held a variety of beliefs and opinions, but the majority were probably *scientific materialists*. In other words, they were only interested in "this world". Why else would Jesus and Buddha exhort them to look for the "other world"?

The early shamans, who pre-dated organized religion by centuries if not millennia, taught that there was more to life than scientific materialism. They taught people techniques and practices designed to transcend the brute fact of materiality and access higher states of awareness. Shamans, prophets, philosophers, gurus throughout the ages, Moses, Socrates, Lao Tzu, Buddha, Shankara, Jesus, Mohammed, all pointed to a deeper and greater life than the ordinary one given to us in the OSC. They taught a radical duality and nonduality which promised emancipation from the dreary round of materialism.

Dualism presents its own problems, but monism is really a regression to a more primitive state of being, not a sign of progress. The great majority of people, the silent majority, have always been scientific materialists, since the earliest dawn of humanity. It's just that their science was so bad. Just because science has improved does not necessarily mean that scientific materialism, as a belief system, is right. Just because we know more about "this world" does not mean that there is therefore no "other world". It marks an advance in scientific understanding, but not an advance in religious understanding. Reason does not supplant faith. It supplants reason.

Science has certainly progressed enormously, particularly over the past few centuries, for which we should be extremely grateful, but so has religion. The understanding of dualists and nondualists is far greater and far more sophisticated now than it ever was in the past. Of course there are ignorant dualists and stupid dualists today, as there always have been, and there are ignorant and stupid monists (it's harder to find stupid nondualists but I'm sure they're out there somewhere). If you must compare, you should compare like with like.

Throughout history, there have been those that have heeded the call of the shamans, prophets and priests and have embarked on their own journey to "the other shore", and there are those, the majority, who haven't. Atheism and monism are nothing new. In a sense, they are the default position of an unreflective humanity. The modern myth that scientific materialism is a historical advance on religion has things precisely backwards. Human spiritual progress does not proceed from dualism to monism. It progresses from monism to dualism to nonduality.

*

Scientific materialism is not an option. So we are back with the seemingly intractable puzzle: duality or nonduality. Which shall it be? Or could it be both?

Yesterday, I somehow passed into another reality far more real than my ordinary, everyday reality. I passed through a "portal of God", or what the Zen tradition calls "the gateless gate". But today I found myself back on the outside again. From the outside, there is clearly a gate between *this* world and *that* world, which needs to be unlocked and opened and passed through in order to get from *here* to *there*. There is duality. But yesterday, on the other side, there was no gate.

Once through the gateless gate, I had turned to look behind me and had seen nothing but a vast, unobstructed view in all directions. No gate to be seen. No division whatsoever. Everything was included in the great nondual sweep of my vision, as if the gate I had passed through had vanished into thin air, as if it had never existed. Today, however, not just a gate, but a portcullis, a moat, a thorny forest and miles and miles of dark and treacherous boggy terrain seemed to separate me from this blessed vision of effortless unity.

Meister Eckhart said, "The eye with which you see God is the same as that with which He sees you."[7] Is this not another way of saying the same thing? The eye with which you see God is the "gateless gate". From the dualistic point of view, there is a "gate" between "you" and "God". And "strait is the gate". Only the most determined can pass through. Looking back from the other side, however, you are no longer seeing with your own eyes, but with "the eye of God".

Looking back at yourself, it is God that sees you. Looking back at the world, it is God that sees the world.

The eye is the same eye, but it is, as it were, a reversible eye, or a reversible lens. Looking up at Heaven from Earth as though through a telescope, you perceive a duality between Heaven and Earth, God and yourself. Looking back through the telescope from Heaven to Earth there is no duality, no separation, no boundary. All things are seen as part of One Existence. From this side, there is an eye. From the other side, there is no eye. There is only seeing.

4. Pantheism is not Sexed-up Atheism

"God does not play dice", said Einstein, famously. Was Einstein religious then? Religious people like to think so, and there are, indeed, plenty of instances where he does sound pretty religious. However, Einstein also apparently said that he was "a deeply religious non-believer"[8], which suggests that, while he may have occasionally had religious feelings, he didn't believe in God as such.

In *The God Delusion*, Richard Dawkins quite plausibly claims that Einstein's "deeply religious" feelings had nothing to do with traditional religious belief but were actually directed at the physical universe. He calls this "natural" as opposed to "supernatural" religion. Dawkins uses Einstein's case as a way of laying down the battle lines in his personal war against "supernatural" religion:

"As I continue to clarify the distinction between supernatural religion on the one hand and Einsteinian religion on the other, bear in mind that I am calling only *supernatural* gods delusional."[9]

"Einsteinian religion", according to Dawkins, is "natural religion" because it doesn't believe in anything outside or beyond the natural laws of the natural sciences. Einstein's God is not part of the God Delusion, because it's really just another name for Nature. Einstein liked to use the word "God" as well as the word "Nature", because, although he was a scientist, he had poetic sensibility. So when Einstein talks about God, it is just poetic license to more forcefully express his sense of awe and wonder in the face of the great mystery of the universe. Also, he was Jewish (though Dawkins doesn't make anything of that).

Apparently, Dawkins has no problem with this kind of thing. Here and elsewhere, he is at pains to stress that he too has poetic sensibilities. He is not just an unfeeling egg-head, but is also moved and inspired by the wonders of the natural world, so much so that he could even describe his feelings as "religious".

The Magic of Reality, a beautifully illustrated book for older children, in which he presents a series of supernatural myths about seemingly inexplicable phenomena followed by the corrective, scientific explanation, is an example of Dawkins' avowed intention to show how science is not only truer, but also more magical than any supernatural myth or religion.

*

At the time of the Enlightenment in the eighteenth century, the scientific revolution ushered in by Copernicus, Galileo, Francis Bacon, Isaac Newton and co. led educated people to question their traditionally held religious beliefs, and the Christian churches in Europe became understandably alarmed at the resulting spread of deism, atheism and pantheism in their congregations. Newton was a deist, who believed that God created the world, but then left the world to get on with it, along rational lines. This was a not unusual view in the more liberal of the young Protestant churches.

The temptation, following Newton, was to see the universe as a giant clockwork machine, running according to a pre-designed plan. God was like the clockmaker and evidence of his technical prowess and ingenuity was visible everywhere, and especially in the mathematical precision of its lawful workings. It is, of course, a small step from deism to atheism, since it is perfectly possible to marvel at the wonder of the "clock" without constantly (and boringly) invoking the "clockmaker". The result is a perfectly unsupernatural, mechanical universe.

Those of a more romantic nature, such as the "Romantics", baulked at this soulless, mechanistic vision. Spinoza's pantheistic philosophy inspired them to develop their own versions of a God-filled universe, as opposed to a God-forsaken one, and to find God in Nature. However, the distinction was a theological nicety in the view of traditional blinkered theists, and Spinoza was himself accused of atheism and excommunicated from the Jewish faith.

Dawkins agrees with the excommunicators. He describes pantheism as completely antithetical to traditional "supernatural" religion, again because it is really about Nature, not God:

"Pantheists don't believe in a supernatural God at all, but use the word God as a synonym for Nature, or for the Universe, or for the lawfulness that governs its workings."[10]

Apart from their predilection for God-talk, pantheists are therefore fundamentally no different in their beliefs from atheists. They are just "Romantic atheists", or, if you like, "sexed-up atheists". Dawkins seems to sum up the whole theological debate in two pithy witticisms:

"Pantheism is sexed-up atheism. Deism is watered down theism."[11]

In Einstein's God-talk, according to Dawkins, what at first sight looks like "Religion" with a capital "R", is in fact nothing of the sort. It is "Einsteinian religion", which is, basically, the same thing as "natural religion", which is actually what is usually called "pantheism", which is, after all, as we just saw, nothing but "sexed-up atheism", which, I think we can all agree, is really, deep down, just good old-fashioned "atheism". So Einstein was an atheist. QED.

Who cares? Dawkins' target is not really Einstein at all. Whether he was or wasn't an atheist is neither here nor there (apart from claiming support from one of the greatest minds that ever lived, that is). The *real* point of the argument is to show that pantheism is the same thing as atheism. Why?

With pantheism on side, as it were, he can simply forget about it and get on with the business at hand: refuting and ridiculing superstitious, deluded religion. After dispatching pantheism in this way, it is never referred to again in the whole of the rest of the book. Why should it be? It's a friend not a foe. Dawkins neatly kills it with kindness before the argument has even begun.

*

Is pantheism really the same thing as atheism? Isn't it really closer to theism? Atheism and theism are like two teenage boys fighting over a girl.

What if pantheism is actually at the very heart of religion? Robbed of pantheism, religion is like a bone without a marrow. Without pantheism, religion loses all trace of nonduality, and all credibility, because God is only allowed to exist in another world, not this one. Dawkins is like a dog with a bone, and it's easy to crush a bone as brittle as that.

Religion only makes sense if pantheism is taken as read. And if pantheism is on the side of religion, not atheism, there is no "God Delusion", as Dawkins himself admits, because then we're talking natural religion, not supernatural religion. Like Prometheus, he steals the fire of pantheism from the gods, not for the benefit of atheist mortals, however, but just so that he can hold up a cold, hollow religion for their general derision and amusement.

Of course there are superstitious people who believe in the supernatural, and there always will be. But to claim that anyone and everyone who believes in God is by definition a superstitious person who believes in the supernatural is to misunderstand what God means and what religion means.

True religion is not supernatural. It is natural. This is because true religion is built on the foundations of pantheism. Pantheism is the root and the flower, the beginning and the end, of the great tree of religion. This is the secret to understanding religion. Read the scriptures, doctrines and liturgy of Christianity with a pantheistic eye and it shines with truth and beauty. It makes perfect sense. Read with suspicion and skepticism, with no knowledge or understanding of pantheism, and it creaks and bends under the unbearable weight of illogicality and impossibility.

I am tempted to rewrite Dawkins' theological witticisms in the light of this understanding. I think it would be more correct to put it this way:

Theism is sexed-up pantheism; atheism is watered down deism.

Anyway, let's leave Dawkins to have his way with his imaginary supernatural friends, and see what Einstein has to say about natural religion instead.

*

"A human being is a part of the whole called by us universe, a part limited in time and space. He experiences himself, his thoughts and feeling as something separated from the rest, a kind of optical delusion of his consciousness. This delusion is a kind of prison for us, restricting us to our personal desires and to affection for a few persons nearest to us. Our task must be to free ourselves from this prison by widening our circle of compassion to embrace all living creatures and the whole of nature in its beauty."[12]

Einstein was a pantheist, but he was a religious pantheist, not an "atheist pantheist". The crucial difference is that Einstein believed that it was possible to see the unity beyond the separateness of the "optical delusion of consciousness". He believed that it was possible to intuit "the whole called by us universe" and to "embrace all living creatures and the whole of nature in its beauty".

An atheist might say that "the whole of nature" is all there is, so we might as well call it "God", but this is not the same thing, because he cleaves to the idea of separateness. Accordingly, "the whole of nature" represents only the sum total of all separate living creatures; it doesn't represent an actual unity. But to experience anything as separate, including God, is precisely what Einstein meant by "a kind of optical delusion of consciousness".

Pantheism, which asserts that the world is God, is implicit in the conventional theistic view. It wouldn't make sense otherwise. The belief that God is a supernatural being separate from the world is actually a heretical belief in all the major world religions. Jews, Christians and Muslims all stress belief in One God, and worship and pray to God as though He were a separate Being, but this does not mean that they believe that He *is* a separate Being. It's just that prayer only works through radical duality. The nonduality is implicit.

Orthodoxy asserts that God is "All and Everything". We can relate to Him both as *the All* and as *Everything*. It is a mistake, a heresy and a delusion to believe that God is *the All* but not also *Everything* (transcendent but not immanent). So, in order to avoid misunderstanding and escape accusations of atheism, pantheism must be understood to include the transcendence as well as the immanence of God. Some pantheists have, for this reason, taken to using the more explicit, though somewhat cumbersome term *panentheism* to emphasize the point. God is both *pan* and *en*, part and parcel, within and beyond, the world.

*

Pantheists believe that God is everything and everywhere: it's "all God" (pan-theos). For pantheists, Nature is God and God is Nature. Adi Shankara expressed this as simply as possible when he said that, "Brahman is the world". Hinduism, bewilderingly complex and variegated as it is, is considered to be pantheistic, although it has more than its fair share of supernatural deities, because it *is* pantheistic. Pantheism is the fount and foundation of the Vedas, made explicit in the Upanishads, the Bhagavad Gita and the Vedanta. Everything else is elaboration and decoration.

Shankara was obviously a pantheist. Was he an atheist or a theist though? If the statement, "Brahman is the world" were the whole of it, we might be tempted to call him a "sexed-up atheist" (although he was celibate!) but, crucially, this statement comes as the culmination of a tripartite formulation:

"The world is illusion; Brahman is the only reality; Brahman is the world."[13]

This formula provides us with the missing links that enable us to draw a definitive line between pantheism and atheism. For the atheist, the world is real and God (Brahman) is unreal. So when an atheist says, "God is the world" or "the world is God", he is saying no more than absolutely nothing.

Both these statements are basically empty of any meaningful content. They are just rhetorical flourishes, because he is not a real pantheist, but one of those atheist pantheists, who "use the word God as a synonym for Nature, or the Universe, or for the lawfulness that governs its workings."

When a true pantheist says, "Brahman is the world", on the other hand, he says it with the prior understanding that, "the world is illusion" and that "Brahman is the only reality". Only after affirming both the illusory nature of the world and the reality of God is he able to say that God is the world. Until you see God, you cannot see the world as it is in reality. When you see God, you see that the world itself is God.

*

Gazing at the endless succession of patterns on the surface of the water, I understood that "the world is illusion". Observing that the body of water under the surface was one and the same water, I concluded that, "Brahman is the only reality." Realizing that the endless succession of patterns on the surface of the water was in fact the play of one and the same body of water, I realized that, "Brahman is the world."

When I looked up from my water meditation, I found myself in a world transformed. I felt as though I had torn the veil of illusion and had entered paradise. The world had not physically changed in any way – I was not seeing things that were not there – but everything was, as it were, infused with a living spirit. It was the same world, but seen in a completely different light. I saw the wonder of existence, the fathomless mystery of the universe, things that a more religiously minded soul than mine would not hesitate to call God.

Pantheism is not sexed-up atheism. Perhaps an atheist sees waters as waters, and a pantheist also sees waters as waters, but there is a world of difference between the two. Let the Chinese Zen Master Ch'uan Teng Lu explain:

"Before I had studied Zen for thirty years, I saw mountains as mountains, and waters as waters. When I arrived at a more intimate knowledge, I came to the point where I saw that mountains are not mountains, and waters are not waters. But now that I have got its very substance I am at rest. For it's just that I see mountains once again as mountains, and waters once again as waters."[14]

5. Something that our Mind cannot Grasp

We are all connected. We are all "a part of the whole called by us universe". From our tiny, limited point of view, we are separate. From the point of view of the universe, we are one. However, since we habitually live our lives from the perspective of the separate ego, we constantly and continuously consolidate and confirm our limited, dualistic outlook on the world. Perhaps because Einstein spent so much of his time contemplating the universe, he could gain a wider perspective and see through this "optical delusion of consciousness".

Einstein said that, "this delusion is a kind of prison for us". Why is it a kind of prison? Most people do not feel that they are in a kind of prison. Or do they? Whether or not they express it in this way, I would wager that most people don't feel really, truly, completely free. I'm not just talking about external social and political freedom, but a sense of *inner* freedom. However congenial and propitious our outer circumstances, however successful, rich, famous and powerful we are, however free to do what we like when we like, we are still prisoners of *ourselves.*

Most people may intuit this in a vague, undefined way. Perhaps most people don't. As G.I. Gurdjieff pointed out, "If a man in prison was at any time to have a chance of escape, then he must first of all *realize that he is in prison.*"[15] Fair enough. But how can we realize we are in prison unless we know what it means to be free?

For Einstein the key is the realization that we are "a part of the whole called by us universe". This is indeed a grand vision. A little less ambitious in scope, and a little less grand, is the realization that we are "a part of the whole called by us Earth". In my case, I am also, at the time of writing, "a part of the whole called by us England". The important point is simply that I am not separate: I am part of a larger whole.

Does this mean that the universe is my prison? Or that Earth is my prison? Or that England is my prison? If so, I can think of worse prisons! No, this just happens to be where I live. It's definitely not a prison.

To fully and truly realize that I am part of England, part of the Earth and part of the universe, is actually *freedom*. Freedom from what? Freedom from myself. I am my own prison. But what is this prison I call myself?

In a sense, I am a prisoner of my own mind. I am imprisoned in a tangled web of thought. What are these thoughts? Some seem to come from me, and some seem to come from other people. Some are old thoughts, and some are new. I can't say for sure whether my old thoughts were originally mine, or whether I got them from somewhere or someone else. As for my new thoughts, I might call them "my" thoughts, but where do they come from? All I know is that they are the product of a lifetime of social conditioning.

I was born, forty-four years ago, into a society that predates me by millennia. Ever since the moment I was pulled from my mother's womb, I have been systematically indoctrinated and socialized, first by my parents, then by my nanny, grandparents, relatives, nursery teachers, children, school, friends, books, films, etc. etc. As William Wordsworth put it in *Intimations of Immortality*, "shades of the prison house begin to close upon the growing boy." Language, thought, feeling, even the way I hold myself and move my body, even the way I think and the way I write, everything about me is ultimately the product of social conditioning. This is my "prison".

Society is all in the mind. The mind is society. We carry it around with us wherever we go. It defines how we see the world, how we think and how we behave. Freedom cannot be found by "dropping out", however, as though society was a bucket and you could just fall through a hole in the bottom. You would still carry it with you, even into your hermit's cell. No, freedom cannot be found in social amputation. It can only be found by "widening your circle" to include all your "sisters and brothers": family, friends, acquaintances, colleagues, fellow citizens, compatriots, and the whole of the human family.

The wider our circle of compassion, the wider, and more spacious, is our prison house. But we will always be in "a kind of prison" as long as we identify ourselves as members of some kind of society, however broad or wide.

True freedom, absolute freedom, is found only when we transcend *all* human societies, and identify with the Earth as a whole: "Our task must be to free ourselves from this prison by widening our circle of compassion to embrace all living creatures and the whole of nature in its beauty."

*

The Hindu pantheist Shankara proclaims that *the world is illusion*. This is the world seen through the lens of the separate, dualistic mind, "a kind of optical delusion of consciousness." This illusory world is the world of the prison house. The Hindus call it *maya*. Next, he proclaims that *Brahman is the only reality*. Brahman (God) represents the *whole*, which for us humans is the Earth (Gaia). This whole is *one*. It is a unified whole. Not just the sum of its parts, but a synthesis of a higher order. What can this mean?

Take a human being. The "whole" of a human being is more than the body, and more than the mind or personality. There is an unchanging essence that persists through all the physical and psychological changes in the body and the mind. What is this essence? We might call it the "Self" or the "Soul". We might call it "the Unified Consciousness of the Organism as a Whole". But where does this unified consciousness come from? For that matter, where does *consciousness* come from? How are we conscious at all?

In attempting to answer this question, the obvious place to look is neuroscience and the philosophy of mind. Clearly, it must have something to do with the brain. So what is the brain exactly? Well, it's mass of cells called neurons. But the brain is not just a bunch of neurons sitting in your skull detached from the rest of your body. It reaches down into every part of you via the sympathetic and parasympathetic nervous system. If you were to slice off the top of your skull and pull your brain out, it would come trailing a huge you-shaped mass of dangling nerves, the longest of which reach right down to the tips of your toes. So although consciousness is clearly associated with the brain, and brain cells, it must also be connected with the rest of the body, and body cells.

The human body is made up of thirty trillion eukaryotic cells, and the human brain is made up of ten billion neurons, highly evolved and highly connected eukaryotes. All of these cells communicate with each other, especially the neurons. All these cells are alive. They are alive and they communicate. In a rudimentary sense, therefore, they display all the hallmarks of *consciousness*. Working together as one organism, through complex and intricate networks of communication, through what is known as "organic functionalism", all these trillions of separate, individual mini-consciousnesses produce one unified field of consciousness, one "Unified Whole", which we experience as our "Self".

The Hindus call the "Self" the *Atman*. And they call the "Higher Self" the *Paramātman*. What is the "Higher Self"? Evolution has already produced the unified consciousness of organisms, including human organisms, through the organic functionalism of eukaryotic cells. What if the same process, using organisms as the new units of organization, produces the same result on a higher level? Cells organize into "societies", just as organisms do. What if societies of organisms produce a higher synthesis, like societies of cells do? What might this higher synthesis look like?

Well, it would look like a "Self", but a "Higher Self". It would look like the "Self" of the whole of life on Earth, like the "Soul of the World", the *Anima Mundi*. Human beings, as the most highly socialized organisms, would then be the equivalent to neurons on the cellular level. In other words, human societies would form the "brain" of the planet. This planetary brain would be highly connected, and continuously communicative, like the Internet. Considering that the human population of the Earth is projected to reach ten billion by the end of the century, which is approximately the same as the number of neurons in the human brain, this is perhaps not so fanciful as it sounds.

Even if the planet had a "Soul", and exhibited some kind of higher consciousness, we would not necessarily be aware of it, just as individual cells in your body are not necessarily aware of "you". But it is conceivable that some neurons in the human brain are in fact, in some mysterious way, aware that they are part of a greater whole.

These special neurons may even be instrumental in the overall consciousness of the organism, so that your sense of yourself as a unique, unified consciousness might actually depend on them. If they were killed somehow, through brain damage, you might still continue to live and function more or less normally, but you wouldn't be a conscious person any more. You would be a (philosophical) zombie.

Analogously, we could speculate that a few human individuals are responsible for the maintenance of the unified consciousness of the planet. These "special" individuals are the *mystics*, who have expanded their sphere of identity to encompass the Earth in its entirety. This cannot, of course, be a merely rational identity, but a total, intuitive, spiritual one. We need words like "intuitive", "spiritual" and "mystical" to point to a type of experience and a type of knowledge that is qualitatively different from the rational. Rationality and thought are, after all, products of society, which is by definition limited to the human, "brain" world.

The word "religion" (from the Latin re-ligare), like the word "yoga", literally means to bind together, tie together, or yoke together. It points to the unity of nondual consciousness beyond discriminative thought. This nondual consciousness makes perfect sense when the dualism of Self vs. Other is transcended through identification with the whole. From the point of view of the planet, of course "All is One", since everything is part of the one planet. Maurice Bucke's *Cosmic Consciousness* should really have been called *Gaia Consciousness*. The mystics in his fascinating study transcended their identification with themselves as separate persons, and identified instead with the whole, which is more realistically the whole planet, rather than the whole cosmos.

*

In *The God Delusion*, Dawkins quotes Einstein in order to more clearly distinguish his form of natural, "Einsteinian" religion from the traditional religious belief in a "supernatural" God:

"To sense that behind everything that can be experienced there is a something that our mind cannot grasp and whose beauty and sublimity reaches us only indirectly as a feeble reflection, this is religiousness. In this sense I am religious."[16]

This rather vague profession of religiosity suits Dawkins fine, albeit with an important caveat. Dawkins writes:

"In this sense I too am religious, with the reservation that 'cannot grasp' does not have to mean 'forever ungraspable'."[17]

Dawkins believes that any gaps in our present understanding of the universe will be filled by the ineluctable march of scientific progress. What cannot be grasped today will one day be grasped by the scientific minds of the future. But Dawkins is wrong when he says that he too is religious in the sense that Einstein is religious, because with this reservation, he clearly shows that he has completely missed the point.

Whatever can be "grasped" by the mind must be grasped as an object of thought. Empirical scientists and rationalist philosophers can grasp empirical data and intellectual concepts, but the "something that our mind cannot grasp" alluded to by Einstein is by definition "ungraspable", precisely because it cannot be treated as an object, whether physical or mental.

What is this "something" which can be sensed "behind everything"? If it cannot be grasped, it is because it is not a "thing" to be grasped, not because it is a thing we haven't quite got around to grasping yet. What could that be? A "something" that is "nothing"? We're in mystical territory again! Well, the two obvious candidates for absolutely ungraspable things that are neither "things" nor "no-things" are *God* and *Consciousness*.

The vagueness of Einstein's profession of faith might prompt us to plump for *God*, the ultimate in vagueness. However, *Consciousness* also satisfies his criteria. It is impossible to "grasp" consciousness, because it is always consciousness that is doing the grasping.

Consciousness is always *subject*, never *object*, and can only ever be inferred by its effects, never experienced directly. It is like an eye trying to see itself. The "I" is beyond the reach of scientific investigation, because, like a receding mirage, it constantly eludes capture: "I am not that which can be observed".

Hence the Vedanta practice of "Self inquiry" proceeds through the radical negation of "I", just as the Christian apophatics, following pseudo-Dionysus, proceed by negating "God". By dismissing and discarding each object of awareness with the words *neti, neti* (not this, not this), the yogi excludes all superfluities and objectifications and backs up, so to speak, into pure Self Consciousness, or Self-Realization. Ultimately, God and Consciousness point to the same thing. God is *Paramātman*, the Higher Self, which is just another word for Higher Consciousness.

In modern philosophical terms, this is basically *Panpsychism*, which posits that consciousness is integral to and constitutive of the very fabric of the universe. A panpsychist is essentially a "property dualist", which means that she considers consciousness to be an inherent property of matter, not just an emergent property or an epi-phenomenon (but who says matter isn't actually a property of consciousness?)

From this point of view, all living organisms are conscious thanks to their component cells, and all living cells are conscious because of their component atoms. Consciousness grows in intensity with each level and order of magnitude, but is present throughout. We cannot draw a line anywhere, even between sentience and insentience, if we want to explain the existence and origin of consciousness as we know it. It is "turtles all the way down". *Everything* that exists is conscious, in its own way, even if, to our eyes, the degree of consciousness is vanishingly small.

If evolution is not interrupted by some cataclysm and continues along the same trajectory, the next logical step in its unfolding must be the unified Self-consciousness of the planet. Planet Earth is either already conscious or is becoming conscious, as a result of the interactions of its trillions of component living organisms, just as individual organisms are themselves conscious due to the interactions of their trillions of component cells.

Speculating further into the future, we would expect Self-conscious planets to form societies between themselves, eventually resulting in a unified, conscious universe. In other words, we are all active participants in the evolution of consciousness of the universe, which we could call *the evolution of God*, whether we like it or not, and whether we know it or not.

*

This understanding of the nature of the universe is basically pantheistic because it sees "God" as being present in nature and the universe. Theists generally don't like pantheism, because they think it collapses the distinction between Creator and Creation. In a sense, if God is everywhere, then He is nowhere. Atheists like Richard Dawkins like this understanding of pantheism for the same reason. It collapses the distinction between the natural and the supernatural, thereby excluding the possibility of a transcendent God beyond. But beyond what? Beyond material processes? Beyond biological processes? Beyond psychological processes?

Biology certainly seems to transcend physics in many important respects. One of the most obvious is the reversal of entropy through the creation of homeostatic systems. Our bodies exist according to rules that transcend the rules of physics. And our minds exist according to rules that transcend the rules of biology. Is there perhaps a mode of existence that transcends the rules of human cognition?

When we understand that the universe is organized holarchically, which is to say, as a nested hierarchy of transcendent levels of reality, we can begin to understand how "God" can be both "within" and "beyond" existence, or at least beyond any particular level of existence. We might say that the cell is "God" for its component atoms, that the organism is "God" for its component cells and that the planet is "God" for its component organisms. But why stop there? There is presumably also a "God" for living planets. And at the other end of the scale, how do we know that an atom isn't "God" for its quantum subjects? From where we are standing, we can already see a nested holarchical system of five levels of existence with five "Gods".

This is a more sophisticated view than the simple caricature of pantheism as a simple belief in the inherent divinity of Nature. Whether or not people take this low resolution version of pantheism seriously, either for or against, it's abundantly clear that as soon as you begin to unpack this idea, you are forced to articulate a more nuanced view. As I mentioned in the previous chapter, this more nuanced view is expressed in the slightly more complex (and clumsy) word, "panentheism", which makes explicit the assumption that God must be both within and beyond, immanent and transcendent. But the word "God" (theos) is obviously a heavily loaded term with all sorts of positive and negative associations. It is also, as atheists often point out, horribly vague. What exactly do we mean by "God" anyway?

Well, of course it's vague. If it were easily definable, it wouldn't be transcendent. It wouldn't be "God". However, having said that, what if we were to substitute the word "Consciousness" for "God"? Would that help or hinder matters? We have some idea of what consciousness is, although we can't define it precisely. We can experience it in our own lives, and can infer its presence in other lives. At the very least, we have a theory of other minds. But as soon as we universalize consciousness, and imagine that it may be something that actually exists across the entire holarchy of existence, then we approach something of the magnitude, majesty and mystery of the traditional conception of "God".

We intimately know our own personal portion of consciousness, which we think of as the essence of our Self, what the Hindus call *Atman*. What if this same consciousness exists throughout everything? When we entertain this possibility, we begin to get a sense of what the Hindus mean by *Brahman*, something like "Universal Consciousness". We can call this view "pantheism" or "panentheism", but perhaps "panenpsychism" is a better word, because we're talking about *Consciousness*.

Do we lose anything important with this substitution? I don't think so. The Being of God, so to speak, is preserved in the "pan" bit of the formulation. In other words, Consciousness is embodied or actualized in Form. It is not just a disembodied Spirit. So this view is not susceptible to accusations of Gnosticism (which sees Spirit as trapped in Matter).

According to panenpsychism, Spirit and Matter (Consciousness and Form) are "not-two": they co-exist in a state of "property dualism", even if at the very limit, Consciousness is believed to transcend Form. But then again, for all we know, it doesn't. How could we possibly know for sure, since we are irrevocably embedded in Form? Either way, the "en" bit of the formula works fine as a pointer to the transcendent nature of consciousness across different levels of the holarchy. My Self-consciousness transcends my biological reality, for example.

If we add to the idea of panenpsychism the holarchical arrangement of existence unfolding through time, which is basically what "evolution" means in its broadest sense, then we can more clearly define this philosophical understanding of reality as "evolutionary panenpsychism" or if you prefer, "holarchical panenpsychism", depending on whether you want to emphasize structure or process.

To be fair to Dawkins then, who is perfectly justified in using the reductive version of pantheism if he wants to, I should really qualify my claim that "pantheism is not sexed-up atheism". What I meant to say was, "holarchical panenpsychism is not sexed-up atheism". But who listens to holarchical panenpsychists?

6. A Walk in the Forest

Watching the brilliant points of fire
Dancing on the water, weaving endless forms,
Orion, Las Vegas, Cleopatra's burnished throne,
I think of Thales sitting by an Aegean stream
On such a luminous day as this, struck
By the same certainty: the world is water.

Since the beginning of time, the same stream flows,
And the same stream Thales saw, I see now:
A perpetual flux, movement without pause,
Sparkling, shimmering, infinite, eternal.

The world is water. It never stops moving. The form the world takes in one instant is instantly superceded by another, then another, then another. To grasp the nature of the world is like trying to grasp a waterfall. Seen from our human vantage point, it is forever ungraspable, because it is forever and infinitely mutable. Seen from the perspective of the world as a whole, however, it is easily grasped: one waterfall, one world.

When we look at the world through the eye of "I", we see *maya*, illusion. This does not mean that what we experience is not real, like a mirage in the desert. It *is* real, but refracted through the shattered prism of duality. Like the light of the sun on the water, broken up into thousands of tiny points of light by the ripples on the moving surface, we see the world divided into thousands of separate beings and things. We live in an infinitely complex world of duality and multiplicity.

When we look at the world through the eye of "Gaia", on the other hand, it is like seeing the light of the sun as one, unbroken, light. It is like seeing the full moon reflected on a perfectly still lake. The full moon, like the sun, is a symbol of the fullness of nondual consciousness. When we look at the moon in the night sky, we are not looking at the light of the moon, of course.

We are looking at the light of the sun reflected off the moon's surface. The moon is like a giant celestial mirror. We cannot look directly into the sun without burning our eyes, but we can look directly at the moon, which partly explains the enduring popularity of moon worship. The moon is the intermediary between us and the sun. It "cools" the extreme energy of the sun, so to speak, making it more accessible to human communion.

We cannot look directly at the sun, just as we cannot look directly at the source of consciousness. But we can see it indirectly reflected in the things around us, on water and in the moon, just as we see evidence of consciousness in the objects of our awareness. When we commune with the sun, by meditating on its reflection on the water or in the moon, we begin to take on the same unified perspective, as if we were taking a sun's eye view. As we turn our attention to the world around us, we now see a "full Earth" as well as a "full moon". In other words, the Earth is experienced as One World. This is the essence of nondual awareness, or "Gaia Consciousness".

In nondual awareness, the world is no longer divided up into subject and object, self and other. There is no separation between "me" on this side of the line, and the "world" on the other. A skeptic might counter that that's all very well, but that the objective fact of the matter is that there *is* a "me" over here and a "world" over there. Blurring the line between the subject and the object is just blurring a line that actually exists.

*

But what is "the world" anyway? Does it really have any independent, objective existence? Or is what I call "the world" really just my *idea* of the world? It took the genius of George Berkley to definitively spell out the inescapable fact of *immaterialism*: we cannot ever know anything directly, but only the representation of things in our minds. This startlingly obvious idea is also at the heart of German Idealism, most clearly stated in Immanuel Kant's distinction between the phenomenon and the noumenon. Arthur Schopenhauer used this insight as the foundation of his philosophy, which he succinctly describes at the beginning of his masterpiece, *The World as Will and Idea*:

"'The world is my idea': this is a truth which holds good for everything that lives and knows, though only man can bring it into reflected, abstract consciousness. If he really does this, philosophical discretion has evolved in him. It then becomes clear to him, and certain, that he knows not a sun, and not an earth, but only an eye that sees a sun, a hand that feels an earth; that the world which surrounds him exists only as idea – that is, only in relation to something else, the one who conceives the idea, which is himself."[18]

To understand this is to understand that, ultimately, *the world is illusion*, and that this illusion is a projection of the self, an "optical delusion of consciousness". In Eastern spiritual traditions, this is called *maya*. Maya is only overcome by seeing it for what it is. It is *the illusion of objectivity*. We think we live in an objective world, and as a result, end up living in a hopelessly subjective one. Recognising the illusion of maya is the first step to freeing ourselves of it. As soon as we see the absolute subjectivity of the world, we free ourselves from our unconscious subjectivity and, paradoxically, begin to see the world more objectively. Ultimately, of course, the distinction is an artificial one.

When I look at a tree through the lens of my self, I automatically assume that there is consciousness located in my body, probably somewhere in my brain, which somehow reaches out to grasp the tree. I assume that I am a conscious subject over *here*, and that there is an objective tree over *there*, with a distance of several metres between us. If I think about it from a scientific point of view, I can imagine a kind of tree-like pattern of light travelling through the intervening space between "me" and "tree" landing (upside down of course) on my retina, to be flipped over and presented to my awareness as a pretty good likeness of the actual, objective tree.

But if I picture the process in this way, I end up holding two trees in mind: the actual big tree several metres away, and a small picture of it on my retina. Am I looking at the small picture or the big picture? If the small one, then what's that big tree I can see over there, plain as plain?

A Walk in the Forest

It's the *same* tree. I am not looking at some cramped little bonsai tree in my head. The tree over there *is* the tree in my head. It is nothing but my idea of the tree projected outwards, beyond my body, in three-dimensional visual space.

Whatever I look at in my field of vision is an *idea* in the sense that it is *in my mind*. But "in my mind" does not mean in my skull, in this "meatball head". My mind reaches out to the furthest horizon every which way. The world around me is in truth nothing other than my mind. Every sense experience, smell, taste, touch, sound as well as sight, all of them are in my mind.

The apparent gap between the tree *over there* and the image I have of it *over here* doesn't actually exist. There is no gap. The sense of distance and space between us is just part of the same visual content of my mind. Me and the tree and the space between are all part of the same idea, the same simple act of consciousness.

*

Here's a thought experiment for you. Imagine you are happily dreaming and then, all of a sudden, you "wake up" in your dream. You start *lucid dreaming*. This means that you continue dreaming whatever it was you were dreaming, except that now you are fully aware that you are dreaming. You know that it's not real. You know that, however convincing and realistic, it is all just a projection of your mind.

One of the most striking things about lucid dreams is their extraordinary detail. Normal dreams seem hazy and vague in comparison, like a fuzzy old black and white TV set compared to the latest high spec, high res, high definition 3D flat screen surround sound entertainment system (or whatever they call them these days). Lucid dreams are almost as real as real life.

Imagine you are lucid dreaming that you are walking through a forest. Everything around you, the trees, the leaves, the blue sky, and whatever else you can see, is experienced with exquisite precision and in glorious technicolour. Yet you know that you are not really walking through a forest at all. You are fully aware that you are in fact walking through your *mind*.

You know that there is no gap between your subjective consciousness and the "objective" world around you. The sense of distance, as you come out of the forest and survey an ocean stretching for miles beyond the edge of a cliff, is also just a figment of your imagination. The tiny ship on the horizon is just as much *here*, in your mind, as the stone by your foot. Waking consciousness is no different.

Here's another experiment. Try walking through a real forest. As you walk (slowly and mindfully please), imagine that you are "headless". There is no need to assume a "meatball head" over *here* looking at a forest over *there*. Your immediate, direct experience of the actual state of affairs is that you are, indeed, headless. Imagine that you forgot that you ever had a head. According to the evidence of your senses, there is no head, there is only the world in all directions.

The late, great Douglas Harding, stumbled upon this simple observation, which, he claimed, is the common experience of mystics of all times and places. He teased out the implications of "headlessness" in a series of brilliant, disarmingly accessible books. *On Having No Head* is one of the great spiritual classics of the twentieth century.

At the end of the day, whether we experience it as "no mind, only world" or "no world, only mind", we are inhabiting the same nondual universe. Either way, it is "not-two".

When everything is seen as permeated by and contained within one consciousness, "things" take on a special quality of Being. They radiate Being as expressions of the one, universal Being. "There is no self anywhere; there is only Gaia". This is really the same thing as saying, "The world is illusion; Brahman is the only reality". Reduced to just two words, which can be used as mantra or koan, we have, "Maya; Gaia". No longer taken in by the illusory play of images projected onto the surface of the water, we take in the full body of water beneath. My consciousness is not my personal, individual possession, as though it were just one shining light among millions. It is the universal "Gaia consciousness" shining through me. When I experience this egoless state of nonduality, I can honestly say (with apologies to St. Paul), "Not I, but Gaia lives in me."

*

From the point of view of eternity, life is like a flash of lightning, or a bubble on a stream. This age-old lament is laconically and beautifully expressed by Ernest Dowson:

"They are not long, the weeping and the laughter,
Love and desire and hate;
I think they have no portion in us after
We pass the gate.

They are not long, the days of wine and roses:
Out of a misty dream
Our path emerges for a while, then closes
Within a dream."[19]

However, life goes on. As the Beatles sang on their Sergeant Pepper album, it goes on "within you and without you". We are like the proverbial light bulb screwed into the eternal current of life, which will one day burn out and be replaced by a new one. The electric current is not mine. The light is not mine. The bulb is not mine. *Life* is not mine. What are this body and this mind, after all, but temporary, fleeting expressions of life and consciousness, of "Gaia".

If you are reading this, we can safely assume that you are alive and conscious. *Here* and *now*, you are alive. Think about the time before you were born and after you die, though. Time stretches back into the past, to all intents and purposes, to infinity (or 13.8 billion years if we're going to be pedantic about it), and likewise into the future. If we could randomly select any time in the life of the universe, the chances are that at that time, *you don't exist*. The same goes for your existence in space. You exist at this point in space, but not at any other point in this infinitely expanding universe. At any other time and space, anywhere else on Earth for that matter, or at any time in its long history and long future, you simply are *not*.

Is this a depressing thought? Shakespeare certainly doesn't give us much cause for cheer in Macbeth's famous soliloquy:

"— To-morrow, and to-morrow, and to-morrow,
Creeps in this petty pace from day to day,
To the last syllable of recorded time;
And all our yesterdays have lighted fools
The way to dusty death. Out, out, brief candle!
Life's but a walking shadow, a poor player
That struts and frets his hour upon the stage
And then is heard no more. It is a tale
Told by an idiot, full of sound and fury
Signifying nothing."[20]

But flip life and death around and suddenly, you are released from the existential burden of mortality.

One final thought experiment: imagine you are walking through a forest again. You are painfully aware that your life is as transient as the dew on the grass. In the grand scheme of things, your life is completely meaningless, "a tale told by an idiot". However, you know that the pain of this acute consciousness of your own mortality is in your attachment to this fleeting life.

What if you were to give up this attachment? Since most of the time, and in most places, you don't actually exist at all, what if you simply "cut out the middle man" and acted as though you don't exist *now* either? Since your life is so vanishingly small compared to the enormity of the universe, this shouldn't be too difficult. All you need to do is project yourself a mere hundred years into the future or a hundred years into the past. What happens?

You don't exist. But you are still here. So you cease to identify with this temporary "light bulb" that is "you", and allow the infinite current of life and consciousness to pass through unimpeded. A lifetime's work of ego building evaporates in an instant. You are still alive and conscious, but this life and consciousness is unfiltered, undiluted, unattached. Furthermore, it is *immortal*. You walk calmly through the forest like a "dead man walking", and the whole forest, and the whole world is alive in the blissful glow of eternal life.

7. Spiritual Autism

In his Introduction to *The God Argument: The Case against Religion and for Humanism*, A.C. Grayling claims that,

"...history is moving in the right direction from the point of view of those who wish to see the human mind liberated from religion and superstition, ... powerfully aided by the work of Richard Dawkins, Victor Stenger, Daniel Dennett, Sam Harris, Dan Barker, and the late and much lamented Christopher Hitchens and others..."[21]

It is true that most people in the developed world are now atheists and that Christianity in particular is undergoing a major crisis of faith with ever dwindling (and ageing) congregations. Grayling looks forward to the time when we are *all* atheists, and "the human mind" (if there is such a thing) is liberated once and for all from its religious and superstitious shackles. He is clearly proud to count himself among this illustrious company, spearheaded by Richard Dawkins, heroically ushering in this future religion-less utopia through sheer intellectual force and scientific rigor.

The New Atheists, as they have come to be called, are the latest in a long line of thinkers who subscribe to the Enlightenment project, begun over two centuries ago, which set out to establish human knowledge on human reason alone. It seems that they feel that the high standards of "the Age of Reason" have begun to slip, and are in need of a new, modern boost. Surely, with their awe-inspiring collective brainpower combined with the amazing advances in recent scientific knowledge, the New Atheists can finish the job and finally put the sinister spectre of religion to eternal rest?

In this ambitious book, Professor Grayling attempts the seemingly impossible: to do battle with God and win. Can he do it? He quickly discovers, to his evident consternation, that, not only does God not play dice, He doesn't much go in for boxing either:

"…contesting religion is like engaging in a boxing match with jelly: it is a shifting, unclear, amorphous target, which every blow displaces to a new shape. This is in large part because the religious themselves often do not have clear ideas, or much agreement amongst themselves, about what is meant by 'religion', 'god', 'faith' and associated concepts. And this is not surprising given the fact that these concepts are so elastic, multiple and ill-defined as to make it hard to attach a literal meaning to them."[22]

It turns out that 'God' is not such an easy target. He is just too vague and too jelly-like to knock down once and for all. What exactly is 'God' (or 'god')? What is 'religion'? What is 'faith'? It seems that the religious can't even agree amongst themselves. They don't have "clear ideas" about the meaning of these concepts, presumably because, being superstitious, they are chronically fuzzy-headed. Since this (admittedly somewhat ill-defined) group of people, "the religious", can't properly define these crucial concepts for themselves, the first job in the battle against religion and superstition, is to define them for them. This is clearly a job for a philosopher, and as a Professor of Philosophy, Grayling is more than qualified for the task. But he has his work cut out for him, since "these concepts are so elastic, multiple and ill-defined as to make it hard to attach a literal meaning to them." Hard, maybe, but for one of his philosophical acumen, surely not impossible!

*

In the battle against religion atheists have no problem defining concepts like 'god' to their satisfaction, whereas the religious are never satisfied. Because atheists believe that 'god' is just an idea, a human invention, with no independent reality outside the human mind and human culture, to refute the idea of 'god' is to refute 'god'. Annoyingly, however, the sneaky religious keep moving the goal posts. Every time one version of 'god' is floored, another version is rolled out from the wings. The atheist must patiently and diligently knock them down one by one, until the religious, one day, simply run out of ideas and so out of 'gods'.

The use of the lowercase 'god' emphasises the fact that 'god' is just an idea, just a word, like any other, the main difference being that it does not actually refer to anything real. Hence, of course, its jelly-like quality. Since it doesn't actually mean anything in reality, it can be made to mean practically anything in religious fantasy.

For a religious person, on the other hand, the belief that God (with a capital letter and without quotation marks) is a fact, and not a concept, means that He is not vulnerable to logical refutation. Ideas about God can be asserted, debated, refuted, affirmed, debunked, and bandied about ad infinitum (and ad nauseam), but none of this human intellectual jousting has any real bearing on the brute fact of God. We cannot have "clear ideas" about God, or attach "literal meaning" to Him, because He transcends the capacities of human reason. He is "something that the mind cannot grasp".

According to the religious, then, God is "ill-defined" because He is *undefinable*. What about other religious concepts, such as 'religion' and 'faith'? Can 'religion' be defined? Of course, we can come up with some definition of religion if we put our minds to it. Alternatively, we can just look it up in the dictionary. But which dictionary? Which definition will we finally opt for as the definitive one?

If there is no definitive definition of religion, it is because there is no exhaustive definition. Anything we say will necessarily be a simplification. Even if we could include everything that has ever been said and written about every religion that exists now or has ever existed, including, of course, all their associated sacred scriptures, this would still not be sufficient to exhaust all the possibilities contained in the word 'religion'.

What about 'faith'? What about 'hope'? What about 'love'? These concepts are perhaps more manageable, since they point to specific human attitudes, experiences and emotions. On the face of it, they seem a good deal less amorphous than the baggy monster we call 'religion'.

A religious person has 'faith'. How do they experience this 'faith'? Is it an intellectual assent to a set of beliefs? An emotional commitment? Irrational belief? A special "spiritual" faculty? Does the religious person themself even know what 'faith' is?

A common wish in Christian discourse is that we may "grow in faith". In other words, 'faith' is not static or fixed. It is by nature "elastic" and open-ended. Where does 'faith' end? It is inconceivable for the faithful that they will ever reach the end of faith, because there is no limit to the potential for further growth. In this life at least, we can never reach a full and complete understanding of the meaning of faith. Any understanding we may have, even on our deathbed, is provisional.

The same is true of 'hope' and 'love'. Can you imagine a time when you could honestly say, "*Now* I know what love is. That's it. I have nothing more to learn. I've been there, done that"? However much you may have loved, however many lovers, love poems, rom coms, novels, operas, drama, heartache, ecstasy, depths of despair and heights of bliss you may have plumbed or scaled, there is always more. How do you know that the *real* love of your life is not just around the corner and that all your ideas about love will be turned upside down? (again). And that's just erotic love! What about all the other kinds of love?

Love is infinite. It can never be exhausted, or rolled up into a ball and understood and defined once and for all. How can you attach a "literal meaning" to 'love'? Even the most hardened materialist atheist, intent on reducing 'love' to a particular firing of certain synapses in the brain and the release of certain endorphins in the blood stream would have to concede that that's not even half of half the story.

What about the Platonic trinity, 'the Good', 'the True' and 'the Beautiful'? Can we ever finally reach a consensus on the correct definitions for goodness, truth or beauty? Can we ever exhaust the possibilities contained in these concepts?

Consider 'beauty'. Will we ever stop deepening our understanding and appreciation of 'beauty'? If we do stop for some reason, is it not with the full knowledge that we are missing out? The *potential*, if not the actuality, of our ever-deepening relationship with 'beauty' is infinite. Beauty is infinite. That being so, we can "grow in beauty", and "grow in love", just like religious people "grow in faith". There is no end to the potential for growth in this life. Will there ever come a time when I possess 'Truth' in its entirety? Will I ever know everything? Will I ever be perfectly 'Good'? Of course not. There is *always* more.

This is a very Platonic way of thinking. In fact, it is the essence of Platonism. 'Goodness', 'Truth', 'Beauty', 'Faith', 'Hope', 'Love'; these are all *Ideas* or *Ideal Forms*. They are infinite and inexhaustible. They represent an absolute reality that is always beyond us, forever out of reach. Yet we can experience them, taste them, and acquire knowledge and understanding of them, albeit partially, through our interactions and engagement with things here in the material world. But they will always be "ill-defined", because we can never know them fully.

The deeper our understanding of these things, of course, the better will be our definitions, even with the knowledge that our definition does not define completely. How can I define the meaning of 'love'? If I have any real knowledge and experience of love, a logical definition, like what you would find in a dictionary, is not enough. I might define 'love' through poetry, music, painting, sculpture, philosophy, dance, gesture, action, or all of these things. Still it won't come close.

*

Professor Grayling wants "clear ideas" about religious concepts like 'religion', 'god' and 'faith', so that he can engage them in intellectual debate. He certainly doesn't want poetry or art, let alone myth and symbol. The implication is that religion only has any valid claim to truth if it can be expressed in clean, logical, scientific, propositional form. This is the voice of logical positivism. Linguistic signs and utterances that do not abide by these criteria are not fit for serious consideration as statements of truth and have no bearing on reality as described by the natural sciences. From this point of view, true philosophy is not the metaphysical "love of wisdom" celebrated by the Ancient Greeks and their heirs, but simply the handmaid of science, clarifying technical issues of meaning and logic.

This is the philosophy of Dr. Spock from the Starship Enterprise. It is not surprising that Professor Grayling does not engage with any of the stories, myths, parables, allegories, sayings, proverbs, prophesies or poetry from any of the scriptures of any of the world religions, let alone the Bible. From his point of view, it's all "illogical, captain".

The "new atheists" want to stamp out religion with the giant jackboot of science. But science is silent about things like 'god', 'faith', 'love', and "the peace that passeth all understanding". Does that mean that these things don't exist? Or just that science cannot see them? By "science", we usually mean "natural science", which is the study of the material world, physical, chemical and biological. It is really *material* science.

In his book, *Eye to Eye*, the transpersonal thinker Ken Wilber draws on the medieval distinction between three "eyes" of the soul. "The eye of flesh" sees things of the flesh, in other words, material things, and "the eye of mind" sees things of the mind, ideas and images. Only "the eye of spirit" can see spiritual things, and the pregnant infinity behind everything that exists. Science only sees through "the eye of flesh". It is tied to a strict empiricism which is necessarily blind to mental and spiritual phenomena. Adherents of *scientism*, who regard science as sufficient for the comprehensive understanding of reality, therefore suffer from "mind blindness" and "spirit blindness", a kind of "spiritual autism".

Grayling is *against* religion and *for* humanism. Humanism is not scientism of course. It honours and makes full use of "the eye of mind". But it still suffers from spiritual blindness, because it cannot see the infinity beyond its own definitions of what the human standard of the truth of things is. The measure of "humanism" is the measure of man, which is simply the human mind, *manas* in Sanskrit.

Grayling is not championing Renaissance Humanism or Christian Humanism of course, but "Humanism against Religion". And what is "Humanism against Religion" but a line drawn around all traditionally religious concepts, such as 'god', 'faith', 'goodness', 'truth', 'beauty' and 'love', thus cutting them off from their roots in infinity, and claiming them as the rightful property of 'humanity'? But how can we define 'humanity'? If we limit the meaning of any of these things, we only end up by limiting ourselves.

*

Plato's *Ideal Forms* do not only apply to abstract concepts, but to everything that exists. 'Taste' is infinite. It is impossible to exhaust all the possibilities of taste, even if we limit our experience to 'cheese' and 'wine'. Therefore 'cheese' is infinite. 'Wine' is infinite. Our experience of 'cat' is infinite, so 'cat' is infinite. 'Table' and 'chair' is infinite. Our experience of tables and chairs can never be definitively exhausted. We will never have experienced everything and know everything there is to know about tables and chairs. We can "grow in table and chair", just as we can "grow in faith".

According to Plato, everything that exists is infinite, because everything is a present manifestation of an infinite potential. What better way to express this infinity of everything that exists that to say that it all rests in the infinity of God? 'God' is the ultimate concept of infinity that includes all other infinities within it. Everything is infinite, because everything is part of one infinite God. So we can, after all, attempt a definition of 'God': "God is Infinity". But that definition sounds more like a description than a definition, because no definition, however broad, can even come close to exhausting the possibilities of what God is.

None of this makes any sense to the rational, materialist atheist, because for the atheist, none of this exists. 'God' obviously doesn't exist, and neither does 'faith', 'love', 'goodness', 'truth', beauty' and the rest. These are just man-made terms we attach to things to describe our personal judgments and feelings about them. They have no independent meaning apart from the particular objects they refer to in each particular instance. There are no *Ideal Forms*.

This then, is the fundamental difference between atheists and the religious. Atheists don't believe in the infinite "spiritual" potential represented by Plato's theory of the *Forms*. I may have several, perhaps many, similar emotional experiences, which I choose to denote to myself and others with the word 'love', but this does not mean that there is such a thing as 'love' above and beyond those particular experiences.

In other words, an atheist, if he is to be intellectually consistent and coherent, cannot believe in 'love'. There can be no such thing. For a religious person, however, love is a "thing" which can grow and be added to.

Every experience and act of love adds to our deepening relationship to one thing, called 'love'. Love exists. Love is infinite. We grow in love. The religious claim that not only does love exist and that it is infinite, but that "God is love". Unsurprisingly, this definition-description of 'God' is also conspicuously absent from Professor Grayling's treatment.

'Truth' is also considered to be "a spiritual thing" by the religious, because it transcends any particular instance of its manifestation. When I have a eureka moment, or experience a revelation or epiphany, a powerful insight, or just have a common-or-garden thought, I know that it has some truth to it, because it carries a "truth charge", so to speak. Over time, after hundreds and thousands of these experiences, I realise that it is not just about the specific content of the thought I am having at the moment. It is about my on-going "growth in Truth". I become less interested in this one particular truth, and how I can turn it to my personal advantage, perhaps, than in the cumulative store of Truth to which this one thought has added. My sights are set, not just on this one grain of truth, but on the whole mountain.

Therefore my insight is actually a spiritual experience, because it is associated with the spiritual *Idea* of Truth. My sense of goodness, and my experience of beauty are also spiritual experiences, because they are part of the spiritual *Ideas* of Goodness and Beauty. If I view my life in the light of the infinite potential of all my experiences, sacred and profane, *everything* is a spiritual experience, because everything points to the endless unfolding of infinity. Another way of saying the same thing, is to say that I see and experience God in and through everything. "God is everything". This is the religious attitude. Everything has infinite meaning. Nothing has "literal meaning".

*

A few days ago I was baptised and confirmed in the Anglican faith at St Paul's Cathedral. My atheist Jewish girlfriend came to support me, along with two gay friends. She found it amusing that I had brought two gays and a Jew to this solemn Christian rite. It was a moving and beautiful service and I felt that I had indeed been initiated into a new dimension of religious life.

However, I was also aware that my friends and girlfriend probably had quite different experiences. My girlfriend later described how she had felt a little intimidated and alienated by the grandeur of the cathedral and the relentless Christianity. She found that although she was aware that there was beauty there, she couldn't completely connect with it. She felt cut off behind a psychological wall.

My girlfriend habitually described herself as an atheist Jew as well as a feminist, a socialist, an artist, an academic and a vegetarian. On all seven counts, Christianity represented a threat. So I was, of course, very grateful and pleased that she agreed to come along. I was also pleased that she actually enjoyed it. How?

At a certain point in the proceedings, she decided to meditate. As she did so, she relaxed her defences, and suddenly, in an instant, her whole experience changed. The light became infused with a numinous quality, colours were richer and brighter, the sounds of the choir swirled through her like a delicious perfume. Her anxiety abated, she could actually begin to enjoy herself.

One way of understanding this epiphany is to view it as a loosening of the psychological hold of identity politics. Her identity as a Jew and an atheist created a psychological stand-off between her and her sensory experience. She felt that the structure of her identity was fixed, and that the structure of the established church was fixed, and that they were, in a deep sense, antagonists. Therefore she had to defend herself against the enemy forces through withdrawal, distrust and distaste. Only when the hold was loosened could she allow some beauty and grace in.

Ironically, the Church of England has taken identity politics to heart, and upholds the rights of individuals to define themselves in whichever way they choose. Before the service, for example, I had time to look around the gift shop in the crypt, and was intrigued to find a prominently placed book about Christianity and the body. But it wasn't about Christian yoga or Christian shamanism. It was about transgender issues.

The Church of England is renowned for being right-on and "politically correct". Over the past few decades it has striven to be as inclusive as possible in the bewilderingly complex milieu of modern British life, with mixed results.

Although this is an undeniably laudable aim, this subscription to identity politics can appear to weaken and dilute its spiritual message. It is, after all, hard to take the "trendy vicar" seriously when he is more concerned not to give offence than to inspire and instruct.

In the case of my girlfriend, the PC brigade would uphold her sovereign right to maintain intact her chosen (and given) identity. She is an "atheist feminist socialist Jew". This is who she is and anyone who dares challenge her view of herself and the world is a "fascist" (this is not my girlfriend's view by the way). Identity trumps everything (unless you do happen to identify yourself as a fascist, of course, in which case you deserve a sound thrashing!) But is it really who she is? If not, who is she really?

*

"Who am I?" is one of the oldest and most intractable of philosophical questions. It is the shining question at the heart of Advaita Vedanta. It is the essence and substance of the *Self Inquiry* of the great Indian yogi Ramana Maharshi. The former Shankaracharya of Jyotir Math, H.H. Shantanand Saraswati, puts it simply:

"If you begin to be what you are, you will realise everything, but to begin to be what you are, you must come out of what you are not. You are not those thoughts which are turning, turning in your mind; you are not those changing feelings; you are not the different decisions you make and the different wills you have; you are not that separate ego. Well then, what are you? You will find that when you come out of what you are not, that the ripple on the water is whispering to you 'I am That', the birds in the trees are singing to you 'I am That', the moon and the stars are shining beacons to you 'I am That'. You are in everything in the world and everything in the world is reflected in you, and at the same time you are That – everything."[23]

When my girlfriend relaxed the hold of her seemingly fixed identity, she tasted the truth and beauty of 'I am That'. This is only possible because her true essence is beyond all definitions, identifications or fixed meanings.

Who am I? 'I' cannot be fixed in a definition, just as 'God' cannot be fixed, or for that matter, 'religion', 'faith', 'love', 'beauty', 'truth', 'cats' and 'dogs', 'tables' and 'chairs'. Nothing in the world is fixed, because everything is *infinite*, including my 'Self', which is ultimately not "mine", but the 'Self' of everything – 'I am That'.

Am I a Christian, now that I have been baptized and confirmed in St. Paul's Cathedral by the Bishop of Kensington? Is this now my identity? In one sense, yes of course. I am now a member of the Church of England. I am a follower of Christ. But at the same time, I am beyond all labels and definitions. I am also a follower of Buddha and a devotee of the Egyptian goddess Isis. In a sense, I am also an atheist. But with Walt Whitman I can say, "Do I contradict myself? Very well, then I contradict myself, I am large, I contain multitudes".

There are people who cling on to their identities for dear life. There are fundamentalist Christians, for example, who cling to a literal reading of the Bible and to a very narrow definition of what it means to be a Christian. If their beliefs are challenged, they experience it as an assault on their very being. These are the kinds of people that atheists prefer to engage with in their mission against God. They have "clear ideas" and "literal meaning". They do not constantly morph into different shapes like jelly. They will put up a good fight.

Ironically, the first criticism levelled against radical Christian or Islamic fundamentalists by atheists, is precisely that they are so literal minded. They are caricatured as being, in a sense, "intellectually autistic", unquestioningly following the revealed "truth" of scripture but blind to the real truth of science and logic. Exponents of this rigid, inflexible attitude to religion are also, in a sense, "spiritually autistic". They heed the letter rather than the spirit. Somehow, they seem to have missed the point completely. For just this reason, they make perfect bedfellows for radical atheists like Dawkins and Grayling.

*

In "contesting religion", Grayling feels as though he is "engaging in a boxing match with jelly". It does not seem to occur to him that jelly is not meant for boxing, but for *eating*. Eating is at the centre of the Christian faith.

When a Christian receives communion and eats the bread and drinks the wine, she is eating the body and drinking the blood of Christ. In effect, she is "eating God". This is a mystical sacrament, which imparts divinity directly through the grace of God and the faith of the believer.

However, the act of "eating God" can also be understood symbolically as ingesting and digesting the *teachings* of the Christian religion, in other words, the "Word of God". Christ is called the "Word", because He embodies and represents the truth and wisdom of scripture and religion more generally, as expressed through the Church and its ministers, for example. To break down the metaphor further, we can say that to understand the things of God, to understand spiritual things, it is necessary to first take in the teaching of God (the "Word") through reading or listening, then to chew it over, swallow it and digest it.

Those, like Professor Grayling, whose aim is to contest religion, rather than learn anything from it, are unlikely to get beyond the chewing stage, whereupon they will promptly spit God out, with varying levels of decorum. Because Professor Grayling refuses to eat his jelly, but insists on fighting it instead, he cannot begin to understand the nuances of religious belief and practice. Instead, he wrestles with a two-dimensional caricature. His philosophical insistence on "clear ideas" and "literal meaning" is itself a telling sign of what, for want of a better term, I am calling "spiritual autism". Whether this condition is due to some psychological attachment to his personal identity politics, or to something else, is not for me to conjecture.

In any case, the inalienable fact remains that certain people just "don't get religion", whether they choose to shoot it down or not. John Calvin believed, following Augustine, that this was evidence of *predestination*. Evidently, some people receive the Holy Spirit through the grace of God and some people don't. Why? Since we receive this grace as a gift and not through any effort on our own part, the only reasonable conclusion is that God has chosen some to be saved and some to be damned. And there is absolutely nothing we can do about it.

Who knows? It is a powerful if counter-intuitive idea. It seems more reasonable, I think, to suppose that we do have some say in the matter and can choose to open ourselves to the infinite grace of God which continually pours down on everyone without distinction. The saving grace of God as Father, Son and Holy Spirit is there for the taking, always and everywhere, but people just refuse to see it or accept it.

It may be that part of the problem is in fact something like "spiritual autism". Perhaps some atheists do have an actual congenital condition that precludes them from understanding or experiencing spiritual truths. Reading *The God Argument* with mounting disbelief, I found it difficult to come to any other conclusion.

8. The Portal of God is Non-Existence

Since Bodhidharma brought Buddhism to China in the fifth or sixth century, Zen trainees have meditated facing a wall. This "facing the wall" has both a practical and a symbolic significance. On a practical level, it minimizes visual distractions (Zen monks meditate with their eyes open). Symbolically, the wall is a great barrier, apparently immutable, between the trainee and Enlightenment.

I am sitting in silent meditation, facing a blank wall in the Zendo, trying to meditate on Emptiness. Focusing on a point on the wall in front of me, I try my best to empty my mind. But my eyes wander and my mind wanders. I start thinking about the meaning of existence, and the meaning of non-existence.

I start wondering about Emptiness. Apparently, atoms are 99% empty space, or something like that. Didn't CIA agents on acid try to walk through walls in the 60's when someone told them? And didn't they stare at goats as well for some reason?

Why can't we walk through walls? Why does everything seem so solid when it isn't? The size of the nucleus compared to its orbiting electrons in an atom is apparently like a football in the middle of an Olympic-size football pitch compared to a fly buzzing round the outside of the stadium. That's a lot of emptiness!

It's not for want of space that we can't walk through walls then. The atoms in the wall could slip past the atoms in my body easily, if it wasn't for the electromagnetic fields around the atoms, that is. Shame!

*

Chuang-Tzu, the great fourth century BC Taoist sage, was almost certainly completely ignorant of these matters. But he was an expert on Emptiness. After Lao-Tzu, the author of the *Tao Te Ching*, Cuang-Tzu is the best known and best loved Taoist philosopher in China. There are many wise sayings attributed to him, and although there is no God in Taoism (is there Tao in Godism?), he did say that, "The portal of God is non-existence"[24].

Zen Buddhism was greatly influenced by Taoism, and the Mahayana concept of *Sunyata* (Emptiness) was particularly suited to the Taoist approach to spirituality. Of course neither the Taoists nor the Buddhists were talking about physical, atomic emptiness. They were talking about a kind of mystical Emptiness, which is closely related to what the Japanese call *mu-shin*, "no-mind".

Thinking about the actual physical empty space around us is itself quite mind-boggling. There is the microcosmic space within atoms (and how much of the nucleus is empty space anyway?) and there is also the macrocosmic space between atoms, between physical things in space, like this cup of tea and my hand, and between planets, stars and galaxies. Most of the universe is just empty space, not to mention the infinite nothingness beyond the limits of the physical universe. Just take a look at a traditional Chinese Taoist landscape painting and you will be instantly struck by their profound intuition of the emptiness at the heart of existence.

In a sense, this kind of emptiness is relative, because it only exists relative to the forms within and around which it hangs. It is "the space between", the cosmic *akasha* of the Vedas. Even the great yawning inter-galactic spaces are part of the universe, as much as the solid stars, planets, meteors and cosmic dust passing through. Like an empty cup, this kind of emptiness can be "filled". It is like the emptiness inside Lao Tzu's clay pot:

"We shape clay into a pot,
but it is the emptiness inside
that holds whatever we want."[25]

Is this "space between" and "emptiness inside" the "portal of God"? Is this what Chuang-Tzu meant by "non-existence"? There is the eternal dance of yin and yang, and the endless play of being and nothingness, existence and non-existence, emptiness and form. Is he suggesting that we reject form and cleave to emptiness? But wouldn't that be taking sides? Wouldn't that disrupt the T'ai Chi balance?

He must be talking about a kind of non-existence beyond the duality of existence/non-existence. An absolute, rather than a relative, Emptiness.

But how can the idea of *absolute non-existence* make any sense in a manifestly existent universe? Perhaps there was absolute non-existence before the universe appeared, that is, before "the Big Bang". Of course there is no way of knowing what there was before "the Big Bang". Maybe nothing. Maybe God. Maybe both. Maybe "God" is "Nothing". But then "Nothing" cannot be a portal to "God". In any case, now that we exist in an existing universe, isn't the absolute non-existence that might have preceded it just a thing of the past? Like an empty pot, hasn't it been filled by the universe?

Without getting into too much of a logical twist, we can accept the possibility of absolute non-existence by reflecting that space and time are intrinsic properties of the universe, which only emerged with the birth of the universe itself. Therefore, there was neither space nor time "before" the Big Bang. Clearly, we can't even talk about "before" if there was no time, or "beyond" if there was no space. But if the universe is not actually eternal, and did have a beginning in time (around 13.8 billion years ago we think) then we can posit a kind of "before/beyond", even if we can't exactly understand how.

At the very least, we can assert that this "before/beyond" the universe, being also "before/beyond" space and time, cannot itself be displaced by space and time, since it doesn't "exist" in space and time. It is not like the space in an empty pot. When my cup is filled, there is no space for more tea, but the "non-existence" is *still here*.

Lao-Tzu spoke about this mysterious dimension of absolute non-existence two and a half thousand years ago:

"There was something formless and perfect
before the universe was born.
It is serene. Empty.
Solitary. Unchanging.
Infinite. Eternally present.
It is the mother of the universe.
For lack of a better name,
I call it the Tao."[26]

The Tao is absolute non-existence. It is "infinite" and "eternally present" precisely because it is beyond space and time. Beyond space it is "infinite", beyond time it is "eternal". Of course infinity doesn't just mean an incredibly big space and eternity doesn't just mean an unfeasibly long time, although this is how we usually think of it. Beyond space and time, infinity and eternity point to a *different dimension*. Non-existence only "exists" in a different dimension.

Lao Tzu does not say "infinite" and "eternal". He says "infinite" and "eternally present". This is important. As creatures of the universe, we exist in time and space. But there is a "portal of God" within space and time. This window on infinity, this portal, appears at the intersection of space-time and infinity. This intersection is called *the eternal present*.

*

The eternal present includes both spatial and temporal dimensions: it refers to "presence" as well as "the present"; it is both *here* and *now*. When we usually say "here", we mean the place in the vicinity or in close proximity to the speaker. It is "here" as opposed to "there", which is of course further away. This is the conventional usage, which determines locations in space relative to an arbitrary point of reference. Of course if I am standing at one end of the room and my girlfriend is standing at the other, my "here" will be her "there" and my "there" will be her "here". In reality, every point in space is just one "there" relative to any other point.

The same is true of time. When we say "now", we mean a point of time in within a short range of our utterance. We are marking a point in time relative to another point in time. It is "now" because it is not "then". However, as soon as we have vocalized the word "now", it has already become "then", depending of course on the range we have decided on. "Now" can refer to a period lasting a nanosecond, a second, a few minutes, or even a decade or century. It is simply a particular point in time relative to other, more distant points in time. Every point in time was or will be "now" at some point, so defining this particular point in time as "now" is as arbitrary as defining this particular point in space as "here". Space and time are relative.

The *Here and Now* of the eternal present is not relative. Everywhere is *Here* (with a capital H) viewed from its own location, that is, without reference to any other point in space. Therefore it is infinite. Everywhen is *Now* (with a capital N) with reference to its own occurrence. Therefore it is eternal. The intersection of infinity-eternity with the space-time continuum is Here and Now in the eternal present. This is "the portal of God".

How can we pass through this portal? How can we enter into the eternal present? To answer this question, it may be helpful to first consider our ordinary experience of time. We think of time as flowing from the past into the future, intersected at every moment by our immediate experience of the evanescent present. We only ever exist in the present, but we seem to be constantly moving, as if we were on a boat being swept along by an irresistible current.

*

Here you are then, on your little boat, bobbing down the river of time. Everything you can see on the bank of the river is part of the passing show of life. When you look behind you, everything seems to be moving away from you, with the most recent events closer to the back of your boat and the most distant in time further away. Some events you can see in their entirety, as objects with a beginning and an end, others disappear into the distance with no visible beginning, and still others continue past your field of vision into the invisible future.

When you face the bank directly, and view passing and past events sequentially, they look as though they are plotted on a time-line. You can think about past events in relation to each other, and make connections between them and see different patterns and constellations of related events. The time-line ends at your present position on the river, but it is of course possible to use your store of memories and your imagination to predict and project it on into the future. From past experience you know that the future is often determined by the past, and at least partially predictable. But since you cannot look into the future directly, it is impossible to know for sure what will happen next.

You cannot look into the future directly. But what happens if you try? It is as though you are sailing into a thick fog. Even with a light, it is impossible to see anything beyond the prow of your boat. The future is invisible, until the very moment it becomes present. You cannot see or experience the future, only ever the present moment as you gently glide into the impenetrable fog, but the present moment never stays the same. It is continually changing, constantly renewed by the new. And then, as soon as it appears, it disappears, out of view behind the boat.

Peering into the dense fog of the future, there is no time to think about the future or the past because the new present just keeps on coming, moment by moment. It's as though there were neither past nor future, only the ever-changing present. You are in a "cloud of unknowing". You don't know what is coming or what is gone, only what *is* right now. From this vantage point, future events are not experienced as the effects of past causes with the present as go-between. The present is now experienced as the continuous, endless *creation* of an invisible future, and the past is completely invisible, and totally irrelevant.

When we turn to face the future, the chronological sequence of events flows in the opposite direction. Things appear from the future and disappear into the past instead of flowing from the past into the future. Time flips round 180°. But in actual fact, this is how we actually experience the flow of time, before we reconstruct the order of events in our minds.

Try slowly walking across the room, or wherever you happen to be, and pay close attention to how you experience the sequence of events as you walk. With each step, the future comes to greet you. Only in retrospect, which is to say, only in your *memory*, does it make sense to say that your first step was taken before your last. As you were actually walking, each step emerges from the future into the present, and as you take your last step, the first step *no longer exists*.

This may feel a little strange or uncanny at first. Experiences suddenly seem very undiluted, raw and immediate. We are so used to experiencing time and events as though they were rooted in the past. The world seems so much safer, so much more solid and reliable when we view it through the window of the past.

The frighteningly precarious present moment is then experienced as a mere speck, as just the latest addition to the great monument that is the past. In another moment, it too will be past.

It's as though we were constantly adding grains of sand to a great sand dune. The sand dune appears solid and immutable. It has already happened and so is immune to the ravages of time. In a sense, it is immortal, and it is perhaps this that gives us the illusion of immortality and the comfort that goes with it. But this giant sand dune of the past, and all the past grains of sand of which it is composed, is only "immortal" because it is dead. It no longer exists, except as traces of thoughts and images in our mind.

To be in the present and to face the unknown future head on is frightening. Anything could happen. However, sitting safely on our sand dune, we know that anything won't, because, to a greater or lesser extent, it is *us* who determines what happens next. We are not simply passive recipients of the future. We are also *creators* of the future.

If we live in the past, we are conditioned by the past, and in some cases even determined by the past. We are tied to the past by seemingly unbreakable bonds of causality. We are servants and sometimes slaves to karma.

If we find the infinite potential of the future too frightening, we will embrace our slavery, for the simple reason that our past conditioning and habits, our *automatism*, gives comfort and security. Better a scripted life of predictability than a perpetually improvised chaos. Or is it? We seem to be caught in an eternal tug-of-war between the demands of the future and the demands of the past, between life lived and life remembered. Somehow our little boat tacks between the two.

Ben Jonson seems content with small helpings when he writes that, "in short measures, life may perfect be"[27], but T.S. Eliot's *Prufrock* is full of regret:

"For I have known them all already, known them all –
Have known the evenings, mornings, afternoons,
I have measured out my life with coffee spoons."[28]

*

My thoughts spin off in a reverie of drawing rooms, cappuccino and cake. My back hurts and my legs are killing me. How long can this go on? When will they ding the little bell and release me from this torment? I pull myself together and make an extra superhuman effort to bring my mind back into the present. I focus on my breathing. I focus my gaze on the wall in front of me.

What is the meaning of this blank wall? I can't see beyond it. Yet I persist in facing it. In a strange way, it's like the implacable, invisible wall of the future.

"It is serene. Empty.
Solitary. Unchanging.
Infinite. Eternally present."[29]

Facing the wall in the eternal present, I find that I am actually facing the future. Maybe I am actually facing God. My mind wanders again and soon I am thinking about religion and atheism.

*

Atheists like to think of the religious as well-meaning but sadly deluded cowards. Who needs God? Only madmen and weaklings. The existentialist breed of atheist in particular is proud to unflinchingly look a Godless world square in the face and to shower scorn on the God-deluded. However, it may be that deep thinking existentialists like Heidegger and Sartre, caught between *Being and Time* or *Being and Nothingness*, were actually much closer to God than anyone, perhaps themselves included, realized.

Arguments for or against the existence of God mostly consider the problem in spatial terms. If not the hackneyed "old white beard" in the sky, we spatial beings can't help conjuring up vague conceptions of some kind of grand, transcendental spatial Being. But what if we approach the mystery of God not through "Being", but through "Time"?

The freedom and dread so beloved of existentialists are closely related to our existential confrontation with time, since existential dread is the direct result of our acute apprehension of absolute freedom in the face of the indeterminate future. Because the existentialists positioned God in the past, as a superstitious relic of a people bound by custom and ritual, they naturally saw religion as little more than a giant comfort blanket against the stark reality of personal freedom and responsibility. In the atheist tradition of Marx ("religion is the opium of the people") and Nietzsche ("God is dead") existentialists regard belief in God as a conservative and reactionary panacea that keeps humanity enslaved in the past.

Kierkegaard, the original existentialist, saw things quite differently. For him, dread was connected to the radical faith of Abraham, who unflinchingly obeyed God's cruel command to sacrifice his own son Isaac. Abraham's God was not a saccharine God of Victorian hymns and weak tea. He was the God of "fear and trembling".

There are of course those, perhaps the majority, of the religious, who worship the God of the past, the God of comfort and consolation. These are the existential cowards. However, there are also those who worship the God of the unknown and invisible future. These are the existential heroes.

*

God cannot be found in space and time. He can only be found in the infinite and eternal future in the infinite and eternal present. The future has always been Here and Now from the very beginning, and will be until the end of time (if there is such a thing). It is the omnipresent, omnipotent creator of the world, the "mother of the universe". Genesis is not an event in the distant past, but an actual and present reality Here and Now. Creation is *now*, eternally ushering in the future from the infinite shores of possibility and necessity.

Who is "the son of Man?" He who is born of the past. Who is "the son of God"? He who is born of the future. The future is the Father as well as the Mother. The Father begets the Son eternally in the Holy Spirit of the present, just as He has since the beginning of time (if there is such a thing).

And the Son forgives all sins, for in the eternal present born of the infinite future, there is no past, there is no karma, and there is no sin.

9. Seven Gods

The existentialist thinks that he is free because he bravely faces the unknown future of infinite possibility. But he isn't. He is beset by a sense of existential dread, nausea, meaninglessness, absurdity, anomie and despair (and melodrama). Cut loose from the anchor of the past, he finds himself aimlessly drifting on a postmodern sea of relativity. Nothing really matters.

Existentialists think that it is enough to look through the portal of the eternal present. This is what distinguishes them from the inauthentic masses, who blindly and unthinkingly follow the dictates of social convention, and whose values, opinions, attachments, happinesses and sadnesses, and the curious ease with which they seem to live, is, in the eyes of the existentialist, nothing more than a charade, a meaningless pantomime, a theatre of the absurd, a "tale told by an idiot, signifying nothing".

If these innocent simpletons saw the truth of their existential situation, even once, they would see what a pointless, fictitious existence they lead. They would throw away their spiritual crutches and stand on their own two feet, and take full responsibility for every free and self-willed act. They would have no more use for the old moth-eaten props of religion, fairy tale and myth, but would be transformed into mature, existential adults: filled with dread, nausea, anomie and despair.

To be truly free, it is not enough to only *look* through the portal of the present. If you only look, you will be turned to stone, as if you had looked directly at the face of the Gorgon. The nether world between time and eternity is a realm of petrified ghosts: poor existential souls caught in a perpetual existential crisis.

If you really want to be free, you can't stay on the outside of the magic mirror looking in. You must go through it. Enter the eternal present, and everything is turned back to front. The normal chronological order of things is reversed.

Events are "anti-chronological", or "ante-chronological" (since this is the natural order of things before our minds reconstruct them, backwards, in the memory). The world rotates 180°. Time flows towards you from the future, instead of from the past.

So what happens if I try to step through the looking glass? Nothing. I hit a brick wall. It seems that there was a wall behind the mirror after all! So what now? How can I get through the wall?

The wall is blank. The mind is blank. I have entered the dark void of the unknown future. This is as far as the existentialist is prepared to go, and he quickly retreats back to the comfort of his nausea, and the iterative pleasures of his cynicism.

*

Back in the meditation hall facing the wall (after another cup of tea and a chocolate biscuit), I am determined to break through to the other side. I redouble my efforts. I sit perfectly still and erect without fidgeting. My breathing slows down and my mind follows suit. I just sit there, quietly, patiently waiting for something to happen. Waiting without expectation, seeking without seeking. All of a sudden, everything comes to a complete standstill. I have no idea how. Somehow, I've slipped through the portal of the eternal present.

Those incessant reminders of the past, my thoughts, have vanished without a trace. I am in a void: the void of the future. It feels almost as if I am *inside* the wall. Perfect darkness. Perfect stillness. After a few seconds, which already seem like an eternity, I feel a faint flutter of panic in my belly. I think of that Edgar Allan Poe story about a black cat. Will I be trapped in here forever?

*

AMUN

AMUN is an Ancient Egyptian god dating from around the 21st century BC, known as "the hidden one" or "the invisible". He is a god of darkness and mysticism.

The word "mysticism" has its origin in the Greek mysteries. These were secret initiation ceremonies, the object of which was "to break through the world of history and time into that of eternity and timelessness."[30] Secrecy was essential, in order to keep the rites safe from the prying eyes of the uninitiated: "the word 'mystery' (*mysterion*) comes from the Greek word *muo*, to shut or close the lips or eyes."[31] Similar initiation ceremonies were performed in Egypt, centuries earlier, and there is now compelling evidence to suggest that the Greek mysteries were directly descended from the Egyptian.

By strange coincidence (or could there be some mysterious etymological link?), the Japanese word for "nothing" is *mu*. This is a very important word in Zen Buddhism, and has become the object of one of the most famous koans of the Rinzai school. In some monasteries it is chanted aloud as a mantra.

The same "dark wisdom" entered the Christian tradition through Dionysius the Areopagite, and became known as the *via negativa*. Christian mystics were those who turned away from the external trappings of religion and entered into the "divine darkness", the "cloud of unknowing", and the "dark night of the soul", in order to approach more closely the mystery of God:

"We pray that we may come unto this Darkness which is beyond light, and, without seeing and without knowing, to see and to know that which is above vision and knowledge through the realization that by not-seeing and by unknowing we attain to true vision and knowledge."[32]

RA

"In the beginning God created the heaven and the earth.

And the earth was without form, and void; and darkness was upon the face of the deep. And the Spirit of God moved upon the face of the waters.

And God said, Let there be light: and there was light.

And God saw the light, that it was good: and God divided the light from the darkness."[33]

Out of the darkness, suddenly, out of nowhere, an iridescent light. This is the light of RA, the Ancient Egyptian sun god. He is the Lord of Light. He rises from the darkness of the void like the Golden Dawn. The warmth of his bliss-bestowing rays suffuses every cell of the body, filling the body and mind with wave after wave of divine energy.

What is this divine light and divine energy? Where does it come from? It is as much of a mystery as the darkness that precedes it. The tantrikas and yogis of India call it the serpent power *kundalini*, which they awaken and control with their magical tantras and yogas, like the snake charmer in the marketplace. It is the *Chi* (or *Qi*) of the Chinese Taoists and the *Ki* and *Reiki* of the Japanese Buddhists and Shintoists. It is the *Shekinah* of the Jews and the *Holy Spirit* of the Christians.

It is the very same energy the prophet Isaiah spoke of when he said, "No high likeness and no peace of love will satisfy me until I myself am kindled and enflamed in the love of the Holy Spirit"[34] and that which filled the apostles: "And there appeared unto them cloven tongues like as of fire, and it sat upon each of them. And they were all filled with the Holy Ghost"[35].

The Spanish mystic, St. John of the Cross, was as much a mystic of the light as of the dark. After "the dark night of the soul" comes "the living flame of love":

"In this state the soul is like the crystal that is clear and pure; the more degrees of light it receives, the greater concentration of light there is in it, and this enlightenment continues to such a degree that at last it attains a point at which the light is centred in it with such copiousness that it comes to appear to be wholly light, and cannot be distinguished from the light, for it is enlightened to the greatest possible extent and thus appears to be light itself."[36]

The American scientist and LSD researcher Richard Alpert (Swami Ramdas), who collaborated with Timothy Leary in the 1960s and later converted to Hinduism, wrote:

"When the source of immortal joy is opened within us, it flows and saturates every fibre of our being, internal and external, and makes our life at once a waveless peace and ceaseless thrill of ecstasy."[37]

ATUM

Once we have passed through the purgatorial darkness of AMUN and the refining fire of RA, our eyes are opened to the splendor of the Ancient Egyptian creator god, ATUM, "the All".

William Blake wrote that, "If the doors of perception were cleansed, everything would appear as it is: infinite."[38] ATUM represents the earth beneath our feet, the lakes and oceans, the fire in the hearth, the wind on our face, and every object of sense: rocks and trees, birds and flowers, houses and cars.

The world as we know it is not the world as it is. We see it through the coloured lenses and filters of our conditioned minds: "For now we see through a glass, darkly"[39]. We perceive things for their instrumental value, for what use they can have for us, rather than their intrinsic value. As a result, we do not see or hear, smell, taste or feel things fully.

In order to survive in this world, it is enough for us to recognize the things in front of us, without going to the trouble of perceiving them in their entirety.

Everything in our experience is covered with a film of dullness and mundanity. We live in a virtual world, not the real one, disconnected, only half alive. D.H. Lawrence saw how disconnected we were and advocated a return to sensory experience: "We don't exist unless we are deeply and sensually in touch with that which can be touched but not known."[40]

Our utilitarian, instrumental gain is our experiential loss. And what a loss! We forget how to see colour and form, light and shade; we forget how to hear timbre, tone and pitch. Our palates and sense of smell, and the sensitivity of our fingertips and skin, all become muted and dull.

But what a revelation when we emerge from absorption in AMUN-RA! The world of the senses emerges triumphant once again in its original shining splendour. The world is made new, as if it were a new Creation. We feel that we are in Paradise or the Pure Land. Colours are richer and brighter, sounds sharper and more melodious, and everything is suffused with a sense of numinosity and beauty.

Aldous Huxley saw this after ingesting LSD:

"I was seeing what Adam had seen on the morning of his creation: the miracle, moment by moment, of naked existence."[41]

The Vietnamese Zen monk and spiritual teacher Thich Nhat Hanh put it beautifully:

"People usually consider walking on water or in thin air a miracle. But I think the real miracle is not to walk on water or in thin air, but to walk on earth. Every day we are engaged in a miracle which we don't even recognize: a blue sky, white clouds, green leaves, the black, curious eyes of a child – our own two eyes. All is a miracle."[42]

KA

In Ancient Egyptian thought, there are three aspects to the soul, only two of which need concern us here, since the third has relevance only in the afterlife. The first is called KA, which is usually translated as "the life-force". As I am using the term, this refers to all inner sensations, feelings and emotions. Whatever we inwardly *feel* is a direct manifestation of our life-force. From the "sensing" of ATUM, we move up to the "feeling" of KA.

Just as we rarely experience the world around us in its "naked existence", because of our "unclean" senses, so do we rarely if ever experience our feelings in their nakedness and purity. Our inner world is a tangled web of thoughts and feelings. We recognize certain complexes of thought and feeling and judge them as 'good' or 'bad', and attach all sorts of labels to them: 'anger', 'jealousy', 'pride', 'pleasure', 'pain', 'distaste', 'desire', 'love', 'lust', 'disgust', 'boredom', 'excitement, etc.

Just as when we label a tree 'tree', the word, thought or image intrudes between us and the direct perception of the actual tree in front of us, so does it happen with feelings and their mental labels. We begin to actually believe that there are these 'things' in us called 'anger', 'jealousy', etc., rather than seeing that they are just particular configurations of psychic energy, of life-force.

Feelings and emotions are nothing more than energetic configurations of KA. What is the "naked existence" of KA then? What is this energy, before it is transmuted into a feeling? It is a profound feeling of "livingness", of the miracle of simply being alive. If we can stay with this basic energy-feeling of *life*, without changing it into anything else, it soon naturally grows into a feeling of *love*.

When this feeling encounters suffering, whether in oneself or in another, this love manifests as "compassion". Thus KA in its "naked existence", before it is co-opted and appropriated by the ego, is *life-love-compassion*, or *love* for short. Because it is of a different order from the usual 'love' we are used to feeling, it is sometimes called *the love of God*.

"No life can express, nor tongue so much as name what this enflaming, all-conquering love of God is. It is brighter than the sun; it is sweeter than anything that is called sweet; it is stronger than all strength; it is more nutrimental than food; more cheering to the heart than wine, and more pleasant than all the joy and pleasantness of this world. Whosoever obtaineth it, is richer than any monarch on earth; and he who getteth it, is nobler than any emperor can be, and more potent and absolute than all power and authority."[43]

BA

BA is the intellectual part of the soul, what we usually call "mind". However, just as KA is essentially beyond our ordinary feelings, so is BA beyond our ordinary thoughts. This is because our ordinary thoughts, like our ordinary feelings, are the products of the ego.

What is the ego? A complex of thoughts, feelings and sensations that arise in us when we feel, think and behave as though we are a separate self set apart from the rest of existence. It feels very solid and real simply because we have believed in it for so many years, for as long as we can remember in fact. Every minute of every day, year after year, the ego refines and consolidates itself by interpreting all sensations, thoughts and feelings as expressions of *itself*. The ego is constantly building and patching itself up. When you stop doing this, you can say, with the Zen Master, "the house builder has put down his tools."

The mind as we ordinarily understand it, is in the service of the ego, and is ultimately the mouthpiece of the ego. However, the picture is complicated by the fact that we are not really one ego, but many. In quiet moments, perhaps while trying to meditate, we might catch the usually unconscious "voice" in our head, narrating, encouraging, cajoling, criticizing, fantasizing. If we persist in observing ourselves throughout the day and in different situations, we notice that there is not one voice but many, each with a different outlook and personality. These are the "I's" (Ouspensky) or "subpersonalities" (Assagioli) of our shape-shifting, mercurial self.

Struggling with the ego is a game of cat and mouse. You think you have exposed the ego for what it is, and are ego-free, until you realize that both the voice congratulating you and the smug self-satisfied smile as you receive the applause are exactly the same ego you thought you had just overcome. It has just put on a hat, a moustache and glasses and come in through the back door.

BA is not the "ego mind"; it is the "Buddha mind". *Buddha* means awakened. The "Buddha mind" is the *Bodhi*, the awake and aware conscious Observer or Witness, beyond and behind any activity of the mind or body. According to the Buddhists, it is *mu-shin*, "no-mind" and *anatta*, "no-self". According to the Vedantists it is the *Atman*, the true "Self" (with a capital 'S'). In the West, it is traditionally known as the "Soul", and in our modern, scientific age it is most likely referred to simply as "consciousness".

BA is that which is aware, but which can never become the object of awareness. Like the Here and Now of the eternal present, the Self is transcendental in the sense that it is beyond space and time. It is like an all-seeing eye that can never see itself. Who sees? Who hears? Who thinks? Self-inquiry, through an inward "stepping back" or "turning about" of consciousness ends in the direct experience of pure Self-awareness and Self-realization.

"That inner Self, as the primeval Spirit,
Eternal, ever effulgent, full and infinite Bliss,
Single, indivisible, whole and living,
Shines in everyone as the witnessing awareness."[44]

GAIA

The Ancient Egyptians did not have a concept for the Earth as a whole, since they only knew a small portion of it, centred around the Nile delta. But the Greeks did. They counted Gaia, the Earth Goddess, amongst the gods of their own extensive pantheon, and worshipped her as the representative of the whole planet.

In our own time, she has been popularized as the protagonist of James Lovelock's "Gaia Hypothesis", which proposes that the Earth behaves like and perhaps in some sense *is*, a super-organism. As a result of the environmental degradation of the past century and our growing concern over the future of the planet, many people are beginning to regard it not merely as our home, but as a living being, which needs to be respected and cared for as a whole, if we are to survive the ravages of climate change, pollution and the chronic despoliation of ecosystems and biodiversity.

Is some form of Gaia hypothesis (if not Lovelock's version) feasible? Andrew P. Smith, an American neuroscientist, has convincingly argued in a series of essays and two full-length books, that a planetary consciousness is not only possible, but inevitable. He traces the story of evolution from the birth of the universe to the present day, and shows how Nature has repeated the same evolutionary processes over and over again.

In *The Dimensions of Experience: A Natural History of Consciousness*, Smith explains how and why different organisms experience the world as they do, based on the idea of dimensions of experience and levels of reality, ideas clearly indebted to Ouspensky's *Tertium Organum*, but fleshed out with impressive scientific rigour and panache. He shows how the evolution of species actually follows the same broad outlines as the evolution of atoms, molecules and cells that went before, thus exhibiting an astonishing amount of analogical processes between these different levels of existence.

The basic scheme is beautifully simple: atoms organize into ever more complex molecular combinations, until a limit is reached. At this point, the problem is solved by the creation of a higher unit, the cell. Cells then combine into larger and more complex "societies" of cells until again, a limit is reached and a new higher unit is created, the organism. Organisms evolve and combine into ever more complex societies until a limit is reached and again, a new higher unit is created. The next higher unit (or "holon", a term coined by Arthur Koestler) is the planet as a whole.

It is impossible to do justice to the depth of Smith's research and insight in just a few paragraphs. The simple, salient point is just that the possibility of a higher planetary consciousness is in fact, scientifically speaking, perfectly viable. This possibility sheds a fascinating light on the reports of mystics throughout the ages. When mystics speak of a sense of oneness with all things, could this not be the result of a literal, rather than metaphorical communion with this higher planetary consciousness?

The basic hallmarks of mystical states or Enlightenment experiences are ineffability, a noetic quality, transiency, passivity, oneness, timelessness and the loss of ego (Happold). These are all phenomena that would logically be expected to pertain if you shifted your identity from your "bodymind" to the planet as a whole. This is what happened to Eihei Dogen when he exclaimed, "Bodymind dropped!"

It is what he meant when he later wrote:

"To study the Buddha Way is to study the self. To study the self is to forget the self. To forget the self is to be actualized by myriad things. When actualized by myriad things, your body and mind as well as the bodies and minds of others drop away. No trace of enlightenment remains, and this no-trace continues endlessly."[45]

This is a typically measured and matter-of-fact explanation from a refined aristocratic Zen Master. In contrast, here is a description of "Gaia Consciousness" by Thomas Traherne, the seventeenth century Anglican priest and metaphysical poet:

"The corn was orient and immortal wheat, which never should be reaped, nor was ever sown. I thought it had stood from everlasting to everlasting. The dust and stones of the street were as precious as gold: the gates were at first the end of the world. The green trees when I saw them first through one of the gates transported and ravished me, their sweetness and unusual beauty made my heart to leap, and almost mad with ecstasy, they were such strange and wonderful things ...

Eternity was manifest in the Light of Day, and something infinite behind everything appeared: which talked with my expectation and moved my desire. The city seemed to stand in Eden, or to be built in Heaven."[46]

JAH

Jah, Jahweh or Jehova is the biblical name for God. If GAIA is the God (or Goddess) of the Earth, JAH is the God (or Goddess?) of the Universe. JAH is the Lord of lords, the King of kings. He is at once the creator, sustainer and redeemer of Heaven and Earth, and beyond them altogether.

There is no reason to believe that evolution will stop with us humans, or even with this beautiful blue planet. In the far future, if all goes well, and as our technological sophistication continues to improve, we will eventually colonize the moon, Mars, and other habitable planets in this corner of the Milky Way. As we spread further afield into the galaxy and beyond, we might well make contact with representatives of other living planets, thus continuing the on-going process of evolution through socialization on a higher level. Reality is composed of "worlds within worlds". The Earth is only one link in the great chain.

The irresistible conclusion to this mind-boggling narrative of cosmic evolution is that the entire universe will one day become a giant, unified conscious entity. Perhaps this is pure science fiction. Perhaps it is a statistical slither of a faint possibility. Perhaps it is inevitable, or even already the case. How would we know?

Whether JAH exists as a present actuality or as a future possibility, we can use the idea of an absolute God of the universe to our spiritual advantage. From the point of view of the eternal present, beyond time and space, it may be that present actuality and future possibility are one and the same, that all time is held in an eternity of which we can have no clear conception. In any case, whether true or not, real or not, belief in God has a powerful effect on our psyches. We are spiritually empowered when belief is a matter of active choice rather than passive acquiescence.

At the very least, even without any religious belief whatsoever, the thought of JAH as the representative of the universe as a whole, lifts our gaze skyward and widens our horizon to include everything in heaven and earth and beyond, or as much of it as our imagination can handle.

The next level above our own is the level of GAIA. JAH is the level above that. It is so utterly transcendent that it seems completely out of reach. Perhaps it is. But it is important to acknowledge its existence anyway, if we are not to mold God in our own image.

"(To) realize a higher state of consciousness is to leave behind forever the experience of being human. ... Technology, it has been often pointed out, proceeds by automating processes that were previously done by human effort. Evolution, similarly, proceeds by making unconscious processes that were previously experienced consciously. We retain the past in our atoms, molecules, cells, but by abandoning our experience of these levels, we are able to know the world in ways incomprehensible to them. Realization of the next level demands no less of a sacrifice, and provides rewards yet to be known."[47]

10. Light in the Tunnel

"Descend lower, descend only
   Into the world of perpetual solitude
   World not world, but that which is not world,
   Internal darkness, deprivation
   And destitution of all property,
   Desiccation of the world of sense,
   Evacuation of the world of fancy,
   Inoperancy of the world of spirit;
   This is the one way, and the other
   Is the same, not in movement,
   But abstention from movement; while the world moves
   In appetency, on its metalled ways
   Of time past and time future"[48]

Soto Zen represents spiritual practice in its purest and simplest form. It is nothing more or less than a sustained effort to *Be Here Now*. Paradoxically, even the effort to Be Here Now is an obstacle, because it assumes that right now we are not present, and so instantly creates a duality between presence and non-presence. Therefore the Soto Zen practitioner follows the teaching and example of Zen Master Dogen, who said that training and enlightenment are one and the same. Zazen (sitting meditation) is not undertaken in order to achieve enlightenment in the future, but is itself the manifestation and expression of enlightenment here and now. Although this approach avoids the problem of duality, ("even a hair-breadth's difference and heaven and earth are set apart"[49]), it is vulnerable to the heresy of "buji Zen", which points out that since we are already enlightened, we don't need to train.

The challenge of Zen practice is to somehow walk the razor's edge of training and enlightenment. To do this it is necessary to defy the logic of duality and go beyond delusion and enlightenment.

In practice, this means that one must Be Here Now, but without *trying* to Be Here Now. One must make an effort without making an effort, seek without seeking. How is this possible?

Dogen's solution was simple: "sit steadily with the legs crossed, neither trying to think nor trying not to think."[50] In other words, neither chasing thoughts nor pushing them away, the mind naturally finds its own equilibrium. It is the intentional effort to manipulate the mind, which is the function of the "will" or the "ego", which is the problem, not the mind itself. Thus the meditator cultivates the complementary states of *mu-shin*, "no-mind", and *wei-wu-wei* "action-no-action", which express a natural state of being beyond the "metalled ways/ Of time past and time future".

T.S. Eliot distinguishes between two ways or approaches to the kenotic purification of the self. The first way, the way of "internal darkness", is the way of ascetic discipline and effort ("desiccation of the world of sense"). It is a concerted effort to shut out the distracting light of everyday consciousness and to "descend lower" into the dark void of absolute non-existence.

In Japanese, this is called *jiriki*, "self-power". Zen is traditionally regarded as employing *jiriki*, since it depends on the personal efforts of the trainee. However, it is a paradoxical form of "self-power", which attempts to negate itself in the act. This is a subtle form of action performed freely without deliberate intention (*wei-wu-wei*), epitomized in the intuitive movements of the Tai Chi and Kung Fu masters, and exemplified in the traditional Japanese arts of archery, the tea ceremony, flower arranging, etc. Ultimately, this "action through non-action" is no different from that of the concert pianist, who has absorbed and mastered her art to such an extent, that she can play with apparent effortlessness and ease. This is the definition of a Master: someone who has mastered an activity to the point of effortless effort. A Zen Master is someone who has mastered Zen, which is simply the art of *presence*.

The second way is "not in movement" but "abstention from movement". At first sight, this may seem like a "double negative". Isn't the whole exercise about "abstention" anyway? Perhaps Eliot is alluding to something similar to *wei-wu-wei* and the paradoxes of freedom in action.

He may also be pointing to the opposite of *jiriki*, "self-power", which is, predictably enough, called *tariki*, "other-power". (*Ki* means energy in Japanese, like *chi* in Chinese. *Jiri* is "self" and *tari* is "other".)

What is other-power? It's something that seems to come from beyond us. While Zen is associated with *jiriki*, Shin Buddhism, which is the "Buddhism of faith", is associated with *tariki*. Shin Buddhists believe that we can best reach Enlightenment by surrendering to the power of Amida, the "Cosmic Buddha", who enlightens us without the need to get bogged down in the sticky quagmire of the self or ego. We can side step the whole messy business of training and enlightenment and simply put all our faith and trust in Amida. However, this second way is beset by exactly the same internal contradiction. Amida does not compel us to surrender to Him. We must make an *effort* to surrender. Letting go doesn't just happen by itself. We have to actively let go.

Just as there is "non-effort" implicit in the "effort" of *jiriki*, there is "effort" implied by the "non-effort" of *tariki*. They are two sides of the same coin, both ultimately pointing to the state of grace or flow called *wei-wu-wei*. Which is the best way?

According to Jiyu Kennett, founder of a Western monastic Soto Zen tradition,

> "there is room in the world for both viewpoints, the devotional and pietistic and the intuitive, (...) they represent opposite ends of the same tunnel, and that according to one's temperament and character, one goes in at the entrance of one's own choice."[51]

The Way of Soto Zen is *zazen*, sitting meditation. Zen Master Dogen claimed that, "Zazen is the only True Gateway to Buddhism."[52] This is the direct approach of "*jiriki* presence": entering and remaining in the eternal present with effortless effort. However, this is easier said than done. A trainee typically reaches an established state of Enlightenment after maybe twenty years or so of continuous practice.

*

Zazen is an example of formless meditation. Claudio Naranjo, in his seminal study, *The Psychology of Meditation*, distinguishes three broad categories: "form", "formless" and "expressive" meditation. Form meditation is any meditation that focuses on some object. Common examples are focus on the breath, focus on a candle, on a symbol or a mantra. It is generally easier to begin a meditation practice with something to focus on, since the mind is initially very easily distracted and prone to wander.

A Zen beginner is usually instructed to meditate on the breath, counting up to ten and then starting again from the beginning. This is an excellent way to focus and train the mind and learn concentration. It is also very useful in alerting the meditator to a wayward mind. She may realize with a start that she has completely lost count. At some point the attention had wandered and she had become immersed in a daydream. The practice is simply to gently and patiently return to the breath and start counting again from number one. There are variations on this meditation, counting on the in-breath or the out-breath, counting back from ten to one, and finally simply following the breath without counting. The aim is to focus and still the mind by giving it a job to do. With nothing to do, the mind is like a monkey, the proverbial "monkey mind", which randomly leaps from branch to branch of the mind forest, chattering away inanely to itself.

Once the meditator has developed her powers of concentration and sufficiently disciplined her mind, she can progress to the formless meditation of zazen proper. Here there is no particular focus, simply the passive awareness of whatever happens to pass through the mind field. The discipline is to maintain a sustained and alert awareness without drifting off or getting swept away by passing thoughts or feelings. The "observing mind", which is the "Buddha mind" or "Atman" (orthodox Buddhists will quibble), stands its ground and remains impassive and untouched by the passing show.

The third category, "expressive meditation" is the force of this concentrated power and attention working through the bodymind in some action or activity. We see it in the, sometimes bizarre, expressions and gestures of the Zen masters, some of which have been immortalized as koans for study.

It can be free and spontaneous or formal and ritualized. The Zen arts, the martial arts, as well as the performance of religious ceremonial and ritual, are examples. The essential quality in any expressive meditation, as we saw above, is the dual and complementary states of *mu-shin*, "no-mind", and *wei-wu-wei*, "action-no-action".

The altered states achieved through various shamanic practices also lend themselves to expressive meditation. These may include seemingly involuntary physical movements and gestures, dance, song, chanting and speaking in tongues (glossolalia). These practices have also found their way into Christian charismatic churches through the influence of African shamanism.

All three categories of meditation, "form", "formless" and "expressive", are necessary to advance any distance along the spiritual path. They interact and interweave, and take the lead by turns, although they do generally follow the logical sequence of form, formless and expressive. It is, of course, up to each of us to explore and experiment to find the best approach.

*

The following mantras are examples of form meditations on Emptiness:

MU : "Nothing".
AMUN : "The hidden one".
NETI, NETI : "Not this, not this".
NADA, NADA : "Nothing, nothing".
NO SPACE, NO TIME; NO BODY, NO MIND.

These words and phrases depend on *jiriki*, "self-power".
The following phrases are designed to evoke *tariki*, "other-power":

LET GO AND LET GOD
SURRENDER
THY WILL BE DONE
THE GREAT WAY OF ABSOLUTE NON-RESISTANCE
NAMO AMIDA BU

The last is a mantra used by the Pure Land or Shin school of Buddhism, the Buddhism of Faith. Pure Land Buddhists believe that if they practice diligently in this life they will be re-born in the "Pure Land" in the next life, where the conditions for practice and enlightenment are perfect. Although it refers to the afterlife (or next reincarnation), it can also be used to refer to a vision of the transformed world in this life in *satori*. This is the way I use the term, based on the provocative statement of Hakuin, "This very land is the Pure Land"[53].

*

In the previous chapter, I identified seven discreet but interrelated facets of the enlightenment experience. These will occur naturally, whatever the method employed. Hence, a strict adherence to zazen in a monastic context, if it culminates in Enlightenment (satori), will produce, in varying degrees but probably in the same sequence, exactly the same seven experiences as those experienced by a yogi, Sufi, saint or shaman using widely different techniques:

There will be a sense of stillness and quiet, inner light and energy, an awakening of the senses, feelings of love and compassion, awareness of pure Self-consciousness and of the unified consciousness of life on Earth, and there will be intimations of the infinity beyond:

AMUN, *The Ground of Being,*
RA, *The Light of Consciousness,*
ATUM, *The Doors of Pure Perception,*
KA, *The Love of God,*
BA, *The Observing Self,*
GAIA, *The Soul of the World,*
JAH, *The Lord of the Universe.*

How do I know that these seven stages will accompany any Enlightenment experience? Firstly, from personal experience. Secondly, from the reports of others. Thirdly, from simple logic.

Let's suppose that human beings have a generally stable level of energy and consciousness. How is that energy and consciousness used? In the ordinary activities of everyday life we expend our energy on bodily movements, emotional states and thought processes. (We can overlook the energy spent on metabolic processes and bodily functions, although this might also be significant.)

This is the normal, natural use of energy and consciousness, and generally speaking, because it *is* normal and natural, we tend to allow free rein to the body, feelings and mind, and use it up without a second thought. On top of that, we waste energy on unconscious or semi-conscious physical tensions, emotional blocks and thought loops continuously rumbling away in the background.

What happens to our energy and consciousness when we sit still and rein in our thoughts and emotions? What happens when we stop processing time past and time future and step into the present? What happens when we enter the void and open ourselves to the unknown?

As we continue to sit, and persist in a state of emptiness and quiescence, we begin to build up a store of latent energy and consciousness (are they two aspects of the same thing?), simply because they are no longer being dissipated in our usual "worldly" activities. A surplus of energy and consciousness is now made available to us, because we have suspended our normal energy expenditure. AMUN is basically an energy-consciousness battery charger.

Suddenly, we experience a rush of energy and light, RA. This is the release of some of the latent energy-consciousness we have acquired through meditation on and in AMUN. This extra energy-consciousness now illuminates our whole being from within: senses, ATUM, feelings, KA and mind, BA. Finally, through the heightened awareness and sensitivity of our increased energy and consciousness, we experience the unity and wonder of the world around us, GAIA, and are awed and humbled by the enormity and grandeur of the universe beyond, JAH.

Chuang Tzu said, "The portal of God is non-existence" because energy and consciousness can only accumulate in the absolute quiet and stillness of AMUN. As the "accumulator" is filled, the light of consciousness overflows and transforms body, mind and the world beyond. This is the logic of Enlightenment.

11. The Clearing

Without immersing yourself in AMUN, however briefly, there is no hope. In the middle of the psychic forest, intimidated by endless trees in all directions, tangled in brambles and briars and oppressed by flitting shadows, you must find a clearing in which to meditate.

Unless you pass through the portal of non-existence, and empty yourself, however partially, of your psychological investments and attachments, you are merely throwing seeds on rubbish. The rubbish must be cleared and the soil prepared before the seeds can be sown.

Be Here Now. Meditation on these three words is enough to open a clearing in the mind. The first word refers to your essential *Being*, not just your contingent body and mind. The essential Being of all beings is the Self, which is Consciousness. This is the transcendental Subject that can never be objectified. Whatever you can point to is not it: "I am not that which can be observed".

The second word refers to the infinite Presence beyond any and every location in space. Everywhere is *Here*. As Hermes Trismegistus put it, "an infinite sphere, the centre of which is everywhere, the circumference nowhere."[54]

The third word refers to the eternal present, the unbroken, uninterrupted stream of time that is always and forever *Now*. Each of these three little words point to that infinite and eternal transcendent reality beyond time and space, which is near yet far, and closer to us than we are to ourselves.

There are many ways to prepare the ground for the seeds of Enlightenment and clear a way for the Lord. The following is a meditation adapted from Theravada Buddhism. I call it "The Clearing Meditation".

ANATTA, ANICCA, ABHAYA

ANATTA means *no-self*. When you say the word, bring the meaning to mind. Do not treat it as a negation or attack on your ego. Take it to refer to the conscious part of you that is not identified with anything. See if you can connect with a neutral space of pure awareness within you. We start with ANATTA, because if we do not consciously find a neutral space within, and disidentify from the forms of our ego, the rest of the meditation may be hijacked by one subpersonality or other and will lose its effectiveness.

ANICCA means *impermanence*. All things change. Nothing stays the same. Impermanence is a law of nature. We too are here for just a brief time, no longer than a "brief candle". We must let go of the illusion of permanence, which is the central illusion of the ego. The ego is just a temporary psychological configuration, but it maintains itself in being through the illusion of permanence. It is a self-fulfilling belief. Because we believe our ego (which is just another word for "personality") is permanent, we behave as if it were permanent and solid. When we remind ourselves of ANICCA, impermanence, we relax our hold and become more fluid and flexible. This is also a very important attitude at the start of a meditation, because it means we are open and sensitive to change, and not rigid, resistant or defensive.

ABHAYA means *fearlessness*. We must put on the fearlessness of a spiritual warrior as we enter into meditation. This is important to combat the fear that is at the heart of the ego. The ego is afraid for itself. It is afraid of death. Both ANATTA and ANICCA mean death for the ego. If we cannot overcome this fear, we will once again fall back in thrall to the ego. It welcomes us back with obsequiousness and cold comfort: "You did the right thing to give up. Well done. Stay here with me. You're safe with me. We'll look after each other. Don't go out there again. It's dangerous." To break through the shell of the ego, we must be fearless even in the face of death.

KARUNA, KARUNA, KARUNA

KARUNA means *compassion*. Confronting the fear of the ego and fear of death, we encounter suffering. The spiritual journey is beset by hardship and struggle. We cannot avoid great suffering if we are to change and die to ourselves. We need the soothing balm of compassion. Compassion is not pity. It literally means "suffering with": *com passio*. It is the willingness to share the suffering of another, and so help carry the load. We can arouse compassion for our own suffering as much as the suffering of another. We can also receive the compassion of an archetypal "divine being" such as Avalokitesvara, Isis or the Virgin Mary. Perhaps the most powerful visual depiction of compassion is that of the pieta, Mary weeping over the broken body of her son. Bringing this scene to mind cannot fail to arouse deep feelings of compassion in us, which we can then direct to our own sufferings "in Christ".

DOSA NIRODHA, KARUNA

DOSA means *hate* or *aversion*. It is a negative psychological attitude of dislike, disgust, anger, rejection. NIRODHA means *cessation*. So when we say the words "DOSA NIRODHA", we become aware of any unacknowledged negativity or resentment we might be carrying, and gently let it go. If it does not dissipate completely, we are content with lessening its energetic charge and so reducing its hold on us. We bring compassion to the suffering caused by DOSA, and the suffering that caused it. We bring compassion also to our inability to free ourselves of it completely. DOSA, if it does not arise in the heat of the moment, as when provoked by an adversary, is generally connected with past slights and resentments. It is the negative energy of our "unfinished business".

TANHA NIRODHA, KARUNA

TANHA means *thirst* or *craving*. It is the opposite instinctual drive from DOSA, a pulling towards, rather than a pushing away. It encompasses all forms of craving, clinging, neediness, lust and desire. It includes spiritual desire as much as sexual desire or desire for fame and fortune. TANHA can be as distracting and destructive as DOSA. Psychological issues associated with DOSA are those around phobias and traumas, and anger management issues. Those associated with TANHA are addiction issues, substance abuse and obsessive compulsive disorders. By bringing the energetic charge of TANHA to awareness and consciously letting it go with compassion, we can begin to reduce its subliminal hold on our lives.

DUKKHA NIRODHA, KARUNA

DUKKHA means *suffering* or *unsatisfactoriness*. It was the recognition of the problem of DUKKHA as the tragic and inescapable fact of life that impelled Shakyamuni Buddha to strike out on his spiritual quest to find a solution to human suffering. The first of his Four Noble Truths is the self-evident existential truth, "there is dukkha". DUKKHA is broader than physical pain or even psychological pain. It includes "having what you don't want" (DOSA) as well as "not having what you want" (TANHA), but also, more subtly, "not having what you have" and "not wanting what you want". In other words, being generally dissatisfied. Life just doesn't seem to live up to the billing. Free even from the push and pull of DOSA and TANHA, things just don't feel right. There is a subtle background malaise. The psychological issue here is depression. Where DOSA indicates an inability to let go of the negativity of the past, and TANHA indicates an inability to deal with the seductive lure of the future, DUKKHA indicates our inability to enjoy the present.

UPEKKHA, UPEKKHA, UPEKKHA

UPEKKHA means *equanimity*. Equanimity is a dispassionate philosophical attitude. Whatever comes our way is treated equally, without preference or deference. We resist the temptation to react negatively with DOSA or greedily with TANHA. We refuse to react with the dissatisfied indifference of DUKKHA. UPEKKHA is a state of poised equilibrium. It is a condition of spiritual fortitude in the face of the "slings and arrows of outrageous fortune"[55], the capacity to "meet with Triumph and Disaster/ And treat those two imposters the same,"[56]. By arousing the quality of UPEKKHA, we complete and consolidate our withdrawal from hate, greed and suffering and turn to face any eventuality with strength and courage.

KARUNA, MUDITA, METTA

KARUNA means *compassion*. This is the golden thread that runs through the whole meditation. We bring the healing power of compassion to bear on all our psychological struggles and difficulties. The difference here is that we are now in a position of spiritual strength from which we can bring compassion to others. We bring to mind the suffering of sentient beings and send out healing compassion to all.

MUDITA means *sympathetic joy*. Here we share in the happiness and joy of others. It is the positive correlative of KARUNA. KARUNA and MUDITA can be seen as the psychological antidotes to DOSA and TANHA. When we encounter difficulty, pain and suffering, we don't like it, so we instinctively react with aversion, DOSA. But we can bring compassion to alleviate the suffering. Thus compassion is the antidote to hate.

When we encounter success, joy and happiness, we might react with envy, another form of DOSA, or with craving, TANHA. We like it and we want some of it. Or we can bring sympathetic joy to celebrate the success and happiness of the other without wanting a part of it. Thus MUDITA is the antidote to greed.

It is like sharing in the achievement or pleasure of a young child. If they are enjoying a lollipop, it would be ridiculous to desire the lollipop, or we are no better that a young child ourselves. In KARUNA we "suffer with"; in MUDITA we "enjoy with".

METTA means *love* or *loving kindness*. We send love and good will to all sentient beings, whether suffering, happy or indifferent. METTA is the antidote to hate, greed and suffering and blesses both the giver and receiver. Once we have made an inward clearing of our psychological ties to ego, permanence, fear, hate, greed, envy and suffering through self-compassion, we find that love arises and flows naturally and easily. Love is the crown of The Clearing Meditation.

12. The Tent

It was getting light outside. Half the people were curled up or stretched out under blankets and duvets. The others were sitting up talking in conspiratorial, hushed tones. Someone got up to tend to the fire. Although I was tired and cosy under my blanket, I decided to sit up and join in the conversation. There were two birds having what seemed like an interminable domestic argument just outside the tent. I guessed it must have been about five or six in the morning. I tried to follow the conversation. The shaman was holding forth about something or other to do with some ancient prophesy. Something he said had caught my interest, but now he'd lost it again. I observed his body language, and those of his listeners, and looked for clues in their facial expressions. They were hunched and serious. They didn't seem particularly happy.

I looked around the tent. The bedraggled state bore witness to the night's chaotic activities. The shadows of the trees were playing on the canvas as they gently swayed in the breeze. They danced between the tent poles, which were now visible against the lightening canvas. I was half listening to the conversation, but for some reason my attention was drawn to the shadowy shapes thrown onto the canvas. There was a wood-burning stove on one side of the tent, with the flue sticking out through a hole. In the middle of the tent there was a solid wooden pole, which disappeared up through another hole at the top of the tent. The other poles were spaced at regular intervals around the circular base, converging at the top of the middle pole. The shadows of the trees moved and danced between them. The birds and the people twittered on.

It struck me that this was a perfect image of the spiritual quest. Everyone was trying to get to heaven, represented by the early morning sky above the tent. Like the shadows on the canvas, we would occasionally come into contact with one of the poles, representing different paths, teachings and religions, which we would then try to climb.

The Tent

After travelling up a little way, however, we would become distracted by the dancing shadows and move off across the canvas, until we came to another pole. Sometimes we would progress upwards, sometimes we would slip down, as if we were playing an endless game of snakes and ladders. In this way, we went round and round the tent, never reaching the top, but always dreaming about heaven, which became ever more fantastic, the longer we dreamt about it. Soon we forgot that we were even trying to get to heaven, and settled for the ups and downs of our endless perambulations.

I looked at the bodies and faces huddled around me. It occurred to me with great sadness that maybe none of them had ever actually been to heaven, and that perhaps they never would. What had they been doing all night? I felt as though I'd been to heaven and back at least three or four times. I looked at the wooden pole in the middle. It was firm and perfectly vertical. It seemed to represent the "world tree", or the *axis mundi*, connecting heaven and earth.

What was it that connected heaven and earth? It was *me*, and it was all of us. The central pole represented *humanity*. We have evolved into an erect, upright position. We are the descendants of *homo erectus*. Somehow, human beings are the connection between the earth and heaven, heaven and earth. We are the *axis mundi*. We are the "world trees". There was no need to blindly grope around the sides of the tent and follow the shadowy shapes and poles left by people who had been dead already for centuries and millennia. We had everything we needed within us. The surest, most direct way to heaven was not through any external teaching, religion or combination of religions. It was a waste of time to try and climb the shadows projected onto the canvas of our minds. We should forget about the shadows and just climb up the central pole!

*

The central pole of the body is called the *shushumna*. It is the central energy channel of the body, which runs up the spinal column from the base of the spine to the crown of the head. Heaven is neither a real nor an imaginary place outside the tent of our bodies. It is an inner abode of light and bliss.

And the way to heaven is not through mental speculation or intellection but through the energy centres of the body. As soon as we mentally set heaven apart, and ourselves apart from heaven, either by affirming it as an other-worldly spiritual dimension or by denying it as mere superstition, it becomes an irrelevant abstraction.

Spiritual seekers tend to fixate on a supreme spiritual goal or destination, called "Enlightenment" or "Salvation". It is imagined to be a once-for-all achievement, the end-point and culmination of life, which is why it is often associated with the moment of death. The spiritual seeker is looking for a one-way ticket to heaven. She hopes that she will be admitted to an eternity of light and bliss in heaven after the struggles and trials of this shadowy world.

This is a linear, occidental, view of the relation between earth and heaven. If heaven exists at all, it must be in the after-life, because it clearly doesn't exist in this life. There is no real expectation in traditional Western spirituality that we will ever reach heaven in this life. We go round and round the cycle of terrestrial life in preparation for and hope of the life to come. We may look up to the skies with longing and pray to God above, but our action is all restricted to the earth below. Like the shadows on the tent canvas, we flit about a horizontal world, a "flat land", condemned to wander forever among the shadows in the valley of death.

The ancient yogis and tantrikas of India had a very different approach. They found ways to awaken the latent spiritual energy of the body, called the *kundalini*, or "serpent power", and to raise it up through the *chakras* to the crown at the top of the head. For these spiritual adepts, heaven was not a final destination, but a constant, ever-present source of spiritual energy and power, which they could visit as often as they liked. Theirs was a cyclical view. They would ascend to heaven in meditation, and come back down to earth renewed and refreshed. For the Indian yogis, heaven is not such a big deal.

Pondering the symbolism of the tent I was sitting in on that early spring morning, I perceived an analogy between the hole at the top of the tent, through which the central pole poked through, and the symbolic hole at the Sahasrara Chakra at the top of the head.

Above and beyond the shady tent I pictured clear blue sky with wisps of white cloud, and the ever-shining, eternal Sun, the Fount and Source of all life on earth. Sitting in that dim tent, it was as if we were trapped in our heads, like those poor Greek souls languishing in Plato's allegorical cave. The real word basks in the glory of the Sun, while we tarry here in a world of shadows and phantasms.

Judging by their weary appearance, my fellow psychonauts had presumably been going round the psycho-spiritual merry-go-round all night. But, by the grace of the Divine Mother yage (ayahuasca), I had been transported to heaven and back several times, and was full of beans. I felt light and clear, relaxed and happy. I understood that heaven is not the goal at the end of the journey. It does not await us after death, or even in a wise old age, but is ever available here and now.

We are the *axis mundi*. We are here to connect heaven and earth, to bring the energy and consciousness of heaven down into the world, which has never needed the light as much as it does now. Heaven is not the goal. It is the way. And the kingdom of heaven is within.

13. The Chakras

The mind is like a tent. We project images, ideas, words, fantasies, hopes and dreams onto its blank canvas. The dark lines of the eight tent poles are like eight paths to heaven. When we follow a path, it takes us higher up the canvas of the mind. The eight tent poles converge at the top of the tent, so the further along a path we go, the smaller the area of canvas. Therefore there is less space for mental projections, thoughts and fantasies. Since all the paths get closer towards the top of the tent, we can easily hop from one to the other. At a critical point, there is more path than canvas, and at the very top, all paths merge into one.

This is the way of the mind. It requires patience, perseverance, time and effort. The danger is that we may become lost in an expanse of blank canvas or led astray by the play of shadows. Or else, we may become so attached to a particular path as to mistake it for the goal and settle there. Or we may be always looking over our shoulder for a better path than the one we are on. We may become insatiably curious about other paths and spend all our time moving from one to the other, forgetting that the goal lies at the end of each. This is a real danger for New Agers, who have a whole spiritual supermarket of different paths and traditions to choose from. Beware the lure of spiritual materialism and spiritual consumerism!

The way of the body lies in the central tent pole. This is the most direct and reliable way to get to the top of the tent and beyond. Unlike the other tent poles, which represent traditions established by other people, the central pole represents the only path that is unique to you, because it *is* you. You ascend to the summit not along paths trodden by others, but along the path of yourself, which is to say, the path of your body.

The body can be energetically divided up in innumerable ways. Probably the most well-known model is the ancient Indian chakra system, with seven energy centres located at crucial points along the spinal column.

The spinal column is regarded by tantrikas and yogis who practice the art of *Psychosoma or Kundalini yoga* (subtle body-mind energetics) as the primary channel for the activation and transformation of psychosomatic energy. This central energy channel is called the *shushumna*, and the energy that passes along it is called *kundalini*, which is usually depicted as a coiled serpent at the base of the spine, dormant until awakened through special postures and meditative techniques. The serpent rises up through the shushumna like a cobra in thrall to a snake charmer, passing through each of the seven energy centres, or *chakras* in turn, until it reaches the crown.

The kundalini serpent is echoed in ancient Egyptian iconography in the *Uraeus Cobra* depicted on the crown of the Pharaohs, who trace their lineage directly to the first mythical Pharaoh, Osiris. Osiris was the original Egyptian kundalini yogi, representing the ancient art of psychosomatic energy transmutation and sublimation.

Chakra meditation harnesses the power of the mind and the power of the imagination, but it is always rooted in the physical body. As we become more familiar and more proficient with working with our bodily energetic system, however, we may find it necessary to make a distinction between the physical body and the subtle, or "astral" body. The physical body breaths, sighs, yawns, burps, farts, stretches, shakes, tenses, relaxes, moves. The astral body is the *inner* body. It is indirectly related to the fine motor functions of the exquisite musculature of the physical body, including those of the internal organs, but is itself experienced non-physically, as energy, light, colour, sound, and image.

What distinguishes the astral body from mere imagination is precisely the fact that it is rooted in the body. When we daydream, fantasize or picture a mental scene, our conscious awareness is generally located in or around the head or in an unspecified imaginary space outside the body. When we connect imaginatively with the astral body however, our focus is on a specific location in the body, and the energy, light, colour, sound or image is inwardly felt in direct relation with that part of the body.

By focusing on each chakra in turn, it is possible to release the latent energy in that area of the body. This release of energy is experienced as a pleasant inner tingling or as a sudden rush of pleasure coursing through the body. It can be limited to one part or the body, or spread generally throughout the whole body. This pleasurable sensation is called *Ananda*, "bliss". It is usually accompanied by an inner light, and sometimes by colours. These are of course more easily discernible with the eyes closed.

Kundalini yoga is the art and practice of releasing the hidden, spiritual energy of the body, called the "serpent power". There are traditional, time-honoured meditations designed to awaken the dormant *kundalini* and raise it up through the chakras. There are special *asanas*, physical postures, special *mudras,* hand gestures, special *yantras,* geometric symbols and special *mantras,* sound syllables, associated with each chakra for the release and flow of the kundalini. These vary from school to school and between the Hindu and Buddhist tantric traditions.

There is no one magic formula or technique. The essential point is *attention* and *intention*. It is enough to focus on the location of a chakra with a conscious and one-pointed intention to free the energy held there. This can be done standing, sitting, or lying down. Visualisations, mantras and mudras are not indispensable for the activation of the kundalini, although they can greatly facilitate it. They focus the attention more powerfully and allow the attention to be sustained for longer, since the mind is more fully engaged and occupied. They also tap into the body's somatic memory. Through the power of association, certain fixed words and images can evoke the release of the kundalini much more quickly. Once a mantra has become so internalised and embodied as to produce an automatic energetic effect on the body, it works like a "magic spell". The mere utterance of the mantra produces the desired effect, in this case, the release of the kundalini energy.

The magic is created by the magician, which is to say, by the wielder and user of the mantra. It cannot be transmitted directly from one person to another. This is why there is no one magic formula or technique. The magic is created through repeated and sustained attention and intention in meditation.

The Chakras

Any sound or image can theoretically become associated with the release of energy in any part of the body through repeated use. Nevertheless, it is clearly helpful for the mind if there is some logical association with each chakra. Since the kundalini energy is understood to pass from a denser to a more refined state as it passes up through the chakras, it makes sense to visualise this represented in the light spectrum, with the lowest visible frequency at the base of the spine moving up to the highest at the crown.

Thus we have the colour associations of red with the base chakra, orange with the sacral chakra, yellow with the solar plexus chakra, green with the heart chakra, blue with the throat chakra, indigo with the third eye chakra and violet with the crown chakra.

This sequence of denser to finer is also easily represented in the spectrum of sound vibrations, again with the lowest frequency sounds at the bottom rising up to the highest at the top. The seven notes associated with the seven chakras can also be considered as a musical octave, an idea explored in detail by Gurdjieff and his followers. To keep things simple, if we begin with C at the base chakra, we progress up the natural scale with D at the sacral, E at the solar plexus, F at the heart, G at the throat, A at the third eye and B at the crown. This is a logical approach, but arbitrary. We could begin with any note, and need not necessarily progress up through an octave in precisely this way.

A third set of associations is that of the natural elements. Again, we begin with the denser elements and move up through the less dense. Thus, the element of earth is associated with the base (or *root*) chakra, water is associated with the sacral, fire with the solar plexus, air with the heart, and ether with the throat. The higher two are considered to be beyond physical manifestation and so do not have corresponding elements.

The senses also have their corresponding chakra associations. Traditionally, they are arranged as follows: smell for the base chakra, taste for the sacral, sight for the solar plexus, touch for the heart, sound for the throat, and intuition or sixth sense for the third eye. The crown chakra is considered to be beyond any sensory association.

The associated body parts for each chakra are perhaps too obvious to mention, but it is good to remember that we are in fact dealing with the physical body here. Whether they actually exist or not, the chakras serve as a convenient focus for directing attention to the various different parts of the body, and particularly to our internal organs. The base chakra is of course associated with the muscles of the pelvic floor and anus, but as the "root support", is also associated with the bones and skeletal structure. The sacral chakra is associated with the sex organs, the bladder, prostate and womb. The solar plexus chakra is associated with the digestive system and the muscles, particularly the abdominals. The heart chakra is associated with the lungs and heart and the circulatory system. The throat chakra is associated with the mouth, nose, throat and ears. The third eye chakra is associated with the eyes, and the crown chakra with the upper skull, the cerebral cortex, and the skin.

Related to these associated body parts are the glandular connections. This may be an interesting area of future research into the physiological basis for the chakra system, since the glands are key elements in the regulation of the autonomic nervous system. Again, simply by anatomical proximity, the following connections can be made: the adrenals with the base chakra, the ovaries and testes with the sacral chakra, the pancreas with the solar plexus chakra, the thymus with the heart chakra, the thyroid and parathyroid with the throat chakra, the pituitary with the third eye chakra and the pineal with the crown chakra.

These associations should be taken as suggestive rather than literal. They are useful footholds for the imagination. As with any meditation, the more we use them, the more potent and vivid they become.

14. The Presence of God

Brother Lawrence was a lay brother in a French Carmelite monastery in the seventeenth century. He became famous for what he called "the practice of the presence of God". According to Brother Lawrence, "The most holy practice, the nearest to daily life, and the most essential for the spiritual life, is the practice of the presence of God."[57]

So what does this practice entail? Well, it's not rocket science. In fact, its beauty is in its absolute simplicity. To come into the presence of God, all that is needed "is a directing of our spirit to God or a present remembrance of God which can come about either through the imagination or the understanding."[58] A seventeenth century Carmelite brother would be perfectly satisfied with that definition. However, a twenty-first century skeptic would in all likelihood demand to know what exactly is meant by "the imagination", "the understanding" and, more importantly, what he means by "God".

Brother Lawrence worked in the kitchen. He couldn't join the spiritual community as a monk because he couldn't read or speak Latin. So his "God" was "the God of small things", pots and pans, meat and veg. His spirituality was eminently practical and immediate, closer perhaps to Zen Buddhism than traditional Christianity. There are many stories about the opportunities for Enlightenment in the heat of the kitchen in Zen literature. The kitchen is like a pressure cooker. Without the luxury of the leisurely pace of the monks upstairs, the cooks are forced to practice their mindfulness in the hustle and bustle of the kitchen. This is why the *tenzo* (head cook) is one of the most respected and prestigious offices of a Zen monastery.

In the Hindu tradition, this kind of spiritual practice is called "karma yoga", the yoga of works. The essence of karma yoga is that work, or any action whatsoever, is done without attachment to results. Action is done for its own sake, with full presence of mind. It is an end in itself, not just a means to an end. This is very similar to the Buddhist ideal of "right mindfulness".

So is Brother Lawrence's "presence of God" essentially the same as "presence of mind"? There is clearly a close connection between the two. If we are acting mindfully in the present, without worrying about the future, we are in a very different psychological state than the ordinary "worldly" frame of mind characterized by "getting and spending". We may find that we enter a state of effortless, graceful action, or "flow", as Csikszentmihalyi describes it. This is that same condition called *wei-wu-wei* ("action-no-action") by the Taoists. It is the unity, the yoking together (yoga) of actor and action, which is the goal of the karma yoga. In this state of flowing grace, are we not also in "the presence of God"?

Brother Lawrence said that he lived "as if there were only God and he in the world."[59] Although this statement professes a basic and fundamental duality between him and God, it is a very different duality to the ordinary one between "me" and "the world". The implication is that there is no world any more. There is only God. But what does this mean? How does the world turn itself into God, or rather, reveal itself as God?

The Hebrew prophets spoke of *Shekinah*, "the glory of God". It can also be translated as "the presence of God". The imagery is an imagery of light. It is as though the world is illuminated by the presence of God. A veil is parted and a numinous, spiritual light shines through all things. This is expressed emphatically in the *Sanctus* in the Catholic, Orthodox and Anglican mass:

"Holy, Holy, Holy Lord,
God of Power and Might,
Heaven and Earth are full of your glory,
Hosanna in the highest."[60]

The "glory of God" revealed to Moses in the heart of the burning bush was the *Shekinah*. I have often stood in awe before the beauty of a particular tree or bush seemingly on fire with the reflected light of the sun. It seems to me that there is a direct connection between this outer, visible light, and our own inner, "spiritual" light. In a receptive frame, we respond to light in a profound, interior way, receiving "light from light".

Presumably there are physiological things going on in the brain here, which should in theory be scientifically detectable. Perhaps our photo-receptors become over-active and somehow spill over into this experience of inner, "spiritual" light? Is this what happened to Moses? We will never know.

The "glory of God" can be revealed in a bush, but it can also be revealed in a kitchen sink. When we are in "flow", we can experience the inherent spiritual vibrancy, the mystical, because mysterious, inner illumination at the heart of everything. This does not necessarily mean that everything has to be "burning" all the time; otherwise we would soon burn out. There may be occasional and sporadic experiences of intense illumination, but mostly, it is through the imagination or the understanding that we approach God.

For Brother Lawrence, the "glory of God" would have revealed itself in gleaming pots and pans and muddy vegetables. Anything can express the glory of God, when we understand that God is everything:

"Everything was the same to him, every place, every task. The good Brother found God everywhere, as much while he was repairing shoes as when he was praying with the Community. He was not eager to go into retreat, for he found in his common tasks the same God to worship as in the depths of the desert."[61]

*

For the authors of the Hebrew bible, all things and all events were understood as expressions of *One God*. The first line of the Jewish Shema prayer states this unequivocally: "Hear, O Israel, the Lord our God, the Lord is One."[62] Christians are also committed to the idea of One God, as stated in the first line of the *Credo*: "We believe in One God."[63]

Religion can be understood as the attempt to re-tune our awareness to receive the ever-present presence of God, which may have been our natural condition in the past, in the pre-lapsarian purity of Adam and Eve, but which we seem to have lost along the way.

The Jewish tradition has remained faithful to the One God as One, but Christianity has developed the curious doctrine of the One God as *Three*.

How does the Christian doctrine of the Trinity bear on the good Brother's "practice of the presence of God"? We have already looked at the Jewish Shekinah, the "glory of God", as one possible interpretation of what he might have been talking about. This almost incidental concept in the Old Testament is placed centre stage in Christian theology as one Person of the Trinity, "the Holy Spirit". What about the other two?

Engrossed in chopping wood or preparing a chicken for the oven, Brother Lawrence may have been blissfully aware of the presence of God as "the Holy Spirit" shining through everything. But what happened when one of the other Brothers came to him to ask for help with the potatoes? Or to tell him a silly story about an incident with the washer woman? Would this have broken the flow? If so, he might have resented the interruption and barked at them to ask someone else – couldn't they see he was busy?

Alternatively, his flow may not have been interrupted at all. His awareness of the presence of God would have continued unhindered. In this case, he would have seen the presence of God in the Brother. In describing this experience after the event, he might continue to refer to the Holy Spirit, which he had seen shining in the Brother as much as in the wood and the plucked chicken. But he would be more likely to say that he saw Christ in the face of his brother.

There is a qualitative difference between the experience of God revealed in inanimate things and in a human being. If "the Holy Spirit" points to our relationship to God through the medium of the material world, "the Son" points to our relationship mediated through humanity. The Holy Spirit is the secret seed of God hidden in all things. The Christ is the secret seed hidden in all people. If "the presence of God" is not to be confined to wild places, to the desert, the forest, the mountains, where no people dwell, it must include the divinity of humankind as the "children of God", personified in the second Person of the Trinity, Jesus Christ.

The Son of God is God incarnate, God *made flesh*. Brother Lawrence would have seen Christ in the face of friend and stranger alike. But if a dog or wolf came into the kitchen scrounging for scraps, might he not also have experienced it as a "child of God", as St. Francis did a couple of centuries earlier? Does a dog have Buddha Nature?

What about "God the Father"? This, the first Person of the Trinity is, for some, the most difficult to imagine or describe. For others, it is the most intuitively obvious. The phrase "the presence of God" may itself suggest an indefinable sense of Oneness or Otherness, which feels closer to the idea of God as "Father" than as "Son" or "Spirit". Neither associated with specific things, people or creatures, the intuition of the presence of God the Father is of a radical transcendence beyond the manifest world.

Philosophically speaking, the Trinity points to One God as *transcendent* (Father), *incarnate* (Son) and *immanent* (Holy Spirit). As we saw in chapter 4, this is exactly the definition of pantheism (or more correctly, panentheism). The pantheism implicit in Jewish monotheism is made explicit in the Christian doctrine of the Trinity. Can it be made more explicit still? Judaism brought the idea of One God into the world. Christianity brought the idea of the Trinity, "Three-in-One". Whatever next? "Seven-in-One" perhaps?

*

The universe has evolved, and is evolving, through seven levels of existence. The first is the pregnant void, pregnant because it gave birth to the universe. This is AMUN, called "the hidden one", because it is hidden within the fabric of space and time. Since the void predates, postdates, is within and beyond, and in all respects outruns space and time, it is not bound by the laws of physics, and is neither touched nor displaced by space and time. AMUN is always, already *Here and Now*, in an eternal presence beyond the reach of space-time. It is everywhere and nowhere, hidden in the invisible cleft of the present moment.

The second is the level of undifferentiated energy, released into our universe in a Big Bang 14 billion years ago. This is the level of RA, the "sun god".

The sun is our local representative of all the stars, and by extension, all the energy (more or less) in the universe. The sun is enormous. It accounts for 99.86% of all the mass in the solar system and is about 1,300,000 bigger than the Earth. It has been burning steadily for 5 billion years and is projected to burn for another 5 billion. The colossal amount of energy radiating out from the surface of the sun in a single second is hard enough to grasp, let alone 10 billion years worth. And our sun is only one of 100 billion stars in our galaxy, which is only one of between 100 and 200 billion galaxies in the observable universe!

The third is the material level, the world of the elements, represented by ATUM, "the All". This level covers all of the known elements in the universe, immortalised in the periodic table. It includes the lighter elements of the early universe and the heavier elements forged in the furnace of the stars. All the matter in the universe, stars, planets, meteors and other cosmic material, is ATUM. On our terrestrial plane, we experience it most readily through the traditional elements of earth, water, fire and air. It is the domain of physics and chemistry, the province of atoms and molecules.

The fourth level comprises the living world of organic, carbon-based, cellular life. This is the level of KA, "the life force". Whatever other forms of life there may be in the far-flung reaches of our galaxy or in the wider universe beyond, life on Earth has evolved as proKAryotic (bacterial) and euKAryotic (plant and animal) cells. It is the domain of biochemistry and biology, the world of cells.

The fifth is the mental level of living organisms, ranging from the simplest sessile forms, such as volvox green algae, to the most complex human societies. This is the level of BA, "the soul". Every living thing has its own locus of consciousness, however rudimentary, traditionally referred to as "soul". This level also covers the complex web of interrelations and interconnections within ecosystems and the societies of single species, since "no man (or organism) is an island". It is the domain of zoology and animal behaviourism, and in the human arena, of the humanities, especially anthropology, sociology and psychology.

The sixth is a higher-level planetary consciousness, called GAIA, the "Earth goddess". This represents the evolutionary synthesis of all of conscious life on Earth, which may or may not have fully occurred yet, known to the ancients as the *Anima Mundi*, or "World Soul". It is of course beyond the scope of present scientific observation, but has been expressed since the dawn of civilization through pantheist strains in philosophy, myth and mysticism.

The seventh level is the ultimate universal consciousness, the Absolute. I call this JAH, after the Jewish God Jahweh. This utterly transcendent God represents the unified consciousness of the entire universe. From a scientific point of view, it is a purely speculative, although logically tenable, hypothesis, based on the direction and structure of the preceding six levels of evolution. The seventh brings the universe to final completion. Far beyond our comprehension, the disciplines of theology and metaphysics represent our feeble human attempts to understand and articulate this *mysterium tremendum*.

These seven levels together constitute a "universal octave", or a "Ray of Creation". For the Ray to traverse the whole of existence, it must pass from emptiness through energy, matter, life, mind, and onwards and upwards to higher planetary and universal consciousness. Since human beings are the only beings on Earth capable of associating and identifying with planetary consciousness, the Ray of Creation associated with the Earth must necessarily pass through human beings. In other words, the further evolution of the universe on this particular Ray depends on *us*.

*

The three fundamental holons (whole/parts) of which existence as we know it is composed are atoms, cells and organisms. These are the only three holons visible to science: atoms and their molecules, cells and their tissues, organisms and their societies. The world as we know it, and the world as revealed by science, is basically made up of interactions between three levels of existence, represented by ATUM, KA and BA.

For scientific materialists, rationalists and humanists, this is all there is. There is no room for a spiritual dimension in their model of reality, because there is no empirical evidence for it. The material world of objects, the physical world of life and the mental world of organisms (including humans) seem to stand alone, floating like anomalous bubbles in the immensity of space. Having said that, scientists are now probing beyond the atomic level into the "quantum" level. Whether this is an elaboration of our understanding of ATUM or a true inroad into the level of RA is a question that will probably not be answered in my lifetime.

Look far enough into the microcosm, within and beyond the atomic level, and you will eventually touch the spiritual essence of existence, AMUN-RA. The universe has not come out of nowhere. It does not rest on nothing. Existence is not built out of material building blocks, as if atoms were so many manufactured lego pieces. We call atoms and the things of which they are composed "material", without really knowing what we mean by this, other than "not living", "not mental" and "not spiritual".

Materialism takes atoms to be the ultimate foundation of existence. All things are ultimately reducible to their component atoms. Apart from the obvious reductionism of this position, which is blind to the emergent properties of complex (and even simple) associations of atoms, cells and organisms, it also makes an unwarranted assumption about the essential materiality of the atoms themselves. This assumption simply amounts to the denial of any possible interiority, other than the smaller building blocks of neutrons and electrons. This denial is presently being put in question by the paradoxical discoveries of quantum mechanics.

The universe was not built in a day, or even six days. And it's not built out of atomic lego blocks which magically appeared out of nowhere, establishing a purely material, blocky universe. All of the atoms on Earth, and throughout the whole universe, trace their lineage back through the stars to the very beginning. They embody the mystery of the beginning, and the mystery of existence. At the very least, they embody the primordial emptiness and energy of the universe, AMUN-RA. Scientific materialists simply overlook the mystery of the essential nature of atoms by treating them like so many building blocks.

The Presence of God

Materialists, wedded to the theory of evolution (or rather the *fact* of evolution, since it has been proven beyond reasonable doubt), arbitrarily put a limit at the level of organisms. The more reductionist among them even deny that human beings are more evolved that other organisms, including such simple organisms as volvox algae, slime mould and even bacteria. Their argument is that the only reasonable measure of evolutionary success is evolutionary fitness. Greater complexity is not necessarily a better fit, so more complex does not necessarily mean more evolved.

Materialists are blind to the evolution of consciousness that accompanies the structural and social complexity of organisms. They are also blind to the further evolution of the planet as a unified super-organism or consciousness, and of the further evolution of the universe beyond. Just as they cannot see the spirit (or consciousness) within the "material" atom in the microcosm, they cannot see the spirit beyond the "material" organism in the macrocosm.

The illusion of materialism comes from the restricted view of science, which can only see the three intermediate levels of ATUM, KA and BA. As soon as we acknowledge the inner reality of AMUN-RA on the one hand and GAIA-JAH on the other, as immanent and transcendent levels of reality within and beyond the immediately visible, the whole of existence as we know it, matter, life and mind, becomes "spiritualised", "illuminated" and filled with "the glory of God". Only when we truly connect within and beyond to the whole of the Ray of Creation, and not just to a truncated part of it, do we truly begin to live in the presence of God.

*

Brother Lawrence tells us that, "it is right to know that this fellowship with God takes place in the depth and centre of the soul. It is there that the soul speaks to God heart to heart, and always amid a great deep peace in which the spirit revels in God."[64]

Where is this "depth and centre of the soul" exactly? In the body? In the heart? In the mind? In all three? If "soul" is just an old-fashioned word for "consciousness", which the Ancient Egyptians called BA, it must encompass body, heart *and* mind.

From the panpsychist point of view, consciousness is located most powerfully in the brain, but is also present throughout the body. And there is no hard and fast dividing line between brain and body. Brain and the body are inextricably linked through the mediation of the nervous system, especially the central nervous system. The brain reaches down, so to speak, through millions of nerve fibres, via the spinal cord, to every corner, every nook and cranny, of the body, so that the two become, to all intents and purposes, indistinguishable.

The "soul" is not located somewhere in the region of the heart, as tradition has it, and neither is it located in the head, as modern rationalists would have it. It is located throughout the entire body, but most intensely in the brain and central nervous system. In other words, the "soul" is located in what the Indian yogis and tantrikas call the *shushumna*, the central consciousness/energy channel passing through the spinal cord to the top of the head. This, then, is where the "fellowship with God" takes place.

Now if this "fellowship with God" is conceived in Christian terms as a "fellowship with the Trinity", where exactly in the soul does this fellowship take place? We have an important clue in the sign of the cross. When making the sign of the cross, Christians touch the forehead "in the name of the Father", the heart "in the name of the Son", and the shoulders "in the name of the Holy Spirit".

Our fellowship with the Father, according to the Indian tantric model, takes place in the *ajna* chakra, the "third eye" chakra. When we make the sign of the cross, we touch the third eye "in the name of the Father". Our fellowship with the Son takes place in the *anahata* chakra, the "heart" chakra. Both of these physical locations make perfect intuitive and symbolic sense. We approach the transcendent through the higher mind, but we approach Christ through the devotional heart.

So far so good. But what about the Holy Spirit? When performing the sign of the cross, we touch the shoulders in order to complete the shape of the cross on the body. This satisfyingly completes the pictorial representation of the cross, physically enacting the central Christian symbol in a simple gesture, but it fails to complete the hidden, esoteric meaning.

The *kundalini* energy rises up from the lower chakras. It makes more sense, then, to visualize the "fellowship with the Holy Spirit" as taking place in the "sacral", *svadhisthana* chakra, known as the *hara* or *dantien* in Buddhist tradition, rather than the shoulders. The traditional sign of the cross is energetically very top heavy. Is it too fanciful to suppose that the omission of the lower chakras is in some way indicative, or even constitutive, of a general neglect of the body and bodily energy, including sexual energy, in Christian spirituality?

It could be regarded as highly dubious and not a little controversial to determine precise anatomical locations for subtle, spiritual concepts such as the three Persons of the Trinity. The mixing of different spiritual traditions in this way may strike some as eccentric at best and insulting or even blasphemous at worst. Others may find it quaint, and just smile to themselves, as they might smile at Descartes' attempts to locate the seat of the soul in the pineal gland, for example.

The rational mind might take offence, but the spiritual imagination is immune to all such foibles. Ever open to new ideas and new associations, it is the ultimate pragmatist. Do the chakras really exist? Who cares? They exist in the imagination. Perhaps they are just psychosomatic projections. But perhaps that's precisely the point. As Brother Lawrence says, "The presence of God ... can come about either through the imagination or the understanding."

*

Relating the Christian Trinity to the Ray of Creation, the "Holy Spirit" obviously corresponds to AMUN-RA. The material world (or the "natural world") is represented by ATUM. When we experience the "glory of God" in the world, we are experiencing AMUN-RA, emptiness and energy, shining in and through the lineaments and contours of ATUM. We intuit the infinite void and the infinite energy at the heart of creation, which we experience as stillness and peace, energy and light.

The experience of being filled with the Holy Spirit is equivalent to the activation, or the awakening of the *kundalini* serpent, which has its source in the lower chakras and the *hara*, the centre of spiritual power in Buddhism and Taoism (think of martial arts such as Kung Fu, Tai Chi, Karate, Judo and Sumo). If we divide up the Holy Spirit into its constituent parts, we can be even more specific: AMUN is associated with the base chakra; RA is associated with the sacral chakra; ATUM is associated with the solar plexus chakra.

The "Son" corresponds to KA-BA. KA represents life and BA represents consciousness. All living organisms embody this dual aspect of life and consciousness. When we see the light of life and the light of consciousness shining through a person or creature, we experience them, not just as dumb animals or talking animals, but as "children of God". Culminating in the heights and depths of divine love and wisdom, KA-BA finds its fullest expression in the human avatars of the world, represented in the person of Jesus Christ, "the Son of God". Where does "the fellowship with the Son" take place? In the heart. To be more precise, in the heart and in the throat. KA, "the life force", is associated with the heart chakra; BA, "the soul" (as mental consciousness) is associated with the throat chakra.

"The Father" corresponds to the World Soul and the Absolute, GAIA-JAH. In touch with the transcendental unity of the planet as a whole or of the universe beyond, we are in "fellowship with the Father". Where does this take place in the body? Intuition of the higher consciousness of Planet Earth, the "Earth Goddess", GAIA, is naturally associated with the third eye chakra, and intuition of the Absolute, JAH, with the crown chakra.

Brother Lawrence said that, "this fellowship with God takes place in the depth and centre of the soul". We can leave it at that, with reference to the One God, or we can try to be more specific, with reference to the Trinity, and re-write his statement as follows: "This fellowship with the Father, the Son and the Holy Spirit takes place in the head, the heart and the *hara*."

Translating this into the language of the Ray of Creation, we can say: "This fellowship with GAIA-JAH, KA-BA and AMUN-RA-ATUM takes place in the head, the heart and the *hara*."

Breaking it down even further, we can re-write the statement again: "This fellowship with AMUN, RA, ATUM, KA, BA, GAIA and JAH takes place in the base chakra, the sacral chakra, the solar plexus chakra, the heart chakra, the throat chakra, the third eye chakra and the crown chakra respectively."

Of course we know that these things do not literally reside or take place in specific locations in the body. It's just an imaginative way to attune ourselves, full-bodied, whole-hearted and open minded, to the presence of God. The practice of the presence of the Ray of Creation is simply an elaboration of the practice of the presence of the Trinity, which is itself an elaboration of the practice of the presence of God. The *One God* contains the *Three*, and the *Three* contain the *Seven*. The *Seven* are resolved into the *Three*, and the *Three* are resolved into the *One*. With practice, the Word of God as One, Three and Seven is made flesh through the inner alchemy of the central nervous system.

Connect with the base chakra.
Focus all your attention on the base chakra.
Repeat the mantra, AMUN.
Keep your body and mind firmly in the void.
Empty your body and mind.
Keep coming back to Emptiness.

Connect with the sacral chakra.
Focus all your attention on the sacral chakra.
Repeat the mantra RA.
Be filled with light.
Let the thrill of ecstasy flow through you.
Enlighten your body and mind.

Connect with the solar plexus chakra.
Focus all your attention on the solar plexus chakra.
Repeat the mantra ATUM.
Connect with your material form.
Embody your atoms and molecules.
Materialise.

Be filled with the Holy Spirit

Connect with the heart chakra.
Focus all your attention on the heart chakra.
Repeat the mantra KA.
Feel the life-force within you.
Embrace all feeling and sensation.
Come alive.

Connect with the throat chakra.
Focus all your attention on the throat chakra.
Repeat the mantra BA.
Be aware of awareness.
Realize you are one unified consciousness.
Realize your soul.

Be filled with the love of Christ

Connect with the third eye chakra.
Focus all your attention on the third eye chakra.
Repeat the mantra GAIA.
Reach out to Mother Earth.
Sense the unity of life and consciousness.
Be part of the whole.

Connect with the crown chakra.
Focus all your attention on the crown chakra.
Repeat the mantra JAH.
Pray to the universe.
Pray to God.
Surrender to the Absolute.

Be filled with the glory of the Father

15. Words and Things

Words are the greatest of friends and the worst of enemies. They both reveal and obscure the things that we attach them to. A rose, by any other name, would smell as sweet (apparently). But would it smell sweeter without a name? Or might it be that it would smell sweeter if we could name it more precisely, as a "Hybrid Tea Brandy" for example? Can even the word "sweet" do justice to the smell of a rose? Is the smell of a "Hybrid Tea Brandy" sweeter than a "Madam Hardy" because it's "stronger"? Or do we need to distinguish between "intensity" and "delicacy"? Do we experience a complex wine more fully when we know that it's "flamboyant with a hint of gym socks"?

What about colour? Can the words "red" or "yellow" capture the colour of a rose? Perhaps we would experience the colour more fully and immediately without naming it at all. Or perhaps we could come closer to the real colour if we used a more nuanced word such as "lust", "oxblood" or "coquelicot" instead of boring old "red". But wouldn't associating the colour of a rose with sex, death and the French divert us from the pure sensory experience? Is there even such a thing as a "pure sensory experience"? Could we conceivably experience the redness of a rose without some awareness of the concept or even the word "red" hovering somewhere this side of consciousness?

This is not just an academic question for neuroscientists. It's central to our everyday experience of the world, and indeed, of ourselves. Since we were initiated into the world of social intercourse and language at the tender age of 0, our experience of the world has been, to a greater or lesser extent, mediated by words.

But is it true that *all* of our experience is so mediated, or should I qualify that and say that *most* of it, or maybe just *some* of it is mediated by words? And what do I mean by "experience"? Is it anything that we are in any sense aware of at any given time, or is it just those things that we actually pay attention to?

*

As I look around the room in which I am sitting as I write this, I can see lots of things. As I glance away from the screen of the computer, I take in the scene, which is a relief for my eyes, but also for my spirit. It is a beautiful scene, as I can see the garden through the French windows and it is a beautiful spring morning. The light streams into the room and picks out the colours of the furnishings, the brown-red-burgundy sofa, the cream-yellow-lemon curtains, the far-too-intricate-to-describe patterned rug. On first glancing at the room, there are no words, only impressions. All the separate objects are just elements of one integrated scene. When I looked at the white cane chair in the corner, neither the words "white" or "cane" or "chair" came to mind.

The night before last I was sitting in a friend's garden shed with a VR (virtual reality) set on my head. I had momentarily forgotten that I was in his shed. I actually thought that I was in a space pod that had just landed on a jungle planet. (This may have been partly due to the joint I had just smoked).

As I moved my head to look around, I could see all sorts of strange technical equipment with absolute clarity and three-dimensional precision. It was curiously the same but different from the images on the screen I had been looking at before actually putting the headset on. On the screen, I had had a general, vague impression of the interior of a spaceship, with lots of indiscriminate space stuff in it. I had neither the capacity nor the inclination to examine them more closely. It looked kind of boring.

With the headset on, however, everything seemed to jump out at me and clamour for my attention. Although I could not name or put any specific words to any of the strange objects around me, I was fascinated by them, and spent some considerable time examining them in much more detail than I did when they were just on the screen. The others, who were watching my progress on the screen, became impatient and told me to get on with it and open the pod door so I could check out the alien planet.

Words and Things

We make most efficient sense of our environment, whether real or virtual, by perceiving things as either *foreground* or *background*. When I look up at the room and take it in as a whole, the whole is perceived as background. The specific objects in the room are not relevant to my present activity, writing, which constitutes my foreground experience.

As soon as I bring the experience of the room into focus in order to communicate it through my writing, I intentionally focus on the individual objects in the room, such as the chair, the sofa, the rug and the French windows with the trees and garden beyond. As I focus on each object in turn, I pick it out of the general background and it becomes foreground. I can then experience it more acutely and in more detail. As soon as I withdraw my attention, it again blends back into the general background.

This was exactly what I experienced with the strange technical objects in the space pod. As I paid conscious attention to each in turn, they emerged from the undefined general background pod and took on a life of their own. Even though I couldn't put any words to any of them, because I had never seen anything like them before in my life, they took on a certain quality of significance, as a prelude perhaps to my working out what they actually were. It wasn't all just an indiscriminate bunch of weird shit any more.

As I sit here writing, my mind is occupied with the effort to communicate certain ideas through words. My thoughts are in the foreground, and the room, including the computer I am writing on, is in the background. From time to time, I glance at the room to have a break from my thoughts and reconnect with the sensory world of light and colour and beauty, but it is a fleeting connection and I am quickly back in my thoughts again. When the garden is lit up as the sun breaks through a cloud, I have to resist the urge to leave my post and go out and enjoy the sunshine. Sometimes I can't resist. The warmth of the sun, the smell of the grass, the colourful flowers, the wind in the trees, what bliss! But I am committed to this work, and must sacrifice these garden pleasures.

Words and Things

I am not a gamer and I am not particularly interested in computer games. Once the novelty of the three-dimensional immersive virtual reality experience had worn off somewhat, I realized that if I was to actually progress through this jungle planet world, I would have to actually play the game. This meant that I would have to identify certain objects in my environment and use them to solve puzzles. Ultimately, this was no different to the adventure games I had enjoyed as a child. It was also the same process I had to go through whenever I had to solve a real problem in the real world.

Was this *play* or was it *work*? Is playing games a sort of rehearsal for work? A kind of pseudo-work or quasi-work? The night before last, trudging around an alien jungle planet looking for clues as to what I was supposed to do suddenly felt too much like hard work, so I handed the headset to someone else.

The German existentialist philosopher Martin Heidegger wrote about the human habit of treating things in the world in the manner of "equipment". In other words, we only ascribe importance or significance to things in so far as we can find some use for them.

This is certainly true in the case of computer games. I knew that if I were to play the game properly, I would have to go back into the space pod and properly check out my equipment. If I were to play the game properly, I would have to shift out of "aesthetic appreciation mode" and get stuck into "problem solving mode". Now I had a job to do and a mission to accomplish, whatever that was.

Likewise, sitting here now on this beautiful May bank holiday afternoon, I have work to do. I have to solve the problem of how to express myself clearly and interestingly enough for you to keep reading, and for me to keep writing. It is hard work, but it is also an enjoyable game. How can I clear a path through the jungle of my thoughts without succumbing to too many hackneyed metaphors, like "the jungle of my thoughts", or being side-tracked by irrelevant self-referential observations?

I know that I shouldn't take too long or too circuitous a route to my destination, but that neither should I arrive too quickly, without enjoying the scenery on the way. I need to find a balance between seriousness and playfulness that is neither too dry nor too facetious.

Whether I succeed and "win" the game I have proposed for myself, is not entirely up to me to decide, but neither is it entirely up to you.

*

In the garden there is a vegetable patch in a wooden box that has a clump of tall grass growing in it. If I focus on this clump of grass, I can distinguish each individual blade of grass. Each blade of grass is then a separate *thing*. If I need a pretty green ribbon to wrap a small present for my girlfriend, or if the mischievous thought pops into my head that I could sneak up behind her as she is working in the next room and tickle her on the back of the neck, then one of these blades of grass becomes *equipment* for me. It is then very clearly distinct from the class of long blades of grass of which it is a member.

From another point of view, however, I experience all the grass in the garden as *one thing*, not a multitude of individual, separate objects. I can pick out one blade out of thousands and regard that one blade as one thing, but actually, it is just a small part of one mass of grass.

When I look at the other plants, I can see that they are all distinct and individual things, but also that, from another point of view, they are one with the other plants, with the flowers and the grass, with the whole garden, in fact. I can say the same thing for the bushes and trees. They are both separate and individual, if I pull them into the foreground of my awareness, but also inseparable from the garden as a whole if I let them blend into the background. It's only through my artificial classification of all these things that they become separate and individual *things*.

How should we divide up reality? Does the scientific classification of kingdom, phylum, class, order, family, genus, species do justice to the complexity of reality? Does it really matter how we divide it up? In the Isha Upanishad it is written, "This is perfect. That is perfect. Take perfect from perfect, the remainder is perfect." However our minds divide and parcel up reality, it is always perfectly real. If we look at reality only from the point of view of *labels* and *equipment*, however, then only those things are real which have meaning and value for us. Everything else is background.

If all the world is a stage, then the things on the stage are just props and backdrop and set. Our focus and interest is on the human drama, specifically *our* human drama. Drama is narrative, stories, meanings, relationships, understandings and misunderstandings, work, play, gain, loss, elation and despair. The dagger, the handkerchief, the king, the fool, together weave the tapestry of the drama, which we experience as the warp and woof of life. Success, failure, victory, defeat, intrigue, betrayal, sacrifice, devotion, happy endings, unhappy endings. We solve problems; we fail to solve problems. We change the world and the world changes us. We travel from the cradle to the grave, create, destroy, laugh, cry. Sometimes we pause to smell a rose.

We live as though the human drama were real and the world was just a painted backdrop. What if the opposite is true? What if the world is real and our human drama is just make-believe? We put all our little foibles, attachments, interests and obsessions firmly in the foreground of our awareness, and everything else, "all living creatures and the whole of nature in its beauty" recedes into the background. What if all our little dramas, what if even our big dramas, were experienced as background and the world itself, which we usually regard as nothing but the "set" and "stage" of the story of our life, was the foreground?

What if the life we think we are living is just as virtual a reality as the game we enter when we put a VR headset on? We select the objects in our environment according to their functional, utilitarian benefits. We even treat other people, work colleagues, family, friends, even romantic partners as "equipment" for the solving of the puzzles and problems of our life.

The dozen roses my friend had delivered for his partner's birthday are meaningful and significant because of their symbolic value. The transactions between grower, distributer, seller, buyer and receiver can be perfectly well carried out without any direct sensory experience of the actual roses by any of them. Which of them actually smelt the roses or appreciated their beautiful colour? The roses are equipment. Even the delighted recipient experiences them as equipment: as a means of communicating love.

There is a close relationship between language and equipment. When words are used to communicate something, they are the equipment of communication. Graphic icons, *emojis* and images can also be used as communications equipment, as can roses. Words, images, roses, chairs and blades of grass, then become part of a linguistic virtual reality that exists apart from the real world.

We exist in both worlds, flitting between the two, just as I flit between writing this and appreciating the garden. When I focus my attention on the white cane chair in the corner, its reality emerges from the background and it stands (or sits?) in the spotlight of the foreground of my attention. However, as soon as I label it as a "white cane chair" for the purposes of communication (with you, dear reader), the words substitute for the reality adequately enough for my purposes, and the reality of the chair again recedes into the background.

What is the significance of the famous painting of a kitchen chair by Vincent Van Gogh? It is a brave attempt, in oils, to communicate the reality, the *essence* of the chair in itself, beyond words. For Van Gogh, it is our connection with the essence of reality that constitutes the meaning of life, not the stories we spin around ourselves, and our chairs.

Both Van Gogh and Shakespeare were great artists, one using the medium of paint, the other of words. Did one experience reality more fully or more truly than the other? Who are we to say? Both are revered as geniuses, because both express something essential about reality, and at times seem to break through the veil of our illusions. We could say the same about any number of great artists, who point away from the trivia of our petty human dramas to something greater, truer, more beautiful because more real.

Is this the difference between the aesthetic sensibility as set against the utilitarian? This is also at the heart of Arthur Schopenhauer's philosophy. Pure aesthetic experience is possible only when we suspend our habitual attitude of exploitation in the service of our "will to life". When we don't ask or demand anything from a particular object, such as a painting, but experience it on its own terms, then we can penetrate into the essence of the thing as it is in itself, beyond any ideas of personal gain, use or equipment. This was also the sentiment behind the "art for art's sake" of Walter Pater and Oscar Wilde.

*

As a precocious young teen, I was fascinated by Zen, which claimed to be "a direct pointing to Reality outside the scriptures". I knew that I didn't experience reality directly, but through the filter of my own mind, and I was acutely aware of the problem of words. Words seem to both reveal and obscure reality. On the one hand, it's difficult to imagine fully experiencing things you didn't have words for. Doesn't the fact that Icelanders have so many different words for snow mean that they experience snow more fully than we do? Doesn't someone with a wide vocabulary experience the world in more depth and detail than someone with a limited one?

On the other hand, words necessarily take our attention away from bare sensory experience into a kind of mental simulacrum, a verbal virtual world. So is it better to cultivate a sensitive and nuanced use of language to more accurately map reality, and have a better chance of finding the *mot juste*, as the best poets do, or to just point directly to Reality without the need for any words or poetry at all?

But what would this pointing consist of if not words? What are the scriptures if not pointers? The expression, "a direct pointing to Reality outside the scriptures" alerts us to the dangers of an over-reliance on words. It reminds us that the map is not the territory and the menu is not the meal. But we needn't take it too literally either. We try for the best map and the best menu to better appreciate the journey and the meal, although ultimately words will always fail us.

> "Words strain,
> Crack and sometimes break, under the burden,
> Under the tension, slip, slide, perish,
> Decay with imprecision, will not stay in place,
> Will not stay still."[65]

In *The Doors of Perception*, Aldous Huxley describes an LSD trip in his garden. He describes in intimate detail his experience of looking at a hedge, which he calls the "dharma hedge". It's just an ordinary hedge, but under the influence of LSD, it's anything but.

Words and Things

    We might imagine he experienced all sorts of crazy psychedelic hallucinations, but it turns out this is not what impressed him about the "dharma hedge".

    What impressed him was that the hedge was just a hedge. Most importantly, it was *just* a hedge. In other words, there were no words. No words, no thoughts, no random mental associations. There was just the essential is-ness, being-ness, or *suchness* of the hedge. If you've never had this experience, it might sound a little trite. "The hedge is just a *hedge*, man". Yeah, cool dadio! Far out!

    Mind stops. Time stops. Words are irrelevant. Things are as they are. Mountains are mountains and rivers are rivers. A state of perfect simplicity. This is the essence of Zen. It's not tripping. It's arriving.

16. Word Magic

The Magician is an ancient archetype. Unfortunately, in our modern scientific age, it has fallen somewhat into disrepute. The magician of the popular imagination is more Tommy Cooper than Merlin. We automatically think of the magic tricks of illusionists and entertainers. For us moderns, "magic" is synonymous with "trick" or "con". We know that there is no such thing as magic, but we can enjoy being fooled into thinking that there is.

Yet most people today still hold on to a vestige of belief in magic, at least in the wider sense of the "extraordinary" or "miraculous", which need not necessarily break any actual physical laws. We are all, in one way or another, in search of the miraculous. We all want a bit of magic in our life.

The Magician is an adept at word magic. He can invest certain words and phrases with magical power, and he can cast spells. A spell is a verbal formula that produces a specific, or near-specific effect. Because of the popular depictions of magicians in books and films and the magical entertainment of professional illusionists on stage and on TV, it is easy to suppose that this means an effect on the physical world. Something is made to levitate or disappear, or some other physical impossibility is performed. However, this is a distorted view of magic. Real magic is not something that is performed on objects in the physical world. It is something that is performed on *people*.

There are several levels of mastery in spell casting. In the first level, the Magician develops the ability to create a specific effect on the mind. This is so commonplace as to seem unremarkable. We do not consider it "magic" when a certain organization of words creates a particular thought or image in our mind. This is, after all, the function of language. Is "The quick brown fox jumps over the lazy dog" a spell or a sentence? If we see it as nothing more than a collection of words that include all the letters of the alphabet, or a simple statement of fact, it is a sentence. If it produces a vivid image of a fox jumping over a dog in our mind's eye, it is a spell.

The magic is in the transformation of the words on the page into an image in the mind. In *that* sentence (the one before this), the magic is in the transformation of words into *thought*.

In the second level of mastery in the magical art of spell casting, the Magician learns to create a specific effect on the emotions. The Magician is a poet, a novelist or a playwright, if he is in the business of creating new spells, that is. The world is already replete with emotional spells, which the Magician casts on himself, or on others. Here is part of a simple spell, courtesy of Philip Larkin:

"The trees are coming into leaf
Like something almost being said;
The recent buds relax and spread,
Their greenness is a kind of grief."[66]

This is a spell of a higher order to "the quick brown fox jumps over the lazy dog", because it produces a particular emotion, not just an idea or an image. It may be that you are not feeling it right now. The Magician feels it. He is receptive to the emotional power of words. This is why he is able to cast spells, and perhaps even create them if he has the skill and artistry. Most importantly, though, he is able to fall under the spell of words himself. The Magician is not so much the creator as the enjoyer of magic.

In the third level of mastery, the Magician formulates spells that create a specific effect on the body. This is really just an extension and intensification of the second level. There are certain words that carry an energetic charge strong enough to penetrate through the mind, through the emotions and into the body. Let us take just three words to illustrate the point: "dog", "grief" and "peace".

The word "dog" conjures up an image in the mind's eye. It is (probably) a fairly neutral image, so will only get as far as the mental representation. The word "grief" conjures up a particular feeling associated with the experience of loss. Depending on the intensity of the feeling, it may also have some bodily, physiological effect, such as a dull ache in the chest area. The word "peace" also refers to a kind of feeling (or the absence of feeling), but it can also be experienced as a physical state of relaxation.

The Magician sees the dog clearly in his mind. He feels the grief keenly in his heart. He experiences peace in his body. But the third level is where the real magic lies. Let's have a closer look at the word "peace". The word "peace" has certain associations related to the absence of war and conflict and the absence of stress and tension. We might think of symbols of peace, such as a white dove, or collocations such as "world peace", "peace be with you", "war and peace" or "peace and love". So far we are at the first level of mental representation. As well as reaching for general meanings and associations, we can also relate the word to our own personal experience. We can remember times when we have felt peaceful and connect with those feelings now. This is the second level of emotional connection.

If we have been involved in some form of spiritual practice for some time, the word "peace" will also have a deeper significance for us. We may have experienced a sense of profound peace in the depths of meditation, for example. In this case, the word "peace" will carry a special power for us, which can be triggered in us, just be saying the word. This is "the peace that passeth all understanding", but it is also "the peace that passeth all feeling", because it has its effect directly on the body.

The mantra OM SHANTI SHANTI has this power. This is precisely the meaning of "mantra": a sound word that has power. Mantras are magic spells designed to have direct energetic effects on the body.

"A Mantra is Divinity. It is divine power or Daivi Shakti manifesting in a sound body. The Mantra itself is Devata (Divinity)."[67]

PEACE is a mantra. LOVE is a mantra. They are both "words of power". When the energy is missing, they collapse into cliché. We could perform the same tripartite linguistic analysis on the word "love". It is a mental concept and an emotional feeling, but beyond those, it is a receptacle of spiritual energy, something like the chalice of Christ's blood, *the holy grail*, in Malory's legend.

The word "love" can contain as much or as little as we are able to pour into it. At a certain point of intensity, we may feel that we need to qualify the energy of the love we receive by describing it as "the love of God", in order to differentiate it from the ordinary emotional love of the second level. In any case, the words "peace" and "love" will never be clichés for the Magician, because to him they are sacred receptacles full to the brim with bottomless spiritual power.

*

Ortega y Gasset defines romantic love as "absorption and surrender due to enchantment"[68]. This is as true of the magic of meditation as it if of the magic of love. In mantra meditation, the mantra works as a spell, creating a specific form of enchantment. The meditator, if she has sensitized herself sufficiently to the "Devata", the Divinity of the mantra, will become deeply absorbed in the mantra as she surrenders ever more completely to its influence. If she is capable of being enchanted in this way, she can rightly be called a Magician.

"Falling in love" is a passive emotion because it happens to you without any intentional, willed action on your part. Ortega y Gasset's definition above describes only the passive aspect of romantic love, which is experienced as an enchantment. However, in a successful romantic relationship, there must also be an active element present, which is the deliberate and conscious assent to loving another. He describes this as "cordial affirmative interest", which unsurprisingly, sounds a lot less romantic. If there is no conscious, active assent, then if the feeling of enchantment dissipates, there will no longer be any basis for persisting in the relationship.

Both the passive and the active elements of love are essential. If only one is present, the love feels unconvincing and compromised. Together, they are mutually reinforcing, so that each lasts longer, and is stronger, than it would otherwise.

Meditation also requires both an active and a passive element. The active element is called *jiriki*, "self-power" and the passive element is called *tariki*, "other power". Mantra meditation typically begins with jiriki. In the Hindu tradition, this is called *japa*.

Japa involves the mechanical, self-willed, intentional repetition of the mantra. The meditator actively initiates the meditation simply by applying some effort and injecting some conscious energy into the repetition of the sound.

The meditation would bear little if any fruit if things simply continued in this active vein. After a while, the meditator must shift gear and withdraw his active energy and intention. Now he becomes passive. He surrenders to the mantra and lets it go its own way. Instead of the meditator leading the mantra, the mantra now leads and the meditator follows. This is called *dharma*. The meditator simply follows the dharma of the mantra, following faithfully wherever it may lead him.

The dharma stage is the passive stage, but it is not yet a condition of complete absorption, surrender and enchantment. This is the third stage, to which the dharma stage points and leads, called *yoga*, the culmination of the meditation. In the state of yoga, which is a state of unity, the meditator abandons the mantra and is abandoned by the mantra. In perfect stillness, he enters into absolute quiescence and absorption, *Samadhi*, the ultimate synthesis of the active and passive elements of love and peace in the depths of the great ocean of universal consciousness, which is the goal and destination of all true Magicians.

Magicians are masters of enchantment and spell-casting. PEACE and LOVE are universal, time honoured spells that will never go out of fashion. But there are others. The most popular, because the most powerful, are those that invoke God directly. This special class of mantra is called a *Divine Name*.

"The Divine Name, revealed by God Himself, implies a Divine Presence which becomes operative to the extent that the Name takes possession of the mind of the person invoking. Man cannot concentrate directly on the Infinite, but by concentrating on the symbol of the Infinite he attains the Infinite Itself."[69]

There are of course many Divine Names scattered throughout the world's religions and spiritual traditions. The devotee of each Name imbues it with spiritual power by the very act of invocation and meditation, so that it may be that the actual form and sound of the Name itself is ultimately of no consequence: "a god by any other name would sound as sweet". However, most mantra yogis invest great significance in the actual sound and form, *namarupa* of the Name.

Divine Names invoke the spiritual essence of the Universe ("the Creation") taken as a whole, conceived as either personal or impersonal: God the Father or God the Absolute. However, there are also Names that refer more specifically to particular aspects or qualities of this ineffable, unknowable Godhead. A collection of these, more limited, Divine Names can flesh out the positive, conceptual content of the Being of God, in a way that the generalized, universal Names cannot. This is known as the *via positiva*, which is complementary to the more mysterious *via negativa*, and provides the rationale for the Seven Mantras presented in this book, which are in effect seven Divine Names of the ultimate mystery of God.

*

The Ancient Egyptians used the term *heka* to refer to the magical power of spells. Each of these Divine Names has its own *heka*. However, just as important as the individual magic of each is the collective harmony and alignment between them. In Ancient Egypt this harmony between the members (*maat*) was seen as absolutely essential to the welfare of the whole. Therefore the Pharaoh was duty bound to achieve and maintain *maat* throughout the Kingdom.

We could say that "love" is the source of magical power, *heka*, and that "peace" is the essence of harmony, *maat*. Through *heka* and *maat*, love and peace, the Magician invokes the Divine Names of God in order to more fully embody the qualities contained in them. Each mantra contains the breadth and depth of his current understanding and experience, and, like a bottomless well, is always filled but never filled up. In this way, the Magician magically transforms himself and, like an Alchemist, tirelessly transmutes the lead of ignorance into the gold of wisdom.

17. In Dreams

For the psychoanalysts Freud and Jung, dreams were the royal road to the unconscious. Dream analysis could provide clues and insights into the psychological issues of their analysands by revealing personal truths through symbol and metaphor that the rational, conscious mind was unable or unwilling to accept. Dreams offer a way into the invisible, repressed material of the unconscious precisely because the usual controlling and repressive functions of the ego are asleep. Unable to reach conscious awareness through the usual channels, these hidden parts of us must find another way through.

When you are dreaming, you are not completely unconscious. Parts of you are asleep, and parts of you are awake. The only time when you are totally, completely unconscious is when you are dead. The Victorian habit of writing "asleep" on their gravestones speaks volumes about the difficulty of coming to terms with the reality and the finality of death. From the Christian eschatological point of view, the rotting corpses under the ground are only asleep because they will be woken again at the end of time when Christ comes again in glory. The word "asleep" implies a temporary condition. What is asleep can presumably wake up again.

Even in deep sleep, you are not completely asleep. Your vital organs are still awake and functioning. Your heart keeps pumping and your lungs keep breathing. Even your senses are awake enough that you can be alerted to a sudden noise, light, smell or movement. There are, of course, degrees of deep sleep. If you are in a coma, have fainted or been knocked out, or are under general anaesthetic, you will not stir even in the middle of an earthquake. Or if you are suddenly and violently roused from normal deep sleep, you may experience "sleep paralysis", where you find that you are physically unable to move. This is simply because the natural order of waking up has been reversed and the mind is awake while the musculature of the body is still asleep.

In the dreaming state, the rational, thinking mind, based largely in the frontal lobes and the neo-cortex of the brain, is asleep, but the imagination is awake. When you dream, the imagination has free rein, unhindered by the strictures and dictates of reason, which is why dreams are often so bizarre. There seems to be a sliding scale of surrealism across different dreams, depending on the level of activity or inactivity of the rational mind and the imagination. Sometimes there seems to be no rhyme or reason whatsoever to a dream, but more commonly, there is a vestige of a faint and tenuous reasoning faculty in the background, vainly straining to bring some semblance of order and meaning to the chaos.

Dreams where the rational mind is completely asleep are difficult to remember on waking up. It may be that they cannot be remembered, and that we only remember those dreams where there is a vestige of rational consciousness present. There are also dreams where the imagination and the reasoning faculty seem to find a kind of equilibrium and can work in tandem. This occurs in the tenebrous state between sleep and waking, called the *hypnogogic* state. This is a state of consciousness/unconsciousness greatly sought after by artists and other creative thinkers, where seemingly insoluble problems are effortlessly unraveled and resolved. The most famous example is probably the case of James Crick, who solved the problem of the genetic code sequencing in DNA after dreaming of two intertwined snakes.

*

When we are asleep, some of our faculties, such as the senses and the rational mind, are asleep, but some faculties, such as the imagination, are awake. The same holds for the waking state. Any of our faculties, our senses, desires, feelings, will, memory, imagination, thought processes, etc. can be awake at one time and asleep at another, conscious one moment and unconscious the next. We are constantly moving in and out of different modes of consciousness as one faculty takes the stage and the others withdraw into the wings.

Who is moving in and out of these different modes? You might be thinking one minute, talking the next, daydreaming, remembering something, craving a coffee, watching, listening, wanting, deciding, imagining, thinking again. One minute, your thinking mind is awake, the next, it's asleep. One minute your imagination is asleep, the next, it's awake. But through all these wakings up and fallings asleep, surely there must a constant someone or something behind it all, which is always awake. But who? Or what?

I notice that sometimes I am aware that I'm thinking, talking, remembering, imagining, looking or listening, and sometimes I'm not. Sometimes my "I" is awake, and sometimes it seems as though it's fast asleep. It seems that the constant something or someone behind all my activities and experiences, which I might as well call "me", "myself" or "I", is not always conscious and awake either.

If I make a concerted effort to be conscious or "mindful", which is to say, aware of myself being aware of something, whether that something is a thought, a feeling, or a rose, only then can I say with all honesty, "Yes, I am conscious. My "I" is awake." In this moment of conscious, mindful awareness, I am *self-remembering*, as the Gurdjieffians say. I am aware that I am aware. A simple visual illustration of this state of mindful, self-awareness is a two-headed arrow pointing simultaneously at the subject and the object of awareness, the "self" and the "other".

If I can, with some conscious effort, "remember" myself, then I must ordinarily "forget" myself. Usually, the arrow of my attention points in only one direction: outwards to the object of my awareness. My awareness of myself, my sense of "I", recedes into the background and becomes unconscious. I am conscious of the object, but I forget myself. My "I" falls asleep. Although to all intents and purposes, I am awake, and continue to think, remember, dream, desire, etc., my "I" is asleep. I am not aware of doing any of these things. I just do them unconsciously, on automatic pilot. I am like a philosophical zombie.

"What sleepwalkers we are!" exclaimed Basho in one of his more philosophical haiku. The clarion call of all the Eastern spiritual traditions, from Advaita Vedanta to Zen is that we must *wake up*. We must be conscious and aware of ourselves and of our surroundings.

We must be mindful at all times. This is, of course, easier said than done. We may wake up for a time, but then quickly fall asleep again, as Ouspensky found to his great surprise and consternation when he stopped to buy a cigar at a kiosk in St Petersburg.

*

When the "I" is asleep while I am awake, I can consciously wake it up by being mindful and "remembering myself". When I do this, my "I" wakes up and my senses wake up, and my discursive mind and my imagination fall asleep. I feel much more awake and present. Everything seems vibrant and alive and all of a sudden, I can see, hear, smell, taste and feel things much more vividly and acutely.

The "I" can be (and usually is) asleep while I am seemingly awake and going about my business, but it's apparently always asleep in actual sleep. Not only that, it's in a much deeper sleep. I might complain that I'm asleep while I'm awake, but I'm obviously not as asleep as when I'm asleep.

So what happens if you wake up the "I" when you're fast asleep in bed? What if you "remember yourself" while you're actually sleeping? Well, that's when you start *lucid dreaming*. Just like in the waking state, when the "I" wakes up, the discursive mind and the imagination fall asleep. There is no more fuzzy background mind activity. Everything is crystal clear. And, just like in the waking state, the senses wake up. Which senses though? Not the external senses obviously, because I'm still asleep with my eyes shut. Not the external senses, but the internal senses. When the inner "I" wakes up, so does *the inner eye*, which is basically what we mean by the "third eye".

Last night I had a lucid dream. I couldn't sleep because my mind was over active and over excited, mulling over some new material for this book, so I decided to meditate in the hope that I would naturally drift off to sleep. But I didn't. The meditation was deep, but I was still wide awake. So I thought I would try a sleeping spell. What would finally switch my wakeful brain off after hours of insomnia? I repeated the words "magic sleep balm" and imagined a white lake covered with soft white feathers.

Suddenly a vivid image of a white plastic covering with a kind of plastic seam on it appeared in my mind's eye. As I consciously tried to sink my mind into unconsciousness, the white plastic turned grey, with a fine grain of darker grey stripes. Suddenly, I was by a canal. It looked absolutely real, as though I had woken up and was standing outside in broad daylight. I was convinced that it was real. Just like in an ordinary dream, I had no awareness that this was a dream.

However, I somehow instantly knew that it wasn't real. I thought I was seeing through the illusion of reality in the "real world" as opposed to the "dream world". I remember thinking, "I'm like Neo (from the Matrix films). I can do anything." So I stepped into the canal, knowing that I could just walk along it without sinking into the water. And I did! I strode along the canal with absolute confidence. My feet sank just below the surface, but they didn't get wet and I walked along the canal with ease.

There was a beautiful arch over the canal, like you might find in Venice. Then I entered a tunnel. A strange vehicle, a bit like a narrow, single carriage of a London tube train went past. I saw a kind of secret entrance in the wall to my left. I went through and found myself in a strange workshop cum garage. There were machines at one end humming and rumbling away to themselves. A man in overalls came in behind me and walked past me. He completely ignored me but I was able to have a good look at his face, which was not quite fully human, a bit like a waxwork model.

I crossed the workshop and pushed through some swinging doors decorated with clowns like in a circus. I experienced some apprehension and not a little curiosity about what I might find, but after only a few steps through a courtyard full of bits of theatrical scenery, I was woken by the screech of a coot outside my window (I live on a boat).

In my experience, lucid dreams rarely last very long. It is clearly difficult to maintain such a level of intensity and concentration. Last night I thought I had another lucid dream (I wrote the foregoing yesterday).

In the dream I was watching a film with my ex-wife. It was a city scene in America, possibly New York. It had a festive, Christmassy feel about it. There was a hotel porter in front of what looked like a large glass-fronted department store who suddenly broke into a Fred Astaire dance routine. Then he started doing all sorts of extraordinary moves, some of which seemed physically impossible.

In the next scene of the "film" I was sitting at a table with my ex-wife. We were having a drink al fresco. I commented to her that we were actually in the film, because if we looked to the sides and behind us, the scenery continued all around us. It was "surround vision" as well as "surround sound". I told her that we were watching a film of the future, which were all like that.

Then, with a queer sense of urgency and with great emotion I told her that actually this wasn't a film at all, but a dream. "Look", I told her, "you will remember this, and then you'll know it was a dream." There were two glasses in front of me on the table. One of them had water in it, and the other white wine. I hesitated between the two, then drank the wine and picked up the glass of water. "Watch!" I said, and proceeded to pour the water over my head.

The dream was extremely vivid and realistic. I was convinced that it was real. I was also convinced that it was a lucid dream. In the dream I knew it was a dream so it must have been! I had many other vivid dreams during the course of the night, which I won't try your patience with here. But reflecting on these dreams the following morning, I realized that although they were all very vivid, none of them was an actual lucid dream. I merely *dreamed* that I was lucid dreaming. I was as lost in the dream as ever. My "I" was still asleep, even while I was dreaming that it was awake.

There may be an analogy here with the waking state. It may be that sometimes we think that our "I" is awake, but actually it is just our mind telling us that we our awake. In other words, we are daydreaming that we are awake. It's almost as if the mind enjoys fooling us. It fools us into thinking that our dreams are real and it fools us into thinking that we're awake when actually we're fast asleep.

*

The "I" is awake one moment, asleep the next. So too is the rational mind and the imagination. So too are the memory, feelings, senses, and body. This is the natural rhythm of conscious human life. Things come to the fore and recede into the background. Part of us wakes up for a while and then falls asleep again. We can't be conscious of everything all the time. It would drive us insane. We can't be fully in our senses, in our body, thinking, feeling, imagining, willing, remembering, all the time and all at once. And we can't be fully self aware with a wakeful and watchful "I" all the time. It doesn't matter that we can't always "self remember". To demand *that* of ourselves is to set ourselves up for a lifetime of spiritual inadequacy and neurosis. Just like the other faculties and functions of human consciousness, the "I" comes and goes, ebbs and flows with the tides of our turning consciousness.

But as long as we are alive, whether awake or asleep, there is a constant Witness behind and beyond all of our experience, real, imagined or dreamed, which is always aware, but of which we can never be aware, just as the eye can never see itself. This is the True Self, the True Atman. It is not the same thing as awareness of "I". It does not come and go. Asleep or awake, this is the core essence of consciousness and life. The Witness lives in all living things. It sees all things, hears all things, thinks all things, bears all things. Only in the true sleep we call death does the Witness finally return to its source in Brahman, the one eternal consciousness. Who knows? Perhaps we are actually all just part of the dream of God.

18. Isis and Osiris

Myths are universal because they are vague and suggestive. They paint with broad strokes, leaving the details to be filled in by the individual listener or reader. They are just stories, and as such, are entertaining, exciting, fun, moving, interesting, or not. If they are good stories, they stimulate our minds and our hearts. They invite us to empathize and feel with the characters, and experience their dramas vicariously through the imagination.

This is true for all art forms. Art is an invitation to participate in the imagination of another, to see through the eyes of another and think and feel with another. Do we see and feel the same things? Does it matter? We are invited into a "sound world" or a "feeling world", or any number of different kinds of "worlds", where we are free to roam and experience things for ourselves. Sometimes these worlds are very closely defined and our responses are narrowly proscribed. Sometimes, they are more loosely defined and we can move more freely within their bounds. Too didactic and narrow and we feel manipulated and constrained. Too open and free and we feel lost. There must be a happy medium, a golden mean. This is perhaps what Nietzsche meant when he said that we must learn to "dance in chains".

There are certain psychological universals, which underpin the structures of our mythical inheritance. There is the association between height, light, and the ethereal or spiritual. This is sometimes referred to as the *numinous*. Then there is the opposite and contrasting association between depth, darkness, and the dense or material, sometimes called the *cthonic*. In a guided visualisation, if your guide leads you up a mountain or up a magical staircase into the clouds, you will naturally be inclined to feel *light*, in both senses of the word. Any beings that you may meet at the top of the mountain or up in the clouds will invariably embody spiritual goodness and wisdom for you.

Alternatively, if your guide leads you down into the depths of the earth, through underground caves, down a deep well or mine shaft, or even to the bottom of the sea, you will naturally find yourself experiencing darkness and heaviness, and any strange beings you meet down there will probably be frightening or disturbing, embodying negative qualities and feelings, evil or even danger of death.

In between the two worlds, the upper and the lower, we have meadows, forests, hills and deserts, or occasionally and grudgingly, villages, towns and cities. Our deeper mythical consciousness seems to prefer scenes taken from the natural world, presumably because this has been our dominant experience in the millennia of our pre-historic evolution. In terms of our shared collective unconscious, urban life is actually only a very recent development. Hence also the surprising prevalence of wild animals in guided vizualisations and shamanic "vision quests".

These three broad realms of mythical experience form the backbone of much mythical storytelling, whether Norse, Greek, Egyptian, Indian, Celtic, Aboriginal or Native American. Often, the story involves a *task* that must be completed in either or several of the three worlds to restore order after a natural or supernatural shock. The homeostatic system of the mythical world has been thrown off balance and a hero or heroine must find a way to set the world right again.

The power of the imagination is a mysterious power beyond the ken of reason or science. It is an evolutionary more ancient and primitive faculty than the logico-deductive neo-cortex, with roots that reach right down to our pre-human ancestors. It is also for this reason much closer to the body, and can cause or trigger changes in the body, which the logical mind cannot so easily reach. These changes may be scientifically observable, such as changes in muscle tension, rate of respiration, heartbeat, and the production of hormones, neurotransmitters and endorphins. They may by immediate and short-term or gradual and long lasting.

If a scene is imagined with enough emotional investment, the brain is easily fooled into thinking that it is really happening, and so responds accordingly.

Thus a chronically anxious person who regularly imagines disastrous and threatening situations actually produces the corresponding hormones, such as adrenalin and cortisol, necessary for "fight or flight" and so becomes chronically committed to a state of anxious readiness. On the other hand, someone who regularly visits a beautiful, relaxing imagined scene, whether natural or supernatural, produces more endorphins such as serotonin and dopamine, the body's natural opiates, which relieve stress and enhance pleasure.

*

Roberto Assagioli was an Italian psychiatrist. He studied psychoanalysis with Freud, who hoped that he would introduce it in Italy. But Assagioli found Freud's psychological model too restrictive and limiting, particularly his conception of the unconscious, and decided to develop his own model, which he called psychosynthesis.

For Freud, the unconscious is, amongst other things, the repository of repressed psychological material from the past. It contains the unacceptable thoughts and feelings that the ego basically can't stomach. This is why so much psychoanalysis is focussed on childhood. Assagioli didn't have a problem with this. In his model, he called it "the lower unconscious". However, he believed that this conception of the unconscious failed to take into account other, higher unconscious potentials. He believed that, as well as a "lower unconscious", there must also be "middle unconscious" and a "higher unconscious".

According to Assagioli, not only do we repress things because they are "below us", but also because they are "above us". He called this phenomenon "the repression of the sublime". The ego protects itself on two fronts, against primitive, animalistic urges (mainly sex and aggression) on one side, and against spiritual feelings and experience on the other. Both represent a challenge and a threat to the control of the ego.

An excessive negative or positive psychic charge impels the ego to repress the experience and push it down either into the psychological cellar or up into the psychological attic. Experiences that have neither a particularly positive or negative charge can still be repressed, or at least forgotten, and end up in the middle unconscious.

Assagioli's psychological model is reminiscent of the traditional division of the world into an underworld (hell), a middle world (Earth) and an upper world (heaven). From the psychological point of view, the denizens of these three worlds are personifications of repressed psychic energies, what Assagioli called subpersonalities, and what Margret Rueffler calls "our inner actors". As we would expect, we find ugly and frightening creatures, monsters and demons in hell, ordinary people and animals in Earth and beautiful angelic beings in heaven.

Transpersonal psychologists have understood the power of myth since the advent of the discipline in the 1960s. The Greek myths and other less well-known myths from around the world have been rescued from the depths of our collective unconsciousness (and cultural amnesia) in order to shed light on psychological processes. Rather than seeing them as tall tales or outmoded, primitive beliefs, they can be more fruitfully approached as repositories of ancient wisdom and psychological insight.

Dante plumbed the depths of hell in *The Inferno* and scaled the heights of heaven in *Paradiso*. The wisdom of the ancients consists in this: to bravely venture into both the darkness and the light, into the depths and the heights of the human spirit. In this way, they could gain access to and re-own and integrate those parts of them that had been split off and banished into the outer reaches of the unconscious. This is what psychosynthesis is all about. Interminable analysis is not enough. What we need is *synthesis*.

*

Modern man, *homo scientificus*, attempts to live in a modern, sanitised world with "no heaven above us and no hell below". Perhaps this is not exactly what John Lennon was getting at with his lovely utopian vision of peace and love, but never mind. From a psychological point of view, to live without heaven or hell means to live without a lower and higher unconscious. But that's impossible. They don't just disappear. They simply become even more unconscious than they were before. Tom Waits sang, "If I exorcise my devils, well, my angels may leave too"[70]. But none of them really leave. They all just become *more unconscious*.

Maybe it wasn't such a good idea after all. We end up more repressed than ever. Our inner devils secretly torment us without our knowledge. Our inner angels wilt and faint from boredom and neglect. We feel weak, neurotic, insipid, uninspired. Life feels flat, monotonous, literal, mechanical. Disconnected from our inner life, we seem to have completely lost our spiritual power. All we have left is the cold comfort of materialism, hedonism and the sure knowledge that, whatever else we might be, at least we're not superstitious!

There is power in the underworld. But we are afraid of power. So we push it down and close the trap door. But it comes knocking in the middle of the night, night after night, until we finally relent and release the genie from his bottle, and relieve the devils of their chains. And suddenly, all the powers of Hell are unleashed on the world, and we are either driven insane or driven to acts of evil, perversion and harm to ourselves and to others. We are as if possessed, and the mild Dr. Jekyll we once were is transformed into the rapacious Mr. Hyde, until the demonic storm subsides and the trap door is forced shut once more.

Most of us are sensible enough not to fling open the gates of Hell. Instead, we expend a great deal of energy on keeping our devils at bay. Strict routine and busyness seem to work best. But still they haunt us in our dreams and nightmares, and we wake up from a night's sleep not refreshed but fearful, uneasy and uncomfortable in our own skin. We go through the day with a dark cloud of irrational anxiety and depression hanging over us. We don't trust ourselves, but keep a constant check for signs that our inner gremlins are getting the upper hand. Desperately, we try to keep them down by self-medicating with drink, drugs, food, TV, music, noise. They always manage to worm their way through the gunk in the end.

We have learned to put up with this dire situation, to accept ourselves as we are: anxious, neurotic, stressed, depressed, obsessive, compulsive, moody, irritable, insecure, exhausted. This is how we are. This is what being human is like. Weak and fallible beings beset by stresses and strains on all sides, hounded, enervated and debilitated by psychological shocks and traumas, we retreat into a world of vicarious pleasure and virtual satisfaction.

The modern remedy for our modern malaise is distraction. We are "distracted from distraction by distraction"[71] as T.S. Eliot pithily put it. Failing this, we talk, usually to a therapist. Failing this, we are prescribed sedatives and anti-depressants. Failing this, we are institutionalized. This is the logic of a world without Heaven or Hell. But there is another way: the traditional way of myth, poetry, magic and the imagination.

Is there a myth that can help us negotiate the heights and depths of our being and deal with our repressed psychic energies? Two things are needful for us, caught as we are between an unconscious Heaven and an unconscious Hell. First, we need to access our inner spiritual energy and power, and second, we need to manage and contain our wayward and rebellious inner forces. But how?

*

In ancient Egyptian mythology, the Lord of the underworld is not evil, like the Devil in Christian mythology. He is none other than Osiris, son of Ra and "Lord of love". Osiris is also Lord of death and Lord of the afterlife. The Egyptian underworld was associated with regeneration, death and rebirth, so Osiris was connected to the natural cycles of vegetation and the annual flooding of the Nile. In death, the Pharaohs would attain eternal life through magical identification with Osiris.

How did Osiris end up as Lord of the underworld? The story goes that when he ruled Egypt with his beautiful wife Isis, his brother Seth became jealous and had him killed. He invited all the gods to a party and at the end of the party, when all the guests had had plenty to drink, he proposed a fun party game.

He brought in a beautiful coffin, inlayed with gold and all manner of precious stones and announced that he would give the coffin as a special going-home present to whomever it fitted most perfectly. Of course, he had already secretly measured Osiris in his sleep, so that when it was his turn to lie in the coffin to try it for size, he fitted perfectly.

Isis and Osiris

Seth slammed the lid shut and nailed it fast. When all the other guests had left, presumably in a drunken stupor, Seth took the coffin, and under the cloak of the night, threw it into the Nile. The plan was perfect. With Osiris gone, he could marry his beautiful queen Isis, and rule in his place.

The only problem was that Isis was powerful. She was the goddess of magic and might be able to use her magic to find Osiris and bring him back to life. So Seth, taking no chances, went back to where he had dumped the coffin. He dragged it out of the river and took out the dead body of Osiris. He cut the body into fourteen pieces and buried the pieces all over Egypt. Surely, Isis would never find them, and he would be safe on the throne.

But Isis, "great of magic", was more powerful than Seth realized. It was her love for Osiris that gave her power. When she discovered what had happened (the tree which had become a pillar of the palace and had grown from the wood of the coffin told her), she wept profusely and vowed not to rest until she had found her beloved. She travelled all over Egypt, retrieving each piece of Osiris' body. Once she had all the pieces (apart from his penis, which had unfortunately been eaten by a fish in the river), she magically joined them back together again (and fashioned a new penis out of clay).

However, her magic was not strong enough to bring him back to life, so the gods decided to give him a job as ruler of the underworld. Although she could not revive him completely, Isis did manage to rouse him long enough to have intercourse with him, and become pregnant with Horus, the future King of Egypt. Isis wrapped Osiris in bandages to stop him falling apart and installed him on the throne in the underworld, which he ruled with great authority and justice.

This is a very potted version of the story, but it will do. Isis is the Queen of Heaven. She is associated especially with the moon, but also with the sun. So after the terrible events of the myth of Osiris' death and semi-resurrection, the situation is this:

Isis and Osiris

Isis reigns in heaven and Osiris reigns in hell. Husband and wife, king and queen, and lovers to all eternity, they are tragically and eternally separated by the cruel, murderous jealousy and greed of Seth, who has usurped the earthly throne and now rules (badly of course) over Egypt. When the baby Horus, son of Isis and Osiris comes of age, however, he avenges his father's murder at the hands of his uncle, kills Seth and is crowned as the rightful Pharaoh of Egypt.

*

What happens next? Let's imagine. Isis is the Queen of Heaven. She personifies the power and magic of the higher unconscious, full of healing and spiritual energy. Osiris is the King of Hell, ruler of the lower unconscious. He is also spiritually powerful. Osiris is a great king, in death as he was in life, but ruling over an unruly demonic mob is exhausting. Inevitably, the strain begins to take its toll, and he literally starts to come apart at the seams.

As Osiris weakens, the devils in hell take advantage of his weakness and begin to foment unrest and open rebellion. There is anarchy and chaos. The demonic uprising spills out onto the shores of the river Nile and slowly works its way through the black land of the Nile Delta and into the red land of the desert. Horus sees what is happening, but is powerless to stop it. Egypt is swamped with devils. He cries to his mother Isis for help.

Isis is swift to respond. She knows she cannot fight the devils back into hell, because they are too powerful, and too numerous. Instead, she flies down to hell herself in the form of a kite. She flies all over hell in search of her husband. But he is not there. So she searches for him in Egypt. His body, fragmented and broken in fourteen pieces, has been scattered by the devils all the way from one end of the Nile to the other.

Again, she must gather the pieces of Osiris together to save him and the fate of Egypt. She finds two pieces in Rosetta at the mouth of the Nile, one in the black land and one in the red land. She finds two pieces in Giza, one in the black land and one in the red land. She finds two pieces in Maidum, one in the black land and one in the red land.

She finds two pieces in Amarna, one in the black land and one in the red land. She finds two pieces in Luxor, one in the black land and one in the red land. She finds two pieces in Aswan, one in the black land and one in the red land. She finds two pieces in Abu Simbel, one in the black land and one in the red land.

Once she has retrieved all fourteen pieces, Isis uses her great magic and her great love for Osiris and pulls him back together again. Isis revives Osiris and he is once again restored to the throne in the underworld. Through his great spiritual power, he recalls all the devils back to hell, and peace reigns once more in his underworld kingdom. Isis returns to her throne in heaven, and Horus returns to his throne on Earth.

*

This is a psychodrama. By channeling psychic energy through the medium of the active imagination, you can use this mythical structure to harness the power of the higher unconscious and pacify the unruly negative energies of the lower unconscious.

Egypt is "the Earth" and represents the middle unconscious and the body. When you feel off-sorts, anxious, irritable, tense, discombobulated, this is a sure sign that the devils are coming. They well us from the depths of the Nile like thick black tar, like a giant oil spill, and overflow onto the banks and poison the streams and tributaries.

Negative thoughts, negative feelings, discomfort, pain and tension in the body. These are the symptoms. The cure is not in fight or flight. The symptoms alert us to the fact that the lower unconscious is getting out of hand and needs the intervention of the higher unconscious to set things right. Osiris, king of the underworld, is weak and desperately needs the saving help of his queen, Isis.

The Nile represents the *shushumna*, the central energy channel passing through the spinal column. The mouth of the Nile opens out to the sea, which represents infinity, at the crown of the head. Calling to Isis for her spiritual aid and magical healing, she enters Egypt (the body) through the mouth of the Nile in the city of Rosetta.

Isis and Osiris

Isis is the Queen of Heaven. In daylight she is in the sun. At night she is in the moon. Call on her with the following incantation:

Queen Isis, great of magic, heal me, as you healed Osiris, king of the underworld!

Imagine her descending on a ray of sunlight in the day or on a ray of moonlight in the night. The light enters through the crown of the head into the astral body (Egypt).

Rosetta represents the crown chakra. Receive her magic power as golden light in the day or silver light in the night. Receive it into the crown chakra with the word *heka*, which means, "magic". Then imagine the light spreading all over the skin of your body, so that you are surrounded by golden or silver light. As you do this, say *maat*, which means "harmony". With this, you have brought together two of the fourteen pieces of the fragmented body of Osiris.

Giza represents the third eye chakra. Again, receive the magic light into the chakra with *heka*. The illuminated chakra is a microcosm of the moon or the sun. It is a sphere of perfect light. With this, you have illuminated the black land in and around the city of Giza. To illuminate the red land, imagine the light radiating out to fill the whole of your head, with *maat*. With this, you have brought together four pieces of Osiris.

Maidum represents the throat chakra. Receive the magic light into the throat chakra with *heka*. Then imagine the light spreading into the red land, your neck and shoulders, with the word *maat*. You have now collected six pieces of Osiris.

Amarna represents the heart chakra. Receive the magic light into the heart chakra with *heka*. Then imagine the light spreading into the red land, your chest area, front and back, and your arms, with the word *maat*. You now have eight pieces.

Luxor represents the solar plexus chakra. Receive the magic light of Isis into your solar plexus chakra with *heka*. Then imagine the light spreading into the red land, your stomach and back, with the word *maat*. You now have ten pieces of Osiris.

Aswan represents the sacral chakra. Receive the light of Isis into your sacral chakra with the word *heka*. Then imagine the light spreading into the red land, your pelvic area and groin, with *maat*. You have now collected twelve pieces.

Abu Simbel represents the root chakra. Receive the magic light of Isis into your root chakra with *heka*. Then imagine the light spreading into the red land, the pelvic floor and legs and feet, with the word *maat*. You now have all fourteen pieces of the broken body of Osiris.

Osiris is made whole again through the love and magic of Isis. He must now be restored to his throne in the underworld. The throne of Osiris is located in the centre of the Earth. Isis must use her magic to transport him safely down through the Earth's crust, through layers of magna and down into the very centre of the Earth's core. There, she revives him and he ascends the throne.

Isis must return to her own throne in the moon (or the sun). The lovers are separated again, but they remain connected by a thread of spiritual silver (or golden) light, which reaches from the moon (or sun) to the centre of the Earth. Imagine that your body is suspended by this spiritual thread between two bright lights: one above and one below. Your body is now the illuminated body of Horus, child of Isis and Osiris and king of Egypt.

The devils are back in their box and magic and harmony are restored in the three worlds. Until the next time…

19. Attention, Attention, Attention

Driving down through the Northumberland hills after a short stay at Throssel Hole Buddhist Abbey, a monastery in the Soto Zen tradition, I was aware of four things: the beautiful scenery, the music on the car stereo, my thoughts and the road ahead. It is common knowledge that we can perform many tasks automatically with minimum awareness. Driving is a good example. Especially on familiar routes, it often happens that we arrive at our destination with no recollection of how we got there. We were on automatic pilot. Our attention was elsewhere, probably lost in thought.

I had been thinking about attention at the monastery and so decided I would try a simple experiment. Could I simultaneously attend to the road, the scenery, the music and my thoughts? I found that I could and I couldn't. I could drive safely and at the same time be aware of the hills in the distance, the music on the radio and my thoughts. However, as I focused my attention on any one of them, I found that the others instantly receded into the background. When I listened closely to the thoughts in my mind, for example, the scenery became background scenery and the music became background music. I could see and hear them, but I was neither looking nor listening. Of course my senses were still working, so there was no sudden blank backdrop or sudden silence, but because I wasn't directly paying attention, the music and scenery seemed less present, more peripheral, less real. Equally, when I listened closely to the music, I found that I couldn't think. When I became fully conscious of my driving, as when there was a sudden hair-pin bend in the road, I could neither think, look at the view nor listen to the music.

This is how the attention works. It is a supremely efficient system. Whatever we attend to moves into the foreground of our awareness, while everything else recedes into the background. As we become more conscious of one thing, we become less conscious of other things.

If we focus intensely on one thing to the exclusion of all else, we become fully conscious of it while becoming fully unconscious of everything else. Usually, however, there is a residual peripheral awareness of everything else. It is a sliding scale.

As my simple experiment clearly showed, we can function perfectly well without full attention. In fact, much of our functioning goes on below the threshold of awareness. And this, I realised, is how we usually experience the world. Our attention is fluid, and fluctuates between different objects of interest. We may believe that we are "multi-tasking", but in fact we are simply flipping quickly and seamlessly between the different tasks. We only have one thing in the foreground at any one time and may have four or five in the background waiting their turn in the limelight. Modern life is increasingly demanding that we splice our attention in this way, since there are so many demands on it. Modern technology has given us instant access to all sorts of interesting and useful things, and we can swipe, skip and jump from one to another in seconds.

The problem with this sort of roving attention is that it does not allow the time necessary for any one thing to come fully into conscious "foreground" awareness, so that everything is ultimately experienced as different degrees of "background". We end up being semi-conscious, half asleep. This is fine as far as achieving our aims is concerned. We will (hopefully) arrive home safely after paying minimal attention to our driving. But we will not fully experience the journey.

The word "Zen" is the Japanese pronunciation of the Chinese word "Ch'an", which is a mispronunciation of the Indian word "Dhyana", which simply means meditation. Meditation is full, undivided attention. It is an offering of the time and space necessary for things to come into the foreground of our awareness and reveal themselves fully. It is a "dwelling upon" with conscious mindfulness. It involves "sati" (concentration) and results in "samadhi" (absorption).

Zen is nothing other than full, undivided attention. This is why one famous Zen master (Master Ichu) when asked about the meaning of Zen simply said, "Attention. Attention. Attention."[72] Whatever you turn your attention to, don't hold back. Pay full, undivided attention to this, then pay full, undivided attention to that.

What should we pay attention to though? Things constantly call for our attention. From a state of equanimity and stability, simply follow the call.

It is wrong but tempting to think that "I" pay attention. We instinctively assume that there is an "I" in here which illuminates different things with the flashlight of attention and that we can vary the strength of the beam. By holding this view, we unwittingly create a division between ourselves and whatever it is we are aware of. There is "I" on one side, "that" on the other side, and attention bridging the two. In full, undivided attention, there is no division between "I" and "that". There is only "that".

With increased attention, there is not only an awareness of "that", but there is also an awareness of the awareness of "that". In other words, one is conscious of being conscious. One knows one is fully awake and aware. This is very different from the automatic, semi-conscious state we are usually in, which, by contrast, is a kind of sleep.

It is not always possible to pay full, undivided attention, or to remember ourselves as we are doing so. However, if we can understand that there are degrees of attention, and that the objects of our experience slide between the foreground and background of our field of awareness, and that there is no "I" apart from attention, then we understand that we cannot *not* be present in the present moment of attention. Zen is seamless and endless. It cannot be chopped and spliced, however much it seems to be.

With this realization, we can relax. When we relax, our attention relaxes. When the attention relaxes, it naturally settles and deepens, and the world emerges from the dark clouds of inattention into bright day.

*

Pure consciousness is "formless" and "empty" because it is the space in which all objects of consciousness exist. It cannot itself be an object of consciousness, because then there would be another consciousness observing it, which would be the "real" consciousness. There is an infinite regress. As soon as you try to make consciousness into an object, that is, to "see" it or experience it in some way, consciousness recedes into the background as the seer or experiencer.

Your inner consciousness, which can only be inferred by the objects of consciousness, and never experienced directly, is the Self. It is variously called the "Witness", the "Observing Self", the "Soul" in Christianity, or the "Atman" in Hinduism. To remind ourselves of the pure, untainted nature of the Self, we can use mental formulas, such as, "I am not that which can be observed", or more simply, "not this, not this", which is the meaning of the famous Vedanta mantra *neti, neti*.

There is therefore an important distinction to be made between the Self as pure subjective consciousness, forever untainted by any objects of consciousness, and the phenomenal self. The usual convention in spiritual circles is to capitalize the former. The Self is the *noumenon*, the "spiritual" essence of all things, which can never be directly known. The self is a *phenomenon*, a "psychological" entity that we can be aware of, if not completely. That which we experience as "self", as opposed to "not-self" or "other", is simply that which we have mentally identified as "self". We cannot even say that it is that which is imbued with Self, because any experience of anything is imbued with Self. My experience of the bottle of water in front of me is held in Self consciousness. It is only my mind that informs me that the bottle is "not-self".

There are three layers to the experience of the phenomenal self. The outer layer is called "mine". I bought the bottle of water in a shop. So it is mine. Although somewhat tenuous and temporary (I've nearly finished it), I have forged a mental tie or identification with "my" bottle and "my" water. All my material possessions and all the people in my life are "mine": my house, my car, my mother, my friend. More abstract identifications also belong in the outer layer: my name, my age, my nationality, my football team, my favourite films, books, singers, etc. as well as my feelings, thoughts, opinions and beliefs. Whatever I preface with the little possessive pronoun "my" has a mental association with "my" phenomenal self.

The second layer is called "me". Whenever I conceive of myself as an object in the world, I experience myself as "me". This is the self-reflexive turn, which looks back at myself from the perspective of a real or imagined other. Too much "me" and I begin to blush and act self-consciously. I lose my powers of speech and dignified locomotion.

This is a typical experience among teenagers who suddenly become painfully aware of how they appear in the eyes of others. Their self-image then becomes a major source of interest and concern, including their physical appearance and clothes, as well as their manner of speech and behaviour. Although the acuteness of the experience of myself as a "me", as an "objectified self" lessens with age and maturity, it is still an important aspect of the experience of the phenomenal self.

The inner layer of the phenomenal self is called "I". This is the feeling of subjectivity and of being a subjective agent. It is not the same thing as the noumenal Self, because it involves some content of experience, some "qualia". This may be a certain feeling in my body which I identify as the feeling of "I", or a general sense of being unique, and experiencing myself and the world around me in a unique way. It is also associated with any conscious, intentional act, such as when "I" am thinking or "I" am walking.

These three layers are associated with different experiences of time. The outer layer of "mine" exists in the extended time frame of past and future, and of indefinite time or permanence. For example, "Sebastian" is and always will be my name (unless I change it), and Chile is and will always be my country of birth. My car is mine until I sell it. The middle layer of "me" exists in the extended present, which lasts as long as people are watching me, or as long as I feel that I am being watched. If I am a narcissist or paranoid, this may last for quite some time. The inner layer of "I" exists only in the immediate present, which is why it is experienced as more intimately personal. Only "I" know what it is like to be "me" in the immediate existential experience of my present Being-ness.

What if I dis-identify from all those things which I call "mine"? It is not hard to see that the essence of who I am has nothing to do with my possessions. If I lose my house and car, all my money, even my family and friends, I am still "me". Of course I do not want to lose all these things, but when I stop viewing them as determining factors of my essential identity, I instantly feel a peculiar but welcome sense of peace, calm and spaciousness.

I realise that although my "possessions" are useful and necessary to live a comfortable life, on a psychological level, they seem to possess me as much as I possess them. I feel like Gulliver, waking up on the beach after a shipwreck, only to find myself pinned down by hundreds of Lilliputian ropes. Each rope is like an attachment to something I claim as mine. As I let go of my attachments, I am released from the psychological captivity of "mine, mine, mine".

What if I dis-identify from the self-image I have of myself, which I call "me"? I have to let go of the labels I apply to myself, positive and negative. I have to give up my mirror image as an accurate representation of who I am. I have to give up the image of myself I intuit in the eyes of my family, friends and acquaintances. I have to let go of my biography, my obituary and my epitaph. It is not so hard to see that all these ideas and images of "me" do not really represent the essence of who I am.

I notice the subtle difference when I am drumming or singing on my own. If I imagine that people can hear me, if I imagine an audience, whether appreciative or irritated, I feel an oppressive sense of "me"-ness. I am aware of what I look like and what I sound like. My drumming becomes self-conscious and strained. If I imagine that I am the only person left on Earth, then the drumming radiates out freely, without a hint of a suspicion of judgment or censure. My hands are free, no longer tied by the projected image of "me".

What if I dis-identify from the intimate feeling of "I"? What if my inner bodily sensations, my familiar points of tension and stress, familiar and intimate thoughts and feelings, are just passing sensations, thoughts and feelings? What if I consciously remove the automatic, habitual "I" labels? Since time immemorial I have claimed these personal, private experiences as "I", but when I observe closely, I see that they are just objective experiences like any other. There is no reason why they deserve the title "I". It is just my own personal whim and lifelong convention and conviction.

I can dis-identify from these three concentric layers of the phenomenal self in turn. Firstly, with the aid of the mantra, "not mine", then with the mantra, "not me" and finally, with the mantra, "not I".

Meditating on "not mine-not me-not I", we arrive at a place of inner freedom and stillness, where the True Self, the inner, pure un-identified consciousness, shines forth. It is the place from which St. Paul could exclaim in wonder, "Not I, but Christ lives in me." This "shining forth" of the True Self, the *Christ Consciousness*, is Enlightenment itself.

20. Earth Medicine

It is difficult to find wide open spaces in the average modern metropolitan city. Not so in London. London's parks and green spaces are legendary. Hackney, Walthamstow and Tottenham marshes, which run alongside the river Lea in North East London are more than parks; they are an oasis of wild countryside smuggled into the heart of the concrete jungle.

Standing in the middle of the wide open space which is Walthamstow marsh on a beautiful summer's day, I was struck by the enormity of the sky above me. As an urban animal, my experience of the sky is largely constrained by window frames if I am indoors or buildings if I am outside. Cities are basically an arrangement of intersecting open-topped corridors, like a maze in laboratory rat experiments. We only ever see slithers and segments of sky and our focus is directed almost exclusively at eye level, or at feet level if we are in a pensive mood. Even when we go to the park on the weekend, we are either playing with our children or chatting with friends or partners. We rarely see the sky in its full glory.

What I noticed on the marshes on my own with the sky laid open before me, was that the sky is not just an amorphous, uniform empty space filled with things like clouds, birds, planes and, occasionally, the sun. This is how it seems to me when I am walking along the street. I look up and there it is: a piece of empty blue sky. But in the middle of a wide, open space, where you have the luxury of an unbroken horizon all the way around you, it is clear that the sky is not just an empty space. It is a giant *dome*.

I stood there for quite some time. The sun began to dip in the sky as evening drew in. This only added to the sense of the domed nature of the sky, as the clear blue began to deepen the closer it got to the apex. There was now a band of light blue over the horizon, gradually darkening to a deep indigo colour directly above me. It occurred to me that this wide blue dome was somehow related to the inside of my skull. I felt a connection between the microcosm of my inner world and the macrocosm of the outer.

Following this line of reasoning, I realised that the colour of the sky on that clear summer evening did in fact reflect the colours of the traditional Tantric chakra system, with light blue at the throat chakra, indigo at the third eye chakra, and violet at the crown chakra. This was, after all, the higher end of the light spectrum, so it was perhaps an unsurprising correlation.

The horizon, which formed a perfect circle around me, was almost entirely made up of trees. It was a lush green band of green. Extending the microcosm/macrocosm idea, I naturally related this green band to the heart chakra, traditionally visualised as green. As I listened to the gentle rush of the wind in the leaves, it also made perfect sense that the presiding element was *air*.

But what about the solar plexus chakra, which is supposed to be yellow and related to the element of *fire*? Well, to the west of the marshes runs the river Lea. As the sun dipped further in the sky, it suddenly transformed it into a shining, burnished gold, as the rays struck the water. I wondered whether the original Indian Tantrikas developed the chakra system meditating by a lake or river, perhaps even by the river Ganges herself, on beautiful clear evenings such as this. I also wondered whether they might have sat around an actual fire.

I guessed that the orange and red of the lower two chakras, the sacral and the root chakra, would then be associated with the glowing embers of the fire, or else the colour of the soil at the sadhu's feet, or both. The element associated with the root chakra is, predictably enough, *earth*, and that associated with the sacral chakra is *water*. As the sun approached the horizon, I wondered whether the deeper golden colour on the surface of the water could actually be the orange of the sacral chakra and the yellow sun itself could be the solar plexus chakra. In any case, the red/brown earth was clearly associated with the root chakra.

The ancient Vedic term for the experience of spiritual Enlightenment is *Satchitananda*, which is usually translated as "Being-Consciousness-Bliss". The Enlightened state encompasses and expresses all three qualities. As I meditated on the scene before me, I saw in a flash that both the macrocosm and the microcosm are divided in the same way, corresponding to the triune *Satchitananda*.

The world is divided into Earth, Horizon and Sky. The "Horizon" is in fact everything between the Earth and the Sky. We could call it the *biosphere*, between the *geosphere* and the *atmosphere*. The body is also divided into three: head, torso and the lower body, from the waist down. *Sat*, "Being", corresponds to the earth beneath my feet and to the lower body. *Chit*, "Consciousness", corresponds to the sky above me and to my head. *Ananda*, "Bliss", corresponds to the whole of life between the earth and the sky and to my own heart.

This meditation requires an open space, an open sky and an open heart. Connect with the lower body and with the earth and with a sense of pure Being and repeat the mantra *Sat*. Then connect with your head and with the sky and a sense of pure Consciousness and repeat the mantra *Chit*. Finally, connect with your heart and torso and with everything on the horizon, everything between the earth and the sky, and connecting with a sense of pure Bliss, repeat the mantra, A*nanda*. Repeat this cycle a few times until the boundaries between your body and the world, and your sense of Being, Consciousness and Bliss, begin to blur and dissolve into one all-pervading *Satchitananda*.

*

Use the power of Nature to heal and enliven you. Use the free gifts of the natural world to free you from your manmade prison. Use your senses. Use the natural elements. You will discover magic that you never dreamed of.

There is magic in the river. There is magic in the forest. There is magic on the canal, in the park, in the garden. Look for it on the ground, in the sky. It is in the sights, sounds and smells of the city as well as in the countryside. Avoid mechanical noise; avoid cars and motorbikes; avoid crowds. Look for the quiet, empty spaces. Look for the green places.

There is magic in water. Watch it move. Water is infinite and eternal transformation in action. It is one body, then several, many, then an infinite variety. First placid and unbroken, it just requires a change in the current, a light gust of wind, a passing water fowl, a surfacing fish, or a stone or twig to ruffle its immutability. All the secrets of philosophy are contained in the infinite movements of water.

There is magic in wind. Listen to the wind rising and falling, sighing and whistling. Listen to how it gives voice to the trees, how they talk with one another and with you. Follow the phrases of the wind as they move around you in forest, glade or garden. Follow it from beginning to end, from the gentle swell of the sound to the gentle hush. The grand, flowing music of the wind in the trees exists on a different time zone to the erratic, staccato of your thoughts. Allow your mind to follow the wind. Allow your breath to synchronize and merge with the breath of the trees.

There is everything to discover and experience as if for the first time: the shades of blue sky in the morning, afternoon and evening; the stately progression of the clouds; the green of the grass and trees. There is light, shadow, movement, contrast, rhythm, strength, gentleness, beauty. There is the sound, sight and feel of the wind on the ears, trees, skin. There is coolness and warmth. There is the feel of the solid earth beneath your feet, or soft moss, hard rock, grass, undergrowth. There is the feel of the firm branch and the delicate leaf and flower.

There is the magic of fire, licking its infinite dancing forms over stick and log, smoke, sparks, glowing embers, yellow, orange and red. The smell, the warmth, crackling light and shadow. There is magic by the sea, on the mountains, in the hills and fields and meadows, moors and villages and farms. There is magic in the sun. There is magic in the moon and the stars. There is magic in the light of the sun or moon on the water, magic in the light and colours of the sun-setting clouds.

It is impossible to get bored of Nature, just as it is impossible to get bored of food or sleep, because it nourishes us. Only when we are spiritually sick and dissociated from the natural world do we cease to enjoy the sight of a bee or the taste of honey. Eating disorders and insomnia are contemporary maladies appearing alongside the loss of our feeling for Nature. We are out of joint when we cannot enjoy the simple things in life: a good walk, a good meal, a good sleep.

It is all medicine for the soul. The elements, the senses, colours, insects and animals, birds and birdsong, sun and wind and rain. All is Earth medicine. We need only open our hearts, minds and souls in order to receive the infinite gifts of our eternal divine Mother Earth, *Pachamama*.

*

As a species, we are destroying our beautiful planet, our beautiful home. We are alienated from our true nature as the sons and daughters of Nature. Collectively, we are committing ecocide and deicide on a terrifying scale. We are killing the Earth and we are killing God. If we fail to stop this worldwide rape and pillage of our Divine Mother, we may imperil the future evolution of God in this corner of the universe, and abort the great adventure of life and consciousness that has unfolded here for millennia.

We are the *axis mundi*. We are the world trees connecting Heaven and Earth. It is up to us to maintain and uphold this connection for the sake of all of life now and in the future. We must reconnect with our spiritual values, and reconnect with our spiritual strength and power, in order to resist the forces of rampant materialism, consumerism and unrestrained capitalism which are devastating our world.

We must redirect our accumulated wealth and technical and industrial power to protect and conserve our precious, fragile environment, and put a stop to the mass extinction of species and desecration of the Earth's biodiversity. And we must invest in research and find real, practical solutions to the energy crisis, the water crisis, and the plethora of other environmental crises confronting us, on local, national and international levels.

At the same time, we need to learn to live in harmony with Nature and with each other, and wean ourselves from our over-dependence on and addiction to material goods, wealth and luxury. We are taking too much, more than we need, creating enormous social inequality and environmental degradation in the process.

We all know this, of course, but in the absence of a living spirituality based on the direct experience of our true spiritual relationship to the Earth, we just don't seem to care enough to do anything about it. Care comes from love. We won't save the planet unless we cultivate *oikophilia* and learn to love our home, our country and our planet with all our heart, soul, strength and mind.

The Earth provides us with medicine, both materially and spiritually. It is time we returned the favour, and transformed the poison of our human greed, hate and delusion into the medicine of love, compassion and wisdom. Only then can we hope to reach the Promised Land, which is the Pure Land, and establish the Kingdom of Heaven here on Earth.

21. Three Trees

I have noticed a certain spiritual arrogance in the New Age worldview, which I have often been guilty of myself. It is partly a chronological superiority complex, stemming from the fact that we are part of something "New" and therefore "Better" than what went before. This sense of chronological superiority is obvious in labels like "Modernism" and "Postmodernism", not to mention "the Enlightenment". The *Enlightenment*! How arrogant can you get?

The arrogance of the Enlightenment is arguably due to a "subtraction story". All you have to do is take away the superstitions, myths and fairy tales of humanity, so the story goes, and the pure light of Reason will shine unhindered over the "real world". The problem with this particular story is that "man cannot live by bread alone". There is Wisdom and Truth in ancient stories that Reason cannot fathom nor substitute. But that's another story.

There is a story that the New Age tells itself about itself, which results in a certain spiritual arrogance, spiritual hubris, or "spiritual materialism", as Chogyam Trungpa called it. It goes something like this: There are many different religions with long traditions spanning centuries, if not millennia. Each religion is the repository of spiritual truth, but also of a great deal of nonsense. There is a beautiful, mystical element in each religion, which is spiritually liberating, but there is also a repressive, punitive element built into the institutional nature of traditional religion. If we can subtract the nonsense and the repression, we will be left with the pure, spiritual core of each religion. By distilling this spiritual core and combining it with the spiritual core of the other religions, we will therefore create the truest, freest and best spiritual culture in the world.

Why ever not? It makes good sense. There clearly is a lot of overlap across the different world religions, and we have had some success in collating and compiling variations on the "Perennial Philosophy", as it's generally called. Comparative religion in general is unarguably a fertile ground for new insights and understanding across traditions.

The New Age story that we can take the best of the past and drop the worst is another subtraction story. Just subtract the bad and you will be automatically left with the good. Skeptics liken this approach to a spiritual supermarket where you can just pick and choose according to your own personal whim. On what basis do you pick and choose? Do you pick the reasonable bits and leave the unreasonable bits? Do you pick the bits you understand and leave the bits you don't understand? Keep the nice bits and throw out the uncomfortable bits? The bits you like but not the bits you don't like?

The obvious criticism is that if I am the final arbiter and judge of what is true and what is good, and choose what I already understand and what I already desire, then all I am doing is justifying the way I already am. Is this not just a recipe for narcissism? Like Narcissus, I am in love with my own reflection, and find it, in this case, in the mirror of religion.

This isn't really how it works, of course. Hardly anyone picks and chooses all by themselves. That's too much work and too much responsibility. People still need to follow advice on what they should choose, so over time, a New Age consensus establishes itself. A new creed and a new dogma emerges. Of course it is a very broad church with many branches and twigs, but the core value is clear: Freedom.

On this point, New Age philosophy dovetails nicely with classical psychoanalysis. Mental health (and spirituality) depends on freedom from repression and freedom of expression. Not the expression of opinions only, but the expression of feelings and desires. Not the freedom from external repression and constraints only, but freedom from inner ties.

Are all New Agers hopeless hippies? Are they all weird superstitious shamanic pagans into the occult and extra terrestrials? Obviously not. There is a colourful, lunatic fringe, but the mainstream is arguably the dominant religious group in the Western world. People who are basically interested in spirituality, but not in traditional, formal, institutional religion. The sorts of people who might be interested in this book, for example.

It's difficult to say exactly what New Age beliefs are, because there is no central text, no sacred scripture or Bible to refer to, in order to find out.

But then again, just as the Judeo-Christian Bible is a compilation of many books, which were written and compiled over a long period of time, might not a "New Age Bible" emerge in the same way? There is no unanimously accepted canon as yet, but it's still early days. The New Age has been around for decades, not centuries. Whether it will ever happen, whether there will ever be a New Age Bible, we can speculate about the kind of things that would go into it. It would probably be a collection of self-help books.

The teachings would, at the very least, have to cover the three broad areas of metaphysics, psychology and ethics, just as all religions do. So what would these be? Well, New Age metaphysics would be based on the choice cuts from the Perennial Philosophy. In other words it would be a "best of" of the world's existing religions. The core beliefs would have to be an affirmation of the divinity of the individual, free will and the basic goodness of uncorrupted human nature. In this, it would be very close, if not identical, to the core beliefs of liberal humanism. New Age psychology would be of paramount importance and would obviously have to be consistent with the metaphysics. Ethically, the rule would be: everyone is free to do what they want, as long as it doesn't curtail anyone else's freedom. This is basically liberal humanism again.

What about morality? If ethics is about how to rub along best with our neighbours, morality is about how we should behave. Are some ways of behaving better than others, even if they don't seem to affect anyone else? Are some ways of behaving better for *us*? This is a pragmatic question. What kind of behaviour is best for our own spiritual flourishing? What kind of behaviour leads to real spiritual freedom? We are, of course, free to tie ourselves in knots, but in the final analysis is that really freedom?

I have a good friend who has just started attending SLAA meetings to help him with his sex and love addiction problems. I have several friends who go to AA meetings to try to get a handle on their drinking. Another friend is really grateful for her co-dependency (CODA) meetings. A couple I know are chronically addicted to marijuana, although they would never think of going to NA. And everyone seems to have a cocaine habit.

What's going on? Why is everyone addicted to something? If it's not sex, drugs, booze, fags, food, or relationships, it's shopping, social media, YouTube or box sets.

How free are we really? We've had our sexual revolution, our social revolution and our spiritual revolution. But are we any happier? Nowadays, as Yuval Harari points out, "more people commit suicide than are killed by soldiers, terrorists and criminals combined."[73] His point is that the ravages of war are becoming a thing of the past, which is obviously a good thing (if it's true). But on the flip side, why are so many people killing themselves? Why are so many people on anti-depressants? Why are so many people in affluent cultures in therapy or in a recovery group? Why so much stress, depression and addiction? Shouldn't we all be spiritually and psychologically sorted by now? What ever happened to "the New Age"?

The spiritual arrogance of New Agers is that we think we are so spiritual that we don't need to curb our appetites. Just do your spiritual practice and everything will be fine. Be free! Enjoy yourself! Your spiritual practice will protect you.

But no amount of positive or wishful thinking can circumvent the need for serious moral discipline and responsibility. You can't have your cake and eat it, no matter how many patisserie gods you pray to. Whatever spiritual practice you have, if personal morality isn't part of it, your wax wings are sure to melt. You might pay lip service to your "shadow", but unless you behave yourself, your "light" won't amount to more than a fairy light, and your "spirituality" to a tinseled bonsai. Just because you don't like the word "sinner" doesn't mean you aren't one.

*

The seven deadly sins are Lust, Gluttony, Greed, Sloth, Wrath, Envy and Pride. Pride is considered the greatest sin, from which all the others flow. Why? Pride is another word for "spiritual hubris". You think you are beyond good and evil. You think you're an exception to the rule. You think you're above morality and "sin". So, obviously, you sin. What does this mean exactly?

LUST

Let's start at the bottom (no pun intended). The first sin is lust. It's not an abstract thing. It's not just spiritual or psychological. Lust is something rooted in the body. Where? Well, at the root chakra, between the anus and the genitals. This is the locus of our sexual energy. If our sexual energy is going to be distorted or corrupted anywhere, it's here.

Is there a difference between lust and normal, healthy sexual feelings? The ascetic end of the religious spectrum says no. Hence the strict celibacy of monastics and religious fanatics. But sex is natural. It can even be a transformative and spiritual experience. So let's not throw out the baby and the bath water. Let's assume that sex itself is all right. So what's the difference?

Lust feels different. It feels "dirty". It feels exciting. It makes you feel like an animal. Well, you are an animal. But somehow lust makes you more animal and less human, or rather less human animal and more non-human animal. Why? Because it turns you into predator or prey, dominator or dominated.

Of course you can't have sex at all without some element of power play. Someone has to take the initiative. Someone has to go on top. And although, for obvious anatomical reasons, it makes sense for the man to take the dominant role (in a heterosexual relationship), there is plenty of room for manoeuvre. Otherwise sex would be boring as hell.

We all have a masculine and a feminine side, whether we happen to be male or female. And the intricate power dynamics played out in healthy romantic relationships can of course find satisfying expression and resolution in the bedroom. But the normal, playful working out of power relations, which is such an important part of human sexual behavior, is not the same thing as the dominance – submission complex I am referring to in relation to "lust".

Whether or not the dominance – submission complex is just the extreme end of one sexual spectrum, with more equal relations in the middle, it is qualitatively different to conventional sexual experiences. A line is crossed where one's body or the body of the other person becomes an object of domination and violence.

There is an important transgressive element here, whereby the limits of the sovereignty of the individual over their own physical being are disregarded and trampled over. Even between consensual adults, the two (or more) parties are colluding in an act of physical violence and invasion of conventional personal space and sovereignty.

This is the simple logic of sadomasochism. Some people get sexually excited by the idea of overstepping the mark of another person's autonomy and dignity, some people get excited by being overstepped, and others get excited by both. You want to dominate or be dominated, humiliate or be humiliated, penetrate or be penetrated.

Lust is about power and the abuse of power. It is about transgression and the crossing of personal physical boundaries, which is why it is so fixated on human orifices. These are after all the only places where your physical body can be invaded (apart from being stabbed or mutilated in some way). But it is also about breaking social, emotional and psychological taboos and smashing the delicate balance of human sexual intimacy with the unleashed force of naked animal brutality.

Lust is experienced as "dirty", partly because it can be literally unhygienic, but also because it is psychically unhygienic. It disrupts the normal functioning of the psychosomatic energy system, so that the individual is more prone to invasive thoughts and feelings of a sexual and often disturbing nature, and to fractured psychic energy. In this condition, it becomes very difficult to focus, discipline and harmonize consciousness. This is a claim that may well be contested by the "sexually liberated", but ultimately, it is something that can only really be substantiated through personal introspection and observation.

GLUTTONY

The second deadly sin is Gluttony. Although this traditionally refers to our relationship with food and drink, I would extend it to all forms of "substance abuse". Where Lust is created by the power dynamics of domination and submission, Gluttony emerges from the push and pull of pleasure and pain.

A "glut" of something is too much of a good thing. A "glutton" is someone without restraint who takes far more than what is appropriate or reasonable. Therefore the term "gluttony" leans towards the positive end of the polarity, which is to say, towards an inordinate consumption of pleasure. The stereotypical image of the glutton is the fat man stuffing his face with pies, and this is not a trivial example, nor is it a trivial problem. For the first time in history, worldwide more people die of obesity than of starvation.

But there are two poles to the disordered appetite. There is the excessive and deficient, the obese and the anorexic. Just as submissive, masochistic sexual proclivities result in lustful feelings and experiences as much as dominating sadism, so does anorexia result in gluttony, broadly speaking. And gluttony is not just about food. It equally applies to sex (again!).

A sexual glutton wants more and more. It's not an issue of quality but quantity. Whereas lust is about "kinky" feelings, gluttony is about common-or-garden pleasure, just *more* of it. It could be more sex, but it could be more chocolate, more wine, or more cocaine. It can even be more friends and more love. What about the sexual anorexic or the social anorexic? They want less, not more. Although at the opposite end of the polarity, this is equally a condition of a disordered appetite.

The problem is that treating ourselves and denying ourselves are equally addictive. We can become addicted to immediate gratification and to endlessly delayed gratification, to piling on the pleasures of self-indulgence and to enduring the pain of self-deprivation. In either case, we disrupt the natural balance of pleasure and pain by trying to force the issue one way or the other.

GREED

Greed is a more subtle phenomenon than gluttony. Where gluttony is about the immediate gratification of the appetite through substances such as food, drink or drugs, or other types of gratification through activities such as sex or TV, greed is about *possession*. It's not about what you do, but what you have.

Most obviously, it is about material possessions. You want more stuff and you want better stuff. Never mind that you live in a perfectly comfortable house that meets all your needs. You want a bigger house in a better area. You long for a better kitchen and a better car. You might rationalise this in terms of needing a more modern kitchen and a newer model of car, because in our fast-paced world, "better" usually means "newer".

This is built into modern technology. New technologies become obsolete at an increasingly fast rate, so that we are continuously compelled to update them. Personal computers and mobile phones are obvious examples. If we are always craving the newest model of everything, chances are we are in the grip of greed. The same is also true of fashion, which works on the same principle. It is even true of relationships. What's going on when a middle-aged man ditches his long-term partner for a "newer model"?

It is tempting to blame capitalism. The capitalist system, being market driven, depends on consumer spending, which therefore encourages materialism, consumerism and greed. Advertising is the cynical manipulation of people's desires. Or so the story goes. But people are not sheep. We are free to buy and free to choose what we buy in a free market but we are not *compelled* to buy anything. It's not capitalism that makes us crave that new handbag. It's our own greed.

It is true that people's greed makes other people richer. There is a system of greed that does seem to have a life of its own, with the most successful in the system taking the lion's share. At this level of abstraction it's not necessary to talk about actual material products like handbags, phones or cars or even property. It's all about *money*. Money is the key to both the capitalist system and the "greed system". But these two systems, though obviously closely related, are not the same thing.

Money makes the world go round, but only when the world lets the money go round. The free flow of capital is essential to the proper functioning of modern democratic societies. Anything else leads to totalitarianism or anarchy. However, this free flow of capital does not necessarily depend on greed. It would work perfectly well if people weren't so greedy.

The modern obsession with continual economic growth founded on consumer spending is a dangerous myth that is putting too much strain on the natural world. Our greed is putting the future of the planet itself at risk.

Everyone knows this. But it's convenient to pass the buck and blame the "system". When the "system" is corrected, or perhaps overthrown in favour of another communist "utopia", then we might be able to sort out the mess. In the meantime, I'll just carry on being greedy like everyone else. I can't help it - I live in a capitalist system!

In truth, the capitalist system is neutral. It is only as greedy as the people living in it. We are as responsible for our own greed as we are for our own gluttony and our own lust. We might feel compelled to buy that handbag because we like the advert (greed). We might feel compelled to eat that doughnut because it looks delicious (gluttony). We might feel compelled to bleep someone's brains out (lust).

This is all compulsive behavior, but that doesn't mean we aren't ultimately responsible for it. You could say we are addicted to lust, gluttony and greed. Is it the "system's" fault? Do we have to blame someone or something else? And do we *have* to succumb to our compulsions? Whatever the reasons for our addiction, we will only overcome it when we actually take responsibility for it. After all, you're not really a sheep or a victim. Unless you think you are, of course. In which case the upside is that at least you don't have to take any responsibility!

LIFE AND BLISS

There is energy in sexual desire. It makes us feel alive. But there is also energy in simply being alive. It is easy to take it for granted that we are alive. The more we take it for granted, the less we feel it, and the more we need other, stronger feelings, like sexual desire, to make us feel alive.

Just sit still. Or stand still if you're standing or lie still if you're lying down. You are alive. Your body is alive. It is animated by life. Can you feel your livingness? Your life force? What is it? It's a kind of subtle energy inside you.

Pay attention to it. Notice it. Give yourself space to feel it. Give yourself time. You don't need to do anything. Just observe. Just open your awareness to how your energy feels right now. Don't try to change it. Don't try to control it. Just observe.

When you allow your life just to be as it is, you are eating from the Tree of Life. Imagine that you yourself are the Garden of Eden. It is a walled garden. The wall represents the boundary between you and the world. Stay in the garden. Stay inside yourself, with no thought for the world outside. Within you there are two trees: the Tree of the Knowledge of Good and Evil and the Tree of Life.

You know that if you eat from the first tree, you will harvest the fruits of lust, gluttony and greed. These are poisoned fruits. So eat from the second tree. You are alive. What does it feel like to be alive?

Stay with the simple feeling of being alive and you will notice that the energy in your body becomes more noticeable. It may be more or less subtle or obvious. It may be pleasant or unpleasant. There may be points of softness and points of acute or chronic tension in your body. You might feel uncomfortable. It might even be unbearably painful. It all depends on your karma, in other words, what state you have got yourself into over the past days, weeks, months and years.

Life is suffering. Even if you happen to be a saint or a master yogi, there will inevitably be a trace of suffering somewhere in there. If you are proficient in spiritual discipline, you will know that the only thing to do is to stay with the suffering. Don't try to get rid of it. Don't try to somehow avoid it or distract yourself from it. You are like the Buddha sitting immobile like a mountain. You will not be moved from the spot of your own existential suffering. You are like Christ on the cross. X marks the spot where you are now and always.

Stay with your discomfort. Stay with your suffering. Bear your own cross. Eventually you will find that the burden is lifted and you will experience relief. Stick with it and you will receive the "consolations" of the medieval mystics. You will experience a rush of energy sweeping through your body like a wave. You will be as though illuminated from within. You will feel a sense of peace and joy. You will feel light and free. It will be Blissful. You will be glad to be alive.

The simple feeling of Life without the push and pull of domination or submission is the antidote to Lust. Bliss is the antidote to Gluttony. When you have Bliss, who needs pleasure? Pleasure always turns to pain. We chase one and run away from the other, like a dog chasing its own tail. We thought this was just the nature of reality, the human predicament. But we were simply looking in the wrong place for satisfaction. What we really want is Bliss and Bliss is the fruit of the Tree of Life, not of the Tree of the Knowledge of Good and Evil.

BEAUTY

The third fruit of the Tree of Life is Beauty. Out of the ocean of Bliss emerges the vision of Beauty, like Venus in Botticelli's painting. When we see Beauty we go beyond form. The form is just a window to the transcendent ideal. It carries Beauty like the shell carries Venus. When we see Beauty itself, we no longer long to possess the shell.

Beauty is the antidote to Greed. Greed is the corruption of Beauty. The wealthy aesthete art collector is possessed by greed. He is not a true devotee of Beauty. The art market is about greed, not Beauty. When the price tag is more impressive than the work of art, and art is treated like a commodity, then we are in the system of greed. This is often true of masterpieces like Botticelli's, when they fall into the wrong hands, but it is most blatantly true of art with little or no aesthetic value. Where there is no Beauty, what is left? Only greed.

SLOTH

The fourth fruit of the Tree of the Knowledge of Good and Evil is Sloth. This is where we inevitably end up when we gather the bittersweet fruits of lust, gluttony and greed. We feel barren, bereft, spent. We feel depleted, depressed, forlorn. We fall into a state of acedie and anomie, into a slough of despond.

After riding the wave of compulsive energy, we crash onto a rocky shore. It's like the comedown from amphetamines or cocaine. The buzz and excitement of the chase for a quick and easy high gives way to feelings of absolute dejection and abandonment.

We have been abandoned by our vices, left to stagger aimlessly in the middle of the desert, or to just sit down and cry. But that gives us no relief, for even our tears are dry.

It's not always that extreme of course. We may just feel a bit lethargic and lazy. We don't have the energy. We can't be bothered. We feel tired and numb. We don't feel anything and we don't feel like doing anything. So it seems that the best thing to do is just to sit in front of a screen and wait for it to pass.

What's going on here? Physiologically, we have messed up our serotoninergic system and are literally depleted. It is exactly like a comedown from speed. In time, we will recover, but it takes longer every time. We have got ourselves into a cycle of boom and bust. In times of "bust" we retreat to the back of the cave and watch Netflix in bed with a hot water bottle and a cup of hot milk. It is of course possible to learn to manage the cycle. We find ways to look after ourselves. And if all our friends go through it, maybe it's okay. Maybe it's "normal".

LOVE

The fourth fruit of the Tree of Life is Love. Out of the simple feeling of being alive emerges the vivifying energy called Bliss. Out of Bliss emerges a sense of transcendent Beauty. Out of Beauty springs Love. This is why Venus is the goddess of Love.

The bitter fruit of Sloth produces dryness of the heart. It produces coldness and indifference. It is impossible to really care about anything or anyone when you are mired in Sloth. Love is the opposite. It is an overflowing of the heart. It is warm and generous. It wells up and flows out in waves of loving kindness, sympathy and compassion. It must be shared because it is too much to contain.

Love is the opposite and the antidote to Sloth. It can't stay still. It is neither passive nor inactive. It is an energetic dynamo that demands action. This is why it is related to diligence. Diligence is the opposite of Sloth. Generosity is the opposite of Greed. Temperance is the opposite of Gluttony. Chastity is the opposite of Lust.

These are the virtues that grow from the Tree of Life. Just let your life force be as it is in the moment without manipulating it in any way. This is the essence of Chastity. Allow your natural Bliss to emerge without chasing after pleasure or running away from pain. This is the essence of Temperance. Allow Beauty to reveal itself in the world without trying to possess it or reject it. This is the essence of Generosity. Let Love flow into you and out of you. Let it power your every activity, whatever it might be. This is true Diligence.

WRATH AND TRUTH

It's not enough to eat the fruits of the Tree of Life. That's the spiritual arrogance of certain New Age types. If you want to make real progress along the spiritual path, you also have to stop eating the fruits of the Tree of the Knowledge of Good and Evil. Don't be lustful. Don't be gluttonous. Don't be greedy. Don't be slothful. And don't be angry.

Modern people don't like hearing "thou shalt not". They'd rather hear about the sweetness and light of spiritual goodies. This is why there is so much spiritual materialism in the New Age. People don't want to give up stuff or stop doing what they enjoy. They want more things to add to their lives. If you feel like something is missing for your life, if you are kind of dissatisfied and disappointed with life, why not take up yoga or shamanic drumming?

However virtuous and beneficial your new spiritual hobby, what good will it do if you don't give up your vicious hobbies? What good are Life, Bliss, Beauty and Love if you spend half your time feeding your Lust, Gluttony, Greed and Sloth? Well, it's better than nothing of course. At least you won't fall completely into the hell of addiction, anxiety and depression. You might even find some kind of equilibrium between heaven and hell. But you shouldn't expect any more than that.

Maybe you disagree with me. Maybe you think I'm being unnecessarily prohibitive. Maybe you think I'm a throwback to religious intolerance and I'm being morally judgmental. Who am I to judge? Who am I to point the finger and blame innocent people for living their lives as well as they can? Maybe there's nothing wrong with a bit of Lust, Gluttony, Greed and Sloth. Maybe they're just *natural*.

If you follow this line of reasoning you will probably end up feeling a bit angry. Keep going and you might blurt out something like, "F off! Don't tell me what to do!" You are convinced that I am wrong. I am wrong and you are right. Therefore you have every right to your righteous indignation.

This is the fifth bitter fruit picked from the Tree of the Knowledge of Good and Evil: Wrath. Wrath is fiery energy that boils over when you feel that you, or someone you care for, has been wronged. Sometimes it is stronger when it's on someone else's behalf. For example, if you spill Degby's pint, he'll punch you in the mouth. If you insult his girlfriend, he'll put you in hospital.

If my pet theory offends you, you might be angry. If, in your view, it offends other people, especially if they are vulnerable people, well, that will make you *really* angry. The defender of the innocent and the vulnerable, and the defender of the faith, whatever it happens to be, is much more justified, in their own view, in expressing and acting on their anger.

More commonly, however, we are angry on our own behalf. I feel that I have been slighted or disrespected. Someone has overstepped the mark and taken advantage of me, or taken me for granted. I have been treated unfairly. "This is a gross injustice and an affront to my very being!" I think to myself. There is no way I am going to turn the other cheek. I am not a doormat! Ironically, perhaps, the perpetrator of this evil and object of our outrage is usual the person who loves us most, such as our husband or wife.

Even if we turn into the Incredible Hulk at the sight of some perceived injustice, deep down we believe that we are doing the right thing, because we are right and on the side of right. Wrath flares up when your sense of rightness or your sense of justice is challenged or attacked. If you are convinced that you are fighting a worthy cause, you will rationalize your anger as fuel for the cause. If you are a "Social Justice Warrior", for example, this is obviously as it should be.

It is very difficult to have a calm, rational conversation about politics with an SJW. It is very difficult to have a calm, rational conversation about religion with an American fundamentalist or a Jihadi.

It's hard to talk to a communist about capitalism. It's hard to talk to a radical feminist about gender. You probably won't get away without being shouted at or having something thrown at you.

"Tyranny is the deliberate removal of nuance"[74], said Albert Maysles. Where is the nuance when the red mist descends? Wrath is a tyrant that obliterates the possibility of rational debate and the quest for Truth. It is the first and last resort of the ideologue.

But what about Truth? Shouldn't we stand up for it by all means necessary? What about Justice? Are we not duty-bound to fight for it tooth and nail? Yes of course. As Edmund Burke (supposedly) said, "The only thing necessary for evil to triumph is for good men to do nothing." But what exactly should good men do? Fly into a rage? Organize an angry mob?

The Truth exists somewhere beyond my personal opinions concerning what is right and what is wrong. My adversary (who I firmly believe is completely wrong) may still know something I don't. They may have something valuable to teach me. The thing may not be quite as simple as I think. And if I lose my temper whenever my position is challenged, the chances are I haven't thought very much.

Thinking requires patiently weighing different and conflicting view of a subject. If you can't consider it from multiple points of view, you are not getting the full picture. I love John Keats' definition of "Negative Capability":

"I mean Negative Capability, that is, when a man is capable of being in uncertainties, mysteries, doubts, without any irritable reaching after fact and reason."[75]

Negative Capability is precisely the ability to not jump to conclusions, take a rigid position, or fly off the handle at the slightest provocation. It is the essential precondition for a dispassionate enquiry into the Truth of the matter. It is a conscious temporary bracketing of prejudice, the prerequisite for an open mind.

This mental condition of openness is obviously much easier to assume from a place of Love. If you are replete with loving feelings, if your positive mood endorphins are flowing plentifully, you will have no difficulty in allowing the Truth to manifest itself as it will.

Your investment in your own opinions will be far outweighed by your sincere and loving respect for Truth.

On the other hand, if you are languishing in the arid desert of brittle indifference, you will hold onto your ideas as if your life depended on it. To shift metaphors, you are like a drowning man clinging to the mast of a sinking ship. All you have left is your opinions. You have to be right, otherwise your self-esteem will sink until it disappears below the waves.

The five bitter fruits of the Tree of the Knowledge of Good and Evil we have looked at so far are: Lust, Gluttony, Greed, Sloth and Wrath. The five sweet fruits of The Tree of Life we have looked at so far are: Life, Bliss, Beauty, Love and Truth. And their corresponding virtues are: Chastity, Temperance, Generosity, Diligence and Patience.

ENVY

Envy is deeper than anger. You could say that anger is the symptom and envy is the disease, at least in a lot of cases. Lets say that I am angry because I feel that I am being treated unfairly. What's wrong with that? I have a right to be angry. You shouldn't treat me unfairly. No one should treat anyone unfairly.

You can't really argue with that. In fact, experiments with chimpanzees demonstrate that our sense of fairness is not unique to human beings. One experiment went something like this. Two chimps were put in two separate cages next to each other. They were both rewarded for some simple task with a banana. After repeating this procedure a few times, one of the chimps was given two bananas for the same task. When the second chimp was offered only one banana as before, he displayed behavior expressing disbelief and refused the banana.

Even chimps have a sense of fairness. Their complex societies are predicated on it. How far this moral sense manifests in the rest of the animal kingdom is an interesting question. It is more than likely that it plays an important role in many of our non-primate cousins.

Be that as it may, it is clear that our sense of fairness and justice is not just a social construct, but is hard-wired into us. It is a trait which far pre-dates the emergence of human culture.

Unfairness is a fact of life. But it doesn't mean that we should roll over and accept it. We have every reason to fight for our rights. And if our feelings of outrage and righteous indignation have evolved in order to defend us from injustice, then we cannot just disregard them because they are uncomfortable feelings which contradict our idealistic worldview.

It's not quite as simple as that, however. Jordan Peterson has convincingly made the case that "dominance hierarchies" are embedded in the very fabric of biological evolution. The dominance hierarchies of chimpanzees have been well documented, but Peterson's point is that it is even deeper than that. We can see them at work even in lobsters.

Lobsters have been around for 350 million years. Our common ancestor is even earlier than that. But the basic structure of our brains is so similar that anti-depressants work on lobsters in exactly the same way as on humans. This is because we share the same serotonergic system. In other words, serotonin enhances the mood of lobsters and humans.

The important point is this: serotonin levels reflect status in the dominance hierarchy. Lobsters are very territorial because territory is essential for survival. When there is a dispute over territory, only one lobster can win. However, if the lobsters engage in physical combat, they both lose. This is because the victor will still probably come away with serious if not fatal injuries. Then a third lobster could easily come onto the scene and take the spoils.

It is not in either of the lobsters' interest to fight. So they have to work out who would probably win if they did fight. How do they do this? By signaling to the other lobster how powerful they are. The bigger lobster is probably more powerful, but not necessarily. The real power comes from the level of serotonin. If the lobster's system is awash with serotonin, it will display an impressive power dance. It will rear up and make itself appear frightening and formidable. It will also release powerful chemicals into the water which can be detected by the other lobster.

So the weaker lobster is the one with depleted levels of serotonin. It will not feel so confident and will communicate this in a more submissive posture. If the difference between the two is very marked, there's no contest. The weaker lobster will quickly scuttle away and the stronger lobster will claim the prize.

However, the real prize is not the territory. It is greater access to serotonin. Incredibly, the brain of the defeated lobster actually "dissolves" and reforms with less capacity for manufacturing and processing serotonin. It therefore physically embodies its lower status in the dominance hierarchy. Conversely, the victorious lobster is serotoninergically boosted after the battle.

If the two lobsters are very closely matched in status, it is possible that the dispute will escalate to actual blows, but only in the last resort. Even a slight difference in status is enough to resolve the dispute one way or the other without physical harm to either party.

So what does this mean? What it means is that because our nervous systems are basically wired the same as a lobster's nervous system, we also experience a direct correlation between mood and status. If we have a high status in any given hierarchy, we will embody that status in our deep physiology and will express it in our posture and body language, as well as our behavior and articulated speech. Any conflict between high status and low status people will be strongly weighted in favour of the high status individual.

However, the stronger individual will not always win. This is illustrated by Peterson's other example about rats. It seems that rats, especially adolescent male rats, like to play rough and tumble, just like human infants. They engage in a form of wrestling, where the winner is the one who pins the other to the ground.

Observations in the laboratory have confirmed that not only do rats enjoy wrestling, and that is a form of play, but that they also *play fair*. In almost all cases, the bigger rat wins (if it is at least ten percent bigger). After the initial bout, when the rats meet again, it is the defeated rat that invites the winner to wrestle. The winner then either agrees to fight or not, depending on their mood. The chances are that the bigger rat will win again. The extraordinary point is that if the bigger rat always wins, then the loser will stop asking to play.

Why would the loser want to keep losing? There's nothing in it for them. So they stop playing. But wrestling benefits them both. They enjoy it and it's good exercise. It has definite survival value for both of them. Where the lobsters want to avoid fighting, the rats actually want to fight. So what happens? The bigger rat wants to fight. It's not fair if he always wins. If he always wins, they will stop playing the game, and he wants to play the game.

So, incredibly, the weaker rat wins. If the weaker rat wins at least one third of the bouts on average, it will keep asking to play. If it wins significantly less than that, it won't play any more. So the bigger rat *lets* the smaller rat win. It's exactly the same with human fathers and their young child. Of course the father is much bigger and stronger and cleverer than the little boy (or girl). But if he always wipes the floor with him when they play, the poor thing won't want to play any more.

Putting these two findings together, we can begin to get a clearer picture of what goes on with us. We have an inbuilt sense of our status, according to our serotonin levels, in any particular hierarchy. When we clash or compete with someone else, we get a sense of their status and behave accordingly. Games are the most obvious social arena where this dynamic plays out.

I am fairly good at tennis, I think. This means that I have an implicit sense of my status in the tennis hierarchy and feel fairly good about it. However, I am not a professional, I don't take lessons and I never play in tournaments, and my serve is pretty erratic. If I did play in the local tennis league, I would have a ranking and have a much clearer sense of my status in the hierarchy. If I was professional, I might even be seeded.

I know that I wouldn't enjoy playing a top seeded tennis player. It would be embarrassing. I also wouldn't enjoy playing a beginner. It would be boring. I am motivated to play well and I enjoy playing the game when I play someone of a similar status as me in the competence hierarchy. And I know that whether I win or lose it's the playing that counts.

It is inevitable across all games and all competence hierarchies that I will encounter and play or compete with people who are higher than me in the hierarchy.

Not only are they more competent, they are more confident. There is a strong probability that they will make me feel incompetent and unconfident, especially if there is a sizable gap between us.

This is a fact of life. Not everyone is equally good at everything and I am seriously deluded if I think I am top dog at anything! I don't need to be the best to enjoy the good that I am of course. I'm not the best tennis player in the world but I can enjoy the skill and ability I do have. I'm not very good at playing the guitar, but I can play a little. Rather than compare myself to John Williams or Rodrigo and Gabriela, I can still enjoy the sounds I falteringly make.

What's the alternative? Envy. I envy Rodrigo. He is an amazing guitarist and he's got an amazing guitarist girlfriend (although they are separated now). I envy Raphael Nadal and Roger Federer. They represent the heights that by right are mine. When I play a terrible shot, I fling my racquet down in rage. When I can't play a cool riff on the guitar I fling it down in fury.

What about people at the top of other hierarchies? I envy the rich lording it over us in their big mansions on the hill. I envy the famous prancing about like peacocks. I envy the political elites strutting their stuff in the corridors of power. They all make me so angry!

So I take sides with the underdog in all hierarchies (even in the football World Cup). Nothing delights me more than when David beats Goliath. My envy transforms into a seething resentment of all the unequal dominance hierarchies in the world. I begin to think that there's something profoundly wrong with the structure of existence. Maybe it's all a big conspiracy. Maybe it's all because of "the Patriarchy"!

If I allow myself to be thoroughly radicalized, I will call for the overthrow of all inequality everywhere. I will not rest until the mountain are laid low and the valleys are raised up and everywhere in all directions is one level playing field. Then, maybe my envy of people higher up than me might be assuaged. Then, maybe we will enter a utopia of equality and sameness where everyone has the same status as everyone else. If it takes tens of millions of corpses, as it did in the Communist experiments of the last century, maybe that's a price worth paying.

This is the logical conclusion of a worldview based on resentment. It needn't go that far, of course, to see its workings in our everyday lives. Think about your partner, if you have one. If not, think about a close friend. If you have a rich and fulfilling relationship, you probably relate to each other in different ways. You probably play different games. Maybe you play tennis. Maybe not. Your relationship might be more intellectual. Maybe you enjoy discussing hot topics like politics and religion. Maybe you like playing scrabble or chess.

The more ways you interact with your friend or partner, the richer your relationship. What do you actually do together? How do you cooperate and how do you compete? Do you enjoy going shopping together? Working together on a common project? Bringing up kids maybe? Do you like dancing together? Socializing together? Climbing? Running? Walking?

It doesn't matter who is the better walker. It doesn't matter who is the better runner. You probably don't need to have an actual race to know who will win. Maybe you are better at some things and your partner is better at others. That's ok. You can live with that. But what about when it comes to negotiating household chores? What about when you disagree about the seemingly trivial things of life like who should take out the rubbish?

One of you might have an overall higher cumulative sense of social status. Things like family and class background will play a large part, as will education. Career status and income are also important factors. If, on top of all that, your partner is better than you at tennis, scrabble and chess, and is smarter, funnier and better looking, you might start feeling a bit miffed.

This is why people tend to find partners of similar social status to them. When the gap is too wide, no amount of romantic idealism is going to paper over the cracks. But it is not easy, or even necessarily desirable to find your exact status replica. It might even make you more competitive!

So what can we do about the status gap? The key is *fair play*. Maybe your partner is more confident than you, for whatever reason. Maybe they think that, all things considered, they are higher than you in the social hierarchy.

If you argue over something inconsequential, they will have a higher level of serotonin in their system. Therefore they will be more powerful. Therefore they will win.

If they keep winning, their serotonin level will increase and yours will decrease. Next time you disagree about something, they will win more easily. Eventually, where you might have had an argument before, there will be the quick and peaceful surrender of the weaker party (you), with no smashed glasses or raised voices.

The advantage of this situation, as with the lobsters, is that no one gets hurt. No one gets physically hurt, but neither do you get emotionally hurt. The downside is that power has been polarized to such an extent that you are living in a tyranny. One of you is the master and the other is the slave. We see this in the submissive, mousy housewife and in the emasculated, hen-pecked husband. Either way, it's not a happy state of affairs.

Like with the rats, unless you are pathologically submissive, at a certain point you won't want to play any more. What's the point of playing if you lose every time? What's the point of a relationship if it's not reciprocal? It's no fun living with a bully. So, eventually the weaker rat stops asking to play, and looks around for someone else to play with.

Who do you want to play with? You want to play with someone who plays fair. Someone who isn't too much better or worse than you, and someone who lets you win sometimes, even when they could win. If they are really good players, they will let you win quite a lot (without making it obvious that they're letting you win of course, because that defeats the object). If you win a lot, your mood will improve. You will become more confident. Your serotonin levels will go up. You will also become more competent. And so the gap between you will close and you will have better games.

GOODNESS

This is what goodness is. Goodness is the deliberate raising up of others. If you are good to people, you will encourage them to raise their game.

This is not the same thing as compassion, or "idiot compassion" as Ken Wilber calls it. You don't just want to be *nice*. You don't want the other person to accept their level in the hierarchy. You want them to *grow*.

Idiot compassion basically says: "You're an idiot. But that's ok. I love you just as you are. And don't let anybody tell you there is anything wrong with being an idiot." This makes idiots of us both. Taken further, it ends up by inverting the competence hierarchy itself. Then the message is something like: "Actually it's good that you are an idiot, because that means that you're not dominating anyone. Your idiocy is actually a virtue and your victimhood actually makes you morally superior to everyone else in the hierarchy." Egalitarianism basically wants to make idiots out of everyone, and so far it has made idiots of a surprising large number of us.

Goodness is not about commiserating with other people's inferior status or patting them on the head for it. It is about helping them improve their status. How do you do that? Not just by "being good". You can only "be good" if you *do good*. But this "doing" of goodness is, as I just indicated, not a patronizing act.

It's not even just about raising people up. It's about creating the best possible conditions for worthwhile, meaningful games. If you are a good player of games, you will play games with people close to your level of competence. If you have the edge, you with help the others to raise their game. You will try to boost their confidence and encourage them to play to the best of their ability. If the other person has the edge, you will encourage them to do the same to you. In other words, you will encourage them to be good.

This is the essence of justice and fair play. No one is equal in anything. But we get better at things by playing with each other, helping each other, encouraging each other, teaching each other. You can conceptualize any unequal game (and every game is more or less unequal), as a competition between a winner and a loser. If you always identify with the winner and only ever think about winning, you will end up being a tyrant and eventually no one will want to play with you. If you identify with the loser and only ever think about losing, you will become resentful and refuse to play.

But those are not the only options open to you. If you are more interested in the game itself, and not in either winning or losing, then the outcome doesn't matter so much. It's not about power, victory and defeat. It's about knowledge. The protagonists are then not "winner" and "loser" but "teacher" and "student". Ideally, in a really good game, both protagonists are teachers and students at different times. The best games are the most reciprocal, which is not the same as equal. If you are equal, then nobody learns anything.

I am, of course, using the word "game" to denote a wide range of human interactions. Actually I am using it to denote the whole range of human interactions. Just because we are serious about some of these, does not mean they aren't games. Games are complex transactions that follow certain explicit or implicit rules. I'm thinking here of *Games People Play* by Eric Berne as well as game theory.

But the specifics are not important. I'm just aiming for the gist. Another useful metaphor is dance. Obviously a good dance is one where the dancers lead and follow each other. Even if one of the dancers is better than the other, part of what makes them a good dancer is their ability to dance at the same level as their partner. If they just spin off in a display of amazing skill, leaving their partner sheepishly shuffling from one foot to the other, what kind of dance is that?

Of course there's nothing wrong with dancing solo sometimes. In the same vein, there's nothing wrong with that guitar solo in the middle of the song. If you have great skill and competence, you can show it off and people will applaud you. The same is true in team sports such as football. Maybe you are the best striker in the world. You have great skills. Your dribbling and shooting skills are legendary. The fans love it when you show off. But if you never pass the ball, their cheers will soon change to boos, and your team will give you the cold shoulder in the changing room.

Being at the top of your game is one thing. You are high up in your competence hierarchy. You are good at what you do. But *being good* is something else. When Messi plays football with his young son in the garden, he doesn't always win. When John Williams plays with the LSO, he is just another musician.

The team, the relationship, the symphony, the dance, the game is what matters. Not winning or losing, but playing the game and learning from it. And hopefully what we learn is not only competence in any particular game, but how to play fair in *all* games, that is, how to be good.

PRIDE

Pride is the cardinal sin on which all other sins are founded. What is pride? Pride is the knowledge of good and evil. Of all the seven deadly sins it is the first and the last. The serpent in the Garden of Eden promised Adam and Eve that if they ate the fruit from the forbidden tree, their eyes would be opened and they would be as gods.

The serpent was later identified with Satan, who was identified with Lucifer. Lucifer was the highest angel in the angelic hierarchy. He was the angel of Light. But because of "overweening pride", as John Milton put it, he was cast from heaven into the deepest pit of hell. Lucifer fell from grace because he had such a high opinion of himself that he thought he was a god.

So in *Paradise Lost*, Milton has Satan pull off the same trick on humanity in a calculated act of revenge against God. If he fell because of his pride, he would make God's favourites fall for the same reason. So when the serpent whispers into Eve's ear that her eyes will be opened and the she will be as a god, he is talking from personal experience. And in his personal experience, thinking that you are a god and thinking that you have the knowledge of good and evil is a recipe for disaster. It means that you have to live the rest of your days in hell.

Why? Because you become the measure of all things. And when you are the measure of all things, all things become extensions of your own limited viewpoint. It is true that Satan is a god. He is god of his own domain. There is nothing higher than him. But for that very reason, his domain quickly becomes hell for him. He is trapped within his own self-proclaimed divinity. His hell is the outward manifestation of his pride.

Luckily for Adam and Eve, God is more lenient with them. Like the curse in *Sleeping Beauty*, which should have resulted in the princess' death when she pricked her finger on the spindle, but was scaled down to eternal sleep instead, the sentence of death and hell is suspended. Adam and Eve are not sent to hell to suffer the eternal torment of Satanic pride. They are sent out into the rough world of history.

For Lucifer there is no redemption because he denies God altogether. He insists on being his own god. Therefore there is no escape from hell. There is no escape from the circle of his own solipsism. As long as he refuses to bend his knee to God, that is, to the Reality beyond his own egocentric conception of it, there is nowhere he can go that is not hell. "Why this is hell, nor am I out of it"[76], says Mephistopheles to Doctor Faustus.

But Adam and Eve are thrown a lifeline. They will have to toil and suffer in the world. They will labour under the belief that they have the knowledge of good and evil. But they will not fully believe it. They will not fully believe that they are gods. The fact that they are not perfect masters of themselves or their world gives the lie to the serpent's claim.

Therefore there is the possibility of redemption. If they become proud, and set themselves up as gods in their own estimation, then they will surely end up in hell. But if they keep their minds and faith in the Reality beyond their own conception of it, that is, beyond "good and evil", then they will be saved.

The story of the Old Testament is the story of the covenant between the descendants of Adam and Eve (the people of Israel) and God. When they remember God, and remember that they are not themselves gods, then things go well for them. When they turn their back on God and behave like they are themselves masters of the universe, then things fall apart and the jaws of hell begin to open.

FAITH

The crowning fruit of the Tree of Life is the fruit of Faith. Faith is the opposite of Pride because it believes in Reality beyond the limits of the circumscribed ego. This is basically what it means to believe in God.

As Hamlet admonished his friend, "there are more things in heaven and earth, Horatio, than are dreamt of in your philosophy."[77] Hell is where we live when there is nothing in heaven or earth except what we think we know. Faith is the sure knowledge that we don't know the half of it.

Faith is often contrasted with Reason. For this reason, it is easily confused with "superstition". What exactly is superstition? As Stevie Wonder put it, it's "when you believe in things you don't understand"[78]. To unquestioningly and unreasonably believe in things you don't understand is what we call "blind faith". According to rationalists and empiricists, these terms are interchangeable.

But it's one thing to believe in stories about God and another to believe in God. If you believe in stories, or propositions, about the nature of Reality beyond your present understanding of it, there is no way that you can know if your belief is true or not. Even if it is true, there is no way of knowing what its being true really means.

But the narrative truth we find in stories is different to the propositional truth we find in scientific theories. Jordan Peterson refers to this epistemological difference as the difference between dream consciousness and articulated knowledge. We can precisely articulate our knowledge about the way the natural world works, because we are, so to speak, looking down on it from a higher ontological vantage point. The material world and the biological world are lower than us in the evolutionary hierarchy. Therefore we can see and analyze them without too much difficulty.

When it comes to understanding how things work on the human level, in human psychology for example, things get more complicated and more nebulous. Because we are humans, we have to take ourselves into account when we try to understand the meaning of a dream, or a story, or a play like *Hamlet*. Meaning is not just floating around in there somewhere for us to discover and articulate. We have to offer interpretations based on a complex range of considerations.

Is there one right interpretation of *Hamlet*? Of course not. For a start, it's packed full of all sorts of different ideas, associations, hints and meanings about all sorts of things. You cannot reduce all of that information to one thing.

The same is true of a Mahler symphony. What does his second symphony mean? I could talk about why it is meaningful for me, and I can try my best to garner and distill as much meaning from it as I can and express it as clearly and articulately as I can. One day, maybe I'll write a book about it. I'm looking forward to reading Roger Scruton's book on Wagner's Ring of the Nibelung, but although I know it will add to my understanding and enjoyment of the music, I also know that it is no substitute for the thing itself. Equally, I know that I will never come close to exhausting the seemingly inexhaustible meanings contained in Mahler's Second.

This is why art is not science. What can a scientist tell me about Shakespeare, Mahler or Wagner? Not a lot. Art cannot be reduced to or captured by articulated knowledge, because it exists in the dream world of the human imagination. Meaning cannot stray too far from this dream world before it fragments and evaporates like a wisp of cloud in a blue sky.

We can grasp scientific knowledge about the material world with a certain amount of concrete certainty, although we probably overestimate what and how we know. The fact that we can make accurate predictions and put our scientific knowledge to use in the development of new technologies, for example, doesn't mean we really know or understand what it is that we are dealing with. Do we really know what an atom is just because we can name it and describe certain regular features of its existence and manipulate it for our own ends?

In the final analysis, we can't really know anything outside our own framing of it, whether our individual, personal frame, or a collective, peer-reviewed frame. We will never attain to objective scientific truth, because it will always be framed by our human limitations. Ironically, perhaps, the scientific claim to objectivity must be founded on a hypothetical monarchical view beyond the subjectivity of any human individuality. "Monarchical" here refers to the idea of One Transcendent View: *mono – arche*. It is indeed a kingly view. But what can this objective view implicit in the scientific enterprise mean? It sounds a lot like God.

Three Trees

The objective stance of science only really makes sense if you assume the existence of a monarchical view of existence, ie. in the existence of God. Without faith in the possibility of this objective view, science is impossible. If we are too proud to bracket ourselves out of the picture in order to take the monarchical view, which transcends our own subjective view, we will be barred from doing science.

By the same token, if we are too proud to admit the perspective of others in the complex hermeneutical games of the arts and humanities, we won't get very far in mining the dream truths of human wisdom and knowledge. If there are higher realities than the human, if we are not in fact the absolute summit of the evolutionary hierarchy, then whatever is above us will be shrouded in even greater mystery than the things around us.

Suppose there is nothing higher than humanity. Are you the pinnacle of humanity? Are you the equal of Shakespeare or Mahler? What about Plato? Einstein? Buddha? Jesus? Does your pride stretch that far? Or do you accept that there are more things in heaven and earth than are dreamt of in your philosophy?

Faith is not belief in things you do not understand. It is understanding that you can't only believe in things you do understand. There is mystery all around you. And the only way to live with this mystery is through Faith.

*

In the Christian myth of the crucifixion and resurrection of the Christ, there are three crosses on the hill of Golgotha. Jesus is nailed to the middle cross. On either side of him are two thieves. One thief denies Jesus and is unrepentant of his sins and goes to hell. The other thief recognizes that Jesus is the Christ, the Messiah. He repents of his sins and is granted entry into heaven.

One interpretation of this story is that these three crosses symbolize three trees. What trees? The cross of the unrepentant thief represents the Tree of the Knowledge of Good and Evil. This tree bears seven bitter fruits, which are the fruits of the seven deadly sins: Lust, Gluttony, Greed, Sloth, Wrath, Envy and Pride.

The cross of the repentant thief represents the Tree of Life, which bears the seven sweet fruits of Life along with their corresponding virtues: Life (Chastity), Bliss (Temperance), Beauty (Generosity), Love (Diligence), Truth (Patience), Goodness (Gratitude) and Faith (Humility).

One tree corresponds to the *inga* channel to the left and the other tree corresponds to the *pingala* channel to the right. Each of the seven fruits of each tree correspond to one of the chakras. The Christ Tree is the *shushumna*, the central energetic channel of the central nervous system. Like the tradition of the Christmas tree, it has a star at the crown, which is the same star that guided the Magi to the birth of the Christ child, which is the birth of Christ Consciousness within you.

BOOK TWO

1. Mystery

Spiritual enlightenment is for those who ask. If you don't knock, it will not be opened unto you. Who to ask though? Where to knock? You could ask Buddha or Jesus, or you could ask God directly. Failing that, you could ask a priest or a monk or a spiritual teacher. But spiritual teachers are no good to you unless they actually know what enlightenment is. And knowing what enlightenment is actually means not knowing. If they think they know, they definitely don't.

There is paradox here, but paradox is good. It points to something deeper than mere logic. Spiritual enlightenment is one of those things that our mind cannot grasp[79]. It is invariably (and paradoxically) accompanied by an absolute conviction that, after possibly hundreds or thousands of lifetimes wondering about it, you now know, at last, finally and incontrovertibly, what reality is, what existence is, what God is, but that a crucial part of that knowing is the certain knowledge that you don't know and can never know.

"Be silent, therefore, and do not chatter about God, for by chattering about him, you tell lies and commit a sin. If you wish to be perfect and without sin, then do not prattle about God. Also you should not wish to understand anything about God, for God is beyond all understanding. A Master says: If I had a God I could understand, I would not regard him as God."[80]

God is a mystery. Existence is a mystery. When religion claims to know what God is, it lies. When science and philosophy claim to know what existence is, they lie. All religion can do is point to the mystery that is God. All science and philosophy can do is point to the mystery that is existence. Ultimately, the mystery at the heart of religion and science is one and the same. But out of the mystery comes understanding:

"Darkness within darkness.
The gateway to all understanding."[81]

There is no *pistis* without *gnosis* and there is no *gnosis* without *kenosis*. In other words, there is no understanding without experience and there is no experience without the openness that comes from emptiness.

Faith in religion is misplaced if you think that religion has all the answers. This was the error of the medieval scholastics and of modern day literalists and fundamentalists. But equally, faith in science and philosophy are misplaced, if you think they hold the keys to the secrets of existence. The central fantasy of the Enlightenment, that through the intelligent application of Reason and Science, humanity could illuminate the darkness and demystify the mystery of existence, has failed.

Where are the Comtean Positivists now? The Logical Positivists? The Utilitarians? The Behaviourists? The Social Darwinists? The Eliminativists? Perhaps it is unfair to say that they are all already in the dustbin of history, but it is certainly questionable that they are on the right side of it. Be that as it may, the practical success or otherwise of theories based on a scientific materialist paradigm say nothing about the underlying metaphysical questions of existence or reality as such.

Nevertheless, the project to construct a scientific morality has failed.[82] The project to create a scientific psychology has failed.[83] The project to develop a scientific philosophy and a scientific religion has failed.[84] The project to explain existence itself along purely naturalistic, scientific lines has failed.[85] So far. A committed naturalist will say we just need more time. Give us a couple of hundred years, or a couple of thousand - science will work it out eventually. This misses the point that infinite time and infinite energy are just as good as no time and no energy when applied to an impossibility.

Early modernity in the Western world is to a great extent defined by loss of faith in religion. After the Reformation, the Thirty Years' War, the Age of Enlightenment, the French Revolution and the publication of the Origin of Species, faith in religion and revealed truth was in tatters. So thinking people shifted their allegiance and put their money on science to tell them what reality was, and to give their lives meaning. But now, at the tail end of modernity, we have lost faith in science, just as we lost faith in religion at the very beginning.

The Faustian fantasy of scientism is essentially over, except for a few diehards. Science cannot explain everything. Of course it goes without saying that the natural sciences as well as the social sciences are good for a lot of things, and have improved our lives immeasurably. Science and technology have transformed the world. However, although they are very good at answering the "how" of things, they are useless at answering the "why". They only deal with relative truth, not absolute truth, which is why we now find ourselves, in the Western world, in the middle of a "meaning crisis"[86].

Science cannot provide us with ultimate meaning. Neither can politics (the Marxist-Leninist church has long since been converted into fashionable apartments for example). Neither can philosophy, psychology, or even religion. Neither can fame, fortune, power, influence, drugs, sex or rock and roll. We cannot put our faith in any of these things, because they are all structurally unstable. It's never a good idea to build a house on sand.

Man's search for meaning[87] leads finally to a dark nothingness, to the great mystery at the heart of all things. This is where true enlightenment is found - not in the harsh glare of scientific observation or the promise of unlimited technological progress, but in the deepest depths of the unfathomable mystery of existence. The solution to the meaning crisis will not be found in any of the answers offered us by science or religion or anything else, but in a cloud of unknowing, in a real and unflinching encounter with MYSTERY.

2. The Divided Brain

Half way through reading Iain McGilchrist's excellent book, *The Master and his Emissary: The Divided Brain and the Making of the Western World*, the scales fell from my eyes. Within these dense pages was a skeleton key with which we could unlock the closet of our original sin and solve the enigma of our spiritual disaffection.

The key point is ridiculously simple: the two halves of the brain experience the world differently. But it's more than a simple division of labour: not so much "what" they do (specific functions are more laterally distributed than previously thought) as "how" they do it. They offer two contrasting but complementary takes on the world, the right hemisphere providing a broad, general view, whereas the left hemisphere gives us a narrow, specialized picture. The right hemisphere perceives the world globally, as a unified synthesis, whereas the left analytically constructs the whole by summing its parts.

The key finding is that the healthy, holistic functioning of the brain is compromised when the activity of the left hemisphere begins to dominate. According to McGilchrist, the right hemisphere is the rightful "master", since it directly and intuitively meditates perceptual reality. The left hemisphere is merely the "emissary", charged with doing the interpretative leg work, primarily through the medium of language.

The collective underlying psychological problem of the modern West is that it has come to culturally privilege the left hemisphere over the right, leading to a host of negative consequences. As people get further drawn into the "computer brain" logic of the left hemisphere, they become increasingly dissociated and alienated from the direct experience of their bodies and feelings, and from nature, art, music and religion. Whatever cannot be understood on left hemisphere terms is deemed irrational and worthless.

As a result, people in Western societies increasingly resemble Vulcans like Dr. Spock, almost as though we were collectively sliding down an autism spectrum. Far left brainers would say we were evolving.

3. The Bitter Truth

"The bitter central truth of the gnostics: the horrifying realisation that the world of the Good God was a dead one, and that He had been replaced by a usurper – a God of Evil . . . It was the deep realisation of this truth, and its proclamation that had caused the gnostics to be suppressed, censored, destroyed. Humanity is too frail to face the truth about these things – but to anyone who confronts the reality of nature and of process with a clear mind, the answer is completely inescapable: Evil rules the world."[88]

In his epic poem *Paradise Lost*, John Milton meditates on the significance of the rebellion of Satan against God. Satan loses in the end, of course, although the Faustian/Promethean undertones made him a sympathetic figure for radicals like William Blake, who famously said that Milton was "of the Devils party without knowing it."[89]

What if Satan had actually won though? Then we would be in the position the gnostics describe: a usurper God, a "demiurge" ruling in the place of the true God. This is analogous to the relationship between the two hemispheres of the brain. In fact, it's the perfect metaphor. Could it be that the gnostics had intuited an important truth about a deep neurological phenomenon? The usurpation of the right hemisphere by the left?

One of the interesting consequences of this process is the rise in the incidence of mental health conditions, such as autism and schizophrenia, which has strikingly similar symptoms to those found in people with right hemispheric lesions.

Louis Sass' classic study *Madness and Modernism* describes in great detail the parallels between modernist (and post-modernist) art and schizophrenia, which fits with the thesis that we are becoming progressively more dominated by a left hemisphere perception of the world. Modern artists like Pablo Picasso, and modern writers such as Franz Kafka for example, derive much of their uncanny power by exposing the madness inherent in left hemisphere dominated modern consciousness.

McGilchrist points to the Renaissance and to Romanticism as two key moments in the modern world where the right hemisphere was in the ascendant, or at least, put up a fight. However, they have since been eclipsed by a strident and arrogant modernism, which believes in its own inherent superiority and feels justified in wiping the past clean in order to build the world afresh. This was most strikingly evident in the insane hubris of the futurist Fascists, Nazis and Communists. In fact, some form of totalitarian control seems to be the logical and inevitable consequence of extreme society-wide left hemisphere dominance.

The collectivist god having waned, however, it is now the capitalist god that is leading the charge in the left hemisphere's project of control and mastery of the world. And with the exponential rise in the power and reach of information technology, and breath-taking global economic growth, right now it looks like an unstoppable juggernaut.

Unsurprisingly, the urbanized world we inhabit is increasingly both the product and the image of left hemisphere perception. Science and technology are the gods of the modern world, not only because they are powerful, but because they reflect back to us the mental landscape of the left hemisphere. If we are increasingly made in the image of the "god of the left hemisphere"[90], we cannot help but make the world in the same image.

It is a positive feedback loop with world and mind co-creating simulations of each other. The more time we spend between glass towers, in front of computer screens and chatting with "friends" on social media, the more accurate our left hemisphere representations of the world are. The wet dream of the transhumanist techno-utopians, the "Singularity", really amounts to nothing more than the total dominance of the left hemisphere in one giant AI super computer world-mind: the perfect Matrix.

This is the gnostic nightmare. Lucifer, the brightest angel in heaven, rebels against God and establishes his own dominion apart from God. The Emissary becomes the Master. We are trapped in the left hemisphere and see nothing but reflections of ourselves wherever we look. The world becomes a hellish hall of mirrors. Perhaps all the grand material progress and accelerating technological advance we are witnessing is not actually a sign that we are moving ever closer to Heaven. It may well be leading us straight to Hell.

4. Faith Never Dies

Is this then the end of Western civilization? Will we become the victims of our own success? Colonized by science and technology to within an inch of our lives?

Obviously we can't really blame the left hemisphere, if that really is the root cause of the problem; we can only blame ourselves for letting it get out of hand. All the warning signs of a decadent civilization in chronic decline are there for anyone who wishes to look: the proliferation of ridiculously complex technocratic and bureaucratic systems of governance, the unsustainable exploitation of natural resources and the despoliation of the natural environment, and the basic amnesia of who or why we are.

Do we really have cause for such pessimism? What about the rational optimism of clever people like Hans Rosling, Steven Pinker and Matt Ridley? Aren't we actually better off now than at any other point in history bar none? In many ways, that's true. Life expectancy has shot up and absolute poverty has plummeted. We have successfully dealt with a whole raft of highly visible problems that at one time seemed insurmountable. This particular problem, however, is potentially a greater existential threat to civilisation, precisely because it is so difficult to see.

The way to cook a frog is not to throw it in a pot of boiling water. It will just jump straight out again. The trick is to put the frog in cold water and heat it up slowly. The frog will never notice. Are we living in a hyper rational, emotionally trivial, spiritually autistic, inhuman technological dystopia? You might think so if you were transported here in a time machine, but not if you grew up here.

One sign of societal decadence and decline is that people stop believing in their gods. This happened to the Egyptians, the Greeks and the Romans. For one reason or another, they just stopped believing. According to the mythology of all three civilizations, the gods not only created and sustained the natural world, but also the social one. (Athena founded Athens for example). The myths point to a fundamental truth: civilizations are sustained by belief in their gods.

G.K. Chesterton wrote, "You hard-shelled materialists [are] all balanced on the very edge of belief - of belief in almost anything."[91] Once belief in God is gone, anything goes. He may as well have written, "When men choose not to believe in God, they do not thereafter believe in nothing, they then become capable of believing in anything" (apparently he didn't.)

It's not possible to literally believe in nothing, obviously, but it is possible to believe in nothing much. People who believe in nothing much are muggles. They basically believe whatever the left hemisphere tells them, which is basically that they live in a dull, materialist, mechanistic universe. People who are capable of believing in *anything* are muppets.

When you choose not to believe in God, you close the door to the unfathomable mystery of existence and in so doing, over-ride the natural primacy of the right hemisphere. The word "God" here is a transcendental signifier – it points to something beyond. It doesn't matter what form the signifier takes (use another word if you must) as long as it points beyond the limits of the world according to the left hemisphere.

So what to do? You can't just click your fingers and believe in God can you? Well, maybe you can. The first step on the path to spiritual enlightenment in the Buddhist tradition is to arouse *bodhichitta*, "the thought of enlightenment". There is no "God" in Buddhism, but there is faith in the enlightenment of the Buddha and the potential for enlightenment in everyone ("Buddha Nature"). You could say that bodhichitta is the Buddhist version of belief in God.

Find a way to believe in the mystery beyond the closed system of your mind and you have found a way to believe in God. The "thought of God", like the "thought of enlightenment" is the chink in the armour of the left hemisphere. It's only the left hemisphere that says it can't be done. For the right hemisphere it's easy.

What are people really saying when they say, "I envy religious people; I wish I had their faith, but I just don't."? They are probably insinuating that, sigh, they are just too intelligent to have the simple minded belief in the supernatural that religious people seem to have.

What they are really saying is, "my left hemisphere encompasses the whole of reality and I bow to its dictates. My right hemisphere is dead to me."

The left hemisphere comes to dominate our world and our lives when we stop believing, and when we forget what belief even means. (The word "belief" means different things to the two hemispheres by the way - see the section on "faux amis" (false friends) in chapter 4 of *The Master and his Emissary*).

Religion loses its power when belief becomes merely a case of passive assent to a set of propositions and dogmas, in other words, when it is becomes left hemisphere belief. A living religion is not based on that kind of belief, equivalent to believing that the Earth revolves around the sun. Right hemisphere belief is an act of faith, an opening to the mystery of reality beyond our limited understanding of it.

Without faith, civilization begins to run down. Everything becomes rigid and mechanical. Empathy and imagination are squeezed out. Magic is dismissed as childish superstition. There is no space for wonder, beauty or faith.

But faith never dies. New gods emerge from the ashes of the old. God is resurrected once more. So it may be true that Western civilization is on its last legs. It may be that we are witnessing *The Suicide of the West* (Goldberg) and *The Strange Death of Europe* (Murray). But there are also signs that a new faith and a new civilization are emerging at the same time.

I don't believe in a facile New Age (because most of the New Age is so facile) but I am hopeful that there are enough glowing embers in the dying fire pit of Western civilization to survive the present decline. All it takes is a spark and the genies will flare up again and usher in a new chapter in the irrepressible march of the human spirit.

5. The Hermeneutics of Faith

Twenty odd years ago (when I was twenty odd) I picked up a beautiful little book of ancient poems by a selection of Tantric adepts translated with a commentary by Thomas Cleary called *The Ecstasy of Enlightenment: Teachings of Natural Tantra*. These highly symbolic verses have hidden within them deep secrets of Buddhist Tantra, and Cleary teases them out beautifully.

One of these secrets has accompanied me on all my various spiritual and philosophical meanderings ever since. It is the teaching on three energetic channels in the body (*nadis*) called the *shushumna*, *ida* and *pingala*. The esotericism is not what captured my attention, however. It was the extraordinary simplicity and explanatory power of the hermeneutical cycle symbolically processed through these three channels.

Thomas Cleary translates the old Bengali terms as "purification", "perception" and "dalliance". The idea is that by purifying consciousness (through immersion in the central shushumna channel) the bodymind is freed up to receive fresh impressions from the world. The doors of perception are cleansed (as William Blake famously expressed it) as consciousness shifts to the ida nadi, located on the left side of the body, representing the *yin* energy of the moon (passive and receptive).

From here consciousness is passed to the pingala nadi on the right side, which represents the *yang* energy of the sun, active and stimulating, the channel of mental-intellectual energy. This is called "dalliance". But it doesn't stop there. Consciousness continues around the cycle, passing back through the "purification" of the central channel to the "perception" of the left channel and back around to the "dalliance" of the right channel, and so on.

Only now, having read *The Master and his Emissary* do I appreciate how brilliant this ancient Tantric knowledge really is: it maps directly onto what we now know about the functioning of the two hemispheres of the brain.

A large percentage of neurons in the corpus callosum which connects the two hemispheres are actually inhibitory. This means that they can stop information passing from one side to the other. It also means that they can inhibit entire neural networks (such as the "default mode network"). Buddhist meditation has the explicit aim of stopping thought, achieving a state of no-mind (*mu-shin* in Japanese). This is what Tantric adepts call "purification", which they locate in their central energy channel, and which passes through the middle of the brain (the corpus callosum) and down through the central nervous system.

The right hemisphere (McGilchrist's "master") is the hemisphere responsible for immediate somatic, emotional and cognitive Gestalt-like integrated experiences. It also controls the left hand and the left side of the body, which is where the ida nadi is located. Remember the ida is the receptive *yin* channel, responsible for "perception".

The left hemisphere (McGilchrist's "emissary") is the hemisphere responsible for language (largely) and the manipulation of things into coherent systems. It is basically where our intellectual processing and system building takes place, what we usually call "thinking". It controls the right hand (the grasping hand) and the right side of the body, where the pingala nadi is located, the active *yang* channel, where "dalliance" takes place.

For the Tantric adept, the goal is not to disappear into a Nirvanic void of "purification" or to remain in a perfect state of mindful "perception". Neither is it (obviously) simply to create models of reality through endless intellectual "dalliance". Rather, the aim is to flow through all three states in a seamless cycle of ever deepening knowledge and experience. Raw experience must be processed in order for it to become knowledge, but that knowledge must in turn be purified so as not to ossify into ideological dogma.

With each cycle, knowledge is refined and experience is enriched. This is how we mature and grow. From this perspective, spiritual development is the approach to Reality (or God) through successive cycles of "purification", "perception" and "dalliance" (or *kenosis*, *gnosis* and *pistis*).

This is the same process McGilchrist describes when he says that the contents of the right hemisphere (the "master") must be passed over (or delegated) to the left hemisphere (the "emissary") but then passed back to the right hemisphere again.

What happens when the flow is interrupted? What happens when the left hemisphere refuses to give up its riches and tries to go it alone? We end up a slave to our egos, and in extreme cases find ourselves in a self-referential world of solipsism, narcissism and schizophrenia. We become progressively more mechanical, stereotypical, puppet-like.

6. All Shall be Well

The problem with social conservatives is that they get easily depressed. Things were always better before and signs of cultural decline constantly pain them. I never thought Roger Scruton and Peter Hitchens came across as the most cheerful of chappies.

But then liberal progressives have their own litany of reasons to be miserable. On the political front, they are depressed by the rise of right wing populism. On the social, they are depressed by the persistence of inequality and the underrepresentation of women and racial minorities everywhere from STEM fields to festival line-ups.

Conservatives are anxious about the constant "red menace" of potential socialist resurgence. They are also anxious about the "pink menace" of the LGBTQIAPK+ movement, the "green menace" of radical environmentalism and the "brown menace" of unchecked Muslim immigration.

Liberals are anxious about the "white menace" of white nationalist, white supremacist neo-Nazis. They are also anxious about anxious conservatives. And about climate change.

It's not good to be depressed and anxious. You don't need me to tell you that. Most of the conservatives' worries are unfounded, as are most of the liberals'. There are, of course, legitimate causes for concern, some of which both sides share, such as the potential negative effects of Artificial Intelligence on the future of society. But most things in life are either mixed blessings or mixed curses.

So don't worry, be happy. Resist the advances of the victim narrative peddlers. Don't be a victim. Remember the words of Julian of Norwich:

"All shall be well, and all shall be well, and all manner of thing shall be well."[92]

7. Filter Bubbles

There has been a lot of talk and anxiety in recent years about the filter bubble phenomenon, where online algorithms create self-replicating versions of the world which push people apart by creating islands of sense-making or "echo chambers". This seems to have resulted in increased polarisation and tribalism as people gravitate to one or other of the dominant ideological algorithm magnets.

Of course there are benefits to being in a bubble. You are among friends for a start. But it is obviously incredibly limiting. How can you know what wonderful worlds may be out there just waiting to be discovered? How do you know you're not in your very own Truman Show?

Apart from online bubbles, there are social bubbles and intellectual bubbles and all sorts of other invisible bubbles. It's only natural. How could we function otherwise? The world would be far too confusing. We can't take in the extraordinary complexity of reality, but need lenses, filter bubbles, maps of meaning or what-have-you to make sense of anything whatsoever. Doesn't our brain filter everything anyway? Aldous Huxley called it a "reducing valve":

"To make biological survival possible, Mind at Large has to be funneled through the reducing valve of the brain and nervous system. What comes out at the other end is a measly trickle of the kind of consciousness which will help us to stay alive on the surface of this particular planet."[93]

Huxley clearly understood this intellectually, but he also understood it experientially. He was literally "red pilled" when he took a strong dose of mescaline in May, 1953 and his reducing valve was temporarily overwhelmed by a tsunami of reality. He would never see the world in the same way again.

As well as his own awakening to the enormity, depth and grandeur of existence, his eyes were opened to just how asleep everyone else was. He saw that what they took to be genuinely real was actually just the measly trickle allowed through the valves of their personal and collective filter bubbles:

"Most people, most of the time, know only what comes through the reducing valve and is consecrated as genuinely real by the local language."[94]

In the film The Matrix, the protagonist Neo is given the choice between taking a red pill or a blue pill. The red pill will wake him up from the Matrix, while the blue pill will send him back into it, erasing all knowledge of the fact that what he reflexively accepts as reality is just a very convincing simulation.

The term "red pill" has been co-opted in recent years by conservatives who perceive that left-wing liberals are living in a fantasy world from which they would do well to awaken. A prominent example in the United States is the conservative activist Candace Owens, whose avowed mission in life is to wake African Americans up to the fact that they are slaves to an unquestioning allegiance to the Democrat Party. Never shy of provocation, she calls it the "Democrat Plantation", branding herself "Red Pill Black".

The progressive left and so-called Social Justice Warriors have their own equivalent term, "Wokeness", appropriated from the 1960's Civil Rights Movement. The idea is basically the same. In this case, people are seen as labouring under unacknowledged, inherited prejudices, primarily racist, sexist and homophobic, which precludes them from seeing society as it is (ie. racist, sexist and homophobic).

Since people have such dramatically divergent visions of socio-political reality, it's not surprising that they begin to conceive of their opponents as blind, deluded or asleep. Otherwise they would have to assume that they were actually evil, that is, intentionally and malevolently perverse in their denial of the truth, which, sadly, is also all too commonplace.

Exactly the same dynamic exists between atheists and religious believers. Sam Harris, a celebrity atheist, called his book *Waking Up*; Daniel Dennett titled his *Breaking the Spell* and Richard Dawkins plumped for *The God Delusion*. All three clearly believe that they are "woke" and that their mission is to "red pill" sleeping, bewitched and deluded religious believers.

On the other side of the aisle, Christian apologists are busy trying to wake up unbelievers and convert them to the true faith, as they have been for centuries. Christian evangelists tend to talk in terms of being born again and seeing the light, whereas New Age evangelists talk more explicitly about waking up.

The problem with filter bubbles is that they create alternate realities which are untouched by other realities. There is an analogy here with the idea of species divergence. When two populations of the same species are separated by some geographical feature, such as a mountain range or a body of water, they may evolve along different lines until the lineage splits and they become different species. The critical point of divergence is when they can no longer mate with a member of the other group.

Imagine if progressives and conservatives and atheists and religious believers decided there was no hope for their deluded antagonists and simply gave up on each other. They would stop listening and stop talking. They would "cancel" or "no platform" each other so as not to be exposed to their toxic "hate speech" and write books titled "why I am no longer talking to x". (Admittedly, one side is guiltier of this than the other at the moment). They would float off in their own bubbles and evolve completely different worldviews. Eventually, they might even become different species.

This is what it feels like sometimes. Increasing polarisation produces near instantaneous communication breakdown, since the very words we use have different resonances and can take on different meanings according to our conflicting paradigms. We are divided by the same language.

Does it matter? Can't we just live and let live and get on with our lives in our respective bubbles? Life would be a good deal less stressful, that's for sure. So maybe it's a good thing that we diverge. Well, maybe, but not if we want to live together. And not if we really want to wake up.

The language of awakening can be used divisively, to put down your opponents, as with the "woke" vs "red pill" culture war. But its original, spiritual usage was about transcending petty divisions and embracing all of reality in a wider, more comprehensive vision. This is what Aldous Huxley was aiming for, which is why he wrote *The Perennial Philosophy*.

However, the duality is intractable (nonduality notwithstanding). If some people really are "enlightened" and "awake", whether permanently or temporarily, then everyone else is by definition "deluded" and "asleep". *Buddha* simply means "the Awakened One", which suggests that the Buddha didn't experience reality via a reducing valve, or through a glass darkly, but "face to face".

If there really are awakened buddhas walking around amongst us, might they be, simply by virtue of the fact that they don't live in filter bubbles, in some mysterious sense, a different species? Is living in a bubble what makes us human, whichever bubble we happen to live in? If so, can we really transcend our humanness? Perhaps on the contrary, Buddha, like Christ, exemplifies what it is to be truly human, and not what it's like to be an exclusive member of a godlike superhuman species.

It may be true that "humankind cannot bear very much reality"[95], but we can probably bear more than we think. What is certain is that the more blinkered we are, the more identified with our filter bubbles, the less human we are, and the more we end up thinking and acting like divas, demons, victims, addicts, muppets and muggles.

8. The Tibetan Wheel of Life

In the most venerable and ancient Tibetan Wheel of Life there are six realms populated by six different types of beings: Humans, Titans, Hungry Ghosts, Animals, Devas and Demons. The Devas live in the *Devaloka*, the Heavenly Realms, the Demons in the *Narakas*, the Hell Realms, and the others in their own specially appointed realms.

I have taken the liberty (with, I hope, sufficient humility, respect and gratitude) of updating these six beings for the modern world. The denizens of the Human Realm I call "muggles"; those of the Titan Realm, "muppets"; the Hungry Ghost Realm, "addicts"; the Animal Realm, "victims" and the Heaven and Hell Realms, "divas" and "demons" respectively.

These beings are not literal beings (in my version at least) but symbolic personifications of different ego states. The Tibetan Wheel of Life is a psychological map as well as a cosmological one, and that's the map I'm using here. I want to explore how, when and why we are possessed by these six archetypal ego states, and what their psychological effects are (by which I mean the whole complex of physical, emotional, mental, spiritual and social effects).

The chief features of muggles and muppets are *ignorance* and *delusion* respectively. The ignorance of muggles comes as a result of ignoring the "signs and wonders" of the world as revealed to us in a state of openness and innocence. They ignore anything that doesn't fit their cosy little worldview and only see what they already know. Hence their immunity to the magic of reality.

The delusion of muppets comes as a result of valuing models of reality above reality itself. Their belief systems cause them to twist reality to fit, until they end up raging against common-sense. As a result, muppets see ideological enemies everywhere and are always spoiling for a fight.

Muggles and muppets are not generally on friendly terms. If you are a bit eccentric and express unusual views, you will quickly be regarded as a muppet by any new muggle acquaintances. They will think you're basically delusional.

If you seem perfectly normal and talk about normal things, you will soon be dismissed as a muggle by your new muppet friends. They will think you're a boring ignoramus.

Muggles tend to be quite naïve, good natured and innocent. Although they might be critical of people who are markedly different from themselves, they generally think the best of people, and assume that everyone is basically, deep down, just like them, in other words "decent" and "nice".

On the contrary, muppets are suspicious and combative. They assume the worst, rather than the best motives for other people's actions, and are most concerned to determine whether they are friend or foe. Basically, if you are not with them, you are against them. It's almost as if they were part of a secret resistance movement in a country under foreign occupation in a permanent, secret war.

If you are a muggle, you live in a world populated by ordinary people, some of which are inexplicably strange (but you don't let it bother you too much). If you are a muppet, your world is full of enemies and spies and you're constantly vigilant and battle ready. At the slightest whiff of provocation, you're ready to fight for whatever it is you believe in. It would be a rare day indeed that passes without at least one argument.

If you are a diva, you see angels everywhere. You seek out the beautiful people, because you sincerely believe you yourself are a beautiful person. The world is a heavenly place, the height of luxury, overflowing with wonderful treats and goodies, full of shiny, happy people. Understandably, you are averse to any sign of ugliness, poverty or unhappiness and try to avoid them as far as possible by giving the less fortunate a wide berth.

If you are unfortunate enough to wind up in Hell, you will see monsters and demons everywhere. You will feel that, deep down, you are a monster as well. If you stay long enough, you won't even have to scratch the surface – you'll know that you are in fact a monster. Your life will consist of torturing and being tortured.

If you are a victim, your world will be full of bullies. If a bully is not bullying you, they will be sure to be bullying someone else. Victims live in constant anxious expectation of being bullied, just as soon as one notices them.

The world is basically divided between two classes of people: victims and bullies. They always take the side of the victims, although, confusingly enough, the bullies themselves often turn out to be victims as well.

Finally, the world of the addict is populated by sirens. Sirens are generally very sexy and very alluring. They are parasitic entities that derive their energy primarily from naked human forms, either real or imagined, but also from other objects of desire such as drink or drugs or sweet and creamy food.

The following diagram sums up the six archetypes and their chief features:

DIVAS
Vanity

MUGGLES	**MUPPETS**
Ignorance	Delusion
ADDICTS	**VICTIMS**
Desire	Fear

DEMONS
Hate

Most people, most of the time, live in Muggle World with "normal people". However, most people also spend some time in Muppet World fighting the enemy, or in Victim World being bullied, in Addict World being seduced or in Heaven or Hell hanging out with angels or monsters.

It makes for a fairly eventful and varied life, but it's not ideal. Luckily, there is another world beyond these, just as there is a world beyond that dreamt of by the reducing valve of the brain, since this is only what the world is like according to the left hemisphere.

9. The Madman's Argument

Unless you are in a state of pristine sanity and enlightened flow on the one hand, or else criminally insane on the other, you are by default a muggle, muppet or diva. These are the three corners of the "ego triangle". If the ego cracks under pressure of madness, however, these three give way to another three waiting in the wings, namely the addict, victim and demon, the three corners of the "id triangle".

In relatively sane people, the three id archetypes have an indirect, unconscious effect. When under the temporary sway of any of the traditional vices of Lust or Greed, Rage or Hate, Anxiety or Depression, a sane person is merely experiencing a leakage of insanity seeping up from their personal underworld. It is only when a person is in the continuous grip of one or other of these mental states, pulled around in a loop as it were by the perpetual motion of insanity, that they can be said to be truly homeless on Earth and have found their home in Hell.

There are, as Dante taught, many levels in Hell, but mercifully few reach the lower rings. However, there are also many levels on Earth. Those human denizens of Earth who consider themselves perfectly sane, are actually in various states of partial insanity. The level of insanity could in theory be measured and graded along a spectrum according to the frequency and intensity of the eruptions of Lust, Hate and Fear into consciousness. A second measure by which to grade Earth people's level of insanity is to determine quite how much of a muggle, muppet or diva they are.

These two measures of relative insanity are of course closely correlated, since the muggle, muppet and diva ego structures must have originally formed as defences against the incursions from the subconscious. Once formed, however, the ongoing ebb and tide of the underground Sea of Hades merely serves to power the ego, like a great hydro-electric plant, with the occasional tidal wave overwhelming the personality altogether and plunging it temporarily into the depths.

The Madman's Argument

In the following I will focus on the internal dynamics of the Earth-bound human ego, the "ego triangle" of muggle, muppet and diva.

Muggles are ordinary people who have no magic, and who either have no inkling that there might be such a thing as magic, or if they have heard rumours, don't believe a word of it. It is of course a derogatory term used by wizards like Harry Potter. In the high drama of the great magical wars between good and evil, muggles are low-paid extras. They unwittingly act as pawns in the game or end up as collateral damage.

The chief feature of the muggle state is ignorance, both in the sense of a lack of knowledge and experience and of an avoidance of knowledge and experience. Muggles ignore anything that falls outside their familiar circle of experience, such as other cultures, alternative states of consciousness (spiritual or psychedelic) or even aspects of their own cultural and religious traditions. The madness of muggles reduces and constricts horizons, even when they think they are expanding them. Take the materialist muggle's conception of the universe for example:

"As an explanation of the world, materialism has a sort of insane simplicity. It has just the quality of the madman's argument; we have at once the sense of it covering everything and the sense of it leaving everything out. Contemplate some able and sincere materialist, as, for instance, Mr McCabe, and you will have exactly this unique sensation. He understands everything, and everything does not seem worth understanding. His cosmos may be complete in every rivet and cogwheel, but still his cosmos is smaller than our world. Somehow his scheme, like the lucid scheme of the madman, seems unconscious of the alien energies and the large indifference of the earth; it is not thinking of the real things of the earth, of fighting peoples or proud mothers, or first love or fear upon the sea. The earth is so very large, and the cosmos is so very small. The cosmos is about the smallest hole that a man can hide his head in."[96]

Muggles are not overly concerned with the meaning of anything above and beyond its immediate value, like a spade or a pretty face. Muppets, on the other hand, trade in the currency of hidden meaning, even existential meaning. But they look for it in all the wrong places, like George Bernard Shaw, who according to G.K Chesterton had "a heroically large and generous heart; but not a heart in the right place."[97]

The madness of muggles is in their easy-going small mindedness, which makes it a rather un-offensive type of madness. The madness of muppets is in their fanatical narrow mindedness, which can make them both infuriating and dangerous. Chesterton's term for muppets is "maniacs". They are characterised not by irrationality as we ordinarily understand the term, but by a form of hyper-rationality divorced from common-sense experience.

"The madman is not the man who has lost his reason. The madman is the man who has lost everything except his reason."[98]

This is one consequence of left hemisphere dominance, which in extreme cases (such as in cases of right hemisphere lesions) does in fact produce symptoms almost identical to those of hyper-rational mental conditions such as schizophrenia and autism. Even in less severe cases, such as with people under the sway of conspiracy theories, it is almost impossible to reason them out of their madness.

"The madman's explanation of a thing is always complete, and often in a purely rational sense satisfactory. Or, to speak more strictly, the insane explanation, if not conclusive, is at least unanswerable"[99].

Muppets abound outside of the lunatic asylum of course, especially among the intellectual elites, which is precisely Chesterton's point. The asylum itself, along with everything else, is now run by maniacs, the most deadly being those who somehow wrest political power for themselves (cue Hitler and Stalin).

Muppets are tribal creatures, which makes them often vituperative and violent. Like their ancestral Titans on the Tibetan Wheel of Life, they are engaged in perpetual warfare, swinging like an angry pendulum between defense and offence. All the talk about "culture wars" in America and Europe is just the most recent manifestation of this eternal battle of the maniacs. More often (thankfully) it actually looks more like a clash of muppets than a clash of Titans. I call it the "muppet wars".

New Atheists and Transhumanists are "nerd muppets"; Progressive Liberals and New Age Stoners are "hippy muppets"; White Supremacists and Antifa both are "radical muppets"; Bible Bashers and Creationists are "fundamentalist muppets". Between them there is more than enough acrimony to keep the muppet wars going.

What about divas? There are the ordinary divas who are rich and famous and live in the lap of luxury, and then there are spiritual divas. Spiritual divas are not stuck in the suburbs like muggles or in the trenches like muppets. They have overcome the ignorance and delusion of muggles and muppets. However, their vanity creates a superiority complex that is very hard to shake off, and which halts any further spiritual progress. This generally manifests as the implacable madness known as "spiritual narcissism".

Believing that they are at the top of the heap, spiritual divas forget that they are not on a heap but a mountain and that the peak is lost in the mists above them. Their vanity causes them to forget what they have learned and, sooner or later, they slip back into the more familiar grooves of muggle or muppet life. And round we go.

As I said at the beginning, we are all somewhere on the ego triangle - we are all either muggles, muppets or divas. Unless, that is, we are in a state of enlightened, wakeful presence and flow; unless, that is, we are on holy ground. Most of the time, however, we are just that little bit mad, ever ready to justify ourselves with a madman's argument.

10. Personality Disorders

Are the six archetypes on the Wheel of Life personality disorders? In their extreme manifestations, I would say, yes they are. In this book I have been treating them as "normal" ego states that we are all susceptible to, but they can become abnormal and pathological when they begin to dominate the personality. It all depends on the severity of the case, but because they are usually "ego-syntonic", that is, consistent with the integrity of the ego, they tend to be seen as normal enough by the person in question, unless they produce extremely problematic or destructive behaviours.

DSM-5 (the Diagnostic and Statistical Manual of Mental Disorders) lists ten personality disorders organised into three clusters. The ten disorders are: paranoid, schizoid, schizotypal, antisocial, borderline, histrionic, narcissistic, avoidant, dependent and obsessive-compulsive. They are organised according to "odd or eccentric" behaviours (cluster A), "dramatic, emotional or erratic" behaviours (cluster B) and "anxious or fearful" behaviours (cluster C).

So how do these map onto the Wheel of Life? Well, cluster A disorders (*paranoid, schizoid* and *schizotypal*) seem to apply primarily to the Muggle-Muppet axis; cluster B disorders (*antisocial, borderline, histrionic* and *narcissistic*) to the Diva-Demon axis and cluster C disorders (*avoidant, dependent* and *obsessive-compulsive*) to the Addict-Victim axis. Based on this categorisation, we might say that muggles are basically paranoid; muppets schizoid and schizotypal; divas histrionic and narcissistic; demons antisocial and borderline; addicts obsessive-compulsive and victims avoidant and dependent.

I don't think this formulation quite works though – some disorders seem closer to other archetypes. Also, addicts seem to be a bit of an anomaly. There is no personality disorder that unambiguously describes the addictive personality. Perhaps this is because addictive behaviours are secondary effects of an underlying personality disorder.

For example, someone suffering from borderline personality disorder will often exhibit addictive behaviours (especially substance abuse), an obsessive-compulsive person may develop an eating disorder, and someone with dependent personality disorder will clearly be susceptible to physical as well as emotional addiction. The results are similar, but the underlying causes are very different.

Addiction is not really a personality disorder in its own right, so, for the present purpose of relating the archetypes to personality disorders, in the interests of simplicity I will put the addict archetype to one side. According to the descriptions proposed by psychologist Theodore Millon,[100] I think the following slightly amended diagnoses for the remaining five archetypes are a better fit than a strict adherence to the cluster model alluded to above:

Muggles are generally *obsessive-compulsive:* "Restrained, conscientious, respectful, rigid. Maintain a rule-bound lifestyle. Adhere closely to social conventions. See the world in terms of regulations and hierarchies. See themselves as devoted, reliable, efficient, and productive."

Muppets are generally *borderline:* "Unpredictable, manipulative, unstable. Frantically fear abandonment and isolation. Experience rapidly fluctuating moods. Shift rapidly between loving and hating. See themselves and others alternatively as all-good and all-bad. Unstable and frequently changing moods. People with borderline personality disorder have a pervasive pattern of instability in interpersonal relationships."

Divas are generally *narcissistic:* "Egotistical, arrogant, grandiose, insouciant. Preoccupied with fantasies of success, beauty, or achievement. See themselves as admirable and superior, and therefore entitled to special treatment. Is a mental disorder in which people have an inflated sense of their own importance and a deep need for admiration. Those with narcissistic personality disorder believe that they're superior to others and have little regard for other people's feelings."

Demons are generally *sadistic:* "Explosively hostile, abrasive, cruel, dogmatic. Liable to sudden outbursts of rage. Gain satisfaction through dominating, intimidating and humiliating others. They are opinionated and close-minded. Enjoy performing brutal acts on others. Find pleasure in abusing others. Would likely engage in a sadomasochist relationship, but will not play the role of a masochist."

Victims are generally *dependent*: "Helpless, incompetent, submissive, immature. Withdrawn from adult responsibilities. See themselves as weak or fragile. Seek constant reassurance from stronger figures. They have the need to be taken care of by a person. They fear being abandoned or separated from important people in their life."

I am not suggesting that muggles are always obsessive-compulsive or that muppets are always borderline, that divas are always narcissistic, demons always sadistic or victims always dependent, or that these labels are simply interchangeable. I do think, however, that the clinical diagnoses of these personality disorders helpfully identify the more severe end of our general psychological dispositions, thus bringing them into clearer focus, and it is these general, non-pathological, dispositions that I have been exploring.

So how would the ten or so major personality disorders fall when applied to the Wheel of Life? I can identify three clusters related to the Muppet-Muggle, Diva-Demon and Victim-Addict axes, although they differ somewhat to the three clusters imported from DSM-5 (I have also included some disorders from the DSM-III-R appendix.)

Let's call the first one, related to the Muppet-Muggle axis, "cluster M". Here I would include obsessive-compulsive, schizoid, schizotypal and borderline disorders. Let's call the second one, related to the Diva-Demon axis, "cluster D". Here I would include narcissistic, histrionic, sadistic, negativistic and antisocial disorders. Let's call the third one, related to the Victim-Addict axis, "cluster V". Here I would include dependent, avoidant, depressive, paranoid and self-defeating disorders.

11. The Iceman Cometh

When Hickey turns up at Harry Hope's drinking salon in Eugene O'Neill's 1939 play, *The Iceman Cometh*, the regulars are expecting the usual party. But Hickey says he has stopped drinking. He says he has woken up from the drunken spell they are all still under. He doesn't try to get them to stop drinking, though. Rather, he tries to convince them to give up their delusional "pipe dreams" and to face the reality of who they are. But it doesn't turn out to be as easy as that. The ones that do give up their pipe dreams are in an even worse state than before.

The three corners of the "ego triangle" are the muggle, muppet and diva subpersonalities. They maintain themselves primarily through ignorance, delusion and vanity. They live on the smoke of pipe dreams, and they have absolutely no wish to be rudely awakened from their reveries.

Just like in *The Iceman Cometh*, it can be dangerous to wake sleeping dogs. The ego triangle keeps us from growing up and fulfilling our potential, but it also protects us from the "id triangle", the addict, victim and demon subpersonalities. It is an important defence mechanism. When we lose faith in the myths and stories that sustain us and the madman's arguments by which we justify our existence, we are apt to fall into existential despair, prey to rage, fear and an insatiable desire for unconsciousness.

"Humankind cannot bear very much reality"[101]: if their illusions are the only thing keeping people sane, then beware of shattering them. When the Iceman comes (always with the very best of intentions of course) those who are not ready to give up their pipe dreams may well find themselves not in a rosy heaven of new life and possibility, but in a fiery hell of bitterness and recrimination.

12. Talk to the Soul

The working hypothesis of Psychosynthesis, the first major transpersonal psychology of the twentieth century, is that every individual is a centre of pure consciousness and will. Every person has a subjective "I". However, from our very first breath, we begin to identify with certain aspects of our experience, initiating the life-long process of ego-building.

What exactly is the "ego"? According to Roberto Assagioli, the founder of Psychosynthesis, the ego is not one, but many semi-autonomous personality structures. A neuroscientist might be tempted to say that they are the expression of independent neural networks in the brain. Assagioli simply called them "subpersonalities".

We are usually unaware that we have more than one personality for two reasons. Firstly, each subpersonality shares the same intimate sense of I-ness, because it is the same "I" which identifies with them all. Secondly, we forget all the other subpersonalities when we identify with one of them. It's a bit like forgetting what cold feels like when you're hot.

There are three central aims in Psychosynthesis psychotherapy: to dis-identify from your subpersonalities, to connect with your "I", and to organise your subpersonalities around it. This is why it is has been called "a psychology with a soul". The therapy works on the assumption that there *is* a soul, a centre of consciousness and will, that can orchestrate and even synthesise the contents of the personality.

Psychosynthesis practitioners generally talk in terms of "identification" and "dis-identification". This obviously puts the agency fair and square in the "I", which is what must be doing the identifying and dis-identifying. However, believing that you are something that you are not doesn't seem like a particularly conscious thing to do. So perhaps "possession" is closer to the mark.

A bit like the 1970's children's programme *Mr Ben* (I'm showing my age here!) it's as though we have a wardrobe full of costumes and when we put one on, we become that person. We are "possessed" by the costumes we put on.

A change in circumstances may prompt us to change costumes, but if we learn how to dis-identify, we can take the costume off at will. If we become overly attached to one particular costume, our personality becomes ever more fixed, inflexible and stereotyped. Eventually, we become a caricature.

So when I talk about being a diva, muggle, muppet, addict, victim or demon, what I mean is that you have put on a diva costume or a muggle costume. Or to put it more esoterically, you are possessed by a muppet spirit or an addict spirit. Or again, more prosaically, you are identified with a victim subpersonality or a demon subpersonality.

These six subpersonalities are a handy way of conceptualising the ego as a whole. Although subpersonalities are legion, they can still be usefully grouped under one of the six types on the Wheel. Whatever their particular, idiosyncratic features, you will still be able to recognise the basic type.

Subpersonalities are very wily. They will try on all sorts of different masks in order to fool you into thinking that this time it really is you. But if you have a basic template of the kinds of masks they might use, then unmasking them is much easier.

When it comes to the masks that other people wear, it helps to recognise what ego state they are in, not in order to unmask them (they won't like that), but in order to avoid getting sucked into unhealthy and counter-productive mind games.

To judge that someone is a diva, for example, is not, therefore, to judge that that person is a diva in essence. It is merely to judge that that person is at this moment possessed by a diva spirit. If they are often possessed by a diva spirit, then you are perfectly justified in pre-judging them. Even before they open their mouth, you will naturally (prejudicially) expect the diva to speak. If they are so completely identified with their diva subpersonality that they always predictably talk and act like one, then you might begin to believe that this person basically *is* a diva.

It is important not to believe that. However strongly identified or possessed, there is always a pure centre of consciousness and will in there somewhere. Beyond the narcissistic or histrionic personality disorder, behind any personality disorder, there is a soul.

If you lose sight of that, you will be lost in ego, whether yours or someone else's. It doesn't matter if the other person can't see it. Treat them as a soul anyway. See the ego but talk to the soul.

13. Soul Building

If you don't believe in the soul, that may be because you don't have one! Gurdjieff for one didn't think that everyone was born with a soul. Perhaps nobody is born with a soul and everyone has to build one from scratch. Maybe having a soul isn't our birth-right, but our life's work.

For what it's worth, I think that everyone is born with an "I", which you could call a "soul". But the "I" is a pure centre of consciousness and will, which is quickly co-opted by the ego, so it isn't a personality in its own right, but the consciousness and will of whichever ego (subpersonality) happens to be in charge. It isn't what we would ordinarily think of as a soul.

I think what Gurdjieff meant be a soul was something like an actualized spiritual personality structure, in other words, a form of conscious life qualitatively distinct from the ego. This spiritual entity is not a given, but has to be consciously created and developed through spiritual practice. Miles Davis knew this, which is why he called one of his albums *The Birth of Soul*.

When Roger Scruton worried about the de-sacralisation of the modern world, he was mourning the death of soul. And of course the death of soul and the death of God go together. For Scruton, God is "the Soul of the World". Kill one and you kill the other.

Then again, it's not so much about killing as refusing to be born. If you don't believe in soul, why bother trying to give birth to it? Scientific materialism is a self-fulfilling prophecy. But if Richard Dawkins or Daniel Dennett can somehow prove that they have no soul that of course proves nothing about the souls of anyone else.

T.S. Eliot wrote about *The Wasteland* and *The Hollow Men*. He was describing the soulless world of modernity, where people have forgotten what it is like to have a soul and a God. The world is disenchanted and de-sacralised, a meaningless wasteland where people are nothing but hollowed-out "dirty computers".

Not everyone, luckily. There are some who have survived the zombie apocalypse, some secret souls picking their way through the debris. The challenge is how to protect the fragile nascent soul and to nurture it so that it is strong enough to withstand the assaults of the droids.

The ultimate challenge, like that faced by the Fab Four in *The Yellow Submarine* is how to turn the wasteland back into a beautiful, blooming "divine milieu", how to beat the Blue Meanies.

It may be true that *All you Need is Love*, but that kind of love doesn't come from the ego, it comes from the soul. And the only remedy for a soulless world is more souls.

14. No Yoga, No Joy

In the worldly world, we seek pleasure and happiness. We are all Utilitarians at heart, trying to maximize our pleasure and minimize our pain, and striving to be as happy as possible. It's what Freud called "the pleasure principle". Very few of us are committed idealists or utopians, so we generally settle for a tolerable balance of pleasure and pain, what Freud called "ordinary unhappiness".

Religious traditions are more optimistic. They speak of "bliss" and "joy", claiming that these are above and beyond ordinary worldly pleasure. Apparently, according to the prophet Isaiah, Heaven and Earth are full of the glory of God. To taste this glory is bliss, *ananda* in the Sanskrit of the Vedic tradition.

Secular thinkers try to define pleasure and happiness either positively, as "positive affect", which includes pleasurable physiological effects caused by the release of dopamine or serotonin for example, or negatively, as the absence of pain or negative emotion. According to them, bliss and joy are merely more intense manifestations of positive affect, different in degree but not in kind.

Religious thinkers, on the other hand, claim that there is a qualitative and not just a quantitative difference between pleasure and joy. They claim it is a peculiarly "spiritual" feeling, or a spiritual "energy". For a secularist, this claim cannot be verified due to the simple fact that they do not have these spiritual experiences to compare to their ordinary experiences.

However, most people, whether or not they profess any religious belief, or consider themselves at all spiritual, have had spontaneous experiences at some point in their lives of pure untrammeled joy, which are clearly pleasurable experiences, but somehow much more than that. Whether or not there is a qualitative difference, it is undeniable that there is some continuity between the experience of pleasure and the experience of joy.

So what *is* the difference? I would say that pleasure and pain are associated with the ego and that joy is associated with the soul.

No Yoga, No Joy

Pleasure is clearly the raison d'être of the addict. But there is also pleasure (as well as pain) in the other realms. There is a certain sadistic pleasure for the demon, a masochistic pleasure for the victim, a complacent pleasure for the muggle, a self-righteous pleasure for the muppet and a vain kind of pleasure for the diva. These are all unstable pleasures which can easily turn sour and produce pain.

Joy, on the other hand, is not just a pleasurable feeling. It is also associated with *meaning*, which is itself associated with *self-transcendence*. Jordan Peterson talks about walking the line between the known and the unknown, between order and chaos. That's one way of thinking about it. New meaningful experiences expand the horizons of the known. Another way is in terms of our orientation towards a goal or *telos*, which, although forever receding and ultimately unattainable, confers value and meaning to our endeavours. This is known as the "progress principle". That can be a pleasure, but not necessarily.

Meaningful self-transcendence is called "yoga" in India. The four traditional yogas described in the Baghavad Gita are *Karma Yoga, Bhakti Yoga, Jnana Yoga* and *Raja Yoga*, which roughly translate as the yoga of action, the yoga of devotion, the yoga of knowledge and the yoga of Self-inquiry (the "royal road").

There is bliss and joy in the practice of each of these disciplines, if undertaken in the right spirit. There is joy in selfless action without attachment to results (karma yoga), joy in devotional practices, such as the singing of kirtan and bajan (bhakti yoga), joy in the insights derived from philosophical contemplation (jnana yoga) and joy in Self-realization (raja yoga).

The four yogas correspond to four archetypes: the Warrior (karma yoga), the Monk (bhakti yoga), the Philosopher (jnana yoga) and the King (raja yoga). Each has its own peculiar joy. There is also the joy of the Mystic (dhyana yoga) and the joy of the Shaman (kundalini yoga).

When you grasp an important insight, when you make connections and synthesize some new piece of knowledge, when the penny drops and you finally get it, when the eye of understanding is opened and you cry "Eureka!" a small burst of bliss is released. There is joy in wisdom. The pursuit of Truth turns out to involve following your bliss as much as the pursuit of Self-realisation. To follow this way is to follow the way of the jnani yogi, the path of the Philosopher.

However, to be a true philosopher, a jnana yogi, you must be open to the Truth in whatever guise it may take. You must be prepared to engage with ideas contrary to your own and to maintain a healthy skepticism regarding all points of view, without falling into radical skepticism, cynicism or relativism. You must strive for objectivity and maintain a discipline of dispassionate inquiry, free from emotional attachments.

In other words, you can't be a muppet. You can't insult your adversaries, use ad hominem attacks, emotional reasoning, negative filtering, overgeneralizing, dichotomous thinking and a whole host of other cognitive distortions. You can't fall for confirmation bias and silence opposing voices on ideological grounds.

Equally, you can't be a raja yogi if you believe in Identity Politics. If you really think that you are nothing but your externally observable immutable characteristics, such as sex, race, ethnicity, shoe size, etc. then you obviously cannot be a raja yogi. This way is by definition closed to you: your true Identity as a sovereign soul, as a King or Queen, is beyond all that. And muggles, who never think to inquire into their essential nature in the first place, can't be raja yogis either.

There is some pleasure in being a muggle or a muppet. But there is no joy. Meaningless, "ignorant" or "deluded" pleasure always gives way to pain in the end. But where there is meaning, there is joy (and where there is limited, truncated, pseudo-meaning, there is limited, truncated, pseudo-joy). The level of joy in meaning, or meaningful joy, is your measure of proficiency in jnana yoga and raja yoga.

Where there is sensual pleasure, but no devotion, there is no joy. Where there is activity, but no surrendered action, there is no joy. Have you experienced the joy of bhakti yoga and karma yoga? Have you felt the special bliss of a Monk or a Warrior? Or do you always take your pleasure joylessly, greedily stimulating yourself or grumbling at work, as addicts and victims do?

Without self-transcendence, there is no joy. There is either utter meaninglessness or the micro meanings provided by false idols. Of course there will be pleasure as well as pain and there will be happiness mixed in with our ordinary unhappiness. But no yoga, no joy.

15. After Virtue

I have been interested in philosophy and psychology ever since I didn't study them at university. Recently, I've been delving more deeply into moral philosophy, which straddles both disciplines. I reread *After Virtue* by Alasdair Macintyre, a book which impressed me when I first read it over twenty years ago, and am more convinced than ever that his diagnosis of the crisis in morality is right: we took a wrong turn in the Enlightenment when we tried to base morals on a purely rationalistic foundation.

Before the Enlightenment, morality was all about virtue, and the key philosopher was Aristotle. But with the advent of Immanuel Kant with his Categorical Imperative and Jeremy Bentham with his Utilitarianism, morality became more a question of rational deliberation than about the development of good character.

The two main modern schools of moral thought are "deontology" (the ethics of obligation) and "consequentialism" (the ethics of outcomes). Although they differ in their approaches and conclusions, they are both more interested in hypothetical moral problems than in moral qualities. They try to answer the question, "what should one do in such and such a situation?" by applying a rule or a calculus of maximum benefit and minimum harm. The focus is on the action and its consequences, and not so much on the agent of action.

Moral thinking has consequently shifted from "character ethics" to "quandary ethics". It doesn't matter who is in the quandary. All that matters is what the right course of action would be. And the right course of action is ultimately the result of a rational process. So, on this basis, it is perfectly conceivable that in the future it would be possible to invent an app that could calculate the best course of action in any given situation.

I wasn't entirely surprised to learn that Bentham was probably on the autism spectrum and that Kant might have been as well. That got me thinking about the Logical Positivists, who dominated philosophy in the first half of the twentieth century and the Behaviourists, who dominated psychology.

Were they on the autism spectrum as well? They certainly had a suspiciously narrow view of reality.

Considering the rise and rise of science and technology in the last two hundred years, and the meteoric rise of computer scientists in defining the culture (many of whom are definitely on the spectrum), I couldn't help worrying whether this might be part of a larger trend. What if moral philosophy, and philosophy and psychology more generally were re-creating humanity in the image of logic machines?

If we think of ourselves as machines, might we not become like machines? Viewed as rational "soft machines", human beings are granted a mind and a body, (software and hardware), but that's basically it. Rational machines make moral choices according to rational considerations, perhaps with a little tug-of-war between "head" and "heart" first. But they soon starts to look uncannily like philosophical zombies or robots, once "head" and "heart" are reduced to clever algorithms.

Traditional humans have more options open to them than the modern ones. They can think and feel, but they can do other things as well. They can "believe", for example. Not in a merely intellectual sense (which is just rational assent to a particular proposition in the absence of compelling evidence), but as a completely distinct psychological capacity. "Belief" in this sense is not an act of reason but a leap of faith, or a "leap into faith" as Kierkegaard put it. It is no accident, therefore, that the advent of High Modernity was accompanied by the "death of God" and the psychological atrophying and neglect of our capacity for belief.

In the West, we live in a post-Christian world, a world "After Holiness". The word holiness is no longer part of our collective cultural lexicon. Only the historical stragglers, the handfuls of congregations who have failed to keep up with the times, are concerned about being holy, "growing in faith" or coming closer to God.

We are also, as MacIntyre argues, living in a world "After Virtue". The language of virtue is as good as dead. As long as you are nice to people and don't offend anyone, you're fine. Few people deliberately cultivate the virtues anymore, or even know what they are.

It seems that we are also living in a world "After Wisdom". In matters of specialist knowledge, we defer to experts. In everything else, we defer to the dogma of relativism, which obviates the need for serious thought. When the idea of objective truth falls on hard times, wisdom inevitably hits the doldrums.

Imagine if a child when asked what they want to be when they grow up replied, "holy, virtuous and wise." We would probably smile indulgently, and not a little condescendingly. Imagine if an adult when asked about their aspirations in life answered the same way. Could you resist a smirk or snigger? Our cynicism runs so deep that the very idea of holiness, virtue or wisdom is laughable.

But what is a man (or woman) without these things? Even if he is the nicest person on Earth, there is a lack of depth to his character, a shallowness which makes any meaningful meeting of minds impossible. In Brave New World there is nobody you can have a decent conversation with.

MacIntyre is perhaps uncomfortably close to the truth when he concludes his magnum opus by comparing our modern world with the Dark Ages following the fall of the Roman Empire:

"What matters at this stage is the construction of local forms of community within which civility and the intellectual and moral life can be sustained through the new dark ages which are already upon us. And if the tradition of the virtues was able to survive the horrors of the last dark ages, we are not entirely without grounds for hope. This time however the barbarians are not waiting beyond the frontiers; they have already been governing us for quite some time."[102]

16. Vive la Resistance!

It's not easy to resist temptation, even when you know it's bad for you. Ask any smoker or coke addict. But just as charity begins at home, so does resistance. Resist that cheeky biscuit. Resist that click bait. There are hundreds of opportunities to build up your resistance every day.

But temptation is not just about greed or lust. It's also about fear and loathing. When we are crossed, we are tempted to stoke up our indignation and resentment to more satisfying levels of seething anger and hatred. When we are thrown off balance, it's tempting to give the ants (anxious negative thoughts) free rein.

Fear, hate and greed: the three temptations of the victim, demon and addict.

Be not afraid. Whether it's terrorism, knife crime, climate change, Brexit, populism, socialism, surveillance capitalism, artificial intelligence or the zombie apocalypse, be not afraid. Love your enemies. Don't let hatred get the better of you. And whatever the advertisers are peddling at the moment, don't let greed lead you astray.

But if you really want to be free, you really should also resist muggle, muppet and diva temptations. The muggle temptation is conformity and being normal ("perfectly normal, thank you very much.") The diva temptations are fame, fortune, power and influence. The muppet temptation is rebellion.

It may sometimes look hopeless, but there is in fact a spirited resistance to the muppet rebellions. There is renewed interest in Christian apologetics, for example, as a counter to the excesses of the New Atheism, which was itself originally a robust rebuttal of religious fundamentalism. And there is growing resistance in academic philosophy and political theory to the excesses of postmodernism and the recent resurgence of far left and far right ideologies.

The best forms of resistance, however, are direct recourse to the Warrior, Monk, Philosopher and King archetypes:

The Warrior archetype represents Karma Yoga: the insidious fear of the victim is dispelled through *Virtue Ethics*. As the Stoics taught so eloquently, do the right thing and you have nothing to fear.

The Monk archetype represents Bhakti Yoga: the insatiable greed of the addict is dispersed through *Devotional Arts,* especially music, where desire is directed heavenward and transmuted.

The Philosopher archetype represents Jnana Yoga: the delusional thinking of the muppet is corrected through Traditional Wisdom. The "best that has been thought and said" through the ages trumps the latest intellectual fads.

The King archetype represents Raja Yoga: the false consciousness of the muggle is overcome through *Self Inquiry*. The simple question, "who am I?" digs down far deeper than any trite self-image offered by the ego.

Let *Virtue Ethics, Devotional Arts, Traditional Wisdom* and *Self Inquiry* shield you against the enervating and soul destroying temptations of Modernity.

Vive la resistance!

17. Mind your Q's

There has been a certain amount of skepticism recently about the value of IQ tests. Do they really test intelligence or do they test something else, like the ability to do well in IQ tests? Are they good predictors of success in life or in the workplace? Are they culturally skewed in favour of certain ethnic groups? Are there other forms of human intelligence which are equally if not more important?

I am no expert in these matters. I haven't taken an IQ test myself, and I haven't been interested enough to look into the subject in any depth. However, in my experience a high IQ does not necessarily correlate with anything approaching "wisdom". Which is why, I suppose, people have found it necessary to develop alternative metrics, such as EQ (emotional intelligence quotient) and SQ (spiritual intelligence quotient).

I would like here to propose an extension of these two alternative metrics to six (MQ, RQ, BQ, EQ, PQ and SQ) to represent all six archetypes on the Cross (Mystic, Shaman, Warrior, Monk/Nun, Philosopher and King/Queen).

Each archetype represents a particular human capacity. The Mystic represents the ability to still the mind or to "deactivate the default mode network". If there were a test for this ability, you would obviously score higher according to the extent to which you could quiet down the inner chatter in your mind. How easily and how quickly can you enter a state of meditative absorption (*Samadhi*)? How easily can you stop thinking? This would be your MQ (meditative intelligence quotient).

The Shaman represents the ability to physically relax and heal oneself. We all carry stress in our bodies, which manifests in different ways, usually as physical tension. We expend a great deal of effort, both consciously and unconsciously, in covering up or distracting ourselves from this underlying physical dis-ease. Eckhart Tolle refers to this chronic background tension as the "pain body". The degree to which you can relax and release stress and tension in the body comprises your RQ (relaxation intelligence quotient).

The Warrior represents physical strength and skill. How developed are your gross and fine motor skills? Are you in control of your body and its capacities? Do you have a high degree of dexterity and flexibility? Can you move with power, precision and grace? Can you run, jump, dance and if necessary, fight? Can you be "in the zone" where the body finds its own spontaneous flow without conscious deliberation? To the degree that you are tuned into your body, you will score more or less highly on the BQ (body intelligence quotient).

The Monk/Nun represents emotional intelligence, particularly the higher emotions. This includes devotional and religious feelings, but also aesthetic feelings, which find their highest expressions in music and poetry. The refined feelings and subtle emotions reflected in the works of composers like Chopin or writers like Jane Austen can only be fully appreciated through emotional intelligence. Equally, the religious feelings evoked by the music of Thomas Tallis or the poetry of George Herbert are only accessible to people who have the necessary sensibility. This depends on EQ (emotional intelligence quotient).

The Philosopher represents philosophical intelligence, which is not the same thing as IQ. It depends on the ability to reason coherently, and to avoid cognitive distortions and logical fallacies. It presupposes a commitment to truth above and beyond all ideological positions. Healthy skepticism and open-mindedness are essential. In the West this is best exemplified by the Socratic Method, which proceeds through careful reasoning in good faith, faithfully following an argument wherever it leads. Cleverness is not enough to score highly here - wisdom and common-sense are more important for PQ (philosophical intelligence quotient).

Finally, the King/Queen represents the inherent authority of the soul. What is the soul? It is clearly something more than mere consciousness, which we share with all other living things. Everyone is conscious, but perhaps not everyone has a fully developed soul, and some people may not have a soul at all. A conscious person beyond all ego states or social roles, a pure centre of consciousness and will - that's what I mean by "soul". You'll know it if you have it and the degree to which you have it determines your SQ (spiritual intelligence quotient).

Clearly it would be extremely difficult if not impossible to actually quantify these human capacities. How could you design a universal test or give a meaningful score for such subjective qualities? It may be possible, or it may not, but we can at least measure ourselves against ourselves. In any case, if you're serious about (integral) spiritual progress, you'd better mind your Q's.

18. Thus Spoke Ayahuasca

Everything is a teaching.
Lost souls remind you to find your way.
Great souls remind you who you are.
The whispering serpent reminds you not to listen to snakes.
The smiling sun reminds you to smile.

The cosmic battle for your soul is here on Earth.
Heaven and Hell beckon continuously.
It's true.
And yet...
But it's still true.

No one has the last word.
There is no last word.
Learn true learning.
There is no end of learning.
But beware of false prophets.

Rest in great natural peace.
Everything is reconciled.
Remember.
Believe in God.
Have faith in faith.

Be strong in faith.
Be strong in love.
Be natural. Be strong.
Remember the teachings.
Don't worry about the teachers.

19. The Temple and the Pub

Some people go to a temple or a church, mosque or synagogue when things are not going well for them and they feel that they need some guidance or support. When people feel that something is missing from their lives, that there must be more to life, or that they just need to get away from it all, they may end up in a temple or a church, or alternatively, they may end up in the pub.

A few months ago, I decided on neither. Instead, I went to my local shaman and drank some psychedelic plant medicine called ayahuasca. Here's what happened. After my second drink, I sat down in my place in the ceremony room and felt instantly queasy. I tried to keep the medicine down, but it was impossible. So I reached for my bucket and was violently (and I mean violently!) sick. All I remember of the terrestrial world after that is putting the bucket down, and that was it. I was gone.

Where did I go? Well, it's hard to explain. Basically, I was nowhere. There was nothing. It was so nothing that it didn't even feel like nothing. After a while (I couldn't tell you how long), the words "I am immortal" came into my head (although I didn't have a head). This produced a flutter of panic in my stomach (which I also didn't have), but I managed to calm myself down by repeating to myself, "It's okay. I'm immortal. It's okay."

This went on for some time. The vista of infinite nothingness ahead of me, for all eternity, was a terrifying prospect, but I continued to self soothe, and somehow managed not to spin out completely. I knew that I was God. But it wasn't much fun. I was kind of trapped in my own immensity.

Eventually, I started to get a bit tired (not bored exactly) of this endless sameness. Then, slowly at first, I began to have visions. I was shown a procession of images representing binary opposites. I can't remember them all now, but there were hundreds (maybe).

The most obvious ones were light and dark, male and female, good and bad, left and right, up and down, all clothed in religious imagery (the male and female entities were Indian deities, for example, forms of Shiva and Shakti).

This went on for what seemed like another eternity. Then I began to feel a strange sense of discomfort in my body, although I was completely unaware of my body. I felt pain where my ribs would have been, and I felt a curious dry feeling in what would have been my mouth, which I eventually realized was thirst. I began to have visions of a pub as my mind eventually grasped the concept of "drink".

A memory of water pulled me back into the physical world as I remembered that I actually had a bottle of water next to me and might be able to actually drink it. As I slowly came round, I realized that I was lying face down on the hard wooden floor, which explained the pain in my ribs. I found my mattress and took a swig of water. It was like a magical elixir. It was amazing.

I looked around at the dimly lit room and at the other participants in the ceremony. Everything was bathed in a magical aura. I felt buoyant and light. I felt like singing. So I did.

I afterwards learned that I had been "gone" for about two hours (Earth time), and that all the things that I thought I had said in my mind I had actually said out loud, which was a bit embarrassing. All in all, it was not a particularly pleasant experience, but it did provide me with powerful insights into the underlying structure of the mind.

This is how I came to understand my experience. Firstly, the dosage was clearly too high. I was rocketed out of my body into another plane. I lost all sense of physical reality. I forgot who I was and where I was. All I knew was that I was conscious and that I was immortal and that I was God.

On reflecting on the experience in the days and weeks that followed, I was reminded of the fourteenth century mystical classic, The Cloud of Unknowing. It was as though I had been catapulted through The Cloud of Forgetting and into The Cloud of Unknowing, which is where the (anonymous) author says you will find God.

When I arrived there, I had a sense of recognition. It was like, "Oh yes! I remember! I'm God!" It was like Plato's *anamnesis*, literally "unforgetting". In my terrestrial life I had forgotten that I am actually the eternal consciousness behind all existence and now I remembered. (I had had similar transcendent experiences before on ayahuasca, so I was also obviously remembering those experiences).

But remembering God (or remembering I was God) simultaneously meant forgetting everything else. I forgot my past, my ego, my body, and everything and everyone on Earth. It was as though I had to pass through a "Cloud of Forgetting the World" before (or at the same time – it doesn't matter) entering the "Cloud of Remembering God".

After some time, however, I got the niggling feeling that I'd forgotten something, and the more tiresome infinite consciousness became, the more I wanted to remember. Eventually the unity of pure consciousness began to divide itself up into binary opposites, and I started to get glimpses of the world that I had forgotten.

When I realized that I was thirsty and started thinking about the pub, I was struck with an amazing revelation. In this (admittedly somewhat ideal) pub, the choice of drinks was infinite. They weren't binary at all. It wasn't just this or that, lager or bitter, red wine or white. There was rosé and sparkling, and an infinite variety of sweet and dry reds and whites of all sorts and vintages, from all over the world. And there was an infinite range of possible beers and ales to choose from as well, not to mention all the spirits and soft drinks. The infinite variety of possible drinks was mind-boggling.

I realized that the same is true of colour. It's not just black and white. And it's not just the primary colours or the colours of the spectrum. Colours are infinite, because there are infinite combinations and hues. The world of colour is not binary. It's infinite.

I later understood that I had experienced three layers or levels of reality in one cosmic experience, and these three levels were clearly described in Taoist philosophy. First I had merged with the "Tao". Then I had descended from the Tao into a world of opposites, "Yin and Yang". Then, finally, I had landed back in the world of the "Ten Thousand Things".

I saw how this movement between levels had also been traced by Western philosophers. It was the old dichotomy between the "One" and the "Many". But I had never quite appreciated how many the "Many" actually was. It was practically infinite!

Drinks are infinite. Colours are infinite. And so are sounds. And smells. And sensations. All the impressions of our five senses are infinite. You might live to be a ripe old centenarian, but I guarantee that you will still be able to enjoy a meal that you've never tried before in your life. And you will never exhaust the existing corpus, let alone future corpus, of art, music or literature.

So why does it all get so stale? Well, we go to the pub and we order the same beer. We go to our record collection (or Spotify) and listen to the same tracks. The infinite "Many" is too much for us. "Ten Thousand Things" is a few thousand too many. So we filter it all down, according to our own particular binary "Yin/Yang" algorithms.

But the binary world we live in, which is the world as conceived and constructed by the human mind, gets boring. We begin to develop a yearning for transcendence (some more than others). We begin to dream of the great shining Temple in the sky, where God lives, and where All is One.

Many people live their whole live dreaming of the One. It becomes a part of their life narrative, of their binary code. They dream of it, but they never reach it. They might even just give up and hope they'll get there in the afterlife (if they're good).

But some people do get there in this life. We generally call those people "mystics". But the interesting thing is that they don't just stay there in a perpetual samadhi trance-coma. They come back. And when they come back, they see the world with new eyes. It's not all binary any more. It's infinite and unique and miraculous. By forgetting the world and remembering the "One" and then forgetting the "One" and remembering the "Many", the world reveals itself in all its resplendent and infinite glory. The world is born again.

It's not really just about the Temple in Heaven. It's also about the Pub on Earth. The Mystic must come back down from the "One" and become a Shaman, and experience the "Many" directly, instead of through the filter of the "Two".

We like to think that the spiritual path is a one-way street. We seek and seek for God and then, in the final climactic scene, we find Him, and live happily ever after. Roll credits. But the reality is very different. It's not so much a linear path as a cycle of remembering and forgetting. We forget the world and remember God; we forget God and remember the world. Each cycle counts as another life, because each time, you are born again. If you move through the cycle often enough, you might even find what the Taoist Masters found: immortality.

20. Remembering and Forgetting

In the last chapter I described an intense ayahuasca experience in which I lost all sense of myself and the world. I suppose you could say that I died and went to heaven. Except that heaven wasn't the particularly blissful or even pleasant place one would expect it to be. And it was severely under populated. In fact there was only one thing in it - me. And then again, not even me, because there was no awareness of "me" to speak of. There was just consciousness, with barely two thoughts to rub together: "I am immortal" and "I am God".

I wouldn't say it was a particularly enviable position to be in; in fact it was verging on the nightmarish. I knew that I would never die, that I would go on and on and on forever, "world without end". And that was a terrifying prospect. I remember realizing with horror, at the age of seven or so, that one day I would die and just cease to be. The realization, forty or so years later, that I wouldn't, was equally horrifying.

I felt the unbearable persistence of being. But, luckily for me, I soon forgot all about it. I forgot that I was God and that I was immortal. I started to think about other things instead, and it was as though I had descended into another plane of existence, outside this silent "cloud of unknowing" I had been suspended in for an unspecified eternity.

This was the plane of binary opposites. But it wasn't just opposites. It was basically a realm of abstractions, represented as much in images as in words, many of which I experienced as arising with their opposites attached, so to speak. Or rather, with their opposites arising out of them.

At first, I was just a passive spectator. I was being shown all these images, one after the other, each illustrating an abstracted aspect of reality. The male/female polarity loomed quite large in this display, but there were many other elements of the human condition as well, such as youth and age, life and death.

Then I could reason again, and think about the things being shown to me. And that's how I reasoned my way back to the particulars of the physical world and the real bottle of water by my side. Eventually, I "woke up" and "re-membered" the world.

I described some of my thinking about pubs and temples in the last chapter. It was all very abstract, "temple" in the abstract, and "pub" in the abstract (although, having said that, I did picture a particular pub in Tottenham near the river Lea). I thought about "drink" in the abstract and "people" in the abstract. I understood that the pub was the place where you found drinks and people. That was the basic definition of "pub".

Not a genius realization, I know. But for me, it was a revelation. The people you can meet in a pub and the conversations you can have, are basically infinite, and so are the drinks you can drink. The "pub" symbolized something like infinite experience, whereas the "temple" represented unity.

My reasoning went a bit like this. I thought about the general category of "drink", and then broke it down into the sub-categories of beer, wine, spirits, fruit juice and cordials. Then I broke those down further into lagers, bitters, stouts, ales, wheat beers, red and white wine, and so on.

It was like tracing the branches of a family tree. And I realized that the final tips of the smallest twigs were infinite in number and that they were growing all the time. New craft beers with new flavours were being created all over the world every day. So that the potential sensory taste experiences of "my" consciousness are, to all intents and purposes, infinite. And that's just beer.

The infinite variety of sense experience is infinite. But they are meaningless if we can't relate them to some abstract idea. This is why, as T.S. Eliot said, "humankind cannot bear very much reality". We can only bear as much reality as we can understand, as is meaningful.

So the world of the "Many" does not and cannot exist for us completely divorced from our maps of it. We may like to think that we can be completely Zen all the time with no mind mediating and interfacing our direct experience of the world. But that's just a naïve fantasy. Zen Masters know it's not really like that.

All sense perceptions must be attached to the family tree of our mental categories for them to be meaningful. Which isn't to say that we can't experience the "Many" relatively free of these attachments, just as we can experience the "One" relatively free of them at the other end. The shaman achieves the former, and the mystic achieves the latter. But pure sense experience is as impossible for human beings as pure consciousness, except, perhaps, very fleetingly.

Plato was right. There is a world of Forms up there (or "in here" – does it matter?) There is the Form of "beer" and the Form of "wine" and the Form of "glass", of which all particular beers and wines and glasses are concrete expressions in the concrete world.

The world of Forms is the realm of Archetypes. "Ideas" or "Forms" or "Archetypes" are really different words for the same thing. As they interact together, they create associations and family trees and maps and stories. They create what Jordan Peterson calls "Maps of Meaning". They create the myths we live by.

What is the Platonic Form of the people in the pub then? Well, just like with the drinks, there are categories of Archetypes floating around up there, and we experience individuals as embodiments of one or more of those Archetypes.

And what about the Archetype for human beings as such? Or the Ideal human Archetype? Peterson would say Christ. If you asked someone in Asia, they would probably say Buddha or Krishna. The fact that they are all men is a bit problematic, and is obviously the result of male dominated religions. In my ayahuasca visions, they did appear strangely androgynous, which is interesting.

In any case, it seems that when we forget the One, we forget the Many, and end up living almost exclusively in a world of ideas, an intermediate world of sense making. We mistake the maps of meaning for the territory. We forget about the trunk of the tree, rooted in Heaven, and we forget the tips of the branches, flowering in the five senses down here on Earth. We spend nearly all our time, like the proverbial monkey mind, swinging endlessly from branch to branch of the cosmic tree.

If you are tired of swinging, and yearn for the One and the Many, and long to return to the Source and taste the fruits of Existence, then the only thing for it is to do what Mohammed suggested, and "die before ye die", or, a little less poetically perhaps, "inhibit your default mode network".

21. Three, Two, One: Heaven, Earth, Hell

In the first two chapters of Book One, I describe my experience of three completely separate realities, approximating Heaven, Hell and Earth. The first chapter is about a *satori* or enlightenment experience I had by the river Isis in Oxford on LSD. For the few hours I was in this alternate state, I felt like I was in the "Pure Land". The second chapter describes a bad trip I had a couple of years previous at a drug-fuelled all-night rave in Wales, in which it seemed to me throughout the night that I was descending the rings of Hell.

The morning after my heavenly river experience, I was disappointed (to put it mildly) to find that I had come back down to Earth. I felt like Adam must have felt on being expelled from paradise. Apart from a splitting headache, everything was just as it was before. The morning after my hellish Welsh bad trip/psychotic episode, I also came back to Earth with a splitting headache, but I was so relieved to be alive and (relatively) sane that I didn't care.

A superficial reading of this tale of youthful folly is that the ingestion of certain psychoactive compounds altered the chemistry of my brain resulting in two distorted versions of reality. In this reading, my ordinary "Earth" experience (including the headache) was really real and both the non-ordinary "Heaven" and "Hell" worlds I stepped (and danced) into were unreal hallucinations. But maybe it's not as simple as that.

My enlightenment experience had all the classic hallmarks of mystical experiences described the world over. The LSD may have been the catalyst in my case, but since many people have had the same or similar experiences without taking drugs (myself included), we can put the drugs to one side for the sake of the argument.

So forget the LSD. What we're really talking about is unitive mystical experience. What is this state like? Well, there are several salient features, non-duality, ineffability and a sense of timelessness among others. But perhaps the simplest way to describe it is in the words of Mechthild of Magdeburg:

"The day of my spiritual awakening was the day I saw and knew I saw all things in God and God in all things."[103]

This is not your ordinary common-or-garden supernatural theism. It is an expression of "panentheism": God both immanent and transcendent in creation. Although this is a profoundly nondual experience with no clear demarcations between subject and object, self and other ("All is One"), it is ultimately a Trinitarian vision. If it were monistic, if it was one "thing" called "God" in all directions for all time, it would be static and uniform with no dynamic relations. It would be infinitely boring (maybe something like my experience in the Temple above). But nondual enlightenment is far from boring.

Let's unpack this using some famous Trinities. In Kashmir Shaivism, the basic trinity at the heart of enlightened consciousness is *Parashiva, Shiva, Shakti*. In Taoism, it is *Tao, Yin, Yang*. In Advaita Vedanta it is *Sat, Chitta, Ananda* (Being, Consciousness, Bliss). In Christianity it is Father, Son and Holy Spirit.

"God the Father" is *Parashiva*, *Tao* or *Sat* (Being). This is the transcendent Godhead which sustains the whole of creation. It is the God Mechthild was referring to when she said "all things in God".

"God the Son" is *Shiva*, *Yang* or *Chitta* (Consciousness). This is the immanent divinity present throughout creation, akin to the *Logos* of the Ancient Greeks and Stoics or the "ubiquitous sentience" of modern-day panpsychists. It is the God Mechthild meant when she said "God in all things".

"God the Spirit" is *Shakti*, *Yin* or *Ananda* (Bliss). This is the energy which we experience as existence or "matter". Ultimately, matter is an abstraction without any real substance beyond the qualities that make up our perception of it, as George Berkeley (perfectly adequately and convincingly in my opinion) demonstrated. According to quantum physics, there is no such thing as "matter"; there are just interacting fields of energy. Mechthild's "things" in the above quote are also part of God, also made of "God-stuff", if you will. They are the play of Shakti energy - the whole creation is experienced as a blissful expression of Spirit.

Anyway, that's how reality appears when you are in "Heaven". What about here on Earth? Well, Earthlings going about their business, whatever their professed beliefs, act AS IF reality was composed of two fundamental elements: Mind and Cosmos or Consciousness and Form. Earth people are basically Substance Dualists like René Descartes. You can divide it up however you like: Mind/Brain, Mind/Body, Mind/Matter, but the basic split is the same.

This version of reality works fairly well. We can experience things "out there" in the world like trees and stones and cats and other people, but we can also experience things "in here" like thoughts and feelings, music and dreams. Sometimes we're "out there" and sometimes we're "in here". Sometimes we can flit quickly between the two, for example when we're talking to someone. It's a little bit schizoid sometimes, but it's okay.

Instead of the three dynamic elements of the Trinitarian vision of reality, we have only two elements in the Dualistic vision. We've lost one. Which one? Well, we experience the world simply as the duality between *Shiva* and *Shakti*, *Yin* and *Yang*, *Chitta* and *Ananda*. So we've lost the transcendent element, *Parashiva*, *Tao*, or *Sat*. We've lost God the Father.

In the West, this loss was made philosophically explicit through the gradual demotion of God the Father in three steps through the seventeenth and eighteenth centuries, from the active God of classical theism to the absent God of deism and finally to the non-existent God of atheism. All that was left was God the Son as "Soul" or "Mind" and God the Spirit as "Nature". Enter the Romantics.

The Romantics were basically pantheists. They believed in the interpenetration of Soul and Nature. They believed in the immanent God but felt they had no need for the transcendent one. Their main worry though, was what might happen if the Enlightenment philosophy underpinning the Scientific Revolution should continue further down the materialist path it seemed to be treading.

Galileo had intentionally split the objective world from the subjective world in order that science could focus exclusively on concrete phenomena. This was a good move. It is what made science so powerful.

But Galileo himself had no illusions about the limits of the new natural sciences. They were designed only for one side of the subject/object divide and had nothing to say about the other side. What if this useful dualism was collapsed into monism though? What if the Soul of the World was taken out as well?

The meteoric rise of the natural sciences led people to suspect that if God the designer was an unnecessary fiction, then maybe the "ghost in the machine" doesn't exist either. Maybe it's just machine all the way down. It could be that what we experienced as Soul or Mind was actually an illusion produced by lots of little machines. The invention and development of ever more powerful microscopes certainly seemed to suggest that. Look at all those little invisible things we're made up of! They may be little, but they're still *things*. Telescopes revealed a universe of massive celestial bodies which moved with clockwork precision, like a machine. What if Reality is actually made up of machines within machines? This is what the Romantics were afraid of. No wonder William Blake had nightmarish visions of "dark satanic mills".

Thus was born the dominant modern worldview of scientific materialism. There is no such thing as Mind or Soul. There is only Matter. That worldview is fine for the scientist busy in his lab, but when he goes home, he falls back into the ordinary dualistic view. He doesn't treat his wife and kids like machines. He may deep down believe that his own experiences and those of his family are just an illusory product of material processes, but he acts as if they were real. If he didn't, he would go mad. He would wind up in Hell.

Scientific materialism reduces the duality of Mind and Cosmos to the monism of only one thing, Cosmos. Mind is thrown out and we are left with a purely material universe. The philosophers called it "ontological reductionism". Everything is understood as a manifestation of one basic substance, called "Matter", or failing that (strictly speaking there is no such thing), "Energy".

So now with naturalism, not only have we lost God the Father, we have also lost God the Son. There is no more Soul, no more *Shiva*, no more *Chitta*. There is no room for any Consciousness at all in this materialistic, mechanistic vision of Reality. All that is left is the intricate, complex play of energy, *Shakti*.

She is not experienced as Bliss (*Ananda*) any more, however. Divorced from *Shiva*, her eternal lover, *Shakti* loses all sense of meaning, and eventually becomes a source of pain and despair, showing her other face, the face of *Kali*.

The Hell of paranoid schizophrenics is often experienced as a soulless world of machines. Hell is not other people, as Sartre supposed; Hell is other machines. Now, if you were a denizen of Hell and I asked you about the nature of Reality, you would tell me that it is all just infinite forms of Matter or Energy, nothing else. I wouldn't be able to convince you otherwise, because you would be right. But you would only be right about Hell.

If you were an Earth dweller, based on your own experience you would give me a dualistic description of some sort, even if you professed belief in God and followed a religion. Whether you think Reality is best understood as Mind and Cosmos, Soul and Body or God and Creation makes no difference. It's the same duality. Again, you would be right. But you would only be right about Earth.

(From a neurological point of view, we could say that Earth people have a good working relationship between the two hemispheres of the brain, whereas people in Hell live only in the left hemisphere. People living in Heaven have access to both hemispheres but also enjoy a higher integration of the two.)

If I asked an enlightened person in the Christian tradition, they would explain that Reality is an eternal dance between the three persons of the Trinity: Father, Son and Holy Spirit. If I asked a Taoist Master, they would tell me about the cycle of Yin and Yang within the unity of the Tao. If I asked a Kashmir Shaivism guru, they would tell me about the love affair between Shiva and Shakti in the bosom of Parashiva. If I asked a Self-Realised Hindu rishi, they would tell me all about Sat-Chit-Ananda.

And they would all be right. But here's the thing: would they only be right about Heaven?

22. How to Make Hell on Earth

Heaven and Hell (and Earth for that matter) are just states of mind. Three people sitting on the same bench in a park can be living in three different worlds. As I described in the last chapter, you are in Heaven when you experience the world as trinitarian, in Earth when you experience it as dualistic and you're in Hell when you experience it as monistic.

The Kashmiri Shaiva doctrine of *Parashiva, Shiva, Shakti* I think expresses the trinitarian idea most clearly. Shakti is energy. It is also the whole manifest universe, which is basically energy expressed in a bewildering variety of forms. Shiva is consciousness. It is that which experiences form. So Shiva and Shakti always go together. Any phenomenon presupposes a conscious mind experiencing it. Wherever there is Shakti, there also is Shiva. Try it out for yourself. Can you experience Shakti without Shiva? It's obviously impossible.

However, it is possible to withdraw Shiva from Shakti. You can sit down, close your eyes and clear your mind, withdrawing your awareness as much as possible from all objects of consciousness. Even better, you can lie in a floatation tank, and enjoy almost perfect sensory deprivation. It's like floating in the infinite void. Then you can withdraw from all bodily sensations, thoughts and feelings. If you are lucky, or if you are an experienced meditator, you will eventually enter a state of absorption in pure consciousness, called *Samadhi*.

Spend long enough in Samadhi and you will realise that your consciousness is co-extensive with a greater, universal consciousness. You will touch the pure transcendent consciousness, "Parashiva". Shiva depends on Shakti just as Shakti depends on Shiva, but Parashiva doesn't depend on anything. It is the Absolute. In deep meditation, you realise the identity of Shiva with Parashiva (*Atman* with *Paramātman* or the Soul with God).

When you return from this state of pure consciousness, you return to Shakti. Shiva and Shakti are re-united in a joyful, loving embrace. This is why they are depicted as lovers. Just like mortal lovers, so with the archetypal lovers of creation: absence makes the heart grow fonder.

Shakti shines with a greater radiance and a greater beauty. The world is renewed, made fresh, born again. This is the elixir of life. It is how creation achieves immortality - through the eternal cycle of the trinity.

Earth beings are mortal because they do not or cannot access pure consciousness, Parashiva. They live in the dualistic world of Shiva and Shakti, not in the close embrace they enjoy in the non-dual trinitarian vision, but apart, like a slightly estranged couple. If we think of it as a marriage, over time the partners get a bit bored of each other and become more like companions than lovers. Then, at the tail end of their relationship, they grow old and die alone.

Earth is not a bad place to live. There is no God and there is no immortality, but life is definitely worth living. There are good times as well as bad. There is joy and wonder and beauty. There is art and music and magic. There is pleasure as well as pain. There is romance as well as estrangement. This is the world celebrated by the Romantics, who passionately urge us to love Shakti with all our Souls.

But there are dark, sinister forces at play in our little corner of the universe, which the Romantics vainly struggled against. These are the forces bent on making Hell on Earth. They are determined to tear the Soul out of the World. They are determined to banish Shiva from the world forever, leaving Shakti alone and bereft.

I mentioned the ascendant ideology called "scientific materialism" in the last chapter. Since the dawn of the modern period, with the great advances in science and technology ushered in by the Scientific Revolution in the seventeenth century, scientific materialism has taken over the hearts and minds of people in the West and all over the world. There is no God. But more than that, there is no Soul. There is nothing but material processes. Nothing but energy. Nothing but quantum oscillations in the void.

This is the first horseman of the apocalypse. The second horseman is a product of the first. Because scientism (the belief that the whole Reality is ultimately explicable by the natural sciences and reducible to material processes) directly challenges religion, religion must fight back.

So religion fights back. But in doing so, it incorporates the scientistic paradigm. It treats religion as a science instead of an art. Nuanced interpretations of scripture just don't seem resilient enough to deal with the powerful threat posed by materialist science. We must fight fire with fire!

The second horseman is therefore religious fundamentalism. It is the literal interpretation of ancient texts in a desperate scramble for certainty and safety in the face of the oncoming charge of the terrible horseman of science. The first two horsemen of the apocalypse are locked in a demonic embrace, each strengthening the other while pretending that they are enemies. They are like two heads if one Beast with long necks intertwined.

The third and fourth horsemen are also intertwined. The third has many variants and goes by many names. The most easily recognisable umbrella term for it, is "postmodernism". Like the first two horsemen, it rips the Soul out of reality by reducing everything to an inter-texual relativistic world of pure Shakti. There is only the play of Shakti endlessly and narcissistically pointing at itself. In literary theory the "death of the author" basically stands for the "death of the soul". There is no intentional mind behind the surface appearances of the text, and there is nothing outside the text. Shiva is banished to the dustbin of philosophy.

The fourth horseman comes to re-create the world as a perfect utopia where all individual Souls are subjugated under the iron rule of the collective will. Where the third horseman tries to dissolve the Soul in the acid of deconstruction, the fourth horseman tries to stamp it out with the boot of totalitarianism. Like the first two horsemen, who pretend to be enemies, but are in fact in league together, so the two sworn enemies, fascism and communism, are actually two versions of the same thing.

23. Training and Enlightenment

Virtue Ethics is about becoming virtuous by behaving virtuously; establishing Good Habits is about habituation; Zen Training is about training; Spiritual Practice is about practice.

Overcoming bad habits and nurturing good ones doesn't happen overnight - it takes time and effort. But it does get easier. At a certain point you begin to notice the influence of what Rupert Sheldrake calls "morphic resonance". Patterns of thought and behaviour which resonate with established patterns, whether individual or collective, come more readily and naturally. Which is why it's much easier to meditate or do yoga in a group, and why it's easier to be good if you keep good company.

Treating the world as nothing but meaningless aggregates of Matter is a bad habit. Whether you agree with them or not, reading sacred scriptures literally is a bad habit. Relativizing everything is a bad habit. Politicizing everything is a bad habit. These four bad habits are easy to maintain because they resonate with established bad habits in the culture, as a result of the tireless work of the four horsemen (see above).

These are four examples of bad habits of thought. It's what makes us think and act like muppets. But there are also bad ego habits, which make us behave like muggles. Our self-image and sense of identity is limited and distorted. We are like Lion Kings who think we are warthogs.

There are bad habits of will and appetite. When the will is compromised we become lazy, apathetic and weak. We start to see ourselves as victims. We are easily disheartened and depressed, and may develop chronic anxiety disorders. When we surrender to every passing desire, we allow our natural appetites to dominate us and develop unhealthy addictions. We become addicts addicted to bad habits, bingeing on everything from coffee and chocolate biscuits to pop music and porn.

The four positive archetypes, Warrior, Monk, Philosopher and King represent the opposite forces, good habits that can potentially overcome the bad ones. We can train ourselves to be warriors instead of victims, monks (and nuns) instead of addicts, philosophers instead of muppets and kings (and queens) instead of muggles.

Alignment Meditation requires practice, training and intention. It's not "positive thinking", although it is a form of "positive psychology". We try to avoid and refrain from acting out and feeding bad habits, but we also try to cultivate good ones. What distinguishes it from ordinary types of moral or psychological developmental systems, however, is the training in mysticism and shamanism.

What is mysticism? Simply stated, it is the practice of retreating from the world. This is why retreats are called retreats. What this actually means is that your consciousness retreats from the objects of consciousness, or in the mystical language of Kashmir Shaivism, Shiva withdraws from Shakti. This retreat or withdrawal of consciousness is the essence of meditation. It leads to a state of quiet meditative absorption, SAMADHI.

Consciousness without an object is called Parashiva. It is absolute, universal consciousness. Wherever there is Shiva there must also be Shakti. But where there is no Shakti, there is only universal consciousness, Parashiva.

To be a mystic is to practice merging Shiva in Parashiva, like a drop of water in the ocean. It is done through forgetting and unknowing. To remember God, you must first forget yourself. You must enter a Cloud of Forgetting and then a Cloud of Unknowing. In the Alignment Meditation system, the mystic archetype represents the union or communion of the Soul with God, Shiva with Parashiva.

This is not the end of the story - it's just the beginning. Mysticism opens the way to shamanism (as well as vice versa). Because Shiva has retreated into Parashiva, Shakti is left to her own devices. Not completely of course, because where there is Shakti there is Shiva, but relatively. It is as though Shiva has fallen sleep, allowing Shakti to wake up her dormant powers.

Broadly speaking, for present purposes, let's say Shiva is the mind and Shakti is the body. When the mind withdraws from the body the body "wakes up". A kind of intuitive body intelligence takes over. To a casual observer, this can look as though the person is possessed by a demonic spirit, as some Christian missionaries believed when they saw the ecstatic dances of African shamans. The body moves spontaneously in accord with some mysterious impulse. It shakes and moves in extraordinary ways. The shaman may make strange sounds or start speaking in tongues.

Of course these unusual (to us) phenomena are not the result of completely involuntary and unconscious processes. Shiva is not completely asleep. We are not witnessing the ravings of a madman or the strange contortions of a zombie. In altered shamanic states, there is always a subtle consciousness and will guiding and responding to the promptings of the body. There is still the dance of Shiva and Shakti, but on another, subtler level. The shaman is the one who has mastered the dance. Hence the expression "the dead can dance". When the mind is "dead", the body can dance.

Mystical and shamanic practices connect us to Parashiva and Shakti respectively. As the mind withdraws from the body and consciousness from the mind, Shiva realises his essential nature as Parashiva. As the body is released from the controlling mind, it connects with the deep well-springs of its life energy and Shakti realises her intrinsic nature. We don't call this state "Parashakti", because she is not transcendent. She is still dependent on Shiva for her existence. Nevertheless, the Shaman experiences Shakti in all her fullness and glory.

Again, this is not the end of the story. Once we have experienced Shiva and Shakti in their pure forms, they can be re-united refreshed and invigorated. Absence makes the heart grow stronger.

When Shiva and Shakti are re-united after being separated, they will not let their restored lover out of their sights. They will not forget each other. This is what is meant by *Self Remembering*. Self Remembering is the simple practice of holding in awareness simultaneously both the object of awareness and the subject of awareness. You are aware of something, such as the words in front of you, but at the same time you are aware that you are aware.

Mindfulness is really just another word for Self Remembering. In both cases, you are simultaneously aware of your consciousness, Shiva ("mind" or "self") and the contents of your consciousness, Shakti (the "world"). Normally we are identified with the objects of our experience - we are in a "world trance". But with the separation of Shiva and Shakti, we can experience them both at the same time, and we feel awake, alert and alive.

Now we are in a much better position to cultivate the character strengths represented by the four archetypes, Warrior, Monk, Philosopher, King. We can mindfully act in accordance with the Warrior virtues and train the will. We can mindfully act in accordance with the moral virtues of temperance and self-restraint represented by the Monk and train our appetite. We can mindfully think in accordance with the intellectual virtues of the Philosopher and train ourselves in the right use of reason. We can mindfully comport ourselves with the sovereign dignity and authority of a King or Queen and train ourselves in authentic assertiveness and ego strength.

Each of these four (good will, good desire, good reason and good ego) find their expression through the skilful and loving dance between Shiva and Shakti. The will of the Warrior is not just a strong will, but also a skilful will and a loving will. The same is also true of the appetite, reason and ego. They follow hidden intuitive promptings rather than explicit rules. The cultivation of good character is an art not a science.

24. Pachananda

If you don't believe in God or Nirvana, it's highly unlikely that you will spend much time praying or meditating. There is no reason to retreat from the world in order to commune with nothing. It's just a waste of time and effort.

If you do believe, you will be much more likely to turn you attention to the transcendent beyond. As C.S. Lewis put it, "If I find in myself a desire which no experience in this world can satisfy, the most probable explanation is that I was made for another world."[104] Your longing for this other world will lead you to pray and meditate.

In the last few chapters I have been exploring the trinitarian doctrine of Kashmir Shaivism, which consists of *Parashiva*, *Shiva* and *Shakti*. Parashiva is the transcendent God (God the Father in the Christian trinity), Shiva is immanent consciousness (the Logos or the Son) and Shakti is the manifest energy of existence (the Holy Spirit). I described how meditation (and prayer) involves the gradual withdrawal of consciousness from all objects of consciousness, which can be understood as the withdrawal of Shiva from Shakti.

Without this intentional process of separating consciousness and form, there is such a fusion of awareness with the objects of awareness, that Shiva and Shakti cannot be distinguished. So the world and the self are experienced as an undifferentiated field of action. It's all just stuff: things and thoughts, feelings and events. It's just "one damn thing after another".

Whether you are theoretically a monist or a dualist, that is, whether you believe that minds are reducible to physical processes or not, you will experience the world in a similar way, as a collection of stuff and experience. That's if you live on "Earth". If you live in "Hell", everything will be tinged with the implacable malevolence of the Great Machine, but we don't need to concern ourselves with that right now.

So what happens when you pray to God or meditate on Nirvana? Your individual consciousness withdraws and merges in absolute, universal consciousness. Shiva merges in Parashiva. What happens when you return? You come back "trailing clouds of glory". You retain something of the experience of pure consciousness and develop a taste for it.

The more often you pray or meditate, the more often you "commune with God", the stronger this sense of pure individual consciousness becomes, the stronger your Soul becomes. Shiva emerges from Parashiva. This is how God makes Souls.

Eventually your life becomes suffused with Soul. You become simultaneously aware of experiences and aware of your awareness of experiences and develop a capacity for Self Remembering or Mindfulness. Wherever you go, wherever you turn, you see both Shiva and Shakti, consciousness and form. This is what I call Pachananda, the "Bliss of the Earth". This is the Pure Land, the Kingdom of Heaven.

25. Jacob's Ladder

"Then he dreamed, and behold, a ladder was set up on the earth, and its top reached to heaven; and there the angels of God were ascending and descending on it."[105]

What or who are the "angels of God"? They seem to be some kind of intermediaries between Heaven and Earth, God and Humanity. Are they messengers? Are they couriers? Do they bring things down to Earth from Heaven and take stuff back up again? They are continuously ascending and descending, as if they were on a conveyor belt. If Jacob had lived in the twenty-first century would he perhaps have had visions of an escalator instead of a ladder?

The angels create a connection between Heaven and Earth, a bridge to the stars. Where the connection was once broken, where the way to transcendence was severed, the angels can re-connect us. Interestingly, the etymological root of the word "religion" has precisely that connotation: *re-ligare* means to "re-bind" or "re-connect" (the word "ligament" comes from the same Latin root).

Jacob's ladder is like a ligament connecting Heaven and Earth. If it was in a brain, it would be a synaptic connection between two neuronal networks. In any case, it is a tenuous pathway between two different worlds, the "earthly" and the "heavenly".

So what is this ladder or pathway composed of? Well, in one word, religion. Religion is a very broad term encompassing beliefs and doctrines but also poetry, music, art, theology, philosophy and even science. But what is it? Where does it come from? A religious person would say it comes from God. It is the Word of God. Perhaps. But who actually speaks the Word? Who tells the stories and writes the poetry? Who sings the songs, plays the music, paints the paintings and icons, builds the cathedrals and expounds the metaphysics?

Us. But not any old us. Religion is the creation of human beings, but it is the particular creation of those human beings who have themselves ascended to Heaven, who have transcended the ordinary, mundane plane of existence.

And they don't come back empty handed. They bring gifts and souvenirs from their travels. And these gifts, whether in the form of words, images, sounds, gestures, actions, these are the "angels of God". This is what we experience as "religion" in the broadest sense.

There are basically two types of art: art that comes from "Heaven" and art that comes from the human will, from "Earth". The first type is generally called "sacred art" and the second is "secular art". The same is true of philosophy, music, dance, and all the human arts. The same is also true, in a more restricted sense, of what we call "science". There is such a thing as "sacred science", although we are much more familiar with the earth-bound secular variety.

The tragic predicament of modern people is that not only have we lost our belief in God, we have also lost our belief in religion and art. However many angels descend from Heaven, we are unable to ascend with them unless we actually believe in them. We have lost the "eyes to see" and the "ears to hear".

Do you believe in Bach? If you believe, you will allow his music to escort you on angelic wings to the highest Heaven. You will ascend the ladder on an "angel of God". If you don't believe, you will stay exactly where you are, cynical and bored. Do you believe in the transcendent power of the Catholic Mass and the transformative power of Holy Communion? If you do, it will lift you up to God. If not, it won't.

If you believe in the thing that sacred art and religion are pointing to, then you will believe in art and religion. If you believe in God you will believe in the angels of God. This means that you will make a conscious, intentional effort to put yourself in an open, receptive state of mind. You will allow yourself to be vulnerable. You will surrender. You will be humble, passive, willing. And the angels will carry you.

Then, if you continue to allow yourself to be carried, ascending and descending with the angels, you may even find that you eventually become an angel yourself, bringing gifts of great joy and splendour from God to His people on Earth. But you would do well to remember Chesterton's words of caution: "Angels can fly because they take themselves lightly."[106]

26. The God of the Living

Imagine you have access to an electron microscope. You train it on the tip of your little finger. As you increase the magnification, you see the skin cells, the cell membrane, the mitochondria, the nucleus, the proteins and peptides, perhaps actual atoms. You zoom in through the realms of biology, chemistry and physics, apparently passing from the animate to the inanimate, from the living to the dead.

Now imagine that next to the electron microscope is a telescope. You look through the aperture and zoom out into the immensity of space, past the moon, past Mars, Jupiter and Saturn, out into the Milky Way and beyond. It looks awesome, but you know deep down that it's all just an immense wasteland of cold rocks and burning stars pointlessly spinning through the infinite void.

Between the microscope and the telescope, you find yourself precariously balanced between two infinities, a sliver of conscious life between two immensities of unconsciousness. Perhaps this is what Prospero meant when he said, "We are the stuff as dreams are made on, and our little life is rounded by a sleep"[107]. Bounded by inanimate matter on all sides, we are like a tiny bubble of life floating on an infinite sea of death.

But what if you were to look through a panpsychist lens? Then you would see not an endless expanse of inanimate matter, but worlds within worlds of infinite consciousness. Then you would no longer be an anomaly, a weird aberration, a strange exception to the rule of universal death and nothingness. You would be a living part of a living universe, and your God would be "not the God of the dead, but the God of the living."[108]

27. Infinite Matter or Infinite Consciousness?

Few people are convinced by rational arguments for or against the existence of God. Atheists assume that the burden of proof is on the believers: "You say there is a God - prove it!", but of course they can't. It is impossible to prove the existence of God beyond all reasonable doubt the way you might prove a scientific theory, because God clearly does not exist in the way material objects exist. But neither can atheists prove that there is no God.

However, there is no reason why the burden of proof should be on the theists. Human beings have lived for millennia with an explicit or implicit belief in the existence of God or some kind of spiritual dimension to life. For most people throughout history, this has been an integral part of their experience of the world. Only fairly recently has atheism seriously challenged this worldview. For believers the existence of God is self-evident and is not in need of external proof, so for them the burden of proof is on the atheist.

In the absence of incontrovertible proofs either way, we have to make do with arguments based on plausibility and probability (if we limit ourselves to rational arguments about the existence of the material universe that is). Which is more likely, given what we know about the universe, a purely contingent, naturalistic universe or one dependent for its existence on something beyond the natural order, ie. "God"?

I won't go into all the details here, but the problems a naturalistic explanation of the universe must overcome include some seemingly intractable ones. In short order: 1. The origin of the universe. How can something come out of nothing? 2. The fine-tuning of the universe. Why are all the physical constants in the universe so perfectly "fine-tuned" for life? 3. The origin of life. How can organic cellular life spontaneously arise in a pre-biotic environment? 4. The hard problem of consciousness. What is consciousness and how can it be created from non-conscious elements?

5. The problem of reliable rationality and value. How can human minds apprehend truth, goodness and beauty? How can we make any claims at all about the nature of reality if our brains are merely the products of natural selection and random mutations? 6. The phenomenology of spiritual experience. Is it reasonable to discount the accounts of millions of people in all times and places who claim to have direct apprehensions of divinity? Particularly if this correlates with positive affect and positive behaviours like compassion and altruism?

Scientists and mathematicians have calculated the probability of the fine-tuning of the universe and the emergence of life on Earth through physical processes and chance alone. The numbers they have come up with are mind-bogglingly small, small enough to qualify as "basically impossible". For example, the probability that the universe expanded at just the right rate at the Big Bang for life to be possible is estimated at 1 in 10 to the power of 55 (ie. 10 followed by 55 zeros). The only way to account for this infinite improbability is to postulate an infinite number of universes. The one universe (lucky us!) that is capable of supporting life would then be statistically possible. But of course there is no scientific evidence for a near infinity of universes.

Materialists, in order to preserve their materialist worldview, must posit an infinite multi-verse. What they have done is to make a god out of Matter, by making Matter infinite.

To all intents and purposes, here on Earth we live according to a basically dualistic understanding of reality: Matter and Mind, Form and Consciousness, Body and Soul. We might not fully understand how these two different realms interact, but we act as if they are real. It is a working and workable hypothesis, which we unconsciously take for granted in our day-to-day lives. The theist explanation of reality as a whole takes one side of the duality (mind or consciousness) and raises it to infinity. This is what is generally meant by the word "God" - infinite Consciousness. In philosophy, this is called Idealism, which is basically the opposite of Materialism.

For transcendental Idealists and theists, both the form and consciousness of all individual sentient beings are contained within a larger sea of consciousness.

In Kashmir Shaivism, this is expressed as the triune God, *Parashiva, Shiva, Shakti*. Parashiva is the transcendent God (infinite consciousness), Shiva is the embodied consciousness (soul) and Shakti is the manifest form (matter/energy).

The only way to prevent the atheist worldview from collapsing under the weight of infinite improbability is to assume an infinity of universes, in other words, infinite matter. So atheism has its own trinity which rivals the theist one. Instead of infinite consciousness, we have infinite matter. We can also express the atheist Materialist trinity in terms borrowed from Shaivism, as "Parashakti", "Shakti", "Shiva", with Shiva (soul or local consciousness) demoted to the status of epiphenomenon.

We cannot prove either hypothesis. But which seems more plausible? Which is easier to imagine and contemplate? Infinite consciousness or infinite matter? When we do imagine and contemplate, we are of course experiencing states of consciousness, not matter. As we reach beyond ourselves in the attempt to understand, we may even forget about our bodies and our surroundings, so that as we introspect and meditate on the ultimate nature of reality, we naturally move towards an experience or intimation of infinite consciousness, not infinite matter. On the other hand, it is perfectly possible to imagine that everything, including consciousness and imagination, is the product of material processes.

However, it seems that our "intrinsic nature" is in fact consciousness, as Bertrand Russel and Arthur Eddington argued. It is the subjective first-person experience of being. So we naturally feel at home in consciousness (some more than others of course). And it is difficult to draw a boundary around consciousness, since it is not a physical object and doesn't have any spatial qualities. Therefore the idea of *infinite* consciousness is not really that much of a leap.

It is possible to imagine an infinite expanse of space containing infinite matter, but this is a counter-intuitive, unnatural thought, since matter is defined by physical limits. Something can be very big, but it can't be infinitely big. Infinite matter seems like a logical contradiction. It also doesn't feel like home. It is difficult to imagine feeling at home as physical organisms in an infinitely extended physical universe, the way we feel at home as conscious beings held in infinite consciousness.

The materialist would have to concede that there is no meaning or purpose in the existence of his multi-verse. There just happens to be infinite and eternal stuff lying around for no particular reason. If one asks "how?" or "why?" all he can do is shrug his shoulders and say, "It just is".

The theist also has to accept that the ultimate nature of reality is shrouded in mystery. Infinite consciousness is by definition beyond the limits of our finite minds. But it is a more optimistic mystery. Beyond the limits of our knowledge, and even beyond the limits of our brief lives, there is not the eternal darkness and death of infinite matter but eternal life, light and consciousness.

28. Bad Science, Bad Religion, Bad Philosophy and Bad Politics

Reality comes in many shapes and sizes. But how can we know what's "really real"? Is that even possible? Science holds out the promise that behind all the illusory appearances of human social constructs there is the "really real" reality described by physics and mathematics. If we can only unflinchingly peel away the surface appearances, we will transcend our human illusions and live on the firm foundations of hard science alone.

Then what? Then nothing. Either we'll have to socially construct a whole new set of appearances or we'll fall into a pit of meaninglessness. We live in a world of appearances. And we can't live without them. The attempt to reduce the complex tissue of our social fabric to a few scientific "facts" is not science. It's pseudo-science. It's science overstepping its bounds.

There is science which is bad because it's wrong. The methodology is faulty. Then there is science which is bad because it isn't really science. Freudian psychoanalysis is pseudo-science. It is psychological speculation dressed up as science. Phrenology is pseudo-science. Eugenics is pseudo-science. Marxist economic theory is pseudo-science. Evolutionary psychology is pseudo-science.

The natural sciences have nothing to say about anything beyond the carefully delimited sphere of material processes and observable behaviour. Philip Goff has pointed out that the success of science rests on the bracketing out of all subjectivity from scientific inquiry. This was the explicit move made by Galileo at the dawn of the scientific revolution, which was subsequently forgotten in the following centuries as the extraordinary success of science tempted some of its practitioners to apply it to all phenomena whatsoever.

This scientific hubris is generally referred to as scientism, scientific reductionism, scientific imperialism, or simply scientific materialism. The belief that there is "nothing but" physical matter is bad science because it is not science at all. It is a metaphysical claim based on a circular argument.

Science is the observation of the behaviour of physical matter. A scientific test of the proposition "there is only physical matter" will obviously result in the affirmative, simply because that is all that science can observe.

What scientism really boils down to then is the claim that science is the only source of valid knowledge about reality. Anything else is not "really real". Since the subjective experience of reality itself was bracketed out at the beginning, scientism in effect must reduce all subjectivity to observable, objective phenomena, precisely what Galileo said couldn't be done. Consciousness, subjectivity, qualities (rather than quantities), values and meaning are all beyond the scope of scientific inquiry.

Science can only see the "outside" of things. It is blind to the "inside". Scientism is the belief that there is no "inside", there are only smaller and smaller "outsides". There is no "ghost in the machine", there is only the machine. The logical conclusion of this position is eliminativism, which posits that there is no such thing as consciousness, and that what we think of as consciousness is just an illusion. The logical absurdity should be fairly obvious - even illusions require someone to be conscious of them.

Bad science is the inevitable result of "nothing buttery": there is "nothing but" atoms, there is "nothing but" matter, there is "nothing but" energy or information.

Bad religion is also the result of "nothing buttery", but in this case it is "nothing but" revealed truth through a sacred scripture. There is "nothing but" the Word of God and the Word of God is "nothing but" what is written in the Koran or in the Bible and there is "nothing but" a literal interpretation of it. But then who decides what the "literal" interpretation is?

Bad philosophy reduces all philosophy, all the various attempts to understand reality through the ages to only one. The Objectivism of Ayn Rand would qualify as bad philosophy. The Logical Positivism of A.J. Ayer was bad philosophy. On the other end of the spectrum, the New Age ideas of someone like Deepak Chopra is patently bad philosophy. Postmodernism as a whole is by and large bad philosophy.

Bad politics is also necessarily reductionistic. It reduces the complexity of human relations to a simplistic model of social organisation. It involves the twin disciplines of bad economics and bad sociology, with a firm foundation in bad history. It is also relies heavily on bad science, bad religion and bad philosophy.

Radical muppets are experts in bad politics. Hippy muppets are experts in bad philosophy. Fundamentalist muppets are experts in bad religion. Nerd muppets are experts in bad science. However, most muppets are a mixture of all four. Bad science, bad religion, bad philosophy and bad politics form a co-dependent ecosystem of muppetry, each one sustaining the others.

Science is an *emissary*. The founders of modern science, Copernicus, Kepler, Galileo, Bacon and Newton were religious men whose faith in the intelligibility of the universe was founded on their faith in God. The scientific revolution was not in fact as revolutionary as is often made out, but rather evolved in a Christian context as one aspect of the intellectual inquiry into the nature of reality. There was the study of special revelation (religion) and general revelation (science). Both were founded on a vision of divine Creation.

Philosophy is not the handmaiden of science as the high priests of the modern scientific establishment would have it. Philosophy is the handmaiden of God, as are science and religion, and as, ultimately, is politics. These four disciplines are all emissaries. The master is God. When the emissary starts to think it is in fact the master, we're in trouble. The world gets overrun with muppets.

29. Bad Art and No Burgers

UNI BANS BURGERS
NO MORE BEEF TO BE SOLD ON CAMPUS AS STUDENTS COMBAT GLOBAL WARMING[109]

So runs the Metro Newspaper headline. The university in question is Goldsmith's, the University of London arts college in New Cross. Good news? Fake news? There are arguments to be had on both sides. What I most liked about the piece, however, was the last paragraph:

"But ex-student Alex Wood tweeted: 'As if being in the middle of the New Cross one-way system and being full of bad art and pretentious hippies wasn't bad enough, now you can't even get a burger.'"[110]

Which isn't to say that I disagree with the college's decision. Beef consumption is clearly a contributing factor to global warming. I just thought it was quite funny!

In the last chapter, I offered some simple definitions of Bad Science, Bad Philosophy, Bad Politics and Bad Religion. Could it be that they all ultimately depend on Bad Art? Aesthetic judgment is obviously not the whole of rational competence, although it does obviously play a crucial role. Many problems do not have purely rational solutions, especially when it comes to the big questions, so that it's actually good taste or the lack thereof which is often the determining factor in reaching the right or wrong conclusion.

So it's not enough to simply avoid being a muppet by resisting Bad Science, Bad Philosophy, Bad Politics, Bad Religion. You also need to overcome your mugglish tendencies by resisting Bad Art. How? By embracing GOOD art, and by allowing good art to teach you the art of good taste. Only then will you be able to appreciate good science, philosophy, politics and religion.

This is why the unfashionable, un-politically correct term "high culture" is so important. What is "high culture" exactly? It's what Matthew Arnold was pointing to in CULTURE AND ANARCHY with the oft-quoted phrase, "the best which has been thought and said". Let me quote the passage in full:

"The whole scope of [this book] is to recommend culture as the great help out of our present difficulties; culture being a pursuit of our total perfection by means of getting to know, on all the matters which most concern us, the best which has been thought and said in the world, and, through this knowledge, turning a stream of fresh and free thought upon our stock notions and habits, which we now follow staunchly but mechanically..."[111]

Whether or not you find this at Goldsmith's College, the point is that only the best will do if we are serious about becoming the best we can become as individuals and as a society. This was the Victorian hope for moral progress anyway, which took a major hit with the advent of the First World War. It seemed that maybe education and good taste wasn't enough to make the world a better place after all.

Arnold's cultural project was also an attempt to shore up the foundational values of a faithless society. If God really was dead, and all that was left was the "melancholy, long, withdrawing roar" of the "Sea of Faith", then maybe art could take the place of religion? Didn't they touch anyway at the highest peaks of sublime feeling?

Art needn't replace religion, and anyway it's clear now that the Victorians' obituaries for God were a little premature. But without good art, without high art and culture, we are as bereft of the solace and guidance of the Good, the True and the Beautiful as we are without good religion, burgers or no burgers.

30. Book Medicine

If you are sick, it's probably a good idea to take some medicine. If you've taken poison, you should take an antidote. But there are many kinds of poison, and it's not always obvious what the antidote is. And it's not always obvious that you've been poisoned in the first place, especially if you've poisoned your soul.

A healthy soul, like a healthy mind, is naturally quiet. It is like a dynamo running smoothly and silently. Only when something goes wrong does it start making funny noises. Good science, good religion, good philosophy and good politics don't make lots of noise. When they are running smoothly, they fade into the background, sweetly humming away to themselves and letting you get on with the more important business of actually living your life.

It's like good writing. If something is well written, the words retire into the background, allowing the meaning to take centre stage. If the writing is awkward and clunky, attention is diverted away from the message to the medium. The faint whirr of the language centre in the brain goes all clangy cymbally.

Good science should be seen and not heard. When it thrusts itself in the limelight screeching, "look at me! look at me! I know everything!" you know that something has gone wrong. Ditto for religion, philosophy and politics. If they are good, they should do their work in quiet humility, like the Master in the *Tao Te Ching*: "When the Master governs, the people / are hardly aware that he exists."[112]

If you're having them forced down your throat, even if it's you doing the forcing, you know you're going to be sick sooner or later.

Anomie, nihilism, despair, cynicism, depression, anxiety, apathy, cruelty, angst, existential dread, lassitude, confusion, nausea. That's what you get from too much bad science, bad religion, bad philosophy and bad politics. So why bother with it at all?

Well, there is a pay-off. There is a buzz. It's the exhilarating feeling of being special. Even if living in an indifferent, purposeless and ultimately meaningless universe is depressing, at least you are special and clever enough to recognise it as such. Special, clever and brave.

It's an ever present temptation. Mephistopheles is there in the wings whispering to you, "just peel back the surface and you'll see what's really real. Go on, I dare you!" Peel it back scientifically and you will see that everything you thought was real is just an illusion. It's really all just a big mechanical universe run by mini robots.

If you are tempted by an angel on the other hand, when you peel away the surface you'll find that everything you took to be real was actually all just an elaborate illusion created by the devil. The only thing that is actually real is whatever it says in your holy book.

If you are tempted by postmodern philosophers, however, when you peel away the surface, you'll just find another surface. Not only is the world you took to be real an illusion, but every possible world is an illusion. You find yourself in a hall of mirrors where nothing is real.

And if you're tempted by revolutionaries, when you peel away the surface you will find the evil machinery of your corrupt world laid bare. What seemed innocent business as usual is in fact a front for nefarious power hungry monsters busy seducing, exploiting and oppressing hapless brainwashed slaves who don't even know they're slaves.

Well, you can believe that the world is made of mini robots, or that it's the work of the devil, that it's a hall of mirrors, or a front for a powerful elite, but if you do, you'll probably end up feeling a bit queasy and unwell. If you swallow the poison of bad science, bad religion, bad philosophy or bad politics, it will slowly make its way into the blood stream, it will dominate your thoughts, and eventually, it will turn you into a muppet.

Is there an antidote? Well, the poison was a little knowledge, and the antidote is a little more. But not too much, otherwise the medicine itself might become poisonous.

Anyway, here's a little book medicine you might try as an antidote in case you do feel a bit green around the gills:

For the "bad science" poison, try *Mind and Cosmos: Why the Materialist Neo-Darwinian Conception of Nature is Almost Certainly False* by Thomas Nagel; for the "bad religion" poison, how about *The Lost Art of Scripture: Rescuing the Sacred Texts* by Karen Armstrong; for the "bad philosophy" poison, you could do worse than *Fools, Frauds and Firebrands: Thinkers of the New Left* by Roger Scruton and for the "bad politics" poison, there's *Black Mass: Apocalyptic Religion and the Death of Utopia* by John Gray or that old chestnut *The Road to Serfdom* by Friedrich Hayek.

31. Atheist Delusions

Delusion is the root of samsara. If you are to escape from samsara, you must cut the tree at the root. You may have to deal with your demons, with your anxieties and depressions, your addictions, your ignorance and arrogance. But if you don't deal with your delusions, however hard you work on yourself, you will always be pulled back into the vortex of samsara.

All spiritual traditions use the metaphors of sleep and waking and of death and life to point to the radical difference between two distinct states of consciousness. The Ancient Egyptians used the word *mut* to describe the state of the living dead, or the spiritually dead. Although you appear to be alive and awake, you are in fact asleep and dead. You are a zombie.

This insight is revealed at the moment of spiritual breakthrough. If you meditate or pray long and hard enough, if you are still enough, you will suddenly be flooded by waves of energy and light. You will be filled with bliss, *ananda*, and consciousness, *chitta*. You will feel intensely alive and wide awake. In that moment, you will appreciate how dead and asleep you were before.

Death and life, sleep and waking are relative. It's actually a sliding scale. As you board the tube the following morning, you will see in the faces of your fellow passengers their degree of sleep and death, their degree of *mut*. Most of them will be hypnotized, gazing at their phones. Some of them might actually be zombies.

According to Daniel Dennett, we are all zombies in the philosophical sense. We behave as though we were conscious, we may even believe that we are conscious, but in reality, consciousness is nothing but a clever illusion conjured up by the brain. This is of course, as Galen Strawson pointed out, the silliest claim ever made. But it is the logical conclusion of materialism.

Maybe if you believe you are a zombie, you actually start acting like one. Maybe you lose your élan vital and your inner light is dimmed close to perfect darkness. Maybe. This is a plausible consequence of this particular delusion.

It appears to be a self-fulfilling prophesy. Disbelieve in consciousness and you don't experience yourself as conscious.

The same is also true for disbelief in God. Disbelieve in God and there is no God. Surely this is clear evidence that He doesn't exist? If His existence depends on belief, then He is obviously just a subjective phenomenon, another "optical delusion of consciousness" (sorry, I forgot, there is no consciousness!)

But then again, maybe you are in fact conscious, whether you believe it or not, and maybe there is in fact a God, whether you believe in Him or not. You may have a diminished experience of life, consciousness and divinity, but if you are to any degree alive and awake, there will still be some, if only a trace.

I agree with Strawson. The denial of consciousness is the silliest claim ever made. The second silliest is the denial of God. In the end the two denials come to the same thing, as in some mysterious sense, God and Consciousness are identical. This, at least, is the claim of the Indian and Sufi mystics, and, in fact, of all mystics.

I have distinguished four basic types of muppet representing four classes of atheistic delusion. Type 1 muppets are scientific atheists. They are physicalists, naturalists, materialists. Type 2 muppets are philosophical atheists. They are relativists and social constructivists. Type 3 muppets are revolutionary atheists. They believe in a human-made utopia, without any higher, transcendent principles or obligations. Type 4 muppets are religious atheists. They think they believe in God, but they don't. They believe in their *idea* of God - what they really believe in is their religion, not God.

The common denominator is atheism. Muppets are Asuras, "Fighting Spirits", because they are in rebellion against God. As a result, they are cut off from the well-springs of light and life. And without access to the divine source of life, the dark veils of ignorance, arrogance, addiction, depression and hatred spread out over the face of the Earth, which then becomes a breeding ground for addicts, victims, demons, divas, muppets and muggles. All six archetypes on the Wheel of Life ultimately owe their existence to the defining condition of left hemisphere dominance: the mistaken belief that there is no God.

32. Mystical Atheism

Religion goes wrong when it is appropriated by the left hemisphere. Then it becomes strident, inflexible, dogmatic and intolerant. This can lead to the horrors of religious violence and persecution. The mystery of God is replaced by an anthropomorphic "god of the left hemisphere" and the metaphors of scripture are subjected to literal interpretation.

If this is religion, then atheists are right to challenge it. This is the kind of religion that Richard Dawkins and the other new atheists love to hate. It seems irrational, arbitrary and cruel. It stifles the human spirit and terrorises dissidents and free thinkers. It is the enemy of enlightened humanism.

But there are two kinds of religion, just as there are two kinds of atheism. One is the religion of the left hemisphere and the other is the religion of the right hemisphere. The former is fundamentalist and the latter is mystical. Religious fundamentalists are "ideologically possessed". They are convinced of their belief system to the point of obsession. They are willing to kill or die in the name of their God.

Mystical religion, on the other hand, is based not on certainty but on uncertainty, less on knowing than on unknowing. When a fundamentalist declares "I believe in God", they mean something very different to when a mystic says it. For the fundamentalist, the word "believe" is propositional. It is like saying "I believe the Earth is round". For the mystic, it is an action, not a state. It is more like saying "I pray" or "I meditate".

You can see the same difference in meaning with the words "think" or "imagine". If I say "I imagine God exists", it can mean that this is my settled opinion in the face of insufficient information (I didn't say "I know God exists"), but if I say "I imagine God existing" it is clear that I am actively making a mental effort to bring the idea of God into awareness.

But what is "God"? The fundamentalist believes she knows. The mystic knows that she has no idea. For the mystic it refers to an unfathomable mystery. Yet it is a mystery that mysteriously reveals itself in the act of believing. Every time a mystic "believes" in God, it reveals something different. Every time a fundamentalist "believes" in God, it further consolidates the same, fixed belief.

Left hemisphere dominant atheists are also ideologically possessed. They disbelieve in God with the same rigid certainty that religious fundamentalists believe in Him. They also think they know what it is they disbelieve in. They think they know what or who "God" is. Just like their antagonists, they marshal reasons, evidence and proof texts merely in order to defend and confirm their pre-ordained position. They are basically atheist fundamentalists.

Right hemisphere dominant atheists are more like religious mystics than atheist fundamentalists. They don't have the same tell-tale militant certainty about their unbelief, but are more comfortable with uncertainty and unknowing. They are more likely to call themselves "agnostic" than "atheist". They don't dismiss religion or blame it for all the ills of humanity, as atheist fundamentalists often do, nor do they dismiss science as religious fundamentalists often do. They are suspicious of both extremes.

John Gray is a good example of a right hemisphere "mystical atheist". This is how he concludes his neat little book *Seven Types of Atheism*:

"Contemporary atheism is a continuation of monotheism by other means. Hence the unending succession of God-surrogates, such as humanity and science, technology and the all-too-human visions of transhumanism. But there is no need for panic or despair. Belief and unbelief are poses the mind adopts in the face of an unimaginable reality. A godless world is as mysterious as one suffused with divinity, and the difference between the two may be less than you think."[113]

33. Cognitive Filters

In the Middle Ages Europe was known as Christendom. Whatever people's specific views and opinions about the world, whatever their level of education, they saw the world through a Christian lens (apart from non-Christians obviously). They were like C.S Lewis, who declared, "I believe in Christianity as I believe that the sun has risen: not only because I see it, but because by it I see everything else".[114]

The lens or filter through which we see the world is necessarily transparent. We see through it, otherwise we wouldn't see anything else. And we see objects in the world because the sun illuminates them, but we don't look directly at the sun itself. The sun is always behind us, as it were.

But a filter is not completely transparent, otherwise it wouldn't be a filter. And the sun is not completely invisible. If we try, we can make out the basic contours of the filter, and we can make out the brightness, shape and colour of the sun in the sky. A filter is semi-transparent. The sun is also in a sense semi-transparent.

Much psychoanalysis and psychotherapy in general is concerned with bringing the unconscious into consciousness, in other words in focusing on and bringing to light the psychological filters through which we experience our world, especially our relationships. At first, this can make us rather self-conscious as we become simultaneously aware of our experience and our (usually neurotic) filtering of our experience.

But behind our personal ego filters, there is a deeper collective metaphysical filter which orients us to the world on a more fundamental level. In Medieval Europe, this was Christianity. In modern Europe, this is secular humanism or atheism. In the Middle Ages, Christianity was largely taken for granted. It was not an object of inquiry, but the semi-transparent lens through which subjects experienced the world.

However, this all changed with the Reformation and the Enlightenment. The Reformation was characterised by a return to the "purity" of textual scripture. The Lutheran slogan was "sola scriptura". This meant that other forms of religious worship and experience were marginalised or rejected. Out went the mysterious and numinous church liturgies and devotions. Out went the embodied spiritual practices, the pilgrimages, the adoration of relics, saints and martyrs. The Bible was the only trustworthy way to come closer to the truth of Christian revelation, shorn of later superstitious accretions and distortions.

The Protestants of the Reformation were bringing the filters of tradition and the church into conscious awareness. The protest was principally about corruption in the Church, but it soon became more than that. It was a protest against the Church itself, which was seen more and more as an arbitrary and unnecessary filter between the people and God. Would it not be better to give the people access to the Word of God directly? Just get rid of the middle man. Go back to the pristine purity of the original scriptures.

The semi-transparent filters of Church and Tradition were exposed and subjected to direct critical analysis, so that rather than being the lens through which people saw the world, they became an opaque object of intellectual inquiry. Unsurprisingly, the Protestants soon splintered into different factions, because they couldn't agree on exactly how much to get rid of or what the denuded, unfiltered scriptures actually meant.

The confusion ushered in the Wars of Religion, with Catholics and Protestants massacring each other in the millions. It appeared that "sola scriptura" didn't work. Since people couldn't agree based on scripture, which could of course be read in a variety of different ways, maybe they should rely solely on Reason in order to reach agreement on how to live peaceably together. Surely Reason was universal and non-partisan?

The Age of Reason, commonly known as The Enlightenment, quickly took root in Europe. The slogan changed from "sola scriptura" to "sola ratio". This meant that not only were the filters of the Church and tradition made the objects of critical analysis, so now was scripture.

The Bible itself became an object of rational inquiry, an artefact amenable to Higher Criticism. The hope was that we could clear away the superstitious filters of the Bible and discover a purer "natural religion" based on pure reason underneath. Then we would usher in an age of peace and harmony, of liberty, fraternity and equality.

It didn't quite work out that way of course. Soon the filter of Reason itself was subjected to critical analysis, most famously in Immanuel Kant's *Critique of Pure Reason* and David Hume's *Treatise of Human Nature*. Reason was not the transparent filter we supposed it to be either.

It seems that any filter we use to understand reality can become the object of rational and empirical investigation, including reason and the senses themselves. Whatever our "ultimate vocabulary", whatever our unconscious, semi-transparent "Umwelt", we can always expose it to the clinical glare of "objective science". All our foundational assumptions can be objectified, deconstructed and radically relativised.

Look what happened to literary criticism in the twentieth century. Novels and poems were put on the dissecting table and subjected to all sorts of tortuous operations, from Structuralism and Russian Formalism to Post Structuralism and Deconstruction, via New Historicism, Freudian, Marxist and Feminist Semiotics. A poem is intended to act as a window on the world, as a new lens or perspective through which we can make sense of our experience. But when it becomes the object of our interest, it ceases to act as a filter or lens. A watch can tell us the time, but if we take it apart, it can also tell us how watches are made. But then we don't know what time it is.

Seemingly straightforward and unproblematic ideas such as atheism are not immune to this process. The recent spate of books about atheism, by critics and defenders alike, means that atheism is now a "thing", itself an object of inquiry and scholarly analysis, not the implicit invisible basis for serious scientific or intellectual inquiry that it purports to be. It is no longer the "sun" by which "I see everything else". It is historically situated. It has its champions and its detractors, its founding myths, its saints and martyrs. It is no longer the transparent or semi-transparent default lens through which we instinctively see the world. It is a filter just like any other.

Is nothing sacred? Is there nothing that cannot be objectified and deconstructed and turned into the subject of a doctoral thesis? Well, technically speaking, there is one thing that cannot be objectified: the *subject*. We can layer coloured filters over our subjective experience, which can be peeled away and analysed, but we can't peel away and analyse the consciousness which makes our experiences possible in the first place.

This absolute subjectivity which cannot be objectified is called *Atman*, the Self, by the anonymous ancient sages who wrote the Upanishads: "Eye, tongue cannot approach it, nor mind know; not knowing, we cannot satisfy inquiry."[115] (Kena Upanishad). The Self is that which sees but cannot be seen, hears but cannot be heard: "He through whom we see, taste, smell, feel, hear, enjoy, knows everything. He is that Self."[116] (Katha Upanishad).

Self-inquiry leads to the inescapable conclusion that the personal subjective consciousness is co-extensive with and ultimately identical with infinite universal consciousness. Atman is Brahman.

The Universal Self, Brahman, is also known as "Paramātman" in Advaita Vedanta or "Parashiva" in Kashmir Shaivism. The closest word we in the West have to this Absolute transcendent consciousness is "God". Like the Self, God can never become the object of analysis. We can analyse religions, scriptures and our ideas about God, but never God Himself. Likewise, we can only ever know the Self indirectly: "It lies beyond the known, beyond the unknown. We know through those who have preached it, have learnt it from tradition."[117] (Kena Upanishad)

So perhaps we can live with the semi-transparent filters of scripture and tradition after all, as long as we understand that they are always only "fingers pointing to the moon".

The default reality beyond all filters whatsoever is not atheism or any other negatively defined pretense at neutrality. It is God, God being the only "thing" which cannot be unveiled and revealed as just another filter.

34. Sola Ratio, Sola Scriptura

"Sola ratio" means that only reason can give us a reliable and accurate understanding of reality. This was the sincere belief of the Enlightenment *philosophes*, the champions of the Age of Reason. The exclusive nature of "sola ratio" (only reason) leads inevitable to a left hemisphere dominant vision, which ends up distorting or even ignoring reality through excessive attention to rational models, theories and systems.

"Sola scriptura" is the attempt to base reality on the revealed scripture. Maybe our reasoning faculties are faulty, but the sacredly validated truths of scripture are inerrant. They are the Word of God, so they can't be wrong. We must defer our fallible human intellects to the unfathomable mind of the Most High. We must not question the sacred texts, but must uncritically see the world through the lenses they provide for us.

When there is only reason, everything is fair game for rational analysis and deconstruction. Everything is dissolved in the universal solvent of objective scientific observation and analysis into its smallest component parts. Everywhere mechanisms are laid bare. Whether or not the cosmic watchmaker is blind, our job is to take the watch apart to see what makes it tick. In rationally constructing diagrams, maps and models of parts of the "watch" we imagine that reality really is just an infinitely complex machine, without realising that our diagrams, maps and models are the creation of our own minds and may in fact have precious little to do with reality at all.

Followers of "sola ratio" are left brain people. These are the rationalist, scientific materialist, militant atheist, logical positivist, nerd muppets. They are Type 1 Muppets. But there are other followers of sola ratio who took a different path. They do not worship reason in the same way Type 1 Muppets do, but take reason to its logical conclusion so that it ends up undermining everything it touches, including itself.

These are the postmodern, skeptical, relativistic, nihilist deconstructionists, and their pathological symptoms are more schizophrenic than autistic. These are the Type 2 Muppets. In both cases, the worlds of art, religion, nature and the body are de-mythologised and de-sacralised.

Followers of sola scriptura are also left brain people, but instead of rejecting all filters on the world and relying solely on pure reason, the scientific method and radical skepticism, they cling tenaciously to one ideology through which they can interpret reality. Their ultimate commitment and loyalty is to seeing the world through the lens of their chosen "scripture", whether it be a traditional religious scripture or a secular system of thought. They refuse to consider alternative views or try out other "lenses" or multiple "maps of meaning" because that would amount to disloyalty and treason.

Type 3 Muppets are ideologically possessed political extremists. Type 4 Muppets are ideologically possessed religious fundamentalists. Both types are capable of extraordinary levels of violence in the name of their chosen scripture, whether it be *Das Kapital* or *The Book of Revelation*.

For Anglicans, the Truth can be approached only through the threefold revelation of Scripture, Tradition and Reason. This is a sensible and effective safeguard against fundamentalism and muppetry. It is a kind of "triangulation": only those things in scripture are considered true (concerning God) that are in accord with both tradition and reason, only those things in tradition that are supported by scripture and reason and only those things reasoned out that are conformable to scripture and tradition.

Reason itself is of course no simple matter. It is much wider and deeper than bare logic on the mathematical model. And neither is the interpretation of scripture. It is multi-dimensional with several layers of possible meaning. As the Egyptian anchorite John Cassian put it:

"Theoretical science is divided into two parts – the *historical* and the *spiritual* meaning; and the latter into three – *tropological, allegorical, anagogical*. *Tropology* (morality) relates to the improvement of morals; *allegory* to another signification than that of the letter; *anagogy* by the spiritual conception rises to the most sublime and secret things of the celestial mysteries. The four senses may be expressed at once in the same image. Thus, for example, *Jerusalem* literally may mean, the city of the Jews, allegorically, the Christian Church; tropologically, the human soul; anagogically, the celestial city."[118]

35. Tradition, Meditation, Revelation

Pure reason is an activity of the left hemisphere, if not wholly, at least predominantly. It is how we organise our knowledge of the world. When the reasoning faculty loses touch with empirical, sensory reality however, that is, when it ignores the right hemisphere, it goes off the rails. This is what Chesterton meant when he said "The madman is not the man who has lost his reason. The madman is the man who has lost everything except his reason."[119]

In *The Hermeneutics of Faith* I described the healthy cycle of knowledge as one passing across the two hemispheres via the inhibitory corpus callosum. I associated the three elements of this cycle with the three Tantric nadis, whose functions can be described as "purification", "perception" and "dalliance".

How does this relate to the triangulation of reason, scripture and tradition referred to in the previous chapter? I would say that the whole point of "spiritual" cognition is that it is not rational cognition. In other words, it is not predominantly a function of the left hemisphere. So if we reserve "reason" for this specific left brain discriminatory type of thinking, we can bracket that out of the cycle of spiritual knowledge.

So we are left with scripture and tradition. But the line between them is very fuzzy. The specifically Christian scriptures, the New Testament, were written within a pre-existing tradition (the Gospel according to John came out of the Johannine tradition for example). Even Genesis 1 came out of a particular tradition.

On the other hand, although we make a formal distinction between the books of the Bible and the writings of early Christians such as Anselm and Augustine in terms of the divine authority bestowed upon them, on a broader view, there is scriptural continuity. This goes for the formulations of the Councils and the development of Church liturgy as well. Scripture and tradition are closely intertwined.

So at the risk of scandalising Protestant purists, I suggest that "scripture" can be subsumed under the broader category, "tradition". This has the advantage of including all expressions of Christianity in all possible mediums, including music, poetry, painting and architecture.

Engagement with any of these forms I call *pistis*.

In other words, when you read the Bible or participate in a church service, listen to a sermon, listen to sacred music or gaze at an icon or painting, you are engaged with the tradition through pistis. When you empty yourself through prayer or meditation, this is *kenosis*. When you receive an insight, vision or revelation, as if from nowhere (from God?), this is called *gnosis*.

These, then, are the three elements of spiritual cognition: pistis, kenosis and gnosis, or tradition, meditation and revelation. They work together on the micro level, as in the process of mindfully reading a scriptural passage in "lectio divina", and on the macro level, as in attending church, meditating or having a psychedelic experience.

36. Borders

I know some people who advocate open borders. They seem to think that if there were no restrictions to the flow of goods and people between countries, everything would somehow sort itself out. There would be no illegal immigrants, no detention centres, no long queues at passport control, and the law of supply and demand would smooth out the bottle necks. If one part of the world was especially attractive to people, it would become so intolerable because of the huge influx of people, that it would cease being popular and people would move elsewhere.

I've never met anyone who advocated the opposite, which is to say closed borders. But I suppose they must exist. Most people, though, are somewhere on the spectrum between open borders at one end and closed borders at the other. Indeed, this goes for all kinds of borders, not just national ones. Some people seem to be temperamentally more comfortable with clearly defined boundaries, whereas others seem to prefer a more amorphous, flexible existence.

It appears that conservatives are generally more into boundaries than liberals. They seem to like to see everything in its proper place. They will be less inclined to blur the boundaries between the sexes for example. They will be less likely to blur age boundaries and dress like a teenager in their forties. They will prefer their art in a frame on the wall rather than on the floor (apart from the Saatchi brothers). They will probably eat lunch and dinner at lunch-time and dinner-time.

There is no such thing as open borders or closed borders, open boundaries or closed boundaries. They are always semi-permeable, although the degree of permeability varies. Obviously, the phrase "open boundary" is a contradiction in terms. If it is fully open, it doesn't classify as a boundary. A "closed boundary" also implies that it can be opened or traversed. If it were completely impenetrable, it wouldn't make sense to call it a boundary.

There is an Overton window through which we can see the range of reasonable permeability or porosity of any particular boundary, such as a national border. Within this window, it is possible to have a range of views on exactly how open or closed it should be.

Outside this reasonable mid-range, however, are the outliers who would like to see a much more open border on the one hand or a much more closed one on the other. These go far beyond the conservatism of the conservatives or the liberalism of the liberals. I call these outliers muppets.

There are four types of muppet: nerds, fundamentalists, hippies and radicals representing the two opposite poles of the border debate.

Nerds can only function within very clearly demarcated boundaries. They need parameters within which to make sense of the world. They are highly methodical logicians. They may have some degree of Asperger's syndrome or be somewhere on the autistic spectrum. They may display obsessive or compulsive behaviours. They may write in short, repetitive sentences.

Fundamentalists are similarly highly boundaried. They draw very thick lines between people and things. There is a clear division between the in-group and the out-group. Ideas are literally true or literally false. There is no room for ambiguity or nuance. There is no room for poetry or metaphor. They know the difference between right and wrong and no amount of argumentation will budge the high wall between them.

Hippies are the opposite. They believe that "All is One" and train themselves not to even see the divisions between things. They float around without caring about right and wrong or up and down or left and right. They believe that they have entered a New Age, where everything melts into everything else. All religions are the same. Everything is permitted and everything is cool.

Radicals are less laid-back. They are also on the open borders of the spectrum, but only because they see so much division in the world. Instead of just ignoring borders and boundaries like the hippies do, they spend their time and energy tearing them down. Any social distinction between different classes of people is seen as inherently divisive and oppressive.

They are therefore extremely sensitive to class, race, culture, gender, sexuality, socio-economic status, and any other dimension along which people can be distinguished. Any distinction between people is ultimately seen as a form of segregation imposed by a power-hungry elite.

This is how the muppets fall: nerds and fundamentalists on the extreme of the closed borders end of the spectrum and hippies and radicals on the extreme of the open borders end. Everyone else is somewhere in the middle. Of course we all need borders and boundaries, whether physical or psychological, but it's best if they are not too many or too high. We need limits, but within limits.

37. Why Left and Right Disgust Each Other

Why is politics so emotionally fraught? Why this seemingly endless, pointless war of attrition between Left and Right? Why do we hate each other so much? Jonathan Haidt has developed a very elegant and persuasive theory addressing this perennial question in his excellent book, *The Righteous Mind: Why Good People are Divided by Politics and Religion*, where he makes the case that people's political orientations are primarily the expression of deep-seated moral values.

Haidt identifies six moral foundations: "Care", "Fairness", "Loyalty", "Authority", "Sanctity" and "Liberty", which he derives in a bottom-up approach from quite plausible speculations about the survival strategies of our hunter-gatherer ancestors. I won't go into the details here, but will just give you the main finding of the book (spoiler alert!) which is that left-wing liberals are currently almost exclusively interested in the "Care" dimension (with a dash of "Fairness"), whereas social conservatives have more evenly spread moral commitments across all six foundations.

This is an excellent model for thinking about morality and politics. However, I would like here to offer another, simpler analysis of the relationship between morality and politics, with reference to the Tibetan Wheel of Life. From this perspective, polarisation in politics is not only an expression of what we value, but also of what we reject; it's not so much about what we recognize as moral as what we recognize as immoral. Because it manifests as a *disgust* response, it is in fact an application in the sphere of politics of Haidt's "Sanctity" moral foundation.

The Tibetan Wheel of Life can be understood as a depiction of the sins of fallen humanity, a graphic Buddhist alternative to the traditional Aristotelian or Judeo-Christian lists, such as the "Seven Deadly Sins". In *The Tibetan Wheel of Life*, I lay out the characteristic sins associated with each of the six positions on the Wheel, as I understand them.

My version of the Wheel describes six sins (or vices) associated with six ego states - three intellectual and three emotional. The three intellectual states are represented by the Muggle, Diva and Muppet archetypes, associated with the sins of Ignorance, Pride and Delusion respectively. The three emotional states are represented by the Addict, Demon and Victim archetypes, with their corresponding sins, Greed, Hate and Fearfulness.

So how does this model shed light on our moral responses in the present, heated political landscape?

Well, let's start with the supposed immorality of the most powerful man in the world, the president of the United States. Donald Trump is variously portrayed as sexist, racist, a crook, a philanderer, a narcissist, a fool, a dunce, a fascist, a bully, an evil mastermind and, it goes without saying, a greedy capitalist pig. One or several of these accusations may very well be true for all I know - I remain agnostic on the true content of his character.

What I am really interested in is the moral psychology behind the image. Who is this monster so vilified by people under the sway of TDS (Trump Derangement Syndrome)? It seems to have elements of the Addict (greedy, lascivious, hedonistic) but also of the Muggle (ignorant, simple-minded, materialistic). But it also has lashings of the Demon and the Diva: not only is he Greedy and Ignorant, he is also Evil and Full of Himself.

The same image seems to stick to our very own "British Trump", Boris Johnson. It's not just the hair and the eccentricity he holds in common with Trump, it's the monster image: Boris is also portrayed as a monster by his political enemies (or, as I heard a nice well-spoken middle class mother banter with her twelve year old daughter on Hampstead Heath the day after his election as Prime Minister, "a prick").

People on the left side of the political aisle look down on Muggles. They call them "hicks", "red-necks", "deplorables", "white trash" and "racists" in the US. In Britain they are called "twats". But worse than mere muggle simpletons, who are just plain Ignorant, are Muggle-Addicts, who are both Ignorant and Greedy (and probably sexual predators to boot).

And worse than Muggle-Addicts are Muggle-Addict-Demons who are secretly driven by malevolence and evil. Worst of all are the Muggle-Addict-Demon-Divas who are not only Ignorant, Greedy and full of Hatred and Evil, but Proud and Arrogant and all too often unconscionably Rich and Famous.

There is a kind of puritanism underlying all this moral outrage. We've been here before. Remember Cromwell? Remember Danton and Robespierre? Remember Stalin and Hitler? Remember the *Der Stürmer* anti-semitic propaganda cartoons? The Nazis held up the moral depravity of decadent money-grabbing monsters for all to see. And hate.

Clearly, it's much easier to kill monsters than people. Which is why painting people as monsters should ring some warning bells. A Muggle-Addict-Demon-Diva is a monstrous creation which can be destroyed without compunction. But so is its political rival, the Muppet-Victim-Diva-Demon. This is the monster held up for ridicule and attack by Right-wingers. In the US they call them "liberals", "radicals", "commies", "hippies" or "social justice warriors". In the UK they're called "twats".

Worse than mere Muppets, who can be pitied and patronised (they're usually too young to know any better) are the Muppet-Victims, who play into the whole "victimology" narrative of Identity Politics and Intersectionality. Not only are they Deluded, they are also Paranoid and Pathetic. Right-wing pundits refer to this kind of social activism as the "Oppression Olympics", where those regarded as the most socially marginalised and victimised enjoy the greatest standing in the Muppet social economy.

This is not traditional left-wing politics of course. It is "neo-progressivism" or "progressive liberationism", a kind of "applied post-modernism". The basic premise is that everything of value in life is socially constructed, so everything can be deconstructed. With enough political will (ie. force) humanity can re-create itself as a blank slate (everyone equalised and neutralised).

The Right experience this kind of thing with intense moral disgust. The most prominent and vocal exponents of Muppet ideology then come to be seen not only as Muppet-Victims but as Muppet-Victim-Demons, whose activism is fuelled by intense self-loathing and hatred, with their sole aim the destruction of the family and Western civilisation. Worst of all are the self-congratulatory, virtue-signalling Proud and Arrogant leaders, the Muppet-Victim-Demon-Divas, on whom the Right can vent all their spleen and outrage.

Just as the Left project all the sins of the Muggle and Addict (Ignorance and Greed) onto the Right, and then pump the monster up with extra Diva-Demonic steroids, so the Right projects all the sins of the Muppet and Victim (Delusion and Fearfulness) onto the Left and pump their monster up with the same Diva-Demonic cocktail of hubristic evil.

Whereas the New Left freak out at the slightest whiff of bigotry, the New Right freak out at the slightest sign of socialism. Their equivalent to TDS is SDS (Socialism Derangement Syndrome). America has been here before with the insanely paranoid McCarthy era. Both sides of the political aisle police the ideological purity of their position with equal fervour. Both demand "politically correctness".

The Left find Donald Trump and Boris Johnson disgusting because they epitomize the heinous sins of "Capitalism" and the Right find Alexandria Ocasio-Cortez and Jeremy Corbyn disgusting because they epitomize the mortal sin of "Socialism". But it's got nothing to do with politics really: it's all about moral disgust for contrasting negative human archetypes. Trump is the archetypal Muggle-Addict-Demon-Diva in the eyes of the Left and AOC is the classic Muppet-Victim-Demon-Diva in the eyes of the Right.

The moral of the story? "Neither a Muggle nor a Muppet be". If you spend your time shouting down Muggles, you're probably a bit of a Muppet and if you get off on shouting down Muppets, you're probably something of a Muggle. Of course it's important that we call out the errors and excesses of both sides, but please, please, please, not out of hatred and disgust. Mild distaste is fine. Because if we carry on like this, we shouldn't be surprised if it's us who turn out to be the monsters.

38. Where do Bored Muggles go?

The Wheel of Life is a thumbnail sketch of the human ego. By "ego" I don't just mean the distinctive manifestations of selfish behaviour that invariably elicit moral censure in others, I mean the basic structure of the human personality - any personality. Think about your name. What's in a name? Your name somehow contains the whole bundle of ego states which make you who you are. You are a bundle of muggles, muppets, divas, addicts, victims and demons, just like everybody else, though differently configured. Amazingly enough, you can actually dimly sense your own unique configuration, just by saying your name.

On an individual level, the Wheel is the "Ego System". On a collective level, it is what Rastafarians call the "Babylon System". The tricksy bit is that, all claims to the contrary, most religious people are as much part of the Babylon System as everyone else. They have just re-arranged the furniture a little. If they are only nominally religious and live reasonably good, moral lives, they will be predominantly Type 1 or Type 2 muggles ("Home Muggles" or "Work Muggles"). If they are excessively religious, they will most emphatically be Type 4 muppets ("Fundamentalist Muppets").

Rational, scientific minded secularists who think that they see through all the illusions lesser mortals labour under (the self-designated "Brights", or "Enlightenment Bunnies" as I like to call them) are just as wrapped up in samsara as those they patronize with such abandon. Their Chief Feature is Type 1 muppetry ("Scientific Materialism"). Again, if they are nominal materialists, they will most likely live on the muggle side of the street. They will probably call themselves humanists, and may even live as good and morally virtuous lives as religious muggles.

All so-called "exoteric" religions exist within the Babylon System. If they are genuine, well-intentioned and orthodox, they will promote the cultivation of positive, pro-social feelings and behaviours and will help people be good muggles.

They will defend people from too deep or frequent a descent into the addict, victim and demon realms and will divert energy away from the muppet and diva realms.

Exoteric religion is for muggles. Which is a good thing. The more muggles in society, the better. Muggles dont want trouble. They just want to get on with their lives, and generally get along fairly peaceably and harmoniously. They are good neighbours and good friends. They are not to be sneezed at.

However, problems arise when muggles start to get itchy feet. For some restless souls, Muggle Land is just not enough. They want adventure and excitement, or at least something more meaningful than the daily round. Oscar Wilde clearly felt this when he said, "To live is the rarest thing in the world. Most people exist, that is all"[120].

But where can a bored, disaffected muggle dandy go? He could take a trip round the Wheel and enjoy a spot of hedonism and depravity à la Dorian Gray, or perhaps a taste of worldly success or, failing that, some good old fashioned protests and rioting. Alternatively, he could step off the Wheel altogether.

Stepping out of the Ego System is basically ego suicide. The person you thought you were, embodied in your name, disappears. Your old self dies. This is what "esoteric" religion means. You die to your self and are reborn as something else, hence the perennial esoteric motif of death and resurrection (which is why the essence of Christianity is esoteric, despite most practicing Christians being firmly exoteric).

Esoteric religion is also known as "mysticism". A mystic is someone who enters the mystery beyond the egoic world of the Babylon System. In mystical consciousness there is no personality to speak of. What is there then? There is what Buddhists call Buddha Nature, the essential enlightened consciousness within each of us. No matter what twisted configuration of ego states we may play out on a rainy day in Babylon, behind it all is our intrinsic Buddha Nature.

In Christian Mysticism it's called Christ Consciousness. As St. Paul succinctly put it, "Not I, but Christ lives in me". In Vedantic Mysticism it's called Krishna Consciousness.

It doesn't really matter what you call it. The important point is that it is not you. Not your usual you anyway. It is your True Self, your Higher Self, the Atman, Buddha Nature.

If you are ruled by your left brain hemisphere, you are automatically in the Ego System, and by extension, the Babylon System. If you are religious, your religion will be exoteric. It will have nothing to do with deeper spiritual realities. You will be you, identifiable (at least to yourself) by your name.

If you are ruled by the right brain hemisphere on the other hand, you are not that which your name points at. You are a Buddha, an "Awakened One". You have escaped samsara and crossed to the other shore. If you identify with a religion, you will understand it esoterically, as a signpost to a completely different way of being. You will be a Mystic, and also, in time, a Shaman, a Warrior, a Monk, a Philosopher, a King, a Poet, a Priest and a Friend.

And what's more, you won't be bored any more.

39. What's at the Top of the Tree?

The idea of evolution is implicit in religion. If there were no progress, there would be no point. In the Judeo-Christian tradition this is expressed in terms of our personal and collective relationship with God. Spiritual progress is defined by our increasing proximity to God. Spiritual regress is of course the opposite. We made a deal with God, back in the mists of time, a covenant. If we obey God's laws and listen to his prophets, if we do our best to be a godly people and live godly lives, then things will go well for us. If not, not.

Evolution is at the heart of contemporary New Age thinking. The Potential Movement, Transpersonal Psychology and Positive Psychology are all about fulfilling our human spiritual potential by evolving. Ken Wilber's door stopper, *Sex, Ecology, Spirituality* is pointedly subtitled *The Spirit of Evolution*.

Then there's the soporific *Conscious Evolution: Awakening the Power of our Social Potential* by Barbara Marx Hubbard and the worthy *The New Cosmic Story: Inside our Awakening Universe* by John Haught. Haught is writing from a Christian perspective, though in a different vein to Teilhard de Chardin. However, it is Indian religion and philosophy which truly excels at evolutionary spirituality, most impressively in Sri Aurobindo's classic, *The Life Divine*.

My personal favourite in this genre is Andrew Smith's *The Dimensions of Experience*, subtitled *A Natural History of Consciousness*. This is an explicitly panpsychist thesis, painstakingly tracing the evolution of consciousness through the three great domains of matter, life and mind (and beyond). It is a little known masterpiece.

According to these evolutionary narratives, it is the mystics who are sitting at the top of the evolutionary tree. You might call them Buddhas, Enlightened Ones, Saints or Ascended Masters. They're basically Mystics. They have realized the mystery of existence. However, in the secular world, there are other things at the top of the tree.

What's at the Top of the Tree?

Following Charles Darwin, who naturalized the idea of evolution with his theory of natural selection, secular humanists dreamed of other futures. The underlying concept, popularized as "the survival of the fittest", appeared to justify the rule of the strong over the weak as "natural". This led to Social Darwinism, the idea that societies could and should be organised along strictly Darwinian lines. The logical outcome of this was the Eugenics Movement, which believed that only the "fittest" human beings should reproduce, in order to ensure the healthy future evolution of the species.

George Bernard Shaw was famously a eugenics enthusiast, as was Adolf Hitler. The dream of a brighter, healthier future purged of cripples and dimwits cut across all party lines. The great German philosopher Friedrich Nietzsche provided intellectual weight to the idea of a future Superman and Master Race. In his *Genealogy of Morals* he argued against the perverse Christian doctrine of looking after the poor and the infirm and for a return to the steely virility of the pre-Christian pagans, the Greeks, the Spartans, the Romans, and the Saxons and Teutons, the "blond beasts". The Christians had turned the Western world into a smelly sanitorium, a culture enfeebled by the care of the feeble, when it should be a bracing battle field, strengthened by the death of the weak and the survival of the fittest.

Nietzsche was a subtle and brilliant thinker. I feel bad caricaturing him like this. But he undeniably expressed this fascistic idea more forcefully than anyone. What is the "Will to Power" but exactly what it says on the tin? What is "Bad Faith" but a pathetic, pusillanimous, emasculated Christian response to the Will to Power?

There seems to be something of a revival of this way of thinking. The popularity of Ayn Rand, particularly in the United States is testament to the fact. Many self-proclaimed Objectivists or Libertarians are basically advocating for "the survival of the fittest". Take away all the irritating and enervating restraints on individual freedoms imposed by an over-protective nanny state and let natural selection run its course. And let the devil take the hindmost.

This is why Libertarians are the enemies of Liberals. Liberals took a different path from Darwin. But before we get to the Liberals, let's have a closer look at the Communists. Lenin and his acolytes were devotees of Karl Marx. Karl Marx was heavily influenced by Georg Hegel. Hegel's great masterpiece, *The Phenomenology of the Spirit*, is basically an account of human history as the expression of deeper evolutionary currents, which he associated with Geist (Spirit).

New Age thinkers like Ken Wilber like this idea because it maps onto their conception of a spiritual undercurrent to history. This is also why Nietzsche remains so popular (apart from his eloquent Christian baiting). Zarathustra is an ambiguous figure who is both iconoclastic and mystical, and who can be equally appropriated by Nazis and hippies.

However, take away the religious overtones, and you are left with a stark choice: "Left Hegelianism" or "Right Hegelianism". Marx was a Left Hegelian. For Marx, the underlying current of human history was leading inexorably to a classless society. His analysis of Dialectic Materialism suggested that through progressive struggles and revolutions and Class War (the perennial struggle over resources and means of production between the Haves and Have Nots), the workers, the Proletariat, would emerge victorious and usher in a Communist Utopia, where all private property would be abolished and all things shared in common in a great Brotherhood of Man.

In Marx's reading, it wasn't a Superman sitting at the top of the evolutionary tree, it was a Superstate. Instead of power being concentrated in the Powerful, power would be concentrated in one centralised, bureaucratic state, which would be "owned" by everyone. No-one would have any power at all, because the state would have a monopoly of power. Ergo, everyone would be equally free and happy (or rather, equally unfree and unhappy).

For the "Right Hegelians", Darwinism implied the survival of the fittest in the Great Game, where power and resources were distributed naturally according to the laws of the jungle. For the "Left Hegelians", it implied the ultimate concentration and therefore perfect distribution of power through the absorption of the individual into the collective.

Surely this was the most highly evolved social organisation imaginable? For termites maybe.

Anyway, back to the Liberals. The absolute value for Liberals is tolerance. Everyone should be tolerated. Everyone should be free to do whatever they like. Without God, everything is permitted. In this, they are arm in arm with the Libertarians. However, as soon as people are free to do whatever they like, they can't help stepping on each other's toes. It doesn't help much to say "you are free to do whatever you like as long as it doesn't impinge on anyone else's freedom" because it's not just about the odd isolated thing. Over the long term, your freedom to live in a decent society will inevitably be compromised.

So Liberals are morally compelled to safeguard people's rights through a kind of compulsory tolerance called Political Correctness. If you don't like what other people get up to, you must keep it to yourself, for fear of social exclusion. You must tolerate everything and everyone.

Moral censure is of course implicit in any society. There are certain social norms and taboos which, if broken, lead to varying levels of opprobrium and can be punished in extreme cases by exile, imprisonment or even death. The difference in Liberalism, is that there are no social norms. Any attempt to articulate social norms is indeed considered Illiberal.

The chaos and confusion surrounding the transgender movement is perfectly illustrative of this problem. It is not difficult to imagine further, even more transgressive movements in the future, causing even more moral havoc, perhaps under the aegis of Transhumanism. Liberal will be committed to defending them all.

The popular historian Yuval Noah Harari describes the horrific events of the twentieth century as the Humanist Wars. He sees them as the humanist equivalent of the Religious Wars in Europe in the seventeenth century. The rivals for the humanist crown in this war are identified as "Liberal Humanism", "Socialist Humanism" and "Evolutionary Humanism" (by "Evolutionary Humanism" he means Fascism and Nazism, the "Right Hegelians"). According to Harari, the winner is Liberal Humanism. Socialist Humanism and Evolutionary Humanism are dead.

But all three humanisms are really evolutionary humanisms. They are all founded on a naturalistic neo-Darwinian conception of humanity as having evolved from apes sometime in the distant past and currently evolving into an unknown future of infinite possibility. Perhaps Liberalism is the best of a bad bunch and deserved to win, but like its human ape cousins, it also seems to be foundering on the shoals of human vanity and ignorance. It seems to be leading us down some strange and frankly inhuman paths.

Humanists think they can forge humanity in the image of their own favourite idols and stick their own angel on top of the evolutionary tree. But the descendants of Abraham, Isaac and Jacob (okay and Ishmael), the "chosen people", patiently remind us that we cannot mould reality according to our personal whims and ideologies. Whether we know it or not, we have made a pact with God. We are all of us people of God, made in the image of God. We are not the children of apes, we are children of God.

In reality, there is only ever one thing at the top of the tree, and whether it's a star or an angel, it's definitely not the work of human hands, let alone ape hands.

40. Redemption

There is a lot of talk in IDW (Intellectual Dark Web) circles about the "Meaning Crisis". The general claim seems to be that the secular worldview we have inherited from the Enlightenment is insufficient to satisfy the deep human need for existential meaning. The story of material progress and technological advance just isn't a big enough story when it comes to the meaning of life.

So where do we find meaning? Well, on one level, there is no meaning crisis. We can find meaning anywhere. What is the meaning of life for an addict? Getting high. What is the meaning of life for a muggle? Belonging. What is meaningful for a victim? Resentment and self-pity. For a muppet? Fighting the good fight. For a diva? A sense of superiority. For a demon? Death and destruction.

The genius of samsara is that there are different sources of meaning. If one starts to wane, just move round the Wheel and pick up another. Bored of the cosy *sorge* world of muggles? Take a few lines of coke. You might risk the sense of belonging and acceptance you enjoyed before, but even if you get seriously addicted, you know you'll be welcomed back eventually. Or you might decide to attack the muggle world, "the system", and join a band of muppet brothers. Then you'll derive meaning from your struggle for justice and freedom, from a sense of solidarity with your comrades and ultimately, from martyrdom.

But what happens when you see through the whole show? What if all these sources of meaning seem ultimately hollow and meaningless? What if even the fame and fortune, power and influence of a diva seem utterly pointless? That's when you have a real meaning crisis. Then you are in the position of King Solomon in *Ecclesiastes*: "vanity of vanities; all is vanity" or of Camus' existential anti-hero Meursault: "I had lived my life one way and I could just as well have lived it another. I had done this and I hadn't done that. I hadn't done this thing but I had done another. And so?"[121]

This is an uncomfortable place to be. But if you are on a spiritual path, it is unavoidable. If you want to escape samsara, the meaning has to be drained out of it, otherwise you will be continuously pulled back into its orbit. Your desire is directed beyond; your meaning must come from elsewhere. This is fine if you decide to become a hermit or take monastic orders. You can (to a certain extent) remove yourself from samsara. But what if you live in the world?

Jesus said, "If anyone comes to Me and does not hate his father and mother, wife and children, brothers and sisters, yes, and his own life also, he cannot be My disciple."[122] This is a hard saying. It makes sense from a spiritual point of view, but it puts a bit of a downer on everyday life. It's not easy to live hating everyone. There is a serious problem here. It is not peculiar to Christianity, of course, but affects all religions. In order to transcend the world, you need to hate the world, but if you hate the world, how can you be said to have transcended it?

But Jesus was only talking about *disciples*. You should only "hate" everyone if you want to be a disciple. Apparently, Jesus only had twelve disciples, which isn't many. Over and again in the gospels it is made clear that he has one teaching for his disciples and another for everyone else. They are his inner circle, privy to the deeper spiritual knowledge reserved for the elect.

So what were the disciples privy to? And why does it mean you have to hate your mother and father? I imagine it would have something to do with Jesus' dramatic claim that, not only was he the Son of God, but he was actually the same as God: "I and the Father are one"[123]. If we are to take this as the expression of an actual lived experience, as opposed to an abstract, theoretical statement of fact (which would then be the self-appellation of a liar, a fiend or a lunatic), it would have to be an experience of radical unity.

I find the usual Christian view that Jesus called himself the Son of God simply because he was the Son of God totally vacuous. How would you know that you were the Son of God unless you experienced being the Son of God? Or rather, unless you experienced something that warranted those words? Something that the words "Son of God" pointed to? My guess is that an experience of such transcendental insight would be something akin to the experience of unity produced by a high dose of DMT.

If Jesus had such an experience, he would understandably struggle to communicate it. He might say that he was one with God and that he was in everyone and that everyone was in him. But other than sounding pretty, it wouldn't make much practical sense. If he were to say, "we are really all one person", his followers would simply retort, "no we're not". To support their position, they would only need to point out the simple fact that they were patently not one person but different people. Jesus might respond with something like, "alright fair enough, but when you transcend your ego and are united with the Universal Consciousness, then you will see that we are actually the same person, even though it *seems* as though we are different people."

If the disciples had the same experience of unity, they would know exactly what he was talking about and they would be able to see the unity reflected in each other. They would treat each other with deep recognition and understanding, as if they really were in some mysterious sense the same person. Perhaps they had glimpses of unity. They must have at the very least believed that what Jesus was telling them was true and aspired to share in his vision.

But Jesus was clearly the only one who had the full-blown experience of unity. He was the only one who could say with any confidence that he was in everyone and everyone was in him. So in the end, since he was the only one who knew that he was God, he was the only one who could say that he was God (or more modestly, the Son of God). It then made as much sense to say that his disciples were one in Him as it was to say that they were one in God. He was the living proof of the living God.

If the twelve had all completely understood, if they had all had the same experience, there would have been twelve Sons of God, but then again, because they were all one, there would still actually only be the one, "only-begotten" Son of God. St Paul was alluding to this when he said, "it is no longer I who live, but Christ lives in me"[124].

In any case, it seems that only with his death and resurrection did the penny finally drop for the disciples. Until that point, they believed in and followed Jesus, but they didn't really get what he was on about. They knew how difficult it was to achieve and to retain the vision of unity. Which is why Jesus' death and resurrection became the symbol of redemption.

Jesus couldn't destroy the world of samsara, the world of division, but He could redeem it. This great insight at the climax of the Christian story made Bodhisattvas out of his disciples and made Christianity a religion of redemption.

Redemption means that it is okay to be on the Wheel of Life. It's okay to be a muggle, a diva, a muppet, an addict, a victim, even a demon. It's okay to be human. We need to forgive and be forgiven. But this is only possible through Jesus, which means, through the vision of unity with God and all humanity. The ultimate meaning of life is incomprehensible to our petty human minds. It is ineffable. It is impossible to communicate to those who haven't experienced it for themselves. But neither is it possible to remain in that state. We have to come back to the world of duality.

There is a place for spiritual community, where brothers and sisters in Christ can see the unity of God reflected in each other and establish a little Kingdom of Heaven here on Earth, or to use Buddhist terminology, where an Enlightened Sangha can create a Pure Land. This is ultimately what the institutions of Church and Monastery point towards. The hope is that the ultimate unity will be fully realised one day in the Eschaton. Until that day, however, we have to make do with the existential reality we find ourselves in. Until then, we have to accept the world as it is.

The world is redeemed through the vision of ultimate unity, not condemned by it. It becomes meaningful again. There is value and meaning in all six worlds of samsara. It is good to belong. It is good to succeed. It is good to fight for a just cause. Even a bit of greed, hate and fear are okay. But the meanings we derive from these things are not absolute. We can take it all a bit more lightly, with a pinch of salt, in the knowledge that the greater meaning is beyond the wheel altogether. But this greater meaning does not destroy the lesser meanings. Jesus said, "Do not think that I came to destroy the Law or the Prophets: I did not come to destroy but to fulfill."[125]

This is the only real solution to the Meaning Crisis. The meaning of life is not about rejecting the world. It's about redeeming it.

41. Three Orientations to Life

Broadly speaking, there are three orientations to life. By far the most common is the first, which is a naive acceptance of reality, or "the unexamined life". This is tantamount to total immersion in the Wheel of Life. You play the part of a muggle, diva, muppet, addict, victim or demon without the slightest flicker of self-awareness.

The second is a naive rejection of life. This is the condition of people who have examined life and found it wanting. They see through the charade and consequently suffer a chronic crisis of meaning. In the modern West we call this an existential crisis or a mid-life crisis, because it usually takes about forty years or so for the sheen of samsara to fade. These second types may become religious ascetics, puritans, or worse. They are the life-deniers.

The third orientation to life depends on the second. It is also built on a vision of emptiness and meaninglessness. However, it moves beyond the mere rejection of the world for the sake of a higher one. Instead, it discovers meaning in a return from the spiritual plane back down to earth. It is the difference between the Bodhisattva and the Arhat. It is "returning to the marketplace with open hands". It is Jesus Christ as world redeemer.

In the first place, we are lost in samsara. In the second place, we escape from samsara. In the third place, samsara is redeemed. But it should go without saying that this is not a once and for all achievement. We get lost again and again; we have to escape again and again; and we must find redemption again and again.

42. Latter-Day Prophets in the Age of Equality

I was saddened but strangely unsurprised to hear that Roger Scruton had died of cancer at the age of 75. I had somehow been expecting it, although I didn't know that he was unwell.

Reflecting on his life's work, it occurred to me that his famous conservatism was simply a way of expressing in a political idiom a deeper current of thought, which actually has more to do with resistance than conservation. On the face of it, his passionate defence of high culture, for example, is about conserving the cultural riches of the past, particularly in music and architecture, for future generations. It is the expression of his sense of duty to the dead and the unborn. However, it is more than that.

It is a repudiation of *equality*. In aesthetic matters, some things are better than others. Beauty is not just in the eye of the beholder. It is not just down to subjective taste or conventional consensus. There is such a thing as "aesthetic value". This is the corner stone of his whole philosophy, which boils down to being a defence of value against equality.

C.S. Lewis makes the point forcefully through the mouth of the demon Screwtape in *Screwtape Proposes a Toast*, written shortly before his death in 1963. It is a witty piece of satire, with Screwtape bemoaning the blandness of the Tempters' Training College annual dinner meal (of the damned) due to the mediocrity of people's sins. But he goes on to argue that quantity is better than quality and that in the long run it's a good thing, because it at least means that hardly anyone's getting into Heaven.

According to Screwtape, this is because of the prevailing doctrine of *I'm as good as you* masquerading under the guise of "democracy". He might equally have used the word "equality". Because anyone is able to say *I'm as good as you* (without actually believing it of course - it is a perpetual inner deception) there is no incentive to be particularly good at anything or to admire those things or people that are.

There is an obvious flaw in the idea or equality. You cannot raise everyone up to be equally good, on a par with the saints or the great composers. That's clearly highly unrealistic, considering it takes years of sweat and tears and not a little natural talent or even genius. Who would make the effort given every conceivable opportunity? Only a handful. The rest would remain what they were.

The only way to achieve equality therefore, is in the opposite direction, by dragging everyone down to the lowest common denominator. Who was it that said, "people are only perfectly equal when they're dead"? For equality enthusiasts, people are only acceptably equal when they're as good as dead.

The Utopian dream of "equalizers" is a world where everyone has made themselves so insignificant, that no-one can hurt anyone any more. Peace will only truly descend on Earth when no-one can pull themselves out of bed. Everyone is equalized and neutralized. No-one pokes their head above the bedclothes.

Aldous Huxley saw this. He called it *Brave New World*. C.S. Lewis saw it. Chesterton saw it. T.S. Eliot saw it. As did Nietzsche, the raging prophet of the "will to power". Nietzsche was nauseated by the simpering Victorian Christianity he saw degenerating into the abject pathos of flaccid, facile, bourgeois domesticity. People should not be domesticated like cats and dogs.

Roger Scruton is in the same tradition, although unlike Nietzsche he champions bourgeois aspirational values against the onslaughts of the radical socialist equalizers. So is Ken Wilber, another latter-day prophet of value, who gets an awful lot of mileage from the concepts of *hierarchy* and *holarchy*, which are of course anathema to equalizers, in fact, the very antithesis of their worldview. As does Jordan Peterson, the latest prophet on the block.

Jordan Peterson and Roger Scruton are well despised, as all good prophets should be. They are dismissed by equalizers with the two magic words, Right and Wing. But, as I said, this goes deeper than political ideology. This goes to the heart of what it means to be human, which is something to do with standing up straight with your shoulders back.

Nelson Mandela famously didn't say, "As we let our own light shine, we unconsciously give other people permission to do the same."[126] But where does the light come from? Where do genius and inner strength and power come from? When you are inspired, you are *in*-spired. It is as if something or someone has breathed into you. It is as if you are filled with a holy spirit. Why not just go ahead and say you *are* filled with the Holy Spirit?

King Arthur was made King because he pulled Excalibur from the stone. This was evidence that he was filled with the Holy Spirit. When you are King, you don't subject yourself to the demands of "equality" or "democracy". You don't hide your light so as not to offend those who don't shine. But neither do you abuse your power. You do not become a tyrant, because you know that you must obey the King above you, the King of Kings, otherwise the Holy Spirit will be withdrawn from you.

The prophets are on one side of the present fissure in history, exhorting us to wake up from our soft, comfortable, modern sleep and to take our place beside the Kings and Queens of myth and antiquity. On the other side are amassed an army of modern and postmodern ideologies and isms. Don't let them bully you. Don't let them fool you into joining the Church of Nobody. Your sins may be trivial, and your flesh may be tasteless, but you'll still end up on the banqueting table in Hell.

43. Rousseau's Chains

The whole of the progressive agenda originates and is summed up in Jean-Jacques Rousseau's famous and oft-quoted line, "Man is born free and everywhere is in chains."[127]

If you were to sum up the religious belief and commitment of Modernity, it is belief in and commitment to "Progress". Who can possibly argue with that? Progress means advance, betterment, improvement. Surely there is always room for improvement, therefore there is always a need for progress. This is so bleedingly obvious that it is a wonder more people don't recognise how utterly trite it is. The question is, not whether progress is desirable, but what counts as progress.

If you claim to be "progressive" and your opponents as "reactionary" or "regressive", you have simply smuggled in the implicit claim that your idea of progress is right and theirs is wrong. In the absence of any concrete instances, the general principle, as a principle of quasi-religious belief, devolves into the basic view that change is good and stasis is bad. If we believe in progress, obviously we have to keep moving.

Although there is a certain commitment to constant change, or in its extreme form, "permanent revolution", mere change is too empty a concept to provide any definite sense of direction. Even progressives recognise that there are changes for the worse as well as changes for the better. They need a rule of thumb in order to distinguish between the two. Which is where Rousseau comes in.

Whatever changes are unfolding in society, they are bad if they add more chains to people and good if they break them. Human progress on the Rousseauian view is the progressive removal of the chains imposed by society on otherwise free individuals. Thus it would more accurately be called "progressive liberationism".

Rousseau saw that the Catholic Church was a repressive institution. People therefore had to be liberated from the church. This meant they had to be freed from the external control and influence of the priests and functionaries of the church, but ultimately meant that they had to be freed from their inner slavery to the restrictive beliefs instilled by the church from early childhood.

The same logic applied to all social institutions, to educational institutions, government, the legal system, and ultimately to the family itself. Were not the original chains placed on the innocent, unsuspecting infant forged in the nursery by mother and father? All external authorities and their internalisations had to be expunged if man was to be truly free. In England, William Blake sang to this same tune in his lyric poems, *Songs of Innocence and Experience.*

Clearly, this is a powerful, emotive idea and it dominated the Romantic Movement throughout the nineteenth century and into the twentieth. Revolution was in the air, and revolution meant freedom from the chains of all societal strictures and restrictions.

This movement reached its apotheosis in the swinging sixties. "Free Love" was the slogan and the dream, and for the first time since Rousseau wrote those fateful words, seemed within the reach of liberated libertarians everywhere. The hippies were poised to take over the world, not with guns, but with flowers in their hair.

The sixties saw the confluence of several strands of "liberationism", creating a perfect storm of progressive frenzy. First, there was the Social Darwinist legacy of Charles Darwin's theory of evolution, which gave a metaphysical justification to the idea of irresistible progress. Then there was the Marxist call to emancipation from class oppression, the Nietzschean call to emancipation from false consciousness and slave morality and the Freudian call to emancipation from the nasty super ego, which we had mistaken for the voice of "conscience".

The combined promise of these intellectual giants of modernity, Darwin, Marx, Nietzsche and Freud, was that, for the first time in history, we could utterly smash the mental shackles that kept us chained to the past. We could throw off our chains. We could rise up free and glorious and stride naked into the new dawn of the New Age of Aquarius.

But it didn't quite turn out like that. Why not? It turned out that Rousseau's "noble savage" was more savage than noble. Freed from the chains of filial piety, respect for authority, religion, education and morality, people found themselves enslaved in a different way.

There was the problem of addiction. People got hooked on drugs and sex. They became slaves to their passions. There were the twin problems of ignorance and delusion. People ceased to be properly educated in the liberal arts and humanities, but filled themselves with all sorts of strange and exotic liberationist propaganda, from Jean Paul Sartre and Simone de Beauvoir to Jean Genet and Michel Foucault.

The Paris riots of 1968 are the iconic moment of this liberation movement, which, appropriately enough, since it all started with the French Revolution, was spearheaded by French intellectuals. But the movement was quickly translated and soon came to dominate the Anglosphere as well.

The smashing of the chains of bourgeois society resulted in a host of societal ills and psychological problems through the nineteen seventies and into the new millennium: higher divorce rates, higher suicide rates and self-harm, increases in anxiety and depression, domestic abuse, violent crimes and homicide.

What went wrong? The hippy dream seemed to have turned into a nightmare. Where was the "noble savage"? All you could see were vain and self-centred divas, ignorant muggles, delusional muppets, insatiable addicts, disconsolate victims and murderous demons. People seemed more enslaved than ever before.

Was Rousseau wrong? Were our chains necessary for our own sanity and safety? Chains have positive uses as well as negative ones – they connect as well as restrain. Perhaps cutting all our attachments was not the best way to achieve social and spiritual progress. Perhaps the surge of enthusiasm for Buddhist non-attachment, which underpinned all the other liberationist streams was misplaced?

As a psychotherapist, I was always looking out for the underlying need of my clients. Did they need help loosening up? Were they too repressed and emotionally cramped? Did they display obsessive traits? Did they have too much order in their lives? Were their chains too tight?

Or did they need help tightening up? Were their emotions all over the place? Did they need to take control of their lives? Did they need more structure and discipline? Were they too chaotic? Were their chains too loose?

There is no simple answer to the eternal conundrum of human freedom. Sometimes we need "loosening up" and sometimes we need "tightening up". Sometimes, as a culture, we veer too far in one direction and sometimes in the other. There are times and generations which need an antidote to excessive order, but there are also times and generations where what's really needed is an antidote to chaos.

44. Reason and Civility

There seems to have emerged a new mini-genre of books dealing with the difficulty of having difficult conversations. There is Alan Jacobs' *How to Think* and Mick Hume's *Trigger Warning* and more recently Peter Bhogossian's *How to have Impossible Conversations* and Dave Rubin's *Don't Burn this Book*. You could also add Joshua Greene's *Moral Tribes*, Jonathan Haidt's *The Righteous Mind* and Douglas Murray's *The Madness of Crowds* to the list.

What's it all about? I would say it's about the re-assertion of classical liberal values in a post-liberal world. Liberalism is in something of a crisis at the moment (in case you hadn't noticed). In a way it is a victim of its own success, as the "negative" liberalism of John Stuart Mill has somehow morphed into the "positive" liberalism of progressivism. By "negative" I simply mean the principle of "negative liberty", whereby everyone is deemed free to pursue their own version of the good life, so long as it doesn't impinge on the freedom of others to pursue theirs. "Positive liberalism" on the other hand imposes a specific liberal vision onto everyone else through active coercion. This kind of liberalism was the subject of Jonah Goldberg's fascinating book *Liberal Fascism*.

Classical liberalism is minimalist. The aim is to give people as much freedom as possible to live their lives as they see fit within the minimum requirements of public order established by the rule of law. That's basically it. As long as you don't break the law, your morals, your beliefs and your actions are your own business. Moral censure and social sanctions are naturally provided by the communities in which you live, but the state has nothing to say about the private lives of its citizens.

I have the right to follow my own version of the good life, but I also have the right to communicate my vision and even to attempt to persuade people to come round to my way of seeing things. I can write books, give talks and hold meetings. I can proselytize and cajole with all the rhetorical skills I can muster, and use everything in my power to convince people of my position.

What I cannot do is to force people to adopt my beliefs against their will. I cannot use violence or blackmail or any form of manipulation that exceeds the reasonable bounds of ordinary acceptable social intercourse.

What those reasonable bounds are will necessarily be blurred. Excessive force in one culture or context may be judged perfectly acceptable in another. These ambiguities and controversies should also be subject to open debate in a properly functioning liberal civil society. However, as soon as one section of society decides to take matters into their own hands and begins to silence another, through noisy or even violent protest and "no-platforming", as soon as we have "politically correct" vigilantes, we have a problem. Freedom of speech is *the* core principle of liberalism, which cannot be violated without putting the very fabric of liberal democracy at risk.

Evelyn Hall (not Voltaire) put the principle most forcibly with the famous words, "I disapprove of what you say, but I will defend to the death your right to say it."[128] This is the essence of classical liberalism, in contrast to certain modern strains of liberal fascism, which will defend to the death my right not to hear it or let anyone else hear it.

What unites podcasters and YouTubers such as Dave Rubin and Joe Rogan and public intellectuals such as Jonathan Haidt, Steven Pinker and Jordan Peterson is their liberal Enlightenment values, which promote freedom of speech and negative liberty over virtue signalling and positive "liberal" bullying. This is really what ultimately defines the ragtag bunch of thinkers and talking heads known as the IDW ("Intellectual Dark Web"). They stand for open and free inquiry about any and every topic, where anything goes, as long as it's conducted with reason and civility. Respect the subject and respect your interlocutor and the truth will out without any need for self-censorship.

45. The Darkness and the Light

The eighteenth century Enlightenment myth of the Middle Ages was that it was an age of darkness, shrouded in the mists of superstition and mysticism. It was the same charge levelled against the Catholic Church by Luther and the Protestants the previous century. With the Reformation and the Enlightenment, Europe was dragged out of ignorance and into the light of Reason and Common Sense.

Although it was a myth, it was powerful enough to persist up to the present. We still think of the Enlightenment as a watershed in history, as the beginning of the modern age. And in a sense, it is. But the light of the Enlightenment cast a big shadow: first the French Revolution and then the Napoleonic Wars, and then the Twentieth Century.

It is true that the Middle Ages are shrouded in mystery and darkness. But the mistake of the Enlightenment philosophers was to assume that this was a bad thing. There is no light without dark and no dark without light. The Christian mystics of the first half of the second millennium understood this. *The Cloud of Unknowing*, written in the 14th Century, beautifully articulated the process by which the human mind could attain the true light of enlightenment, through unknowing and darkness.

We are only haltingly coming to appreciate this in the modern age, blinded as we are by the phosphorescent lights of Science and Rationality. Part of our re-membering is due to the discovery in the West of the treasure trove of Eastern mysticism. The first chapter of the Tao Te Ching sums it up beautifully:

"Yet mystery and manifestations / arise from the same source. / This source is called darkness. / Darkness within darkness. / The gateway to all understanding."[129]

T.S. Eliot understood that the banishment of mystery and darkness in the modern world was a spiritual tragedy:

"Not here / Not here the darkness in this twittering world."[130]

But there is good darkness and bad darkness. There is the pregnant mystery at the heart of creation and there is the impenetrable veil of ignorance spun by human minds. Of course there was plenty of that in the Middle Ages. But that was what the church was for. Orthodoxy mitigated the descent into madness and confusion that descent into the dark might occasion. Tradition was the ongoing conversation between the ineffable mystery and its representation in word, art, music and doctrine.

In my little Tibetan mind map, the Titans (muppets) can fall foul of either too much artificial light or too much artificial darkness. Type 1 muppets, the scientific materialist militant atheists, live in a false dawn of LED strip lighting. Type 2 muppets, the cultural relativist postmodern nihilists, live in a false dusk of cynical nonsense and obscurantism masquerading as wisdom.

Type 3 muppets, the revolutionary socialist utopians, live in the long shadow of the Enlightenment. Whether Marxist, Leninist, Trotskyist, Stalinist, Maoist, Jucheist, Mussoliniist or Hitlerist, these muppets believe that no amount of darkness can dim the radiant purity of their enlightened vision. Type 4 muppets, the religious fundamentalist jihadists (of all affiliations) likewise.

"O dark dark dark. They all go into the dark,
The vacant interstellar spaces, the vacant into the vacant."[131]

That's what you get when you cut yourself loose from the mystery of your own spiritual tradition.

46. Why Marx was Half Right

"Marx's work is all about human enjoyment. The good life for him is not one of labour but one of leisure. Free self-realisation is a form of "production", to be sure; but it is not one that is coercive. And leisure is necessary if men and women are to devote time to running their own affairs. It is thus surprising that Marxism does not attract more card-carrying idlers and professional loafers to its ranks. This, however, is because a lot of energy must be expended on achieving this goal. Leisure is something you have to work for."[132]

Marx highlighted how grinding poverty robs people of leisure time because they have to work all hours of the day just to survive. Although he pointed to the tragic plight of the busy workers in newly industrialised British cities, this is even truer of traditional agrarian societies. Ironically, it was the industrial revolution and capitalism which began to free people from the servitude of labour and open up new vistas of leisure.

Fast forward to the labour saving devices of the 1950's. Fast forward to the AI revolution and the further spread of automation throughout the manufacturing and even service industries. A bright future of endless leisure beckons. No more slaving over the washing or in the cotton mills. Plenty of free time for "self-realisation".

Are we ready for the communist utopia then? Not quite. Even though we don't really need to work all hours of the day to survive, we still work like dogs. Why? Because we want a bigger house and a better car. We do have plenty of leisure time left over though. But we don't seem to use much if any of it for self-realisation. We'd rather spend it on other things, like entertainment.

This is what "the evil of capitalism" seems to amount to for Marxists. People work all day in bullshit jobs and then spend their evenings being brainwashed by idiotic TV shows and advertising. What kind of a life is that? I call it Muggle Life. Aldous Huxley called it *Brave New World*.

At the end of the day, it doesn't seem to matter how much money you have. You still end up being a cog in the capitalist machine. This is the half that Marx was right about. All his talk of "alienation" boils down to this dehumanising, superficial existence of material production and consumption.

Marx was reticent about speculating on what the communist utopia would actually be like. We know that the communist dystopia looks something like George Orwell's *1984*, as appears to have been fully realised in the Democratic People's Republic of Korea. But why wouldn't the utopian version be something like Huxley's *Brave New World*?

As Terry Eagleton says, "leisure is something you have to work for", which is why Marxists cannot enjoy the fruits of their leisure. They are too busy. Busy doing what? Working for the future leisure utopia of course! And how do they keep themselves busy? Well, they read Marxist tracts. They attend meetings. They go on marches and demos. They talk incessantly about how awful capitalism is.

Marxists are too busy to "self-realise". They will not rest until the communist leisure utopia has arrived. But what if the capitalist leisure utopia has already arrived? What's the difference? Surely leisure is leisure, by whatever means it is achieved?

A committed communist will not rest until everyone has plenty of time on their hands. But how much time is enough time? If everyone had enough time to spare in a capitalist society, would a communist be satisfied? Of course not. They want a communist society not a capitalist one. They don't want capitalists to have loads of time – they want *communists* to have it.

But if you can't rest until everyone has enough leisure time to self-realise, but only if they are communists in a communist utopia, then you will never rest and so will never have enough leisure time yourself. You will never lay down your arms, because human nature being what it is, you will never be able to accept that you have reached the longed for communist utopia, because you never will.

Marx was right about leisure. You need leisure time in order to self-realise. But he was wrong about how to go about getting it.

Perpetual revolution, perpetual Marxism, perpetual class struggle, don't exactly free up time. You just end up swapping muggle pastimes for muppet ones.

Which is not to say you shouldn't work for the material betterment of humanity. Some people are called to help the poor and to fight on behalf of the oppressed. Some of them call themselves Christians; some of them call themselves Marxists. But the poor are always with us. The way society is organised is not necessarily fundamentally corrupt and does not necessarily need to be completely overturned.

The only way to truly "self-realise" is to realise that you are responsible for what you do with your time. You can choose how much to work. You can choose how to spend your free time. You don't really need loads of money, so you don't really need to work your fingers to the bone.

Marx was half right in that we need basic material conditions in order to be able to fulfil our human potential for self-realisation. But he was wrong in supposing that material conditions go all the way. At a certain point, a very close point in fact, the spiritual must take over.

47. Do Not Waste Time

Spiritual practice takes a lot of effort and a lot of time. If you want to get anywhere on the spiritual path, you need to make a serious commitment and make some serious sacrifices. It's impossible to have a "normal" twenty-first century lifestyle. Why? Because you will waste energy and you will waste time. Unless you live in a monastery or a hermitage, the big challenge is how to live "in the world but not of the world".

This is the predicament of the "householder", who must follow the "fourth way" (the first three being the way of the fakir, the way of the monk and the way of the yogi). The householder has limited time and energy left over after family, work and social responsibilities. So the key is in knowing how to save time and energy and how to make the most of the little you have.

It's easy to waste time in Muggle Land, what with family get-togethers, coffee with your gossipy friends or pints down the pub when the football's on. You can end up talking for hours about next to nothing. For muggles it's really the company that matters, not the conversation. But you don't need to be around people to be in Muggle Land – you carry it around in your pocket. Social media and popular television shows take you there in an instant.

At a certain point in her spiritual development, Saint Teresa of Avila couldn't bear to talk about anything but spiritual matters. If people were talking about something else, she longed to be alone. She later understood that this was just a phase of early enthusiasm that she needed to grow out of. So I am not saying that anything but spiritual talk is a waste of time. I'm just saying that talking (and listening) must be carefully rationed.

If you can talk with someone about spiritual things, it can be very useful, as long as they are sympathetic and know something about it. However, it's a waste of time talking to muggles, because they won't be interested and it won't mean anything to them. But it's an even bigger waste of time talking to muppets.

Do Not Waste Time

Don't waste your time trying to convert muppets. You will just end up arguing. Not only will you waste time, but you will waste a lot of energy as well. You will end up drained and perhaps angry and confused. Whether they are Type 1 Muppets (scientific materialists), Type 2 Muppets (postmodern relativists), Type 3 Muppets (political activists) or Type 4 Muppets (religious fundamentalists) you will lose. Not the specific argument, necessarily, but the unspoken meta-game, which is, who gets more wound up?

Does this mean you should give up on people? Isn't it your duty on some level to bring people to God? Wouldn't it be great if you did convince someone with your clever arguments? Of course it's possible, but the odds really are extremely low. In a one-to-one setting, you are pitting one head against another, and the greater likelihood is that you'll end up head-butting each other (figuratively speaking).

However clever and persuasive you are, a one on one with a muppet is a losing game. The only way is through the force of numbers. In other words, you need a community. For many alcoholics, the only way to give up their addiction is to go to AA. The same goes for muppets. The only way they will change is not through confrontation and argument but through osmosis. If they are surrounded by people who can model a more relaxed, spiritual way of being, they may slowly begin to let go. If they are hardcore muppets, however, they will absolutely hate it.

The best way to spiritually help other people is to strengthen your own faith and focus on your own spiritual development. Join a spiritual community, such as your local church or synagogue. If someone shows interest, talk to them about it by all means. Invite them along. But don't waste time proselytising or debating. Above all, avoid treating spirituality as an intellectual game. And it's no good trying to "fix" addicts, victims, demons, muppets, muggles or divas. Nobody likes to be coerced or to lose face. They will come in their own good time if you only show them where the exit is.

48. Tetris and Zen

There are two ways to experience reality: qualitatively and quantitatively. The former is mediated by the right brain hemisphere and the latter by the left. The former is the domain of art and the senses; the latter of science and mathematics. In the philosophy of mind, "qualia" are the irreducible elements of our conscious experience: the redness of a rose, the smell of coffee, the taste of a mint. These are the qualities of lived sensory experience. While they may have neurological correlates in certain regions of the brain, which can be observed to be active when we have these experiences, they cannot coherently be reduced to this activity. To do so would be to discount and deny the reality of our conscious experience, which is patently absurd because there is nothing we can be more certain of than our own immediate conscious experience.

When we think, we abstract ourselves from our immediate conscious experience in order to make sense of the world by manipulating symbols and concepts. We do this most readily through the medium of language. When we think, we are in a virtual world suspended above the sensory world, beyond time and space. In actual fact we enter a second dimension of time. The first dimension is experienced as a flow. When you are in the first dimension, you experience events unfolding sequentially in real time. Time is "live". This is how birds and mammals experience time.

In the second dimension, your sense of time extends into the distant past and the distant future. You are no longer tied to the "animal present". There are memories and future projections. There is a great store of ideas, patterns, stories, conversations to sift through. And the store is growing all the time. It's a bit like Tetris. New shapes are continuously falling onto the great mountain of your mind. If you manage to turn them this way and that as they fall, they will fit neatly into the gaps and synthesize with earlier shapes and disappear. If you don't, the mountain will overflow with rubbish.

We are highly sophisticated creatures. We live in five dimensions: three of space and two of time. The left brain hemisphere specializes in fifth dimensional experience, ie. thinking. The better the thinking, the more you can integrate into your understanding of reality, the less thinking you actually need to do. Your mind is ordered and coherent. Different shapes don't heap up into a tangled mess but rather mesh together harmoniously, like a well composed work of art.

Then you can leave the fifth dimension left hemisphere with a clear conscience, like when you leave a tidy house to go for a walk. You don't need to worry about the dirty laundry on the floor or the overflowing dishes in the sink and you can attend fully to the beauty of your surroundings. When you leave the left hemisphere and step into the right hemisphere, your experience of the world opens out in two directions. You enter the live flow of time, which is the fourth dimension. But you can also enter the dimension beyond the fifth, which transcends all dimensions on our plane of reality: the zero dimensional nondual state called *Satori*.

Immediately given conscious experience mediated through the right brain hemisphere is Zen. Zen is "losing your mind and coming to your senses". It is entering the flow of the fourth dimension. But it is also, occasionally, entering the wide Buddha Field of perfect enlightenment.

Tetris and Zen.
Autumn leaves and a plum.

49. What's Behind the Wall?

"'The world is my idea': this is a truth which holds good for everything that lives and knows, though only man can bring it into reflected, abstract consciousness. If he really does this, philosophical discretion has evolved in him. It then becomes clear to him, and certain, that he knows not a sun, and not and earth, but only an eye that sees a sun, a hand that feels an earth; that the world which surrounds him exists only as idea - that is, only in relation to something else, the one who conceives the idea, which is himself."[133]

Although beautifully expressed, Schopenhauer cannot claim originality for this idea, inherited as it was from George Berkeley, David Hume and Immanuel Kant, but reaching much further back into classical antiquity. The best recent elucidation of this insight can be found in the witty writings of the late, great Douglas Harding.

Forget your knowledge of the world for a minute. Forget your left hemisphere mind maps of the "objective world". What is your immediate experience revealing to you right now? You are not aware of having a head, are you? That is only an inference from seeing other heads. Where is your "meatball head" in direct, present experience? There isn't one.

If you can settle into a purely "subjective" attitude, you will appreciate that the tree outside the window is not a tree but your idea of a tree. The same goes for everything you care to rest your eyes on. The same is also true of any sounds you hear, or any smells, tastes, feelings or sensations. They are all ideas or representations (vorstellung). You do not know the noumenon (the "thing in itself") but the phenomenon.

What is the limit of your vision as you look around you? If you are indoors, it is probably a wall. If you are outdoors it is probably the sky. The wall and the sky are the limits of your mind. Your mind extends outward (it seems) to the limits of the visible world at this particular moment in time. It is not that your mind is "in here" making contact at a distance of several metres with the world "out there".

The tree outside the window is not outside your mind. Your consciousness is right there where the object of consciousness is. There is no gap between them, "not even a hair's breadth difference".

This can be expressed as the union of Shiva and Shakti. Shiva represents consciousness and Shakti represents the objects of consciousness. Wherever your attention goes, there is Shiva, instantaneously and by definition. You cannot catch yourself out. "If you are aware / Shiva is there". Shiva is everywhere bringing the world into consciousness. But He is invisible. The multifarious qualities that you experience; colour, form, light and shade (in the case of vision), are Shakti, Schopenhauer's "ideas". Shiva and Shakti are in a perpetual, loving embrace (if you are as sentimentally minded as me).

The question is, what's behind the wall? And what's behind the sky?

If you answer "the neighbour's bedroom" or "the troposphere" you've completely missed the point. If you answer "nothing" you're on the right track. We're talking about the subjective world of immediate experience, not deductions or inferences about the objective world. Facing you is an "idea" of a wall. This is the limit of your (visual) mind. There is no immediately given visual "idea" of your neighbour's bedroom. In my case I haven't ever seen my neighbour's bedroom so I can't even recreate it in my imagination.

But "nothing" is also not quite right. What is "nothing" anyway? Is it pitch black? But then it's not nothing - it's darkness. And although you are not immediately aware of it, how could it possibly be "nothing"? Whatever you can see right now is somehow produced and sustained by your mind, by consciousness. If there was "nothing" beyond the limits of your visual field, there would be no possibility of visual experience within the field. Nothing comes from nothing.

The persistent illusion is the belief that consciousness resides "in here", in our heads. The world around us is in a sense a projection from this central point. We experience the world as though it revolves around the axis of our bodies. Our head, our brain, is the centre of our world, the centre of our universe. But this is not right. There is a Copernican revolution needed to understand that your consciousness is not a point at the centre of your world (in the pineal gland maybe?) but is an infinite field beyond the limits of your world.

This infinite field is called Parashiva. It is pure mind, pure consciousness without an object. It is the mind-stuff which contains, sustains, creates, and makes possible your experience of the world. It is infinite because it has no spatial qualities to speak of. Space and time only have any meaning within the field of Shiva-Shakti, within the phenomenal world.

If we are to imagine Parashiva as anything, it is not as darkness, but as light, the light of consciousness which lights up the world of experience. It is infinite light, infinite being, infinite consciousness, infinite bliss, "Sat-chit-ananda". Maybe that sounds a bit over the top. Unless you experience those things, they are just hearsay.

We don't know what's "behind the wall". Maybe we can't know. But we can *believe*. If you believe that there is infinite light and consciousness behind everything you experience, and if you believe that it is somehow "good" or somehow the essence of what we call "love", then you are a believer, whatever else you believe.

The curious thing is that if you believe that there is a field of pure consciousness beyond the limits of the phenomenal world, a spiritual light beyond the visual, a primordial sound beyond the auditory, heavenly bliss beyond the sensate, you actually begin to get a taste these things, perhaps as a kind of earthly analogue. Your belief, in some mysterious way, is actualized in your experience.

Anyway, whether you experience it or not, this is what belief in God means. Whether in relation to the microcosm of your subjective world, or the macrocosm of the objective universe, the belief in a mysterious something behind and beyond all manifestation is the foundational belief of all religions.

Belief in a transcendent God, Parashiva, naturally spills over into belief in an immanent God, Shiva. The rays of the Absolute emanate down through the phenomenal world of experience, illuminating and vivifying all things in the process, and waking the spirit of Shakti, which radiates with a numinous, ineffable divinity. Then we experience the sublime heart of existence. You are a child of God, and the world is filled with a Holy Spirit. This is, as Blake put it,

To see a World in a Grain of Sand / And a Heaven in a Wild Flower / Hold Infinity in the palm of your hand / And Eternity in an hour."[134]

50. Waking Up

One summer twenty years ago, by the river Isis in Oxford, I had a profound experience of waking up from my ordinary, habitual "me" consciousness into an extraordinary nondual consciousness, where I felt completely at one with my surroundings and with the whole world. It felt as though I had stepped into a timeless realm, where one instant and ten thousand years were somehow the same and where one glance at a flower was more real and meaningful than my whole life up to that point. The experience only lasted for a few hours of clock time, but once back in the "ordinary" state, I knew that I would have no choice but to dedicate the rest of my life to finding my way back again.

Many others have been there too. For other first-hand accounts of spiritual awakening, check out Evelyn Underhill's *Mysticism: A Study of the Nature and Development of Man's Spiritual Consciousness*, Richard Bucke's *Cosmic Consciousness: A Study in the Evolution of the Human Mind*, William James' *The Varieties of Religious Experience*, W.T. Stace's *Mysticism and Philosophy* and F.C. Happold's *Mysticism: A Study and an Anthology*. Here is an account taken from *The Varieties of Psychedelic Experience* by Masters and Houston:

"The subject, S-1 (LSD), a housewife in her early thirties, was taken by the guide for a walk in the little forest that lay just beyond her house. The following is her account of this occasion:

I felt I was there with God on the day of the Creation. Everything was so fresh and new. Every plant and tree and fern and bush had its own particular holiness. As I walked along the ground the smells of nature rose to greet me - sweeter and more sacred than any incense. Around me bees hummed and birds sang and crickets chirped a ravishing hymn to Creation. Between the trees I could see the sun sending down rays of warming benediction upon this Eden, this forest paradise.

I continued to wander through this wood in a state of puzzled rapture, wondering how it could have been that I lived only a few steps from this place, walked in it several times a week, and yet had never really seen it before. I remembered having read in college Frazer's Golden Bough in which one read of the sacred forests of the ancients. Here, just outside my door, was such a forest and I swore I would never be blind to its enchantment again."[135]

51. The Eye of God

What was it that triggered my satori (Enlightenment experience) twenty years ago? We were stood at a small bridge on the river Isis in Oxford. It was a beautiful sunny day, and as my two companions chatted about this and that, I drifted off, mesmerised by the brilliant dancing point of light on the water. A pair of ducks drifted by, breaking up the ripples into thousands of intricate patterns. I willed myself to "make my mind water" so that I could follow the patterns of light exactly as they occurred without lagging behind. I started to hallucinate endless figures and shapes, which would disappear as fast as they appeared. I remember being impressed by an Egyptian scene with Cleopatra on her barge in full regal splendour.

Once I had tired of this, I began to reflect on the illusory nature of this light show. I imagined Thales sitting on a bank contemplating a similar scene and coming to the conclusion that the world was water. I asked myself, "if all this endlessly changing spectacle is an illusion, what is real?" The answer came fairly quickly: "well, the actual body of water is real." Then, with a sudden shock of realization, I made a further logical step: the body of water *was* the shifting patterns on the surface. They were not two different things.

When I looked up from my meditation, the world was transfigured. "The green trees ... transported and ravished me; their sweetness and unusual beauty made my heart to leap, and almost mad with ecstasy, they were such strange and wonderful things."[136]

It was only months later, as I desperately tried to make sense of my experience, that I came across the following, ascribed to Shankara:

"The world is illusion; Brahman is the only reality; Brahman is the world."[137]

I had passed through the same logical steps as had Shankara in his search for the Ultimate. Somehow I had passed through the "gateless gate". Once through the gate, if you look behind you, there is no gate at all. All is seamlessly One.

The Eye of God

It is the same as when you "see God". How can you see God? God cannot be seen. True, but He can be apprehended, intuited, imagined. He can be "seen" with the eye of contemplation, if not the eye of flesh. So to "see God" is to arrive at a convincing enough approximation of what "God" might be. Convincing enough to be transported to a higher plane. Invariably, when we feel that we "see God" we instinctively look up at the heavens. We may remain like this for some time, rapt in awe and wonder. At some point, we tire, and our gaze turns back to Earth. What do we see? Not the same Earth we were standing on a few moments ago. We see the Earth transfigured. Why? Because we are seeing it not with our eyes, but through the eyes of God.

Meister Eckhart said, "The eye with which you see God is the same eye with which He sees you."[138]

It is the same eye, but looked through in the opposite direction. It is a reversible eye. It is the "gateless gate". From the perspective of the higher Being we call God, All is One. There is no separation anywhere. There is no separation between the world and God because God *is* the world. Brahman *is* the world. And more than that, the world, this planet we call Earth, is God. When we look at the world from God's eye view, we are looking at the world from the World's point of view. We are lending eyes to the world to look at itself. And it sees itself as One. The world is the world, which is the same as to say, as the Cabbalists are so fond of saying, God is God.

What happens when you look at *yourself* through the "eye with which [God] sees you"? You see that you are also part and parcel of the One God. You are a child of God, so to speak, a son or daughter of God. You feel that your soul, your mind, the very cells in your body, are part of the One God. You may feel a rush of energy, of being filled with the Holy Spirit. This is communion. In this moment of communion, your body is the body of Christ.

Seen through the eye with which you see God, the world is the Kingdom of God, and you are the body of Christ. Or, as the Nondual Amida Buddhists would have it, "this body is the body of Buddha; this very land is the Pure Land."

52. The Ray of Creation

There is an ancient story about some blind men and an elephant. Each one felt a part of the elephant and came to the conclusion that it was just as they felt it. The one who grabbed a leg thought the elephant was like a pillar, the one who grabbed the tail thought it was like a stick, etc. The moral of the story is that different people take only part of the scriptures, believing it to be the whole. The contradictions lead to disagreements and religious conflict, but are simply the result of partial understanding.

What if we could feel the leg, the tail, the ear, the belly and the trunk to get a better picture of the elephant? We would have to accept that true as each part is, it is not the whole truth. As a self-professed "blind man", I have made it my life mission to feel the WHOLE elephant.

I have felt seven parts:

I have felt the empty Void within and beyond manifestation, called *Sunyata* in the Buddhist scriptures. I call it AMUN, "the Hidden One".

I have felt the light and energy within manifestation, called *Kundalini* in the Vedas. I call it RA, "the Sun God".

I have felt the material substance of manifestation, called *Prima Materia* by the alchemists. I call it ATUM, "the All".

I have felt the aliveness of my body, the breath of life, called *Prana* by the Hindus. I call it KA, "the Life Force".

I have felt the pure consciousness of the Self, called *Atman* in the Vedas. It is the Witness of our life. I call it BA, "the Soul."

I have felt my connection and identity with the planet, called the *Anima Mundi* by the Neoplatonists. I call it GAIA, "the Earth Goddess".

I have felt the Universal Consciousness, called *Jah* by the Rastafarians. I call it JAH, "God".

These seven "gods" together constitute "the Ray of Creation", which traces the evolution of the universe from the Void to the Absolute. Each "god" contains all the others below it in a nested hierarchy. They are like the layers of an onion, like the *Koshas* (sheaths) of Vedanta. Each "god" denotes the unified consciousness of the realm or level it presides over: Jah is the god of the universe, which contains Gaia, goddess of the Earth, which contains Ba, god (or soul) of the organism, which contains Ka, god of cells, which contains Atum, god of atoms, which contains Ra, god of energy, which contains Amun, god of Emptiness.

Each time I have an experience of one of these parts of the elephant, I think to myself, "this is it!" The experience eventually and inevitably fades and then, at some other point I have a different experience and an equally compelling conviction that "this is it! I must put all my faith and devotion into *this*!"

When I experience one part of these realities, I give myself to it heart and soul, and exclaim with the *credo*, "I believe in ONE God". In that moment of communion, nothing else exists. This is God for me now. But once the experience has passed, I realize that it was only one dimension of something much larger, only one part of the elephant.

There is another old story about a mountain and a mountain climber. It was a very difficult mountain to climb, but the mountain climber was determined to find a way to the summit. After much effort and exertion, he managed to find a way to the top. He had imagined that once he reached the summit, he could plant his flag and be done with it. However, back home again, he felt a strong urge to climb the mountain again, but by a different route. So he climbed up the mountain again. He did this over and over again for years, always climbing via a different route, until he had covered the whole mountain. Only then did he realize that the goal was not after all the summit of the mountain, but the mountain itself.

53. Meditation

Gary Weber has described in detail how the "default mode network" in the brain can be deactivated through meditation. He calls it the "blah blah blah", because it is characterized by incessant chatter, sometimes pointless and inconsequential, but sometimes of seemingly huge import. In Buddhist circles, it is known as the "monkey mind", not because we share it with our primate cousins, but because we jump from thought to thought like a monkey jumping from tree to tree. This is what the mind does when it is "at rest" or "at ease", in other words when it has nothing better to do. Hence the term "default mode". We daydream, we ruminate, we worry and fret. It is characterized by self-concern, and as such has some clear evolutionary survival value. We do need to evaluate the past and project and plan the future. We need to think about our self-image and reputation and those of significant others in our personal and professional lives. That's all normal and necessary. But, unfortunately, it can get out of hand.

If the default mode network is over-active, it begins to interfere with the activity-focused networks. We find it hard to concentrate and perform tasks efficiently and creatively. Attention deficit disorders are neurologically characterized by the inability to inhibit the default mode network. Conversely, highly focused and creative people can silence the "blah blah blah" for extended periods of time. They can engage fully in a task to the point of being completely lost in it – they can enter "the flow". Think of Mozart composing a symphony. Think of the last time you were "lost in music". Where was your "default mode" then?

So the ability to systematically inhibit and even completely deactivate the default mode network is clearly an extremely useful thing to be able to do. Even if it comes back (and it always comes back) taking a brief holiday from it has well documented mental and physical health benefits. Meditation is one of the best ways to effect this deactivation or inhibition of the "default mode network". Prayer, fasting, ecstatic dance and psychedelic drugs are some others, although they each have their disadvantages.

If you've ever tried to teach a class of rowdy children anything, you will know how difficult it is to get through to them. This is why discipline is so important. Only once you have a quiet, attentive classroom environment can any real learning take place. The same is true of our unruly minds. We can still process information with the default mode network rumbling away in the background, but nothing sinks in at a deeper level.

On the other hand, when the mind is perfectly still and quiet, new insights strike us with the force of revelation. We "get it" at a deeper level than the surface "blah blah blah". Imagine you're reading a poem, say T.S. Eliot's *Four Quartets*. When the mind is quiet, the words touch you with a deep sense of meaning and beauty. When the mind is agitated and distracted, it's all just a jumble of words.

Another way to understand this movement is as a movement from the left hemisphere to the right hemisphere. Words are then experienced as alive and profoundly meaningful, rather than as mere signifiers in a system of abstract signs. The word *love*, for example, has merely ideational, conceptual meaning when experienced through the left hemisphere, but carries a deep, inherently meaningful charge and energy when experienced through the right hemisphere. You feel the word rather than just thinking it.

Alignment Meditation is a mantra-based meditation for the deactivation of the default mode network and the cultivation of the virtues. The first part of the meditation is designed to quiet the mind and relax the body. The second part is designed to instil and strengthen positive qualities and virtues, drawn from both Eastern and Western wisdom traditions.

The meditation proceeds through five stages:

1. Grounding
2. Clearing
3. Levels
4. Archetypes
5. Transcendentals

The first two meditations still the mind and connect us with the body and the senses. The following three meditations connect us with positive spiritual energies.

1. We align ourselves with the seven *levels* of "The Ray of Creation", Amun, Ra, Atum, Ka, Ba, Gaia, Jah, corresponding to "the Father".

2. We invoke the seven *archetypes*, Mystic, Shaman, Warrior, Monk, Philosopher, King, Friend, corresponding to "the Son".

3. We call forth the seven *transcendentals,* Peace, Love, Goodness, Beauty, Truth, Consciousness and Bliss, corresponding to "the Holy Spirit".

Each mantra is associated with a specific point in the body, using the seven points on the Christian Orthodox Cross, so that the meditation as a whole is rooted in the body as well as the mind (the seventh point being the heart).

54. Flat Batteries

I spent Christmas Eve morning with a Romanian boat mechanic. My battery was flat so I had to jump start the engine with his. As he fiddled and I hovered, I couldn't help thinking about the deeper lesson.

When we feel depleted, we need to recharge our batteries. We need a holiday. Like Christmas. But why did we get flat in the first place? Flat batteries are caused by leaks. But where are the leaks?

We leak energy all the time. Worry, anxiety, negativity, obsession, over reacting, over thinking. When we are ruled by our inner demon, addict, victim, muggle, muppet, or diva, we leak energy.

We accumulate energy simply by limiting its dispersion. Although negative thoughts and feelings are the biggest drain on our energy reserves, even ordinary thinking is a drain. To plug the leaks, you need to stop having negative thoughts, but ultimately, you need to stop thinking. Stopping thinking is meditation.

The energy we accumulate in meditation is experienced as inner vitality. It awakens the inner shaman. Mystic, Shaman, Warrior, Monk, Philosopher, King. This channel charges your inner energy reserves and defends you from leakage. If you can establish yourself as a "Philosopher King" (or "Philosopher Queen") you will find it easier and easier to stop thinking and acting like a muppet or a muggle. You will stop draining away your energy.

So keep practicing. And stop leaking!

55. Balance and Volume

Notice what happens when you sit down to meditate. After a few minutes (or seconds) you will become aware of your inner chatter. Usually you identify with it. Usually you think that it's you that's chatting (call it "thinking" if you must). But when you meditate, you consciously dis-identify from the chatter and can observe it, or rather listen to it, as if you were listening to someone else's voice.

This inner voice is a distraction. It's annoying. You can't relax, be quiet and meditate with that incessant "blah blah blah" going on. It's as if someone left a radio on in the next room. In this scenario you have three options: either you try to ignore it, switch it off or give up on meditation and go and listen to the radio instead.

A fourth option is to notice what the voice is saying and "who" is saying it. Is it moaning? Does it hate it when you try and meditate? Is it craving something? Is it trying to convince you that what you really need is a bit of chocolate? Is it full of resentment? Is it re-playing some slight and telling you how much you hate so-and-so and how dearly you would love to get your own back?

Your inner voice might belong to your inner victim, your inner addict or your inner demon. It depends which one has the upper hand in that moment. Or it might belong to your inner muggle, your inner muppet or your inner diva. Is it just chatting away inanely about nothing much? Gossiping about your friends? Is it lecturing you about something? Or constructing some devastating argument against your ideological nemesis? Is it re-assuring you how wonderful you are? What a great meditator perhaps? What a wonderfully spiritual person?

These are the elements of your "default mode network": the clamouring voices of your inner diva, demon, victim, addict, muppet and muggle. It's annoying, but it's only natural. As long as none of the voices is too insistent or too hectoring, and graciously gives way to another voice after a while, it's just about tolerable.

The pressure of your cravings are alleviated as your mind wanders and you start thinking about your friend's children; your ennui is alleviated by the excitement of your killer argument which finally proves the existence of God. And round it goes.

You only really begin to experience mental distress when you get stuck. If you just can't get the chocolate or those perfect breasts out of your head; if you can't stop replaying the scene where you push your mother-in-law down the stairs; if you seem to be swirling down a giant plug-hole of self-pity; or if you just can't stem the tide of endless inanities, interminable arguments or vain self-congratulation.

It may happen that one or more of these inner players takes over and starts tyrannizing you. You are possessed by a demon, or a diva, or a muggle, muppet, victim or addict. Your Wheel is off-kilter. It can't turn properly. The more stuck it is, the more anguish you feel. In desperation, you may even consider doing something drastic and destructive, just to alleviate your mental torment. You may seek relief in self-harm, for example.

A healthy Wheel is a balanced Wheel. None of the six spokes should stick out. Ideally, the muggle should be the dominant voice, with the most air-time. If any of the others is dominant, things tend to get unbalanced fairly quickly. Mental health therefore depends in large measure on having a good balance between these six ego states, with the muggle ultimately in charge. In fact, most psychological work and psychotherapy are oriented to this end.

Meditation can also help. As you become aware of the different voices, you can begin to exert some measure of control over them. You can resist one by activating another, for example. By recognising the victim voice, you can consciously decide not to give it any more rope with which to hang you. By recognising the muppet, you can consciously decide to let the matter rest. By recognising the diva, you can consciously decide to eat a slice of humble pie.

Balance is important. But dimming is even better. Think of a dimmer light switch. The lights are on full brightness. Perhaps there are six different colours, all equally bright. As you turn the switch, the lights get dimmer. They have less power. They are softer, gentler.

Or think of the radio. Six channels blare out their six different broadcasts at top volume. But you can turn down the volume. You can even turn it to mute.

Alignment Meditation is about balancing your habitual ego states, but more importantly, it's about dimming them, turning down the volume, *weakening* them. This is done by strengthening their opposites: strengthen the Mystic and you weaken the Diva; strengthen the Shaman and you weaken the Demon; strengthen the Warrior and you weaken the Victim; strengthen the Monk/Nun and you weaken the Addict; strengthen the Philosopher and you weaken the Muppet; strengthen the King/Queen and you weaken the Muggle.

First, balance the Wheel. Then turn down the volume. You will find that, even in the midst of muggle-talk with your friends, your King or Queen will unexpectedly shine through; in the eye of a demon-rage, your Shaman will appear; in the slough of victimhood, your Warrior will rise up. And gradually, the Cross archetypes will take the place of the Wheel archetypes, in your meditation, but more importantly, in your life.

56. Express Yourself

The Chilean transpersonal psychologist Claudio Naranjo defines three broad classes of meditation practice: formless meditation, form meditation and expressive meditation. Mindfulness, vipassana and zazen are formless: you just allow thoughts, feelings and sensations to come and go without trying to force or control them in any way. The mind and body settle naturally. Mantras, prayers and visualizations are examples of form meditation: the mind has a specific object and a specific focus.

Expressive meditation is about embodying and expressing energy, the most obvious examples being singing and dancing. But singing and dancing as expressive meditation is very different from singing karaoke or dancing at a wedding or nightclub. We learn to sing and dance as it were "from the outside", whether we have actual lessons or not. We mimetically acquire the correct vocal inflections and dance moves and mentally impose them on the body. Thus we learn the cultural conventions of song and dance.

If you can allow the body to do its own thing without external imposition, "from the inside" you are doing expressive meditation. The breath is set free. The voice is set free. The usual social constraints and habitual self-repression are temporarily suspended. The body can express itself spontaneously in sound and gesture. It feels liberating. It feels great.

To a casual observer, it can look and sound amazing or completely ridiculous. As with any art form, either the person expressing is an experienced, skilled practitioner or a clumsy novice. But if they are doing it right, even beginners can express beauty and charm. Think of unselfconscious young children. Their sense of freedom and playfulness shines through whatever they do.

Mysticism is about mastering the arts of formless meditation and form meditation. Shamanism is about mastering the art of expressive meditation. Through practice, awareness shifts from the left to the right hemisphere. You learn to think differently, speak differently, sing differently, dance differently.

And you get better at it. You refine your expression. You find the balance between order and chaos. No longer stuck in your head, you can express yourself fully, mind, body and soul.

57. Ghosts, Spirits and Angels

In *The Great Divorce*, C.S. Lewis' prolonged psychedelic trip about the afterlife, the protagonist finds himself on a bus holiday outing to Heaven. At first it is unclear whether the departure point is a particularly dreary corner of the North of England, Purgatory or Hell itself. It turns out it was Hell. And the quarrelsome day trippers turn out to be ghosts.

Ghosts come in many shapes and sizes. There are nasty ghosts, moany ghosts, hungry ghosts, ignorant ghosts, deluded ghosts and superior ghosts. In other words, all six types you would expect to find on the Wheel of Life. They are ghosts because they have failed to fully materialize. They are not quite up to the standard of reality. Which is why the grass in Heaven hurts their feet: it's too real for them.

People lost on the Wheel are basically ghosts. Sometimes they seem like zombies, vampires, werewolves, dolls or puppets, but they're basically ghosts. They're neither fully dead, nor fully alive. They're what the Ancient Egyptians called *mut*, the "living dead".

Spirits, on the other hand, have made the quantum leap from the Wheel to the Cross. They have begun the process of becoming mystics, shamans, warriors, monks or nuns, philosophers and kings or queens. These human archetypes point to different dimensions of the human encounter with reality. They have begun the process of becoming *real*.

Spirits have spirit. They have spiritual discernment and spiritual practices. But they are not fully realized or enlightened. They have not mastered themselves completely. They have not completely surrendered. They may be saints, but they are not yet angels.

Compared to ghosts, and even spirits, angels are infinitely holy, virtuous and wise. They are pure vessels of divine consciousness. It's not often you meet an angel, if ever. And if you do, the chances are you won't recognize them. Only advanced spirits have developed the eyes to see them.

58. The World, the Flesh and the Devil

According to traditional Christian theology, the world, the flesh and the devil are the three principal enemies of the soul. So what exactly are the "world", the "flesh" and the "devil", and why should we be wary of them?

In one of his most celebrated sonnets, Wordsworth wrote, "The world is too much with us; late and soon, / Getting and spending we lay waste our powers"[139]. There is something about the "world" that saps our energy and weakens us. It is debilitating, enervating, emasculating. It has something to do with "getting and spending", the commerce of life, whether in a strictly shopping mall sense, or in a broader social sense.

I think it's fair to say that both Wordsworth and the Christian theologians mean something like the "social world" when they say the "world". They clearly do not mean the natural world, as Wordsworth's next line makes patently clear: "Little we see in Nature that is ours". We are alienated from the natural world because the world of getting and spending, the social world, is too much with us.

If we let the "world" dominate us, we become muggles and muppets. Too much shopping, gossip, social media and light entertainment, and we are muggles living in a muggle world. Too much bad science, philosophy, politics or religion and we are muppets living in a muppet world. We are so entranced by the human world of culture and society that we forget about Nature or God. We are lost in the "World Trance".

Part of the problem is that we love problem solving, even when it's not our problem. Whether it's Jenny's marriage or Jonny's selfishness, there is always something to vicariously sort out and worry about. But it takes a lot of time and energy. Muggle logic rules that this is precisely what you should be spending your time and energy on (because you're a muggle and that's what muggles do).

Muppet logic demands that you focus instead on sorting out and worrying about the world's problems, not just trivial personal ones. The Middle East Crisis, Climate Change, Nuclear Disarmament, Crony Capitalism, Big Data, China, America, Technology, Deforestation, Immorality, Godlessness. These are the kinds of problems you should be solving (even if deep down you know you haven't the faintest idea what the problem is, let alone the solution.) No wonder all this "lays waste our powers".

So what about the "flesh"? That's just the prudish hangover of sexually repressed puritans, isn't it? Maybe so, but is there any truth in it? Should we be on guard against the temptations of the flesh?

It's surely common knowledge, from our own experience as well as the countless examples of others, that if you over-indulge your appetites you will run into difficulties. It doesn't matter what your particular poison happens to be: Moscow Mule, Manhattan, Merlot, Weed, Vape, Coke, Porn Hub, Tinder, Grinder, Burger and Chips, Chocolate Digestives, Café Latte with a Caramel Shot.

Of course the pleasures of the flesh are perfectly innocent and natural, up to a point. But if you're not careful you will end up a slave to desire: you will end up a victim and an addict. As you progressively lose your ability to resist ever more insistent cravings and temptations, you will swing between the highs and lows of the victim-addict cycle, in ever narrowing turns of the screw.

The "world" is represented by the muggle and muppet archetypes; the "flesh" is represented by the addict and victim archetypes; so the "devil" must be represented by the diva and demon archetypes. So what is the "devil"?

The devil is a "demon whisperer". He insinuates discord, enmity, suspicion, hatred, vindictiveness, resentment and simmering rage. But the devil is also a "diva whisperer". He sows the seeds of ego with two simple, seemingly innocuous thoughts: *no-one can tell me what to do* and *I'm as good as you*. With these two thoughts, you are persuaded that there is no authority above you. You are subsequently immunized against all higher learning, but most importantly for the devil's purposes, against all religion.

The genius of the modern-day devil, is that he has succeeded in convincing people that this is actually a great and noble virtue. The intrinsic dignity of modern democratic humanism is that it bows down to nobody. The individual self is supreme. Call it "self-reliance", "authenticity" or "self-determination", the proud humanist counts all of human history, art, literature, science, philosophy and religion as nothing compared to the subjective sovereignty of his "secret, sacred self".

If he decides that Wagner is rubbish, then Wagner is rubbish. If he concludes that Christianity is a big bag of nonsense, then so it is. What pope or priest can claim any authority over his pure humanist soul? He is the self-proclaimed arbiter of his own truth. And you can't argue with that. If he deigns to listen to anyone else, it is only because of his infinite magnanimity and patronage, and only because he secretly likes what he hears.

So our inner "muppet-muggles" are in a World trance, our inner "victim-addicts" are slaves to the Flesh and our inner "diva-demons" are in thrall to the Devil. Could it get any worse? Of course it could. But it could also be a hell of a lot better.

59. Orthodoxy

The first step on the Buddha's Noble Eightfold Path is right view or right thinking. Why? Wouldn't it be better to start with right mindfulness (the seventh practice) or even right samadhi (the eighth)? Clearly, he was not advocating for a strict linear progression through these eight practices. They are inter-dependent and mutually supportive. But neither are they arbitrarily listed. It is no accident that right view comes first.

Right view refers to your understanding of reality. It's about your worldview, your "Umwelt". However much mindfulness you practice, if your world view is wrong, you will continue to delude yourself about reality. The Buddhist Tantrikas called the practice of acquiring a right world view "dalliance". It is one element of a threefold practice of perception, dalliance and purification, which functions as a cycle of knowledge.

It is tempting to align dalliance with the practice of philosophy, except that so much of philosophy is clearly wrong. Philosophy in the basic sense of a love of wisdom or a search for truth is obviously the foundation of dalliance. Dalliance is about mulling things over in your mind, spending time with ideas, in other words, *thinking*. But not any old thinking and not any old philosophy.

There is such a thing as right thinking, which implies right thinkers. Therefore dalliance in the service of right view relies on spending time with right thinkers who themselves hold right views. This may sound obvious to the point of tautology, but it implies something very important about our relationship to truth and reality. There is such a thing as orthodoxy.

The problem is, who defines orthodoxy? The Theravada? The Mahayana? The Catholic Church? The Church of Latter Day Saints? The Church of Woke? The Party? It is tempting to get rid of the concept altogether and live with heterodoxy, or at least with differences of opinion. Can't we all just agree to disagree, live and let live, and follow our own paths and our own orthodoxies?

There's no point blindly following dogmas. If you're not thinking for yourself, you're only as good as a Herdwick sheep. But you can't create your own orthodoxy from scratch either. If you resist the temptation of subjectivism and relativism, you are committed to the idea of objective truth and therefore of right views and wrong views.

Orthodoxy implies heresy. But you can't be a heretic if you don't belong to a tradition. If you don't know the first thing about Buddhism, you are not a Buddhist heretic. You have to be a Buddhist before you can be that. In the East, worldviews grow out of the soil of ancient traditions: Buddhism, Hinduism (for the sake of brevity), Jainism, Confucianism, Taoism, Shintoism.

If you were born in Asia of Asian heritage, you will probably belong to one of these traditions. There are four modes in which you can relate to your tradition. You can be a practicing Buddhist, for example, or a nominal Buddhist, or an apostate or a heretic. If you are practicing, you follow the teachings of the Buddha and his followers to the best of your ability with a certain amount of devotion. If you are nominal, you just go through the motions and attend the major festivals. If you an apostate, you renounce and even denounce your Buddhist heritage. If you are a heretic, you pervert and distort the teachings and stray down wrong paths.

The Abrahamic faiths constitute the major orthodox traditions of the Western world. If you are Jewish, Christian or Moslem, you will also be either practicing (even devout), or nominal, or an apostate or a heretic. But what if you are neither Jewish, or Christian or Moslem? What if you don't belong to any religious tradition, East or West? Then what are you? Are you free to be whatever you like?

In theory, I suppose so. But in practice, who can honestly say that they do not belong to any religious tradition whatsoever? If you are from Asia or Europe, you only need to go back two or three generations to see that you are connected to one of the major world religions. This is because Asia and Europe have had religious traditions stretching back for millennia. Until fairly recently, for example, Europe was known as "Christendom". If you weren't Jewish or Moslem, you were almost certainly Christian.

For Africa and the Americas and Australasia things are a bit more complicated, because the spiritual landscape was, until the arrival of world religions like Christianity and Islam, dominated by a panoply of different indigenous belief systems, tribal, shamanic, and pagan. But then of course, so was Europe and Asia. It's just that the transformation occurred a few centuries later.

Are all the major world religions equally true? Is indigenous "paganism" true? Are modern belief systems true? Many people believe that just as Christianity supplanted the superstitions of primitive peoples (the Saxons for example), secular modern views have supplanted the superstitions of religious people (Christians for example). This is the Enlightenment Myth anyway.

So what is orthodoxy in "post-Christian Europe"? Is it allegiance to a set of post-Christian doctrines? Or to a set of pre-Christian doctrines? Or even maybe to Christian doctrines? Or is it some kind of distillation of the "truths" running through all three?

If you are a Christian, or have a Christian heritage, you either call yourself a Christian, in which case you are devout, nominal or heretical, or you don't, in which case you are an apostate. As Ben Shapiro in *The Right Side of History: How Reason and Moral Purpose made the West* and Tom Holland in *Dominion: The Making of the Western Mind* make clear, in Europe we are all inheritors of the Judeo-Christian tradition, whether we like it or not. So all Europeans (apart from recent immigrants obviously) who do not consider themselves to be Christians or Jews are basically apostates. In fact you could say that atheists the world over are actually apostates, because they have turned their backs on their religious heritage.

So what? What's the difference? An "atheist" would quite understandably throw my "apostate" jibe back in my face. Who am I? The Spanish Inquisition? Beyond the name calling, the deeper point about these labels is that they actually define which is the primary and which the derivative condition.

The term "atheist" is obviously derivative of the term "theist". It is a negative concept, defined by that which it lacks. This is how it was originally meant, and its original usage did indeed carry negative connotations.

These have largely been lost, due to the inversion of the demographic proportions of believers to unbelievers, so that most people hear the word "atheist" as normative and "theist" as exceptional. The term "apostate", on the other hand, is unambiguous - it is a failure of belief, a falling away from belief, a repudiation of belief, analogous to the word "treason" in the political sphere.

A minority of Europeans are now practicing Christians or Jews, in other words, believers. The others are tenuous "nominals" or "apostates" (lapsed Catholics, secular Jews, etc). Apostates and nominals, who either turn their backs on religion entirely or else just don't bother much about it, are basically muggles. Heretics, who either turn their ire against their heritage or hold to a parasitic or bastardised form of it, are basically muppets.

So what would be the modern orthodox counterparts to the four basic muppet heresies in the West? By "orthodox" I mean modern post-Christian beliefs which are in line with Christianity as well as with ancient pre-Christian pagan beliefs, in other words, perennial beliefs which constitute the enduring core of Western civilization.

In the place of militant atheism (H1) I would volunteer panentheism. In the place of moral relativism (H2) I would advocate moral realism and virtue ethics. In the place of political utopianism (H3) I would propose social democracy and classical/conservative liberalism as two sides of an ongoing political conversation. In the place of religious fundamentalism (H4) I would insist on experiential, mythopoetic, contemplative spirituality.

It is right and proper to be a Christian panentheist, a Christian moralist, a Christian democrat and a Christian contemplative, and preferably all four at once. This is right view (in my view).

60. The Magic of Christianity

Religions are always a bit strange. If they weren't, they wouldn't be able to hold our attention for very long. At the heart of every religion is a mystery, which the religion must communicate to us without either normalising it or making it too impossibly remote from our everyday lived experience.

I have been fascinated by the strangeness of Ancient Egyptian religion, for example, ever since my "Egyptian experience" (a psychedelic trip on mushrooms in my twenties). The images and symbols clearly have some powerful esoteric significance, difficult to fathom at this far remove from the living civilization.

The Egyptian religion was explicitly based on magic. There were magic spells and magic amulets to guide the dead in their passage through the afterlife. Many of the spells are collected in *The Egyptian Book of the Dead*. Another magic based religion is that of the Tibetans, with their syncretism of Buddhism and Bon (an older, shamanistic religion). Their magical instructions for the afterlife are known (unsurprisingly) as *The Tibetan Book of the Dead*.

Anthropologists have attempted to classify religious practices throughout the ages in various ways. One such classification, made famous by Jean Gebser, and even more famous by Ken Wilber, traces an evolutionary arc from prehistory to the present. Gebser identifies five broad stages: the archaic, the magic, the mythical, the mental and the integral.

From the vantage point of the mental stage, the stage of Modernity, the archaic, magic and mythical stages seem like primitive superstitions. They seem almost irredeemably strange. But the integral stage beyond the mental also seems strange. Wilber called this situation the "pre/trans fallacy", by which he simply meant that "pre"-mental and "trans"-mental phenomena are easily confused. Someone like Freud would typically reduce transpersonal states to prepersonal states, and someone like Jung would elevate prepersonal states to transpersonal ones.

In the eighteenth and nineteenth centuries, there were highly educated Europeans and Americans whose intellectual Enlightenment sensibilities were offended by the magical and mythical elements of Christianity. Some of them attempted to purge Christianity of its superstitions and thereby create a purely rational modern religion, for example Thomas Jefferson, whose "Jefferson Bible" stresses the moral message of Jesus but without any of the miracles. Many of them would call themselves Deists, if not outright atheists.

Paul said, "But we preach Christ crucified, to the Jews a stumbling block, and to the Greeks foolishness."[140] It wasn't just modern Enlightenment intellectuals who struggled with the extraordinary claims of Christianity. It was already unbelievable at its very inception. We may be tempted to assume that people in the ancient world were generally more ignorant or more gullible than we are, but this is patently untrue. The Jews had a centuries' old, painfully realistic, mature religion and the Greeks boasted a wealth of highly sophisticated philosophers. The world in which Paul preached was not stupid.

As a teenager I was drawn to Buddhism. I had no problem with the claim that the Buddha achieved enlightenment through his own heroic spiritual exertions. Why couldn't someone who meditated for hours every day eventually break through and experience the truth of reality beyond all the obscuring veils of the mind? It makes rational sense. If the mind is your interface with reality, then cleansing the mind, or cleansing "the doors of perception" would presumably bring you to a truer, more intimate relationship with Reality.

It stands to reason. It's only natural. It's not rocket science. Only perverse sophists would dispute this. Now, what if you substituted the word "God" for "Reality"? Would this radically change anything? Not really. Both words point to a mystery beyond the current limits of our human minds. Whether you are a Buddhist and talk in terms of Reality or a Vedantin and talk in terms of God, the process and the results are the same.

The Jews talked in terms of "God". They were the people of Israel, which means "to struggle with God". They were bound by a covenant with God, a commitment to God, which meant that they had to live their lives as much as possible according to the Law of God, which we might translate as something like "the Structure of Reality".

The Jews and the Gentiles, just like the Buddhists and Vedantins, were followers of natural religion. Through religious observances and practices, prayer, fasting, meditation and contemplation, you could by your own spiritual efforts, approach the "Holy of Holies", the mystery at the heart of Reality.

Of course there are traces of magic and mythical thinking in all these traditions, but they are all perfectly rational in essence, if not "integral". As a teenager, I could see that these were all different expressions of the same natural spiritual impulse to greater consciousness and life. It was just the culture, the language and the idiom that differed.

There was Buddha, there was Krishna, there was Socrates, there was Lao Tzu, there was Moses, there was Christ, there was Ramana Maharshi. Why couldn't they all be "sons of God"? Weren't all spiritual masters equally enlightened? They were the spiritual heroes who had broken through to the other side, who had crossed to the other shore. Religions were just the signposts they had left for those who came after.

But Christians annoyingly claimed that Jesus Christ was "the only begotten son of God". I always went silent at that part of the Mass. He wasn't the only one! That was just petty, arrogant and wrong. Many buddhas had appeared in the world, and many more were yet to appear, and Jesus was just one of them. Why be so exclusivist and parochial about it?

The Virgin Birth was silly. The Miracles were silly. The Resurrection was silly. Apart from the exclusivism of "the Only One", these were my three big stumbling blocks. Like the Deists, like Franklin and Jefferson, I could understand the natural theology, but these crazy supernatural claims made a mockery of the whole thing.

It turns out it was me that was arrogant and wrong. I failed to understand the magic of Christianity. And I failed to understand the true meaning of "the only begotten son of God". Jesus was not the only son of God. He was the only *begotten* son of God. Everyone was called to be sons and daughters of God. The saints, the prophets, the enlightened masters, these had all become children of God through their own spiritual efforts. They were ordinary human beings, like Siddhartha Buddha, who had achieved buddhahood.

The Jews and the Greeks had no problem with this of course. Live a holy and devout life, and if you're lucky, you might just make it into the spiritual hall of fame. They were spiritual realists. They had outgrown the superstitious magical thinking of the Egyptians. You couldn't just say the right spell and click your fingers. You had to do the hard spiritual, philosophical and psychological work if you wanted to be a "son of God".

Christianity has been described as the melding together of three separate traditions, the Jewish, the Greek and the Mystery Religions of the Mediterranean. There is a striking resemblance between the Cult of Jesus and the Cults of Osiris, Mithras and Orpheus for example. They were all of divine provenance, performed miracles and rose from the dead. But they were clearly mythical gods worshipped in a mythical context. We might say they belonged to Gebser's "mythical" stage.

Christianity emerged in a very different context, a firmly established "mental" context. The Pharisees and the Philosophers were not weavers of yarns and tall stories. They were serious, meticulous, sober thinkers. So Paul preaching "Christ crucified" must have had very different implications to the magical-mythical claims of the Mystery Schools (although what actually went on there is unsurprisingly shrouded in mystery).

Gautama Buddha is reputed to have attained spiritual enlightenment at the age of thirty-five. His achievement is a great source of inspiration for spiritual aspirants. If he did it, so can you. Meditating on the person of Buddha, perhaps seated in the lotus position with a faint, knowing smile playing over his lips, encourages a state of tranquillity and mental poise. You sit like a buddha, as if you were a buddha, and so manifest the enlightened qualities of buddhahood. It is a focused application of what Jung called "active imagination".

Jesus Christ is reputed to have been *born* enlightened. He died about the same age as the Buddha's enlightenment. Since he only preached for a handful or years, it is conceivable that he in fact achieved enlightenment, like the Buddha, in his early thirties or late twenties perhaps, in which case he was really just another prophet in the Jewish tradition, which is what Jews and Muslims generally believe. In this case, he was just another instance of natural religion.

On the other hand, if Jesus is considered to be "the only begotten son of God", born of the Virgin Mary, then meditating on the person of Jesus carries more weight than meditating on the person of Buddha or of your personal guru. The Buddha was a human being. Your guru is a human being. The Christian claim is that Jesus was essentially a human being but also essentially God, both fully human and fully God.

This is magic. It doesn't make sense on the purely mental level. But it makes sense on the "integral" level. It works a bit like alchemy. Just as the alchemists employed a small quantity of gold in order to catalyse a transmutation process resulting in the creation of more gold, so the early Christians would meditate on the divine "gold" of Jesus in order to catalyse their own divinity. They would use their "active imagination" to share in his death and resurrection, and so be spiritually reborn themselves.

The perennial strangeness of Christianity is due to its magic. Faith, belief and grace are the hallmarks of the Christian method. They depend on the mysterious magic of psycho-spiritual processes, which will always evade our rational understanding. We don't know exactly why, or exactly how, but it seems to work. Not only that, but it seems to work much faster than the usual natural methods, which take years and decades, even lifetimes, of hard graft. This is why Christianity was originally so successful. It's also why it is so misunderstood and neglected now, in this Muggle-Muppet Age of Pure Reason and Irrationality.

There is the *Jesus of History* and the *Christ of Faith*. Most of the misunderstanding of Christianity boils down to confusion between these two different people. We cannot know anything about either of them with absolute certainty. The Jesus of history is lost to us in the mists of time. We cannot hope to speculatively reconstruct him from the meagre historical fragments at our disposal. As a consequence, every age reconstructs him in its own image. However "historically sound", the picture we end up with is always a fiction. The Christ of faith is even more difficult to pin down, as it has morphed and mutated almost beyond recognition over the centuries. In any case, it is impossible to generalise out from such an intensely personal experience. Beyond certain basic similarities, every Christian's experience of the Christ of faith is necessarily unique and individual.

So who was Jesus Christ? In my (speculative) opinion, he was both an enlightened prophet, something like a Jewish buddha (the Jesus of history) and a divine being "eternally begotten of the Father" (the Christ of faith). This is the only way I can make sense of the impact he had during his lifetime and the impact he had after his death (and resurrection). And I see no reason not to believe in both.

61. The Philosopher Monk

How do we know what's true? Do we discover truth or do we create it? It is a mind-bending problem. If you are a naturalist, you have to assume that truth claims and propositions are the result of evolutionary processes, in other words that they emerge from the bottom up. If so, we do not so much discover truth as create it.

There is the perennial intractable problem of *intentionality*: how can any physical process, however complicated, be "about" anything? How can we derive thoughts and ideas from matter? Even if we grant intentionality, how can we associate thoughts and ideas meaningfully, with sound logic? How do we know that one line of argument is true while another is false?

The materialist, committed as he is to a causally closed physical system, is utterly flummoxed. He can't even get off the ground, because he can't account for consciousness in his hypothesis. However, if we grant him consciousness, and allow him some panpsychist wiggle-room, things don't actually look that much better. We can go some way towards explaining the emergence of higher forms of consciousness, but the problem of the right association of ideas to produce "truth" remains. How do we know it's true?

John Keats famously wrote, ""Beauty is truth, truth beauty," – that is all/Ye know on earth, and all ye need to know."[141] Does this help? Well, it does give us a way of approaching what we call "truth" if we think of ideas as *patterns* of thought. Just as words can be arranged in sentences, paragraphs, pages and books, so can concepts be organised and arranged together in sequences and patterns. Could it be that a certain configuration of thought strikes us as true because it's beautiful? We are struck by the rightness of it, the correspondence and harmony of its parts, just as we do when we make aesthetic judgments.

Think of a mosaic: if the tiles fit together perfectly, with each edge lining up just right (a craftsman would say the edges were "true") and all the pieces in their proper place, and the picture corresponds truthfully to some recognisable aspect of reality, we experience a sense of fitness, of rightness, of beauty and truth.

But the mosaic must itself be representing or approximating to some other pattern, a pattern to which it is pointing, and which we see, dimly but perhaps clearly, in the mosaic itself.

In other words, beauty and truth are two aspects of one thing: the reflection of a pattern of reality through some medium, whether natural and "accidental" (as in a beautiful sunset) or man-made and "intentional" (as in a painting of a sunset). Reality is composed of patterns, and it is the task of art and philosophy, of beauty and truth, to find these out. From this point of view, therefore, truth is both created and discovered. We create the form (the "finger") but discover the truth to which it points (the "moon").

The "Philosopher" is a *Jnana Yogi*. She is a lover of wisdom and seeker of truth. The "Monk" is a *Bhakti Yogi*. He is a lover of beauty. The one experiences insight and the other devotion. But the two are ultimately inseparable. If you do separate them, the Philosopher is reduced to dry scholasticism and the Monk to meaningless emotivism. Truth is apprehended in beauty and beauty in truth.

To recognise the lineaments of truth requires exposure to and familiarity with patterns of sense making. It requires *dalliance*. Dalliance means dwelling on truth patterns. In other words, it means doing philosophy, reading and thinking. If they are good patterns, the mind becomes habituated to good pattern recognition. It learns to see the truth.

The same hold for our relationship to beauty and aesthetic appreciation. Only through exposure to patterns of beauty in language, poetry, the visual arts, music, etc. do we become proficient at recognising beauty. We refine our tastes. We begin to see through the semi-transparent form to the transcendent reality beyond.

The Christian monks of the Middle Ages were scholars and artists. They spent their lives studying and contemplating, composing and illustrating. They were Philosopher Monks. However, they were not only that. They were also Mystics. They prayed and meditated. They cleared their minds of all preconceptions. They subjected themselves to self-emptying, "kenosis" and *purification*. This in turn opened the way to "gnosis" and *perception*.

What is perception in the Tantric sense (see *The Hermeneutics of Faith*) but a glimpse of the unmediated patterns of reality? These are the visions and revelations which are in constant dialogue with the reflections of *dalliance* ("pistis"). Pistis is often translated as *faith*. You need to have faith in the patterns, in the objects of dalliance to get anything out of them. This is why the Christian monks practiced "lectio divina", an absorbed, meditative approach to the text.

So what did the monks have faith in? What did they dally with? Well, they rediscovered and translated the Ancient Greek classics of philosophy and drama. But most centrally, and most importantly, they studied the Bible. They wrote hymns and poems, painted pictures and icons, carved statues and sculptures, built churches and cathedrals. They wrote theology and philosophy. They performed rituals and conducted services.

The whole of Christianity can be characterised as a two millennia long dalliance with the Bible. Considering the Bible is itself dalliance with earlier sections of the Bible, this process of dalliance actually stretches back to the early writers of Genesis, some seven centuries before Christ.

Christianity is not a set of propositions, much less a set of injunctions or Thou Shalt Nots. Christianity is the confessions of Augustine, the poems of Thomas Traherne, the music of Bach, the hymns of Charles Wesley, the cathedral of Chartres, Michelangelo's David. It is too many things to even know where to start. It is an ongoing conversation of what it means to be human, and how best to be human, by humans in the Middle East, Europe and North Africa and then, later, throughout the world.

Of course, it is to some extent a matter of personal taste, but in my view the most beautiful architecture in the world was built by Christians to worship their God. The most beautiful paintings and sculptures, the most beautiful poetry and music, the most beautiful religious and mystical writing, were all produced by Christians. Christians founded the public schools and universities. They built Oxford and Cambridge. They established the legal system and laid the foundations for modern democratic government.

Atheists like to take all the credit for "modernity". But the Enlightenment owed almost everything to Christianity. Those who tried to cut themselves off from their Christian roots were cutting their nose off to spite their face. Where will famous atheists like T.H. Huxley, Spencer, Marx, Nietzsche, Freud, Sartre, Foucault, Hitchens and Dawkins be in a thousand years' time? John Lennon famously claimed that The Beatles were bigger than Jesus. Where are The Beatles now, just a few decades later? (and this from a Beatles fan). Where will Lennon be in a thousand years' time?

The anti-theists, one after another, convince themselves and others that theirs is the final nail in the coffin of Christianity. But even the vile persecution and violence against the Church in the former Soviet Union, the mass murders and desecration couldn't completely extinguish the flame. The Russian Orthodox Church is slowly recovering and will live on indefinitely. Where is The League of the Militant Godless now? Where will Lenin and Stalin be in a thousand years' time? Villains in a schoolgirl's history book. Nothing more.

All the brash, strutting self-proclaimed God Killers go the way of Ozymandias in Shelley's poem:

"My name is Ozymandias, king of kings:
Look on my works, ye Mighty, and despair!'
Nothing beside remains. Round the decay
Of that colossal wreck, boundless and bare
The lone and level sands stretch far away."[142]

But Christianity will never die. In a very real sense, this ongoing conversation with the Bible, the central book of humanity, will continue until the end of human history, as John correctly predicted in its last book, the Book of Revelations. The true pattern of reality is there, waiting to be brought out in ever greater clarity and beauty:

"For now we see through a glass, darkly; but then face to face: now I know in part; but then shall I know even as also I am known."[143]

62. The Warrior King

In the last chapter I looked at the relationship between the Philosopher and Monk archetypes, and the intimate connection between truth and beauty. I argued that contemplation of patterns of thought and expression in pursuit of the True and the Beautiful is an exercise in *dalliance*, and that in Christian monasticism, this presupposed both *purification* and *perception* ("kenosis" and "gnosis"), represented on the Cross by the Mystic and Shaman archetypes.

The Mystic Shaman is the foundational core of knowledge and experience, providing right hemisphere, direct, unmediated contact with reality. The Philosopher Monk is engaged in dalliance over truth and beauty. So what about the Warrior King? Where does he fit in?

In *No Yoga, No Joy* I equated the four archetypes Warrior, Monk, Philosopher, King, with the four yogas taught by Krishna to Arjuna in the Bhagavad Gita. The Warrior is a *Karma Yogi*, the Monk a *Bhakti Yogi*, the Philosopher a *Jnana Yogi* and the King a *Raja Yogi*. I discussed Bhakti Yoga and Jnana Yoga, the yogas of devotion and knowledge, beauty and truth, in the last chapter. Here I will look at Karma Yoga and Raja Yoga, the yogas of action and self-inquiry.

The problem with action is that it inevitably leads to more action. It is subject to the universal law of cause and effect, the universal law of karma. Thus if you perform a "bad" action you will have to deal with the consequences: what goes around comes around. The more bad actions you commit, the more bad karma you create. You end up tying yourself up in all sorts of karmic knots, and it takes ten times as much time and effort to untangle to knots as it did to tie them.

Krishna's elegant solution to the problem of karma is to act without attachment to the fruits of action. This is the central practice of Karma Yoga. Through detachment, you train yourself to act dispassionately, and to do your duty without the desire for any sort of reward. As a warrior, you are not looking for glory, honour or riches. You do not fight and kill with hatred or sadism in your heart. You do it in a spirit of non-attachment. You do it with what the Taoists call *wei-wu-wei*, action-no-action.

The point is to minimise the karmic fallout. Ultimately, you may even overcome karma altogether, like a bird that leaves no tracks (unlike a 747). However, this seems like an impossible task. Whatever you do has consequences, good or bad. How can you escape the law of cause and effect? And what about good effects? Shouldn't that be your aim?

Krishna's point is that if you focus on the effects of your actions, whether you deem them to be good or bad, you will inevitably generate more karma for yourself, which you cannot predict or control and which you will have to deal with one way or another. So you shouldn't focus on the effects. You should focus fully and exclusively on the action itself. Just do the right thing and do the best you can. The effects are not your business.

This moral ideal of dispassionate action is present in India and in China. But it is also there in Stoicism and in Christianity in the doctrine of Charity and "Good Works". The point of doing good is not in the reward but simply in the doing of it, inspired for example by Christ's claim that "Inasmuch as ye have done it unto one of the least of these my brethren, ye have done it unto me."[144] In Christian terms, your reward is in Heaven not on Earth.

The Christian version of Karma Yoga is therefore Good Works. However, whether Hindu, Taoist or Christian, the problem still remains: how to act without remainder? How to act cleanly and selflessly without generating more karma? To act with no attachment to the results is easier said than done.

The problem is in the actor not the action. Who is performing the action? Inevitably, it is some ego, with a host of unconscious motivations and agendas. This is what makes it so difficult to do what you know you should do and not do what you know you shouldn't. Some unconscious ego, some diva, demon, victim, addict, muggle or muppet is secretly pulling the strings.

Only when you are free of these ego states, or subpersonalities, can you truly act cleanly and dispassionately. Only when you know who you are, can you do the right thing without remainder. And when you know who you are, you are a King or a Queen. You know that your essential nature is identical with the essential nature of the universe.

In other words, your soul (Atman) is part and parcel of God (Brahman). Or to put it in a Christian idiom, you are made in the image of God. Or again, you are a child of God.

This Self-Realisation is achieved through Self-Inquiry: just keep asking yourself, "Who am I?" until it dawns on you. When the penny drops, you will find yourself straightening up. You will possess a power and authority, a nobility and a dignity that wasn't there a moment before. You will see clearly and judge right from wrong without confusion or hesitation.

Now your challenge is to remain a King (or Queen). How do you do that? By doing the right thing. It may be that there are ten wrong things you could do but only one right thing. You need to choose that one, and do it well. You are of course, free to choose, but if you want to remain King (or Queen) you really have no choice. As soon as you put a foot wrong, make a wrong turn, or neglect to do the right thing for its own sake, you will create the instant karma that will knock you off your throne. You will forget who you really are.

As well as the *dalliance* of truth and beauty, we also need the *dalliance* of consciousness and goodness. We need to remember who we are and do the right thing. We need to remember that we are children of God and brothers and sisters in Christ, and do Good Works in a spirit of faithful obedience and service. And when we go wrong, we need to know that we are forgiven if we truly repent. Then we can write off our bad karma and pick up where we left off.

63. The One True Refuge

As I write, a violent storm is raging. Just back from Sunday Mass, I ran from the car through the horizontal rain, head bowed against the gale, and shut the door with relief against the swirling chaos. The house is empty and quiet, save for the roaring of the wind outside. It feels like a true refuge.

The idea of refuge is fundamental to Buddhists, whose daily vow is to take refuge in the Buddha, the Dharma and the Sangha. Taking refuge both acknowledges the steadfast reliability of the Buddhist way and the inherent unreliability of the things of the world. By taking refuge in the "Three Treasures", you simultaneously reject the refuges offered by the world, such as a house. The archetypal Buddhist monk is a homeless mendicant, which forcefully expresses this exclusive refuge in the one thing that really matters.

The idea of refuge also appears in other traditions, not least the Christian. The Biblical authors exhort us to "Trust in the LORD with all your heart and lean not on your own understanding"[145]. For Jews and Christians, the one true refuge is God. He is the only truly trustworthy refuge.

The things of the world can never satisfy the spiritual longings of the human soul. If you rely on riches and material possessions, you will always be disappointed. Neither will you find refuge from the storms and tempests of the world in fame, fortune, power or influence; you may find temporary relief, but not lasting peace. The fashionable places where Divas and Muggles seek refuge are ultimately neither safe, nor solid, nor reliable.

Alcoholics take refuge in alcohol. They know this is not a safe refuge, but they can't help themselves. There is no safe harbour for dedicated Addicts, Victims or Demons, and there is no true refuge for Muggles, Muppets or Divas. None of our worldly desires and commitments hold up to the infinite power of Reality.

The One True Refuge

There is no ultimate refuge in science, philosophy, politics, religion or art. As soon as you try to make them into a refuge, you inevitably "lean on your own understanding" and turn them into idols. Even if you believe that science will one day explain everything, you cannot take refuge in science. Reality does not consist of explanations, but neither can anything be represented in one way, without taking into account its opposite. The same is true of all other human disciplines, including religion.

Relative truth is founded on opposition and contrast. For example, we should heed the wisdom of our elders, but not to the exclusion of the fresh insights of youth. Age and youth, past and future, conservatism and liberalism; all relative things exist in tension with their opposites. They are like two sides of the same coin that can be endlessly flipped over.

You cannot take refuge in the future any more than you can take refuge in the past. You cannot take refuge in conservatism or liberalism, and you cannot take refuge in Christianity or Buddhism or any other religion. The one true refuge is God alone. Whatever champions one side of a coin and refuses the other is no refuge at all. Reality will not be brow-beaten or bullied. When you dig your heels in and fight for one side over the other, you are in Muppet Land fighting a Muppet War with no possibility of ultimate victory.

It is natural to prefer one side of a coin to the other. Your personal beliefs are like so many coins turned favourite side up. Which way up depends largely on your social conditioning. Your personal likes and dislikes are equally the result of a lifetime of conditioning. In fact, everything on the Wheel is the result of conditioning. It all adds up to your sense of identity, which is really nothing more than the sum total of the things you identify with. Are you a liberal or a conservative? Do you prefer coffee or tea? These are the things that make you who you are. But they can all be flipped.

The Wheel represents the ego in all its complexity. But are you really that? Are you identical with your ego? If you continuously defend and maintain your ego in order to achieve an illusion of solidity and permanence, that doesn't mean that your ego is solid or permanent. Can you take refuge in yourself? Can you find stability and peace? Can you find rock bottom?

Jesus said:

"Therefore whosoever heareth these sayings of mine, and doeth them, I will liken him unto a wise man, which built his house upon a rock:

And the rain descended, and the floods came, and the winds blew, and beat upon that house; and it fell not: for it was founded upon a rock.

And every one that heareth these sayings of mine, and doeth them not, shall be likened unto a foolish man, which built his house upon the sand:

And the rain descended, and the floods came, and the winds blew, and beat upon that house; and it fell: and great was the fall of it."[146]

64. Integral Yoga

Christians take refuge in the Father, Son and Holy Spirit and the rest of the articles of the Apostle's Creed, including "the holy catholic Church, the communion of saints, the forgiveness of sins, the resurrection of the body, and the life everlasting." Saying the creed (*credo* means "I believe") is a declaration of commitment, trust and refuge taking, not just a statement of belief in the common, propositional sense.

"Belief" has different connotations, depending on whether you are talking left or right brain hemispheres (see McGilchrist on "faux amis"). From the right hemisphere point of view, therefore, the creeds (both the Apostle's and the Nicene Creeds) are the Christian equivalents of the Buddhist vow to take refuge in Buddha, Dharma and Shangha.

In the last chapter, I claimed that the one true refuge is God. There is no contradiction here. The particular spiritual tradition doesn't matter. The point is that, whatever the idiom, the follower takes refuge in that which is beyond the ordinary world, beyond the Wheel.

For Buddhists, the ultimate ground of Being is "Emptiness"; for Christians, it's "God". Here there can be no identity, no ego. All supports are taken away. I cannot be a diva, demon, victim, addict, muppet or muggle in the One True Refuge. Who am I then?

In truth, I am nobody. I am no longer an identity, a personality, a self, a body or a mind. I am not defined by what I "am". If someone asked me who I was, I would probably say "I don't know". I don't care who I am. Does it matter? *Should* I be someone? The world is obsessed with "being someone". Life on the Wheel depends on it. Life coaches encourage it. They seem to believe that being human is all about human beings being someone. Is it?

Step off the Wheel and you step off the world. You give up everything; you cut all ties. You give up your self and you give up the world, because self and world are two sides of the same coin. You enter the cloud of forgetting. You forget everything.

Then you enter an even thicker cloud, the cloud of unknowing. You don't know anything. It's all a blank.

When you are in this kenotic state of radical emptiness, although you would hesitate to name it, you are in the silent heart of infinite creative potential. People in this state are traditionally called mystics. So, although it resists all labels, we can helpfully identify this state with the archetypal figure, the Mystic.

You come into the present. Past and future evaporate. Body and mind drop off. Thoughts stop churning. You find yourself in deepest stillness and silence, at "the still point of the turning world"[147].

Then you "enter the dragon". Your consciousness, freed from the endless round of mentation, sinks down into the body. Your breath becomes dragon breath. You are filled with fire. You come alive. Your voice is the voice of all living creatures. Your body is a supple powerhouse of pure energy. You have woken the sleeping dragon, the sleeping serpent kundalini.

Now you are a Shaman. You have the power of healing and power to raise the dead. You can wake up the life force of others. Like an electrical current, the kundalini passes from one body to another. You can jump start people, especially in a sacred, ceremonial setting, and especially under the influence of psychedelics like peyote or ayahuasca.

The trunk of the tree grows out of the Mystic in the sky and the Shaman in the earth. The branches which grow from the trunk depend on the Warrior, Monk, Philosopher and King.

Mystic and Shaman represent the states of radical emptiness and radical aliveness. They correspond to the Egyptian gods *Amun* and *Ra* and the transcendentals *Peace* and *Love*. But you cannot remain in this state forever. So what do you do when you come back down to earth?

You do what needs to be done. You peel onions and wash the dishes. You "chop wood and carry water". Doing your duty without attachment to results, you just do what you are called to do, moment by moment.

When you sit, just sit. This is called *shikantaza* in Japanese. When you walk, just walk. When you fight, just fight. When you dance, just dance. Dogen Zenji taught that training and enlightenment are one. Krishna taught Arjuna the same lesson. He called it Karma Yoga.

Soto Zen is Karma Yoga and Karma Yoga is Soto Zen. This is the true way of the Warrior (whatever the Rinzai may say), pure action in the flow of the unfolding moment.

Everyday activities, making tea or making the bed, can be done with a Warrior spirit, with one-pointed attention and mindfulness. Sports, martial arts and dance should also be done in this spirit. They are a great training in Karma Yoga and *wei-wu-wei* (action without action). The Zen arts of calligraphy, flower arrangement, tea ceremony, archery and martial arts all strive for this condition of effortless effort. This condition is of course not unknown in Western arts, though not expressed so explicitly.

There is a particular class of arts, however, highly developed in the West, which do not aim merely at the absorbed flow of dispassionate action cultivated by the Warrior arts. These are the devotional arts. They are about passion, not dispassion; feeling and emotion, not detached equanimity. These include the arts of music, poetry and painting.

The beauty of great music and poetry arises out of the balanced poise of Karma Yoga flowing over into Bhakti Yoga. It is not quite Wordsworth's "emotion recollected in tranquillity", more like emotion overflowing the cup of tranquillity. Tranquillity is the root and emotion is the flower. Beauty is the overflow of goodness, or "right action". And it is this overflow which inspires devotion in us.

The archetypal figure of the Bhakti Yogi in the West is the Monk or Nun. They are specialists in the devotional arts, in prayer and songs of praise and thanksgiving. When a Warrior walks, he just walks. When a Nun walks, "she walks in beauty".

The Warrior learns to master the will by letting go of the will. The Monk or Nun learns to master the heart by letting go of the heart. Intense beauty, intense wonder, intense sadness and grief, if allowed to penetrate the soul, will either melt the heart or break it. This is how the Bhakti Yogi opens herself to the world, by opening her heart.

The heart breaking stories of the Greek Tragedians open the heart through catharsis, but the ultimate heartbreak is the story of Christ's Passion. This story includes betrayal, injustice, sacrifice, intense physical suffering, humiliation, disappointment, the grief of a mother over her child, and the death of God.

There is nothing so heart rending in all world literature.

But, unlike Greek tragedy, the story doesn't end there. Jesus rises from the dead and ascends in glory. The broken heart flames with love and compassion and new life. God never dies. He will always rise again. So the Bhakti Yogi moves from tears of grief to tears of joy, from sighs of lament to songs of celebration.

Zen Buddhism is primarily a religion based on Karma Yoga; Christianity is primarily one based on Bhakti Yoga. This is why over the centuries it has produced the most exquisite art mankind has ever seen, in music, poetry, prose, painting, sculpture and architecture. Christianity is primarily a religion of beauty and devotion. And the most committed Yogis are of course the monastics, the Christian Monks and Nuns.

But among the monastics were serious thinkers as well as devotees. These were the theologians, Aquinas, Anselm, Augustine (just to starts with the A's). But the study of God (theology) inevitably includes the study of truth through the love of wisdom (philosophy). Indeed, Augustine was heavily indebted to Plato and Aquinas to Aristotle, and Christian theology in general relied both on the Jewish revelation of the Law and the Prophets and on the metaphysics and philosophy of the Ancient Greeks.

Since the late Middle Ages, philosophy in the West has evolved beyond the bounds of Christian orthodoxy, via Renaissance Humanism, the Enlightenment, and the dual streams of contemporary Continental Philosophy and Analytic Anglo-American Philosophy (not all of it good.)

Where the Warrior masters the will and the Monk (or Nun) masters the heart, the Philosopher masters the mind. The particular school of thought is not as important as the commitment to truth, reason and discourse. Ideas must be tested and challenged. False inferences and faulty logic must be rooted out. But this cannot be done without some serious study of the great thinkers. After all, we cannot learn how to think well without models of good thinking. Thinking is an evolved, not an innate capacity. It must be cultivated.

When you are engaged in good thinking, you are actualizing the Philosopher archetype. You are a Jnana Yogi.

However, if this is not rooted in Karma Yoga and Bhakti Yoga, in other words, founded on a free will and an open heart, it will quickly lose its connection with lived reality and degenerate into a dry exercise in abstract theory. It will become left hemisphere dominant.

A true Philosopher stands on a firm foundation. He is first a Mystic, a Shaman, a Warrior and a Monk. If the foundation of your thought is based instead on your Diva, Demon, Victim and Addict natures, however, you can shout you're a Philosopher until you're blue in the face, but really you'll be nothing but a Muppet.

If you want to be a truly Integral Yogi, you must master the human will, the human heart and the human mind, but also the human soul. You must be a Raja Yogi as well as a Karma, Bhakti and Jnana Yogi. You must plumb the depths of your essential nature. Now you can answer the question, "who am I?" Now you can fully embody your intrinsic divinity, your sovereign individuality, your inner King or Queen.

However, nobody can storm Heaven. You cannot find God or spiritual enlightenment through your own self-will, no matter how heroic. But actually, you don't need to find God or enlightenment. Just practice the yogas in all humility and sincerity and God and enlightenment will find you.

65. A Simple Cure for Spiritual Narcissism

New Age groups and cults seem to attract people who think that they are special. Nothing wrong with that, except that a percentage of those people are also narcissists. They have difficulties maintaining relationships because they feel that nobody sufficiently appreciates them or is good enough for them. They find in New Age philosophies the perfect explanation and justification for their social difficulties: they're special; they're "spiritual".

When narcissists find spirituality, they are apt to become "spiritual narcissists". This is obviously not confined to the New Age – you will find them in all religious or pseudo-religious organisations. But the New Age, with its emphasis on individualism and the divine authority of the "secret, sacred self" certainly lends itself to narcissism.

Is there a cure for spiritual narcissism? Psychotherapy offers one possible cure, although this can also be co-opted by the narcissist as further evidence of their psychological self-awareness and superiority over others. "Shadow work" is, after all, just another aspect of their overall personal spiritual development. Traditional religion can potentially offer a more effective cure. The following passage from the Gospels, if taken to heart, is as simple and effective a cure for spiritual narcissism as you will find:

"Master, which is the great commandment in the law?

Jesus said unto him, Thou shalt love the Lord thy God with all thy heart, and with all thy soul, and with all thy mind.
This is the first and great commandment.
And the second is like unto it, Thou shalt love thy neighbour as thyself.
On these two commandments hang all the law and the prophets."[148]

66. I Believe

At the end of the Penguin Books UK conversation between Philip Pullman and Philip Goff on the subject of panpsychism, Philip (Goff) asked Philip (Pullman), "Do you think it's true?" Pullman replied instantly, "yeah".

I remember being asked the morning after an ayahuasca ceremony if I believed in God. Usually I would qualify and prevaricate. On this occasion there was no hesitation. I simply said "yeah".

I have seen extraordinary things on psychedelics. I have seen the Purusha, the "Perfect Person", a single human organism encompassing all humanity, past, present and future. I have experienced the non-dual experience of "Satori", where All is One. I would even go so far as to say I have "seen" God.

Do I think these experiences are real? It's easy to dismiss them as the hallucinations of a drug-addled brain. But somehow, for some reason, they carry the stamp of truth. Do I think they're true? Yeah.

But what kind of "true"? In *Sola Ratio, Sola Scriptura*, I quoted a medieval theologian on the different levels of the interpretation of scripture. The basic distinction is between the *literal* and the *spiritual*. The spiritual then sub-divides into three: the *tropological* (moral), *allegorical* (metaphorical) and *anagogical* (intuitive).

Ayahuasca is considered to be a powerful teacher by the shamans of the Amazon. She teaches on all four levels, literal, moral, mythical and mystical. She shows you where you need "amendment of life" and provides insights into the nature of reality itself.

The same is true of the Bible. The same is true of the Vedas and the Shastras, the Tripitaka, the Guru Granth Sahib, the Koran and the Hadith. The same is true of all the sacred writings of humanity from time immemorial.

All religions point to God, although they use different idioms. All religions point to the divinity of human beings, often personified as a God-Man, Krishna, Buddha and Christ being the most current.

Do I believe that the Buddha was Enlightened? Yeah. Do I believe that Jesus Christ was the Son of God? Yeah. Do I believe that He died and was buried and on the third day rose again and ascended into heaven and is seated at the right hand of the Father? Yeah.

I believe it anagogically, which is to say *mystically*. The same way I believe in Purusha and Satori. The same way I believe in Parashiva, Shiva and Shakti. The same way I believe in God.

I believe in these things with neither blind faith nor absolute certainty. The intuitions of the right hemisphere are enough for me; I don't require the irrefutable proofs of left hemisphere logic. I rely on *negative capability*, "that is, when a man is capable of being in uncertainties, mysteries, doubts, without any irritable reaching after fact and reason"[149]. The miraculous resurrection and ascension of Jesus is inevitably shrouded in uncertainties, mysteries and doubts. But I believe it anyway.

All religions, including the oldest and the earliest religions, the shamanic religions, which use psychotropic drugs as their sacrament, point to a reality and an existence beyond the ordinary, everyday. There have always been those who believe and those who don't. And there have always been those who don't quite believe, but find the whole thing kind of interesting and exciting, and those who would like to believe but can't, mainly because they don't understand what belief is. I used to be one of those. I was too Modern.

Modernity presents us with a curious paradox. Think about the great fuss made over the re-discovery of the Ancient Greek classics (preserved by Arab scholars) in the Middle Ages. Received wisdom is that Europe and Christendom were so impoverished by their absence that the historical period before their transmission is justly called "the Dark Ages" and the periods after, "the Renaissance" and "the Enlightenment".

But now we have not only the Greek and Roman classics, but Egyptian, Mesopotamian and Zoroastrian sacred writings, Gnostic texts, Jewish and Islamic classics, not to mention all the infinite wisdom of the East, Hindu, Jain, Buddhist, Sikh, Confucian, Taoist, etc. After centuries of splendid isolation, the mysteries of Japan and Tibet are now an open book. The esoteric teachings of Tantra and Alchemy, Shamanism and Yoga are an open secret.

The extraordinary richness of the religious teachings of humanity is laid out before us like an exquisite Persian carpet. For the first time in the history of "homo religiosus" they are freely available to anyone who cares to look. Yet most people in the modern West have scant knowledge of Eastern religion, let alone of Greek philosophy. Worse, they know next to nothing about their own indigenous tradition, Christianity. Most people live in a spiritual ignorance far darker than anything you might find in the supposed "Dark Ages".

We have stopped believing. Not only out of neglect, but also abuse. Never before has there been so much indifference to the extraordinary phenomena we call religion: never before have there been so many muggles and apostates. And never before has there been such corruption of genuine spirituality: never before have there been so many muppets and heretics.

We have never been so blessed with spiritual riches as we are today, but equally, we have never been so cursed with contrary forces. In the end, the choice between a spiritual life and a non-spiritual one boils down to one question, the answer to which cuts through the Gordian knot of claims and counter-claims: "Do you think it's true?"

67. The True Vine

"I am the true vine, and My Father is the vinedresser. Every branch in Me that does not bear fruit He takes away; and every branch that bears fruit He prunes, that it may bear more fruit. You are already clean because of the word which I have spoken to you. Abide in Me, and I in you. As the branch cannot bear fruit of itself, unless it abides in the vine, neither can you, unless you abide in Me.

I am the vine, you are the branches. He who abides in Me, and I in him, bears much fruit; for without Me you can do nothing. If anyone does not abide in Me, he is cast out as a branch and is withered; and they gather them and throw them into the fire, and they are burned. If you abide in Me, and My words abide in you, you will ask what you desire, and it shall be done for you. By this My Father is glorified, that you bear much fruit; so you will be My disciples."[150]

In the Hebrew Bible the vineyard is a metaphor for Israel. "Israel" means "to struggle with God". This was the name Jacob received after he wrestled with the angel, who should be understood as a direct manifestation of God in human form. Therefore the people of Israel are those who struggle with God, those who engage with God, who have made a covenant with God. They are connected with the divine mystery beyond. God planted the vineyard and tends the vineyard and the vines bear fruit.

In the New Testament, it is not the people of Israel, but the person of Christ who is "the true vine". The Many become One. The disciples of Christ are like branches connected to the source of life, to the water and nutrients in the soil, by being connected to the vine, which is Christ himself. He is the connection between the people and God.

The spiritual meaning should be clear. If you are connected to God, you have life and bear fruit. If you're not, you wither and die. But perhaps the idea of connection and disconnection also applies on a cultural and even a physical level?

"Israel" represents a people, a community with a shared history, cultural heritage and common destiny. A branch cut off from the vine, an exile cut off from society, is cut off from the source of cultural and social life.

Cut off from Nature, from the elements, the weather, vegetation, animal life, and cut off from our own physical bodies, is there not also, in a very real sense, an atrophying, a withering and dying of our essential vitality? What happens to people who spend their lives in extremely urbanised environments? What happens to people who spend their lives in jail? What happens to people who spend their lives staring at a screen?

Dislocation and alienation are hallmarks of the art and literature of Modernism and Postmodernism. Louis Sass explores the relationship between Madness and Modernity in his book of that title; Iain McGilchrist explores it further in the context of left hemisphere dominance in *The Master and his Emissary: The Divided Brain and the Making of the Western Mind*.

Modern, urbanised people are clearly dissociated from the natural world like they never have been before. This is of course further exacerbated by the rise of information technology, computerised office work and entertainment media. As a result, people suffer from all sorts of stress-related conditions, anxiety and depression.

However, they are also dissociated and alienated from their cultural heritage. The prevailing modern myth is based on novelty and originality, and a severing of the bonds that connect us to tradition. The self-definition of Modernity and moderns is that we are cut loose from the past and can self-create ourselves as we wish. No other period in history has designated itself as "modern" in this way.

However, as Modernity inevitably begins to establish its own canon and its own history, the rug has to be pulled from under it in order to maintain the principle of newness. Hence the need for Postmodernity, which is simply the ongoing undercutting of the past as it is created in the present. It is like a gardener continuously pulling up any young shoots before they have the chance to establish roots and grow into anything.

In radical left-wing politics, this is called "Permanent Revolution". From an anarchist perspective, this is necessary in order to prevent any social hierarchy being established. This principled commitment to a radical divorce from all established social structures and institutions is the same in the political as in the cultural sphere. We might call it, echoing C.S. Lewis, "the Great Divorce".

The main excision of Modernity and Postmodernity, however, is the casting away of religion. The irony is that, in our Faustian hubris, we think we have done away with God or even killed Him, that we have somehow brought about "the Death of God". We think we have simply cut off a dry branch of antiquated superstition and thrown it into the fire. But it's the exact opposite. We have cut ourselves off and thrown ourselves in the fire:

"If anyone does not abide in Me, he is cast out as a branch and is withered; and they gather them and throw them into the fire, and they are burned."

The Great Divorce of Modernity is a simultaneous divorce from Nature, Culture and God, or in the language of the New Age, from Body, Mind and Spirit. The true vine which will heal this dissociation and alienation is simultaneously the body and blood of our saviour Jesus Christ, the vine of the living Judeo-Christian tradition, and the vine of the dead, ayahuasca (or endogenous DMT). And when we are restored and healed, we will be friends again, with ourselves, with each other, with Nature and with God.

"These things I have spoken to you, that My joy may remain in you, and that your joy may be full. This is My commandment, that you love one another as I have loved you. Greater love has no one than this, than to lay down one's life for his friends. You are My friends if you do whatever I command you. No longer do I call you servants, for a servant does not know what his master is doing; but I have called you friends, for all things that I heard from My Father I have made known to you.

You did not choose Me, but I chose you and appointed you that you should go and bear fruit, and that your fruit should remain, that whatever you ask the Father in My name He may give you. These things I command you, that you love one another."[151]

68. The Armour of Christ

In his letter to the Ephesians, St Paul encourages his listeners to put on "the armour of God":

"Finally, my brethren, be strong in the Lord, and in the power of his might. Put on the whole armour of God, that ye may be able to stand against the wiles of the devil."[152]

In other places (Romans 13:14 and Galatians 3:27 for example) he exhorts his listeners to "put on Christ". Although he doesn't say so explicitly, he may well have been thinking about armour here as well. We need all the help we can get in defending ourselves against the "world", the "flesh" and "the devil".

If we are serious about the spiritual path, spiritual progress and the spiritual life, we soon realise that it's not all sweetness and light and plain sailing. There are equally serious forces ranged against us, serious and powerful. Sometimes that can be bargained with, but sometimes, if you don't want to be defeated and overrun, you just have to stand your ground and fight.

In any military engagement, you must look to your defences as well as your opportunities for attack. This is as true of football and chess as it is of war. The primary thing, however, as you square up to your opponent, is to make sure you have a strong defence. You must never leave yourself open and exposed to a counter-attack.

When you enter the spiritual battle, you need to put on your armour if you are to have any hope of survival or victory. As a Christian, you put on the armour of Christ. But what does that mean? Do you just bring Christ to mind? Do you imitate Christ? Do what Christ would do? Imagine you are Christ for the duration of the battle?

It clearly must be something along those lines. We are talking about spiritual armour here, and the royal road to the spiritual is via the imagination. But we can be even more effective in armouring ourselves if we take the imagination a step further.

I describe the perfect God-Man, represented by Christ, as a "Mystic-Shaman-Warrior-Monk-Philosopher-King-Friend". Each of these seven archetypes I associate with a specific point on the Christian Orthodox Cross: the Mystic at the top of the vertical, the Shaman at the bottom, the Warrior at the left end of the lower horizontal, the Monk at the right end, the Philosopher at the left end of the higher horizontal, the King at the right end, and the Friend in the middle.

Imagine crossing yourself in the usual way, from the middle of your forehead to your heart, to your left shoulder, right shoulder and back to the heart. Now imagine doing the same thing, but with a "double" cross which reaches down to your navel. You cross yourself from the middle of your forehead, down to your navel (*hara*), to your left hip, right hip, left shoulder, right shoulder and end at the heart.

(From an energetic point of view, we have extended the cross to cover our whole body. Might the fact that the traditional sign of the cross reaches only as far as the heart chakra say anything about our lop-sided, top-heavy view of ourselves in the West? Isn't it time we included the lower chakras in a more integrated spirituality?)

Now, if you mentally cross yourself while bringing to mind the archetypes at each of the seven points on the body, you will find that you create a sort of mental shield. If you do it repeatedly, the energy of this mental shield will increase, as though you were turning a dynamo. You can think of it like a force field. Any number of Hollywood superhero movies should help you visualise it (think Dr Strange*)*.

The repetition of the mantra is called *japa*. You repeat the sequence at some speed and keep going until it slows down of its own accord. Eventually, it will find its own rhythm and you will find that you are no longer using your conscious will to keep it going, but are merely following it as it continues by its own steam. This stage is called *dharma*. It feels effortless and easy. Finally, the mantra will slow down and come to a natural stop. This final stage is called *yoga*. The mind is still and the body is energised. You have put on the armour of Christ.

69. Holy, Virtuous and Wise

To be holy, virtuous and wise: not a bad aim for a good life, even if it does sound horribly old-fashioned and pretentious to modern secular ears. What do I mean by these words though? It may be worth briefly defining them a little more precisely. By "holy" I mean the capacity specifically for spiritual experience but more generally, for the achievement of *eudaimonia*, the good life. By "virtuous" I mean the development of positive character traits and *arete*, moral excellence. By "wise" I mean the possession of *phronesis*, practical wisdom, essential for the exercise of both holiness and virtue.

The following meditations will help you cultivate holiness, virtue and wisdom and overcome the "devil", the "flesh" and the "world" by inhibiting the ego system and awakening the soul system. They are based on the three lines and seven points of the Cross.

The "holiness line" is the energetic channel running through the spinal column from the ajna chakra (the "third eye") to the muladhara (the "root chakra"). This is the vertical line of the Cross. Visualize it as a channel of pure light running from top to bottom through the core of your body.

Repeat the mantras *Amun Ra* then *Mystic Shaman* then *Peace and Love*.

(This counters the Diva-Demon axis.)

Once the vertical is suitably lit up and you're feeling nice and holy, you can shift your attention to the lower horizontal "virtue line" which runs from the left hip to the right hip. This is the balancing line (think stabilizers on a child's bicycle or ballast on a ship).

Repeat the mantras *Atum Ka* then *Warrior Monk* (or *Warrior Nun*) then *Goodness and Beauty*.

(This counters the Victim-Addict axis.)

When you feel sufficiently strong, grounded and balanced, turn your attention to the second horizontal "wisdom line" which runs from the left shoulder to the right shoulder and finishes at the heart chakra.

Repeat the mantras *Ba Gaia Jah* then *Philosopher King Friend* (or *Philosopher Queen Friend*) and finally *Truth Consciousness Bliss*.

(This counters the Muppet-Muggle axis.)

Shabestari, the 14th century Persian Sufi poet said:

"The journey of the pilgrims is two steps and no more:
One is the passing out of selfhood,
And one towards mystical Union with the Friend."[153]

Pass out of the selfhood of the ego system represented by the Wheel of Life and into mystical union with the soul system represented by the Cross of Life. The more you do this, the more you will weaken the former and strengthen the latter. Then you will develop the strength of character to deal with "the slings and arrows of outrageous fortune".[154] The "world", the "flesh" and the "devil" won't bother you anymore.

The above is a variation of the basic meditation, which is to repeat each of the three mantras separately as you cross yourself, touching each of the seven points with your mind. The first mantra, *Amun, Ra, Atum, Ka, Ba, Gaia, Jah*, corresponds to "the Father"; the second mantra, *Mystic, Shaman, Warrior, Monk, Philosopher, King, Friend*, corresponds to "the Son" and the third mantra, *Peace, Love, Goodness, Beauty, Truth, Consciousness, Bliss*, corresponds to "the Holy Spirit".

Begin by applying some conscious energy to the mantra (japa), then let the mantra go its own way and simply follow (dharma) and finally allow the mantra to fade into silence (yoga) before picking up the next:

Amun, Ra (vertical); *Atum, Ka* (lower horizontal); *Ba, Gaia, Jah* (upper horizontal, ending in the heart).

Mystic, Shaman (vertical); *Warrior, Monk* (lower horizontal); *Philosopher, King, Friend* (upper horizontal, ending in the heart).

Peace, Love (vertical); *Goodness, Beauty* (lower horizontal); *Truth, Consciousness, Bliss* (upper horizontal, ending in the heart).

70. Two Trees

In the Garden of Eden there are two trees: the Tree of the Knowledge of Good and Evil and the Tree of Life. When they ate the forbidden fruit of the Tree of the Knowledge of Good and Evil, our "first parents", Adam and Eve, were banished from the Garden forever.

The "Wheel" and "the Cross" are like two trees. If we connect up the six archetypes of each in the same way, with a central vertical line and two horizontal bars, we get a crude depiction of two trees. One tree is bad and bears rotten fruit and the other is good and bears sweet fruit.

It doesn't make much sense to call them "the Wheel Tree" and "the Cross Tree" though – better to call them "the Ego Tree" and "the Soul Tree". The trunk of the Ego Tree is formed of the Diva-Demon axis and its branches are made up of the Victim-Addict and the Muppet-Muggle axes. The trunk of the Soul Tree is formed of the Mystic-Shaman axis and its branches are made up of the Warrior-Monk and the Philosopher-King axes. These are the "holiness line", the "virtue line" and the "wisdom line" respectively. We might also call this tree *the Tree of Life*.

*

The day before yesterday was Ash Wednesday and I went to an evening service at my local church in Highgate to get "ashed". Ash Wednesday marks the beginning of Lent, the forty days of fasting and penance observant Christians undertake in preparation for Easter. It is a time for self-examination, contrition and repentance, a time for looking into the heart to see what sins are lurking there.

Naturally, I found some. I had been unfair and unkind to someone I loved - I had been under the sway of my judgmental Diva-Demon, I had allowed the insecurity of my Victim-Addict to get the better of me, and I had fallen for the tall tales spun by my Muppet-Muggle.

So I turned to the Bible. What did the Bible have to say about being judgmental, anxious or delusional?

"Judge not, that ye be not judged. For with what judgment ye judge, ye shall be judged." (Matthew 7:1)

"Be strong and of a good courage; be not afraid, neither be thou dismayed: for the LORD thy God is with thee whithersoever thou goest." (Joshua 1:9)

"And he cometh, and findeth them sleeping, and saith unto Peter, Simon, sleepest thou? couldest not thou watch one hour?" (Mark 14:37)

Judge not. Be not afraid. Sleepest thou?

These three maxims can be used as mantras. Bringing them to mind brings the soul back into alignment. We find three other mantras, "magic words", or "words of power", in St. Paul:

"Though I speak with the tongues of men and of angels, but have not love, I have become sounding brass or a clanging cymbal. And though I have the gift of prophecy, and understand all mysteries and all knowledge, and though I have all faith, so that I could remove mountains, but have not love, I am nothing. And though I bestow all my goods to feed the poor, and though I give my body to be burned, but have not love, it profits me nothing.
Love suffers long and is kind; love does not envy; love does not parade itself, is not puffed up; does not behave rudely, does not seek its own, is not provoked, thinks no evil; does not rejoice in iniquity, but rejoices in the truth; bears all things, believes all things, hopes all things, endures all things.
Love never fails. But whether there are prophecies, they will fail; whether there are tongues, they will cease; whether there is knowledge, it will vanish away. For we know in part and we prophesy in part. But when that which is perfect has come, then that which is in part will be done away.

When I was a child, I spoke as a child, I understood as a child, I thought as a child; but when I became a man, I put away childish things. For now we see in a mirror, dimly, but then face to face. Now I know in part, but then I shall know just as I also am known.

And now abide faith, hope, love, these three; but the greatest of these is love."[155]

References

American Psychiatric Association, 2013. *Diagnostic and statistical manual of mental disorders (DSM-5®)*. American Psychiatric Pub.

Armstrong, K., 2009. *The case for God*. Random House Digital, Inc..

Armstrong, K., 2019. *The Lost Art of Scripture*. Random House.

Arnold, M., 1994. Culture and Anarchy. 1869. *Ed. Samuel Lipman. New Haven: Yale UP*, *1*, p.164.

Assagioli, R., 1965. Psychosynthesis: A manual of principles and techniques.

Aurelius, M., 1904. *Meditations*. D. Appleton.

Aurobindo, S., 1993. *The integral yoga: Sri Aurobindo's teaching and method of practice*. Lotus Press.

Aurobindo, S., 1990. *The life divine*. Lotus Press.

Ayer, A.J., 2012. *Language, truth and logic* (Vol. 1). Courier Corporation.

Basho, M., 2006. Narrow Road to the Interior: And Other Writings. Shambhala Publications.

Beck, C.J., 1993. Nothing special: living Zen.

Bentham, J., 1996. *The collected works of Jeremy Bentham: An introduction to the principles of morals and legislation*. Clarendon Press.

Berkeley, G., 1999. *Principles of human knowledge and three dialogues*. OUP Oxford.

Berlinski, D., 2009. *The devil's delusion: Atheism and its scientific pretensions*. Basic Books (AZ).

Berne, E., 1968. *Games people play: The psychology of human relationships* (Vol. 2768). Penguin Uk.

Bible, H., 1982. The New King James Version. *Nashville: Thomas Nelson Publishers.*

Blake, W., 2008. The complete poetry and prose of William Blake. Univ of California Press.

Blake, W., 1975. *The marriage of heaven and hell* (Vol. 321). American Chemical Society.

Boghossian, P. and Lindsay, J., 2019. How to Navigate Contentious Conversations. *Skeptic (Altadena, CA), 24*(4), pp.30-34.

Broughton, J.L., 1999. *The Bodhidharma anthology: The earliest records of Zen.* Univ of California Press.

Bucke, R.M., 1923. *Cosmic consciousness: A study in the evolution of the human mind.* EP Dutton.

Budge, S.E.A.W., 2001. *The Egyptian book of the dead.* Cassell.

Burckhardt, T., 2008. *Introduction to Sufi doctrine.* World Wisdom, Inc.

Burgess, A., 2013. A Clockwork Orange: Restored Edition. Penguin UK.

Burke, E., 1986. Reflections on the Revolution in France (1790). *Everyman's Library.*

Camus, A., 1988. *L'étranger.* Routledge.

Cassian, J., 1997. *John cassian: The conferences* (No. 57). The Newman Press.

Cheng'en, W., 2008. *Journey to the West: The Monkey King's Amazing Adventures.* Tuttle Publishing.

Chesterton, G.K., 2006. *The Complete Father Brown.* Waking Lion Press.

Chesterton, G.K., 2013. *Orthodoxy.* Moody Publishers.

Cleary, T., 1998. *The Ecstasy of Enlightenment: Teaching of Natural Tantra.* Weiser Books.

Dante, A., 2017. *The divine comedy.* Aegitas.

Dawkins, R., 2016. *The god delusion.* Random House.

De Chardin, P.T., 2018. *The phenomenon of man*. Lulu Press, Inc.

Dogen, E., 2007. Shobogenzo. *Trans. H. Nearman. Mount Shasta, CA: Shasta Abbey Press. http://www. urbandharma. org/pdf/Shobogenzo. pdf.*

Dennett, D.C., 2006. Breaking the Spell: Religion as Natural Phenomenon. *London: Allen Lane, and New York: Viking Penguin.*

Descartes, R., 2013. *René Descartes: Meditations on first philosophy: With selections from the objections and replies*. Cambridge University Press.

Donne, J., 1987. *Devotions upon emergent occasions*. Oxford University Press on Demand.

Dowson, E.C. and Symons, A., 1919. *The Poems and Prose of Ernest Dowson*. Boni and Liveright.

Durrell, L., 2015. *The Avignon Quintet: Monsieur, Livia, Constance, Sebastian and Quinx*. Faber & Faber.

Eagleton, T., 2011. *Why Marx was right*. Yale University Press.

Eckhart, M., 1987. *Meister Eckhart, Sermons & Treatises* (Vol. 1). Element Books Limited.

Eckhart, M.J., 1994. Selected Writings, edited and translated by Oliver Davies.

Einstein, A., 2011. *The world as I see it*. Open Road Media.

Eliot, T.S., 1943. *Four quartets*. Houghton Mifflin Harcourt.

Eliot, T.S., 2010. *The waste land and other poems*. Broadview Press.

Ferrari, G.R. ed., 2000. *Plato: The Republic*. Cambridge: Cambridge University Press.

Frankl, V.E., 1985. *Man's search for meaning*. Simon and Schuster.

Fremantle, F., 2000. *The Tibetan book of the dead: The great liberation through hearing in the Bardo*. Shambhala Publications.

Freud, S. and Cronin, A.J., 2013. *The interpretation of dreams*. Read Books Ltd.

Freud, S. and Strachey, J.E., 1964. The standard edition of the complete psychological works of Sigmund Freud.

Galilei, G., 2008. *The Essential Galileo*. Hackett Publishing.

y Gasset, J.O., 1957. *On love: Aspects of a single theme*. Meridian Books.

Gebser, J., Barstad, N. and Mickunas, A., 1985. *The ever-present origin* (Vol. 1). Athens: Ohio University Press.

Giles, H.A., 2013. *Chuang Tzu*. Routledge.

Goff, P., 2019. *Galileo's Error: Foundations for a New Science of Consciousness*. Pantheon.

Goldberg, J., 2009. Liberal fascism: The secret history of the American left, from Mussolini to the politics of change. Crown Forum.

Goldberg, J., 2020, January. Suicide of the West: How the Rebirth of Tribalism, Nationalism, and Socialism Is Destroying American Democracy. Crown Forum.

Gray, J., 2007. *Black mass: Apocalyptic religion and the death of utopia*. Macmillan.

Gray, J., 2015. *The soul of the marionette: A short inquiry into human freedom*. Macmillan.

Gray, J., 2018. *Seven types of atheism*. Penguin UK.

Grayling, A.C., 2013. *The God argument: The case against religion and for humanism*. A&C Black.

Greene, Joshua, 2013. Moral Tribes: Emotion, reason and the gap between us and them. Atlantic Books.

Gurdjieff, G.I., 1964. *All and everything: Beelzebub's tales to his grandson*. EP Dutton.

Haidt, J., 2006. *The happiness hypothesis: Putting ancient wisdom and philosophy to the test of modern science*. Random House.

Haidt, J., 2012. *The righteous mind: Why good people are divided by politics and religion*. Vintage.

Hakuin, E., 1967. The song of zazen.

Hamilton, E., Cairns, H. and Cooper, L., 1961. *The collected dialogues of Plato*. Princeton University Press.

Hanh, T.N., 2016. *The miracle of mindfulness: An introduction to the practice of meditation*. Beacon Press.

Happold, F.C., 2017. *Mysticism a study and an anthology*. Penguin Books Limited (1963).

Harari, Y.N., 2016. *Homo Deus: A brief history of tomorrow*. Random House.

Harding, D.E., 1961. On having no head. *Arkana.[aBM]*.

Harris, S., 2005. *The end of faith: Religion, terror, and the future of reason*. WW Norton & Company.

Harris, S., 2014. *Waking up: A guide to spirituality without religion*. Simon and Schuster.

Hart, D.B., 2009. *Atheist delusions: The Christian revolution and its fashionable enemies*. Yale University Press.

Hart, D.B., 2013. *The experience of god: Being, consciousness, bliss*. Yale University Press.

Harter, S., 1978. Effectance motivation reconsidered. Toward a developmental model. *Human development*, *21*(1), pp.34-64.

Haught, J.F., 2017. *The New Cosmic Story: Inside Our Awakening Universe*. Yale University Press.

Hayek, F.A., 2014. *The road to serfdom: Text and documents: The definitive edition*. Routledge.

Hegel, G.W.F. and Inwood, M., 2018. *Hegel: The Phenomenology of Spirit*. Oxford University Press.

Heidegger, M., Macquarrie, J. and Robinson, E., 1962. Being and time.

Herbert, G., 2007. *The English Poems of George Herbert*. Cambridge University Press.

Hicks, S.R.C., 2004. *Explaining postmodernism: Skepticism and socialism from Rousseau to Foucault*. Scholargy Publishing, Inc..

Hitchens, C., 2008. *God is not great: How religion poisons everything*. McClelland & Stewart.

Holland, T., 2019. *Dominion: The Making of the Western Mind*. Little, Brown.

Hubbard, B.M., 2015. *Conscious evolution: Awakening the power of our social potential*. New World Library.

Hume, D., 2003. *A treatise of human nature*. Courier Corporation.

Hume, M., 2015. *Trigger warning: Is the fear of being offensive killing free speech?*. HarperCollins UK.

Hunter, J.D. and Nedelisky, P., 2018. *Science and the good: The tragic quest for the foundations of morality*. Foundational Questions in Scie.

Husserl, E., 1999. *The essential Husserl: Basic writings in transcendental phenomenology*. Indiana University Press.

Huxley, A., 1998. Brave New World. 1932. *London: Vintage*.

Huxley, A., 2010. *The doors of perception: And heaven and hell*. Random House.

Huxley, A., 2014. *The perennial philosophy*. McClelland & Stewart.

Jacobs, A., 2017. *How to think: A survival guide for a world at odds*. Currency.

James, W., 2003. *The varieties of religious experience: A study in human nature*. Routledge.

Jefferson, T., 1989. *The Jefferson Bible: The Life and Morals of Jesus of Nazareth*. Beacon Press.

Joachim, H.H. and Rees, D.A., 1952. Aristotle: The Nicomachean Ethics.

Jonson, B., 1838. *The Works of Ben Jonson*. Routledge.

Jung, C.G., 2014. *Psychology and alchemy*. Routledge.

Jung, C.G., 1956. *Symbols of Transformation: The collected works of CG Jung*. Routledge & Kegan Paul.

Kafka, F., 1979. *The Basic Kafka* (Vol. 82561). Simon and Schuster.

Kant, I., 1949. Critique of practical reason, and other writings in moral philosophy.

Kant, I., 1908. Critique of pure reason. 1781. *Modern Classical Philosophers, Cambridge, MA: Houghton Mifflin*, pp.370-456.

Keats, J., 2002. *Selected letters.* Oxford University Press, USA.

Keats, J., 1920. *The poetical works of John Keats.* Humphrey Milford, Oxford University Press.

a Kempis, T., 1940. *The imitation of Christ.* Lulu. com.

Kennett, J, 1972. *Selling Water by the River: A Manual of Zen Training.* George Allen & Unwin.

Kierkegaard, S., 2013. *Kierkegaard's Writings, VI, Volume 6: Fear and Trembling/Repetition.* Princeton University Press.

Kinne, B., 1943. Voltaire never said it!. *Modern language notes*, 58(7), pp.534-535.

Kipling, R., 1990. *Gunga Din and Other Favorite Poems.* Courier Corporation.

Koestler, A., 1968. The ghost in the machine.

Larkin, P., 2012. *The complete poems of Philip Larkin.* Faber & Faber.

Law, W., 1978. *A Serious Call to a Devout and Holy Life; The Spirit of Love.* Paulist Press.

Lawrence, B., 2005. *The practice of the presence of God.* Shambhala Publications.

Lawrence, D.H., 1994. *The complete poems of DH Lawrence.* Wordsworth Editions.

Lennon, J., 2010. Imagine. 1975.

Lennox, J.C., 2009. God's undertaker: Has science buried God?. Lion Books.

Lewis, C.S., 2001. *Mere christianity.* Zondervan.

Lewis, C.S., 1947. Miracles; a preliminary study.

Lewis, C.S., 2017. *Screwtape proposes a toast.* William Collins.

Lewis, C.S., 1949. *Transposition, and other addresses*. G. Bles.

Lewis, C.S. and Whitfield, R., 1946. *The great divorce* (p. 64). New York: Macmillan.

Lincoln, A., 1991. *Great Speeches*. Courier Corporation.

Lindsay, J.A., Boghossian, P. and Pluckrose, H., 2018. Academic grievance studies and the corruption of scholarship. *Areo Magazine, October*, 2.

Locke, J. and Nidditch, P.H., 1979. The Clarendon edition of the works of John Locke: An essay concerning human understanding.

Lovelock, J. and Margulis, L., 2007. The Gaia Hypothesis. *New York*.

MacIntyre, A., 2013. *After virtue*. A&C Black.

Mackenzie, B.D., 1977. *Behaviourism and the limits of scientific method*. Taylor & Francis.

Maharshi, R., 2004. *The spiritual teaching of Ramana Maharshi*. Shambhala Publications.

Malory, S.T., Sanders, C.R. and Ward, C.E., 1940. *Le morte d'Arthur*. Wynkyn de Worde.

Marlowe, C., 2005. *Doctor Faustus*. Routledge.

Marx, K., 1972. *The marx-engels reader* (Vol. 4). New York: Norton.

Masters, R.E. and Houston, J., 1966. *The varieties of psychedelic experience* (Vol. 9289). New York: Holt, Rinehart and Winston.

Maurer, N.E., Maurer, N.M., van Gogh, V. and Gauguin, P., 1998. *The pursuit of spiritual wisdom: the thought and art of Vincent van Gogh and Paul Gauguin*. Fairleigh Dickinson Univ Press.

McGilchrist, I., 2019. *The master and his emissary: The divided brain and the making of the western world*. Yale University Press.

McGrath, A. and McGrath, J.C., 2011. *The Dawkins delusion?: Atheist fundamentalism and the denial of the divine*. InterVarsity Press.

McGrath, A., 2007. *The twilight of atheism: The rise and fall of disbelief in the modern world.* WaterBrook.

Mill, J.S., 1963. Collected works.

Millgram, A.E., 1975. *Jewish worship.* Jewish Publication Society.

Millon, T., *Personality Disorders in Modern Life*, 2004. John Wiley and Sons.

Milton, J., 2005. *Paradise lost.* Hackett Publishing.

Mitchell, S., 1988. Tao te ching (lao tzu). *New York: HarperPerennial.*

Murray, D., 2019. *The Madness of Crowds: Gender, Race and Identity.* Bloomsbury Publishing.

Murray, D., 2017. *The strange death of Europe: Immigration, identity, Islam.* Bloomsbury Publishing.

Nagel, T., 2012. *Mind and cosmos: why the materialist neo-Darwinian conception of nature is almost certainly false.* Oxford University Press.

Naranjo, C. and Ornstein, R.E., 1971. *On the psychology of meditation.* Viking Adult.

Nicoll, M., 1980. Psychological Commentaries on the Teachings of. *GI Gurdjieff and PD Ouspensky.*

Nietzsche, F., 1977. *The Portable Nietzsche.* Penguin.

Nietzsche, F., 2008. *Thus spoke Zarathustra: A book for everyone and nobody.* Oxford University Press.

O'grady, P.F., 2017. *Thales of Miletus: the beginnings of western science and philosophy.* Routledge.

O'Neill, E., 2006. *The iceman cometh.* Yale University Press.

Orwell, G., 2017. *1984 & Animal Farm.* Text Publishing.

Osborne, A. ed., 1997. *The collected works of Ramana Maharshi.* Weiser Books.

Ouspensky, P.D., 1997. *A new model of the universe*. Courier Corporation.

Ouspensky, P.D., 2001. *In search of the miraculous: Fragments of an unknown teaching*. Houghton Mifflin Harcourt.

Ouspensky, P.D., 1957. *The fourth way: a record of talks and answers to questions based on the teaching of GI Gurdjieff*. Knopf.

Palmer, W.S., 1920. *The Confessions of Jacob Boehme* (p. 118). London.

Pater, W., 1980. *The Renaissance: studies in art and poetry*. Univ of California Press.

Patrick, G.T.W., 1889. The fragments of the work of Heraclitus of Ephesus on nature.

Perone, J.E., 2006. *The Sound of Stevie Wonder: His Words and Music*. Greenwood Publishing Group.

Peterson, J.B., 2018. *12 rules for life: An antidote to chaos*. Random House Canada.

Pinker, S., 2012. *The better angels of our nature: Why violence has declined*. Penguin Group USA.

Pinker, S., 2018. *Enlightenment now: The case for reason, science, humanism, and progress*. Penguin.

Pirandello, L., 2016. *Six characters in search of an author*. Bloomsbury Publishing.

Poe, E.A. and Lane, J., 2003. *The black cat*. Alex Catalogue.

Pollan, M., 2019. *How to change your mind: What the new science of psychedelics teaches us about consciousness, dying, addiction, depression, and transcendence*. Penguin Books.

Pound, E., 1957. *Selected Poems of Ezra Pound*. New Directions Publishing.

Prabhavananda, S. and Isherwood, C., 1947. Shankara's crest-jewel of discrimination. *New York: New American Library*.

Pseudo-Dionysius (the Areopagite.), 2005. *Dionysius the Areopagite: The Mystical Theology and the Celestial Hierarchies*. Kessinger Publishing.

Pullman, P., 1997. *His dark materials trilogy*. Scholastic.

Ramdas, S., 1994. *In the Vision of God*. Blue Dove Press.

Rand, A., 1963. *For the new intellectual: The philosophy of Ayn Rand*. Penguin.

Rennie, B.S., 1996. *Reconstructing Eliade: making sense of religion*. Suny Press.

Ridley, M., 2012. The rational optimist: How prosperity evolves. *Brock Education: A Journal of Educational Research and Practice, 21*(2).

Rorty, R. and Mendieta, E., 2006. *Take care of freedom and truth will take care of itself: Interviews with Richard Rorty*. Stanford University Press.

Rosling, H., 2019. *Factfulness*. Flammarion.

Rowling, J.K., 2015. *Harry Potter and the philosopher's stone* (Vol. 1). Bloomsbury Publishing.

Rousseau, J.J., 2018. *Rousseau: The Social Contract and other later political writings*. Cambridge University Press.

Rubin, D., 2020. *Don't Burn this Book: Thinking for Yourself in the Age of Unreason*. Signal.

Rueffler, M., 1995. *Our inner actors: The theory and application of subpersonality work in psychosynthesis*. PsychoPolitical Peace Institute Press.

Russell, B., 2009. *The basic writings of Bertrand Russell*. Routledge.

Sacks, J., 2017. *Not in God's name: Confronting religious violence*. Schocken.

Sacks, J., 2012. *The great partnership: Science, religion, and the search for meaning*. Schocken.

Saint John of the Cross, 2007. *Dark Night of the Soul: And Other Great Works*. Bridge Logos Foundation.

Saraswati, S., 1987. *Good Company*. Element Books.

Sartre, J.P., 2001. *Being and nothingness: An essay in phenomenological ontology*. Citadel Press.

Sass, L.A., 1992. *Madness and modernism: Insanity in the light of modern art, literature, and thought.* Basic Books.

Schopenhauer, A., 2012. *The world as will and representation* (Vol. 1). Courier Corporation.

Scott, W. ed., 1924. *Hermetica: The ancient Greek and Latin writings which contain religious or philosophic teachings ascribed to Hermes Trismegistus* (Vol. 2). Clarendon Press.

Scruton, R., 2019. *Fools, frauds and firebrands: Thinkers of the new left.* Bloomsbury Continuum.

Scruton, R., 2017. *The Ring of Truth: The Wisdom of Wagner's Ring of the Nibelung.* Abrams.

Scruton, R., 2016. *The soul of the world.* Princeton University Press.

Seneca, L.A., 1995. *Seneca: Moral and political essays.* Cambridge University Press.

Shabistari, M., 2002. *The Secret Rose Garden.* Red Wheel/Weiser.

Shakespeare, W., 2012. *Four Great Tragedies: Hamlet, Macbeth, Othello, and Romeo and Juliet.* Courier Corporation.

Shakespeare, W., 2007. *The complete works of William Shakespeare.* Wordsworth Editions.

Shankara, A., 2014. *Vivekachudamani.* Gilgamesh Edizioni.

Shapiro, B., 2019. *The Right Side of History: How Reason and Moral Purpose Made the West Great.* Broadside Books.

Shaw, B. and Laurence, D., 1970. *The Bodley Head Bernard Shaw: collected plays with their prefaces* (Vol. 1). London, UK: Bodley Head.

Sheldrake, R., 2012. *The science delusion.* Coronet.

Sheldrake, R., 2017. *Science and Spiritual Practices: Reconnecting through direct experience.* Hachette UK.

Shelley, P.B., 2000. *The Complete Poetry of Percy Bysshe Shelley* (Vol. 2). JHU Press.

Sivananda, S. and Sivananda, 1975. *Concentration and meditation*. Shivanandanagar, India: Divine Life Society.

Smith, A., 2010. *The theory of moral sentiments*. Penguin.

Smith, A., 2010. *The Wealth of Nations: An inquiry into the nature and causes of the Wealth of Nations*. Harriman House Limited.

Smith, A.P., 2008. *The Dimensions of Experience: A Natural History of Consciousness*. Xlibris Corporation.

Spinoza, B., 1910. Spinoza's Short Treatise on God, Man, and His Well-Being. *Trans. and ed.. Wolf. London: Adam and Charles Black*.

Stace, W.T., 1960. *Mysticism and Philosophy: WT Stace*. JP Tarcher.

Stenmark, M., 2017. *Scientism: Science, ethics and religion*. Routledge.

Strawson, G., 2018. *Things That Bother Me: Death, Freedom, the Self, Etc*. New York Review of Books.

Swami, S.P. and Yeats, W.B., 1937. *The ten principal Upanishads*. Faber.

Tobin, F.J., 1995. *Mechthild von Magdeburg: a medieval mystic in modern eyes*. Camden House.

Traherne, T., 2010. *Centuries of meditations*. Cosimo, Inc..

Traherne, T., Dobell, B., Wade, G.I. and Traherne, P., 1932. *The poetical works of Thomas Traherne*. PJ & AE Dobell.

Trungpa, C., 2002. *Cutting through spiritual materialism*. Shambhala Publications.

Tweedy, H.H. ed., 1942. *Christian Worship and Praise*. AS Barnes and Company.

Tweedy, R., 2018. *The god of the left hemisphere: Blake, Bolte Taylor and the myth of creation*. Routledge.

Underhill, E., 1911. *Mysticism*. London: Methuen.

Version, K.J., 1989. *The holy bible*. World Publishing Company.

Vervaeke, J., Mastropietro, C. and Miscevic, F., 2017. *Zombies in Western Culture: A Twenty-First Century Crisis*. Open Book Publishers.

Vogels, J.B., 2005. *The Direct Cinema of David and Albert Maysles*. SIU Press.

Waits, T., 2011. *Tom Waits: original album series*. Rhino Entertainment Company.

Watson, N. and Jenkins, J., 2006. *The writings of Julian of Norwich: A vision showed to a devout woman and a revelation of love*. Penn State Press.

Watts, A., 1999. *The way of Zen*. Vintage.

Weber, G. and Doyle, R., 2015. *Into the stillness: Dialogues on awakening beyond thought*. New Harbinger Publications.

Whitman, W., 1904. *Song of Myself...* Done into print by the Roycrofters.

Wick, G.S., 2005. *The book of equanimity: Illuminating classic Zen koans*. Simon and Schuster.

Wilber, K., 2001. *Eye to eye: The quest for the new paradigm*. Shambhala Publications.

Wilber, K., 2001. *Sex, ecology, spirituality: The spirit of evolution*. Shambhala Publications.

Wilde, O., 1997. *Collected works of Oscar Wilde: The plays, the poems, the stories and the essays including De Profundis*. Wordsworth Editions.

Williamson, M. and Williamson, M., 2005. *A return to love*. Harper Collins Publishers.

Wordsworth, W., 2000. *William Wordsworth: the major works*. Oxford University Press, USA.

Quotations

BOOK ONE

Introduction

[1] Law, 1978

Holy River Isis!

[2] Wordsworth, 2000
[3] Traherne, 2010
[4] Blake, 2008
[5] Traherne, 2010

Heaven and Hell

[6] James, 2003
[7] Eckhart, 1994

Pantheism is not Sexed-up Atheism

[8] Dawkins, 2016
[9] Ibid.
[10] Ibid.
[11] Ibid.
[12] Einstein, 2011
[13] Shankara, 2014
[14] Watts, 1999

Something that our Mind cannot Grasp

[15] Nicoll, 1980
[16] Dawkins, 2016
[17] Ibid.

A Walk in the Forest

[18] Schopenhauer, 2012
[19] Dowson, 1919
[20] Shakespeare, 2012

Spiritual Autism

[21] Grayling, 2013
[22] Ibid.
[23] Saraswati, 1987

The Portal of God is Non-Existence

[24] Giles, 2013
[25] Mitchell, 1988
[26] Ibid.
[27] Jonson, 1838
[28] Eliot, 2010
[29] Mitchell, 1988

Seven Gods

[30] Happold, 2017
[31] Ibid.
[32] Pseudo-Dionysius, 2005
[33] Genesis 1, 1-4
[34] Eckhart, 1987
[35] Acts 2:3
[36] St. John of the Cross, 2007
[37] Ramdas, 1994
[38] Blake, 2008
[39] 1 Corinthians 3:12
[40] Lawrence, 1994
[41] Huxley, 2010
[42] Hanh, 2016
[43] Palmer, 1920
[44] Osborne, 1997
[45] Dogen, 2007
[46] Traherne, 2010
[47] Smith, 2008

Light in the Tunnel

[48] Eliot, 1943
[49] Wick, 2005
[50] Dogen, 2007
[51] Kennett, 1972
[52] Dogen, 2007

[53] Hakuin, 1967

The Clearing

[54] Scott, 1924

[55] Shakespeare, 2012
[56] Kipling, 1990

The Presence of God

[57] Lawrence, 2005
[58] Ibid.
[59] Ibid.
[60] Tweedy, 1942
[61] Lawrence, 2005
[62] Millgram, 1975
[63] Tweedy, 1942
[64] Lawrence, 2005

Words and Things

[65] Eliot, 1943

Word Magic

[66] Larkin, 2012
[67] Sivananda, 1975
[68] Gasset, 1957
[69] Burckhardt, 2008

Isis and Osiris

[70] Waits, 2011
[71] Eliot, 1943

Attention, Attention, Attention

[72] Beck, 1993

Three Trees

[73] Harari, 2016

[74] Vogels, 2005
[75] Keats, 2002
[76] Marlowe, 2005
[77] Shakespeare, 2012
[78] Perone, 2006

BOOK TWO

Introduction

[79] Einstein, 2011
[80] Eckhart, 1994
[81] Mitchell, 1988
[82] See Hunter, 2018
[83] See Mackenzie, 1977
[84] See Stenmark, 2017
[85] See Nagel, 2012
[86] Vervaeke, Mastropieto, Miscevic, 2017
[87] Frankl, 1985

The Bitter Truth

[88] Durrell, *The Avignon Quintet*, in Gray, 2015
[89] Blake, 1975
[90] See Tweedy, 2018

Faith Never Dies

[91] Chesterton, 2006

All Shall be Well

[92] Watson and Jenkins, 2006

Filter Bubbles

[93] Huxley, 2010
[94] Ibid.
[95] Eliot, 1943

The Madman's Argument

[96] Chesterton, 2013
[97] Ibid.
[98] Ibid.
[99] Ibid.

Personality Disorders

[100] Millon, 2004

A Simple Cure for Spiritual Narcissism

The Iceman Cometh

[101] Eliot, 1943

After Virtue

[102] MacIntyre, 2013

Three, Two, One: Heaven, Earth, Hell

[103] Tobin, 1995

Pachananda

[104] Lewis, 2001

Jacob's Ladder

[105] Genesis 28:12 (NKJV)
[106] Chesterton, 2013

The God of the Living

[107] Shakespeare, 2007
[108] Mark 12:27 (NKJV)

Bad Art and No Burgers

[109] *The Metro Newspaper*, Aug 13, 2019

[110] Ibid.
[111] Arnold, 1994

Book Medicine

[112] Mitchell, 1988

Mystical Atheism

[113] Gray, 2018

Cognitive Filters

[114] Lewis, 1949
[115] Swami and Yeats, 1937
[116] Ibid.
[117] Ibid.

Sola Ratio, Sola Scriptura

[118] Cassian, 1997

Tradition, Meditation, Revelation

[119] Chesterton, 2013

Where do Bored Muggles go?

[120] Wilde, 1997

Redemption

[121] Camus, 1988
[122] Luke 14:26 (NKJV)
[123] John 10:30 (NKJV)
[124] Galatians 2:19-21 (NKJV)
[125] Matthew 5:17-20 (NKJV)

Latter-Day Prophets in the Age of Equality

[126] Williamson, 2005

Rousseau's Chains

[127] Rousseau, 2018

Reason and Civility

[128] Kinne, 1943

The Darkness and the Light

[129] Mitchell, 1988
[130] Eliot, 1943
[131] Ibid.

Why Marx was Half Right

[132] Eagleton, 2011

What's Behind the Wall?

[133] Schopenhauer, 2012
[134] Blake, 2008

Waking Up

[135] Masters and Houston, 1966

The Eye of God

[136] Traherne, 2010
[137] Prabhavananda and Isherwood, 1947
[138] Eckhart, 1981

The World, the Flesh and the Devil

[139] Wordsworth, 2000

The Magic of Christianity

[140] 1 Corinthians 1:23 (NKJV)

The Philosopher Monk

[141] Keats, 1920
[142] Shelley, 2000
[143] 1 Corinthians 13:12 (KJV)

The Warrior King

[144] Matthew 25:40 (KJV)

The One True Refuge

[145] Proverbs 3:5 (KJV)
[146] Matthew 7:24-27 (KJV)

Integral Yoga

[147] Eliot, 1943

A Simple Cure for Spiritual Narcissism

[148] Matthew 22:35 (KJV)

I Believe

[149] Keats, 2002

The True Vine

[150] John 15:1-8 (NKJV)
[151] John 15:11-17 (NKJV)

The Armour of Christ

[152] Ephesians 6:10 (NKJV)

Holy, Virtuous and Wise

[153] Shabastari, 2002
[154] Shakespeare, 2007

Two Trees

[155] 1 Corinthians 13 (NKJV)

Printed in Poland
by Amazon Fulfillment
Poland Sp. z o.o., Wrocław